AF594030

Lost Cities

Beauty in Desolation

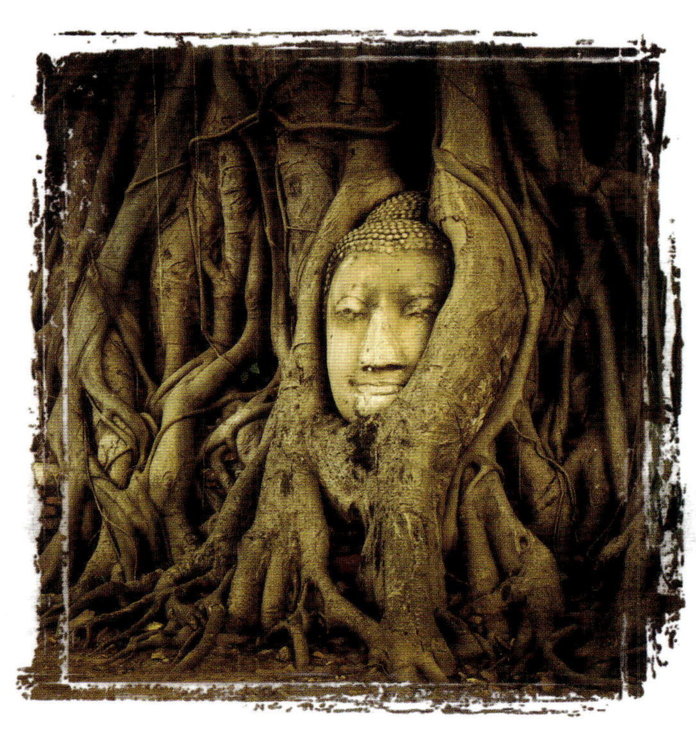

Publisher and Creative Director: Nick Wells
Project Editor: Polly Prior
Art Director & Layout Design: Mike Spender
Digital Design and Production: Chris Herbert
Copy Editor: Karen Fitzpatrick
Proofreader: Dawn Laker
Indexer: Amanda Leigh
Special thanks to: Laura Bulbeck and Carly Laird

FLAME TREE PUBLISHING
6 Melbray Mews
Fulham, London SW6 3NS
United Kingdom

www.flametreepublishing.com

First published 2017

19 21 20
3 5 7 9 10 8 6 4

A CIP record for this book is available from the British Library upon request.

Image Credits: © **REX/Shutterstock** and the following: imageBROKER 51; News Pictures 120; Sipa Press 144; KeystoneUSA-ZUMA 164. © **Shutterstock.com** and the following: Chaiwat Vuttikornvipak 1 & 73; Andrew V Marcus 3 & 134; Anton_Ivanov 4 & 34; Kanuman 6 & 127; Waj 7; Milkovasa 8 & 103; Jorg Hackemann 10; Nejdet Duzen 12; Oleg Znamenskiy 14, 15, 21; Ikpro 17; Yacine Ketfi 18; yanugkelid 19; Tony Cradcock 22; milosk50 24; C Jones 26; David Crosbie 27; Scott Biales 32; Barna Tanko 36; Joakim Lloyd Raboff 37; Stefano Ember 38; Alexey Stiop 39; Victor Baril 43; Jess Kraft 44, 128; zimmytws 45; Sergei Afanasev 49; Yury Birukov 50; Lucian BOLCA; 53; suronin 55; givaga 56; matias planas 58; saiko3p 61; Rafal Cichawa 62; Boyloso 66; jeep2499 68; John Copland 69; Ramillah 70; Sviluppo; 71; vz maze; 74; nhtg 76; HUANG Zheng 77; Hugo Brizard - YouGoPhoto 78; Penny Adams 81; RIRF Stock 82; Andrey Bayda 84; Jon Bilous; 87; Sue Smith 88; donvictorio 89; erwinf 91; Filipe Frazao 92; Steven Schremp 95; Dmitry-T 98; Roberts Vicups; 100; andzher 101; Fotokon; 102; Danita Delmont 105; North Toda 106; kou2341 107; Mikhail Starodubov 108; Joe Gough 109; Gail Johnson 110; Durk Talsma 111; oceanfishing 114; mundosemfim 116; asiastock 119; Frankris; 122; Benny Marty 123; Jose Arcos Aguilar 124; Henryk Sadura 126; matremors 131; Massimiliano Marino 132; Sergey Kohl 135; tupatu76 137; Luis Echeverri Urrea 138; Esdelval 139; dailin 141; ValerioMei 143; Guglielmo Francavilla 145; Dustie 146; Pattie Steib 147; LuisSilvaRodrigues 148; Der Wats 149; Marco Lissoni 150; De Visu 152; Luz-i 153; salajean 154, 155, 177; Francescomoufotografo 156; Olivier Bourgeois 157; Kakabadze George 161; Tspider 162, 165; Yujnyj 163; Oriole Gin 167; Kateryna Upit 168; Tatyana Vyc 169; VasilPetrus 171; Suchart Boonyavech 172; Matus Duda 173; Anton Kudelin; 175; Igor Dymov 176; pedrosala 178, 185; Katoosha 179; Frank Gaertner 180; Pippa Sanderson 181; Sean Pavone 182; staoist520 184; Opachevsky Irina 187; Drop of Light 188. © **SuperStock** and the following: Yoko Aziz/age fotostock 9 & 52; Stock Connection 16; Ian Murray/age fotostock 28; The Irish Image Collection 30; Yoshio Tomii 31; Philippe Michel/age fotostock 40; Jan Wlodarczyk 46; LatitudeStock/Capture Ltd 47; Konrad Wothe 54; Chris Caldicott/Axiom Photographic/Design Pics 60; Michael S. Nolan 64; imageBROKER 72; russellkord.com/age fotostock 86; National Geographic 96; fStop 112; Alvaro Leiva 113; Ingram Publishing 118; Quanthem 130; Mi.Ti. 142; Ed Darack 159; Glasshouse Images 160; Blend Images 192.

ISBN: 978-1-78664-528-9

Printed in China

Lost Cities

Beauty in Desolation

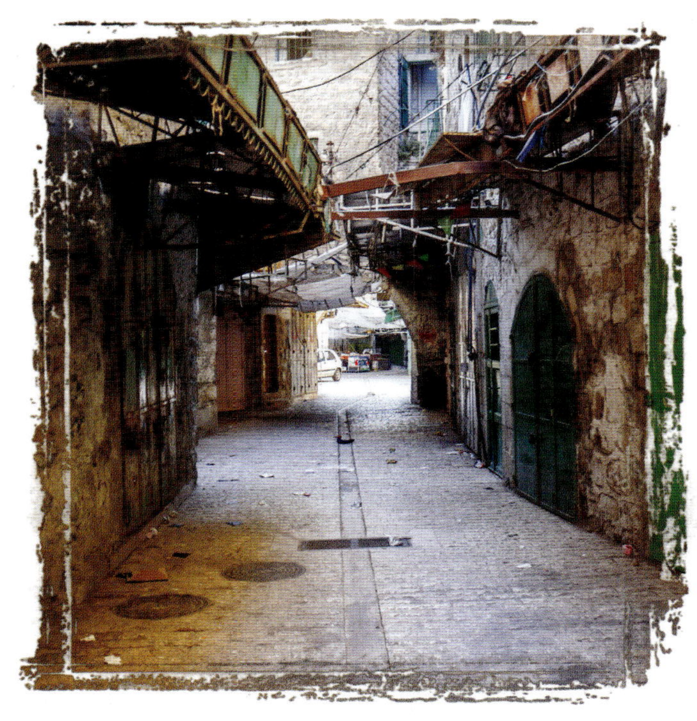

Julian Beecroft

FLAME TREE
PUBLISHING

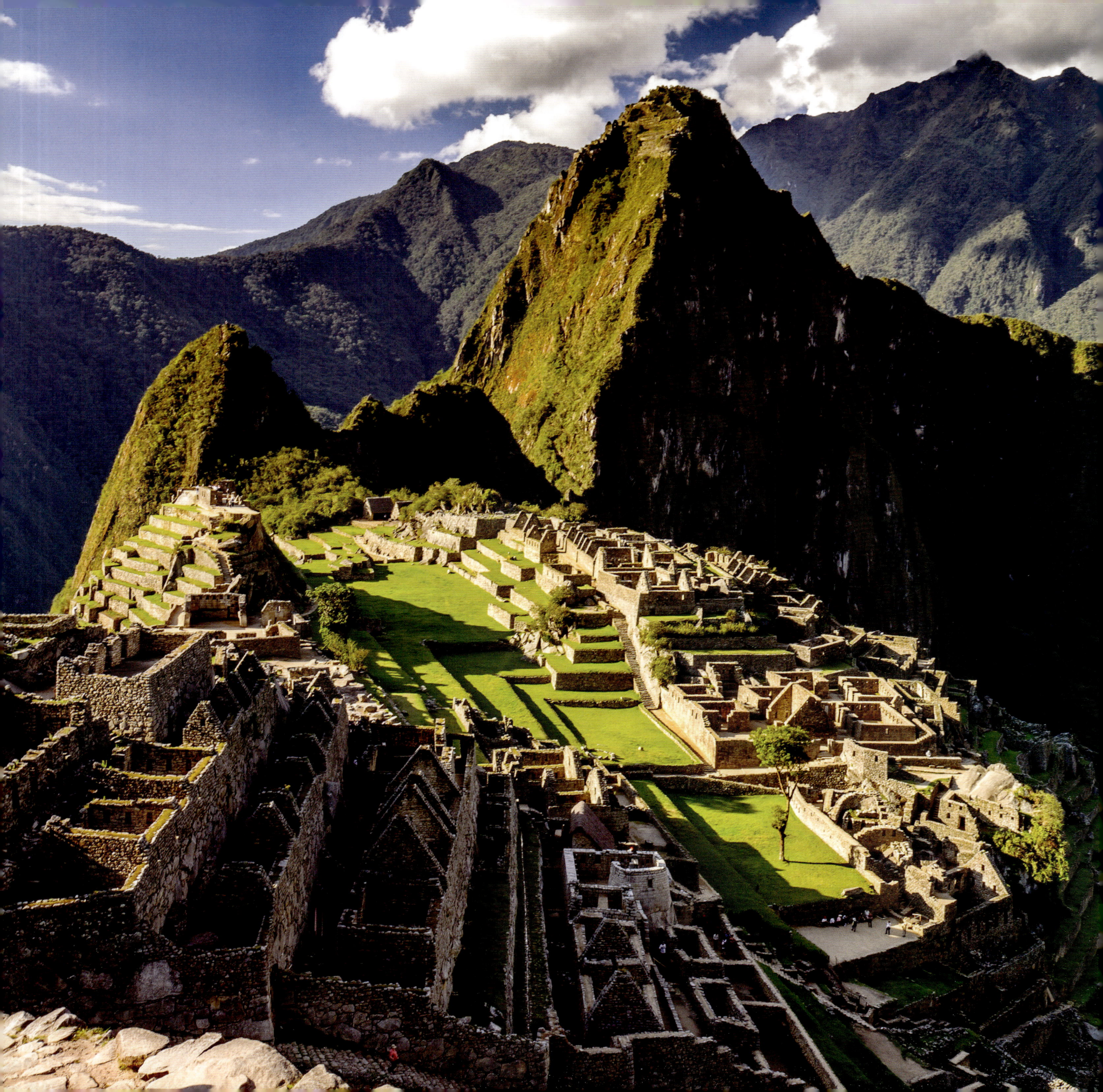

Contents

Introduction

The past recedes behind us like a road in a rear-view mirror. We know it to be real because the people we shared it with – our fellow travellers – confirm our memories, and the places we recall are still there whenever we care to visit them, either as familiar as they once were or indeed quite changed. In our own personal histories as also in the world's inhabited spaces – the villages, towns and cities where people actually live – there's a continuity we all take for granted. We call it civilization, for want of a better word. But abandoned cities, towns and other settlements challenge us with a sense of history broken off, ruptured by forces of various kinds with a common terminal outcome.

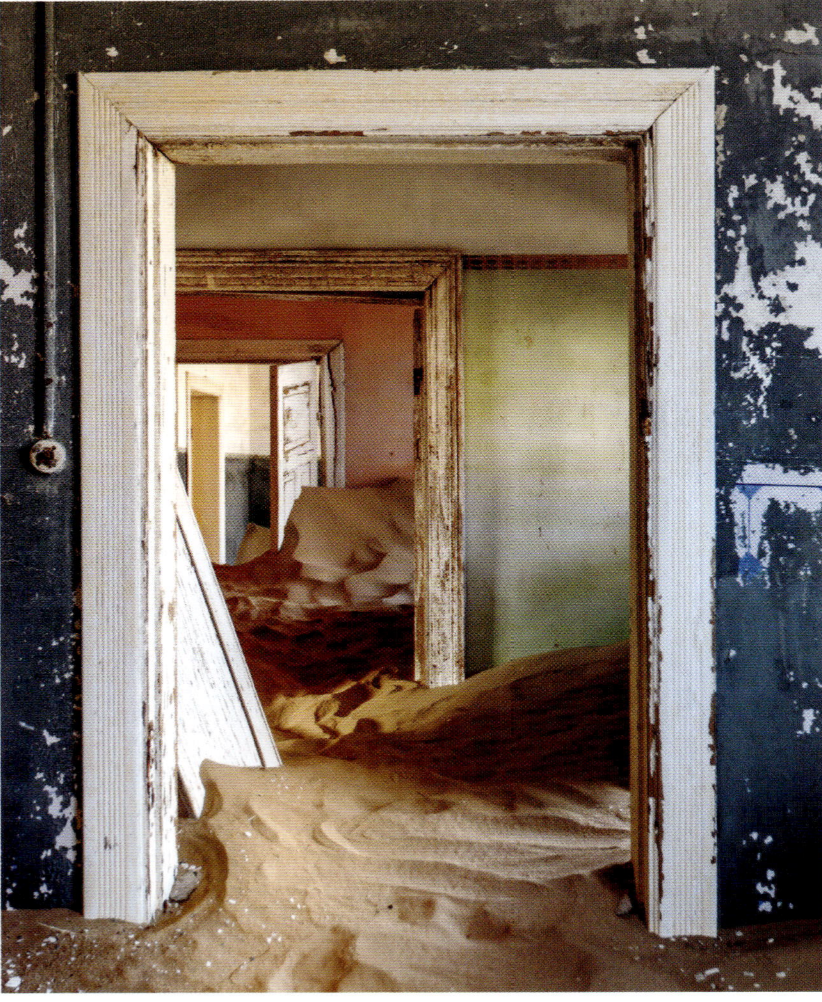

Broken Histories

The sadness of this rupture is in stark contrast to the evidence that does survive. Even in this diminished state, ruined or abandoned places bear witness to the ambition, zeal, vision, resolve and sheer communal effort invested by those in the past who raised them to their pomp. Who could fail to wonder at the system of beliefs which inspired the Pharaoh Khufu and his subjects to build the Great Pyramid of Giza, not to mention the colossal achievement of a monument so marvellous and so structurally secure it has lasted some four and half millennia? Indeed, this and the other pyramids, perched on the edge of modern Cairo, are all the more impressive for standing impassively in the path of encroaching urban sprawl, reminding us of a span of time that makes a mockery of our present worries. For the appeal of abandoned places where people once lived is in part the confirmation they offer of our own mortality in a context much larger than we usually care to consider.

The Immediacy of Ruins

History offers numerous examples of once-proud cities and even whole civilizations brought low by war, conquest, climate change, resource exhaustion and all manner of natural disasters. Ruin and decay is the natural state of manmade things when left untended. We can see it even in places so recently abandoned, like the diamond mining town of Kolmanskop in Namibia, deserted only since 1954 but now being gradually swallowed by sand; or the ghost city of Pripyat, one of several Ukrainian towns and cities completely evacuated after the Chernobyl nuclear accident in 1986, where despite toxic levels of radiation, nature is steadily reclaiming every nook and cranny from which it was banished when the city was built; or in parts of once prosperous cities like Detroit, where mortgage foreclosures since the subprime crisis of 2007 have seen some districts lose a third of the people who lived there just a few years ago, their houses abandoned to the weeds.

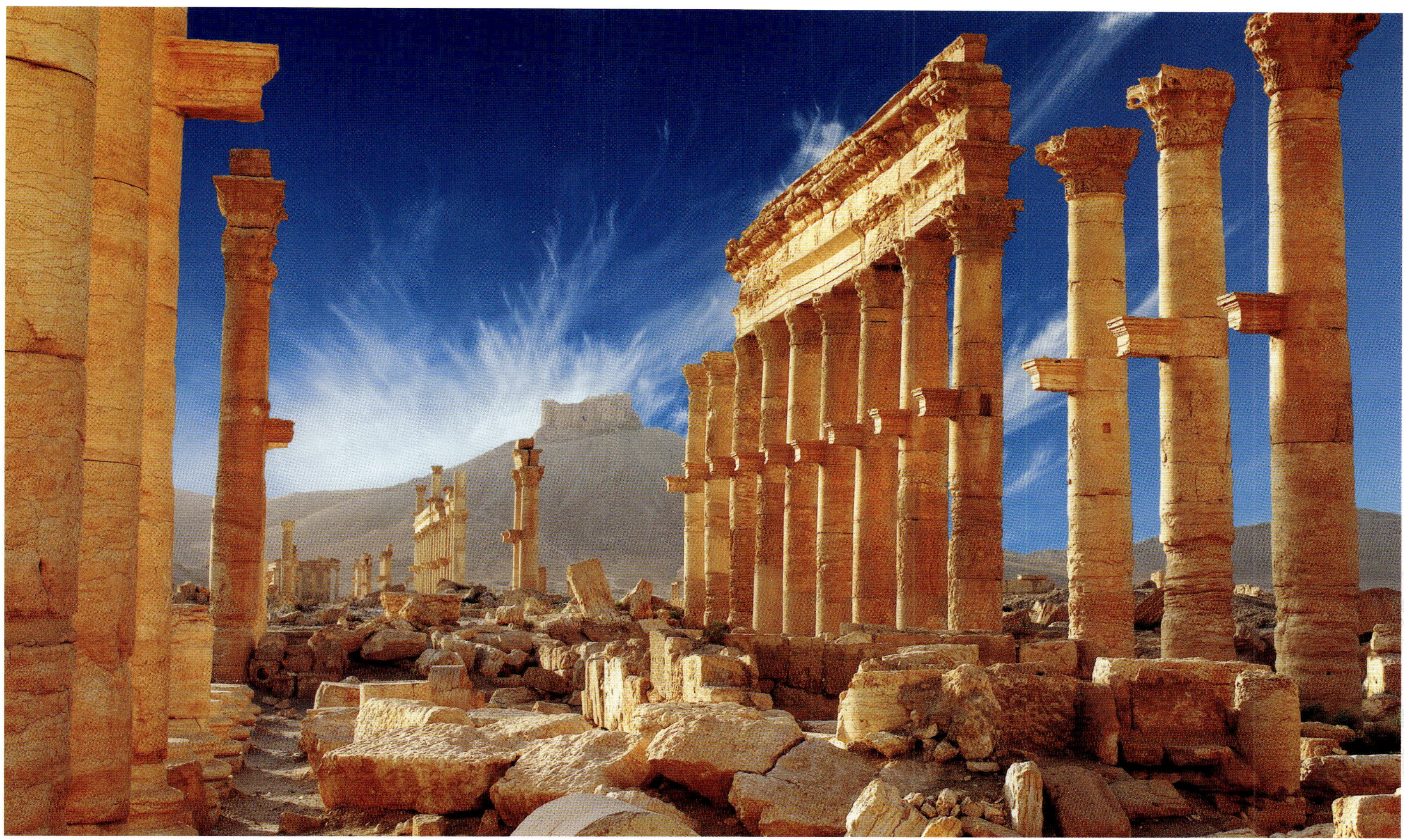

These places, though modern, can seem more desolate than ancient ruined settlements thousands of years older; the trauma of people departing, never to return, almost palpable in the streets and buildings themselves.

A Damaging Present

These recent desertions stem in one case from industrial decline, in another from industrial calamity, in yet another from an economic system gone badly awry. But, just as in the past, these catastrophes can also arise from the misplaced conviction of fanatics in their right to destroy, as recent desecrations in some of the great ancient cities of the Middle East have so painfully reminded us. At such times, when the past is endangered by the present, civilization as a whole seems imperilled. Before their recent, near-complete destruction by ISIS, venerable Assyrian cities like Nineveh or Nimrud in modern Iraq were already partial ruins; but our sense of where we have come from as a world civilization, as a species, is built upon such fragile remnants of an ancient past. Their beauty owes much to incompleteness, to the gaps in a once-magnificent architectural fabric, in the archaeological record, in the space between what is and what was. And the lesson they offer from the past reveals other gaps too – between who we were and who we are and who as a species we still might be.

The Trials of Palmyra

Imagination plays a part in finding beauty in what, from a rational viewpoint is evidence of disaster. Even in places damaged repeatedly over many centuries, like Palmyra in the Syrian desert, enough may still remain there to persuade us to rebuild this glorious ruin; at least in our minds, despite evidence from recent photos of the stones of once-noble temples turned to rubble by the rabid iconoclasts of ISIS.

The desert city was ideally placed along the trade routes between East and West to absorb the range of architectural influences for which it was so admired in its own ancient heyday, not just in ours. A cosmopolitan city it may have been, but neither its mercantile acumen nor its cultural openness was enough to save it from initial destruction at the hands of the Roman emperor Aurelian in AD 273. Rebuilt on a smaller scale, the town became a place of Christian and then Islamic worship, before again being laid waste in 1400 by Tamerlane and his Timurid army. For many centuries more, it existed as a simple village amidst glorious ruins of a golden age; until in 1932, as part of the French Mandate, the city of modern Palmyra was established on a nearby site. That so much of the city of the Roman era had survived not only these conquests, but especially the passage of more than 2,000 years, is owed to a dry climate and the durability of the stone that was used to build it.

A Walk in the Woods

But stones are not sufficient in themselves. Let's imagine we go walking in the woods close to where we live. On this particular day, we decide to take a different path, one we have never tried before. After a little way (as once happened to the author in not dissimilar terms), we come across an old stone wall, which doesn't look like much but even so is not quite in the style of other, archaic structures we are used to seeing hereabouts. Deciding to investigate, beneath a fervid sprawl of brambles we find an

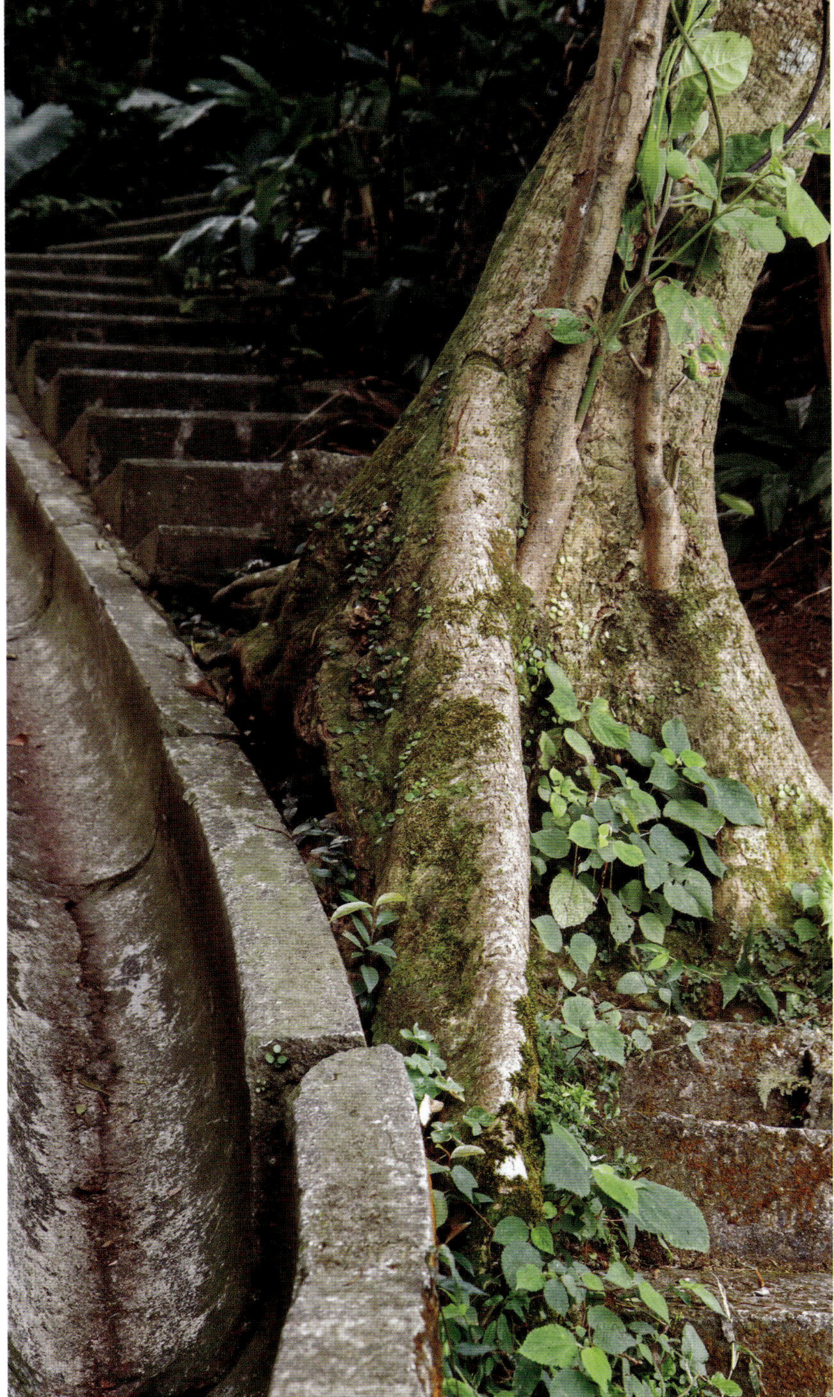

extensive series of walls that point to a significant building which must once have stood here. Returning home, after a little research and expert guidance, we reach the conclusion that the ruins we have stumbled on belong to an old Roman bathhouse that served the people then living in this obscure locale.

Knowing this, our experience of these ruins is transformed. Curious to begin with, now we are fascinated by the thought that Roman soldiers or citizens may have lived in this area that we thought we knew so well; our little local patch is suddenly connected to places far away that we may already know or may not yet have seen – perhaps even to ancient Palmyra. We don't need to return to the site to see it again in our minds and to resurrect the people who would once have bathed there. So while intrinsic mystery attaches to ruined places we know little about – as clearly it did for J.M.W. Turner and John Constable when they painted Stonehenge in the early nineteenth century, when very little was known of the monument beyond what was visible – there is another kind of mystery arising from knowledge itself.

A Common Heritage

Even in the most decimated places, where almost nothing remains, an imagination armed with knowledge can make much of very little. At the site of Xanadu – now Shangdu in Inner Mongolia, a part of modern China – there is almost no trace of the summer capital and fabled palace of Kublai Khan, as described by the Venetian explorer Marco Polo in 1275 and then immortalized in the poem by Samuel Taylor Coleridge more than five centuries later. But that does not prevent those who know either of these accounts, or the formal histories of Khan and his Mongol empire, from seeing in their mind's eye the stately pleasure dome of the poet's imagining rise again from the footings of the palace, which are now more or less all that remain.

More knowledge might even keep these places from further harm. Giving the benefit of any doubt to US-led forces stationed in the ruins of Babylon in Iraq in 2003, had they realized the true significance of the site they were occupying, they might not have vandalized its ancient fabric in the way they so needlessly did. That we feel so keenly the damage they inflicted on the majestic city of Nebuchadnezzar, or the destruction that Palmyra or Nineveh or Nimrud or Parthian Hatra have suffered at the hands of ISIS, tells us something else: that the presence of the past we can feel in such places is not simply the story of the people who have lived there – no matter how different from our own their culture may seem – but a universal tale that involves us all.

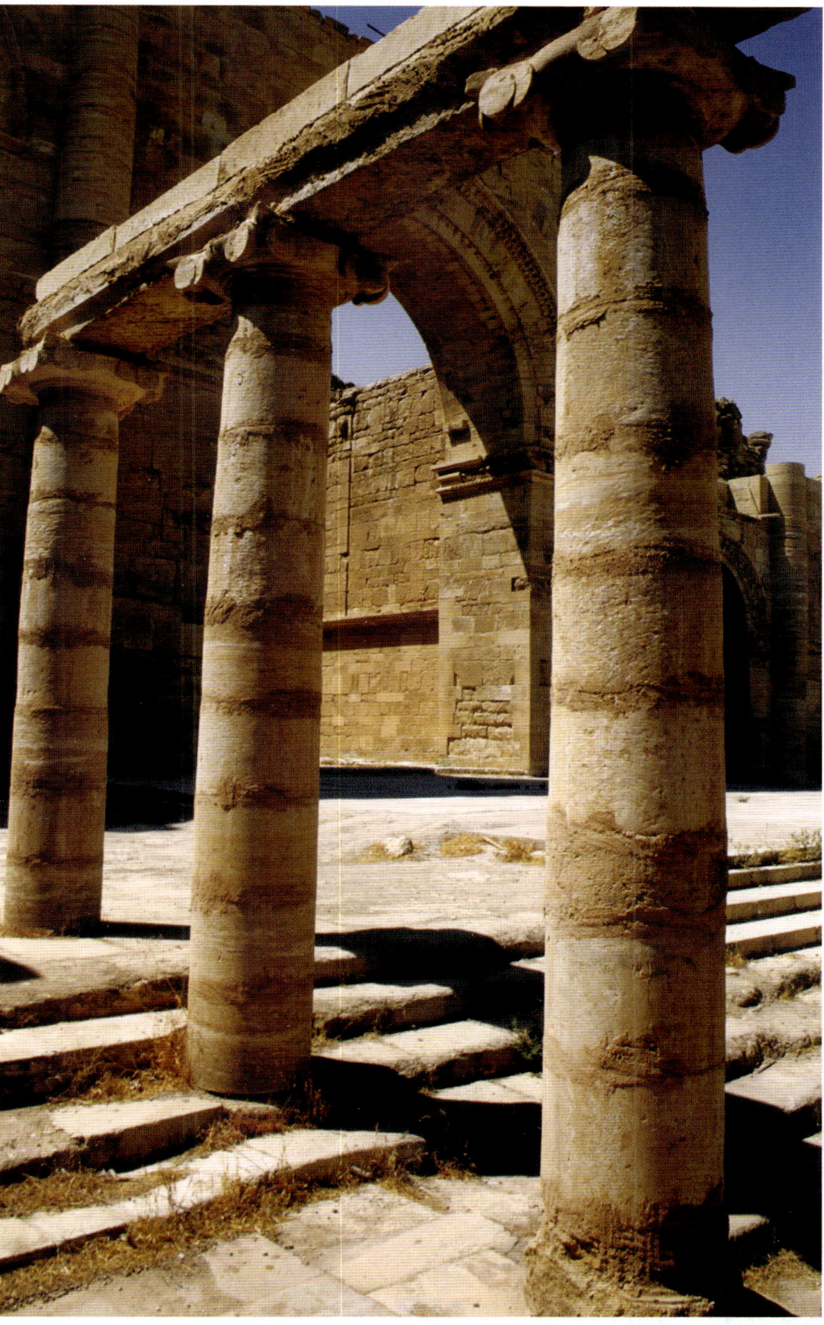

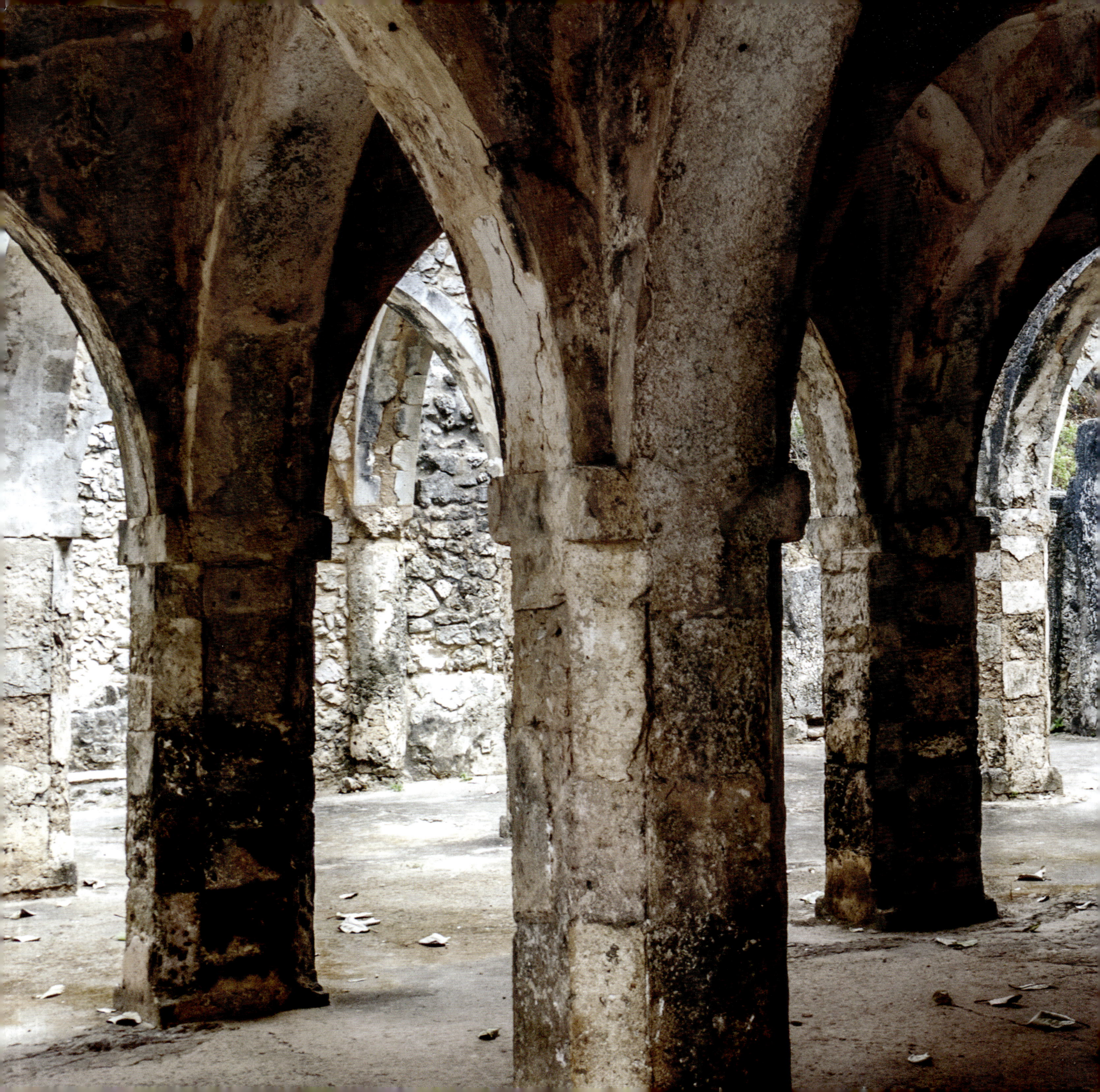

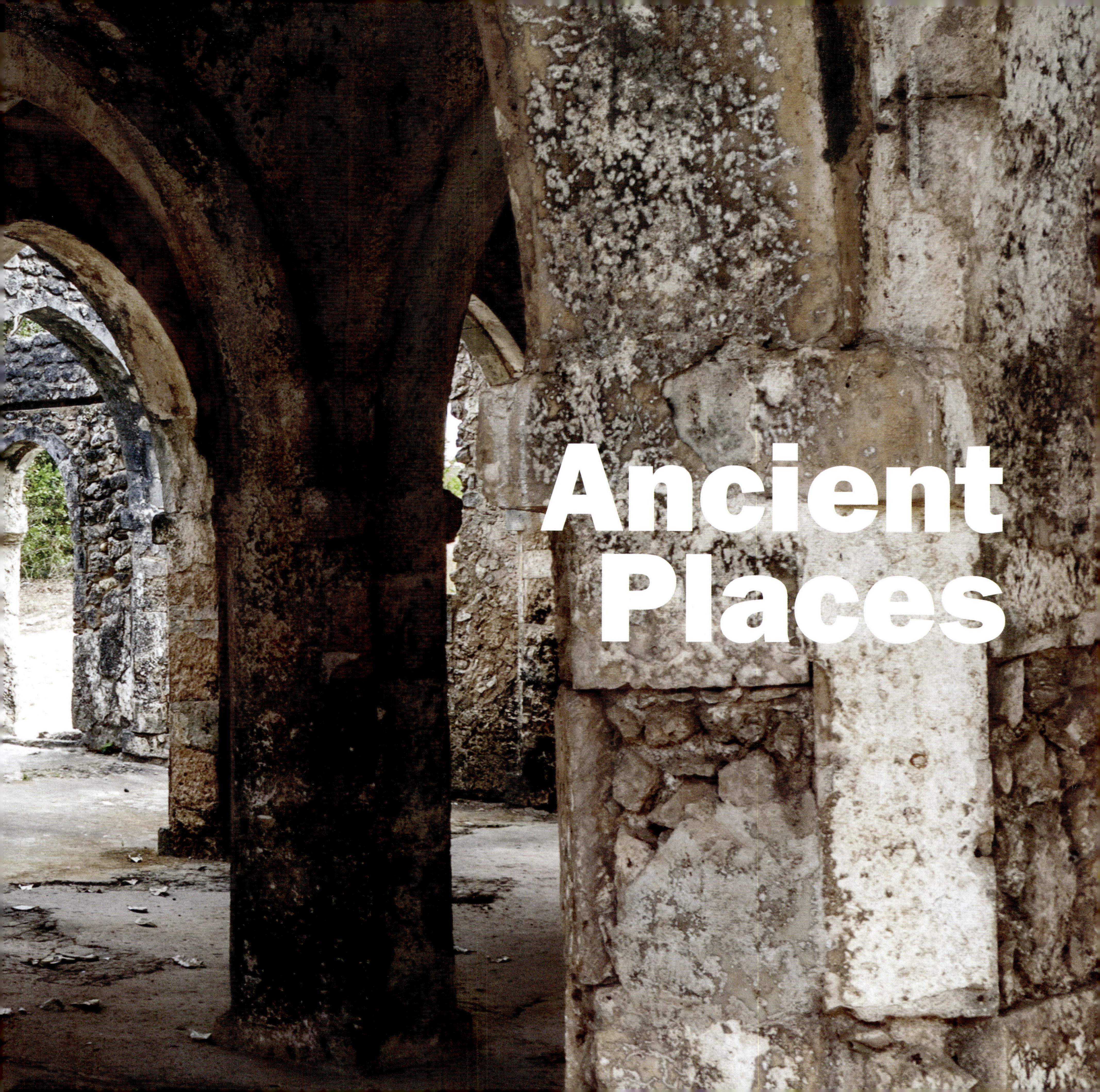

Ancient Places

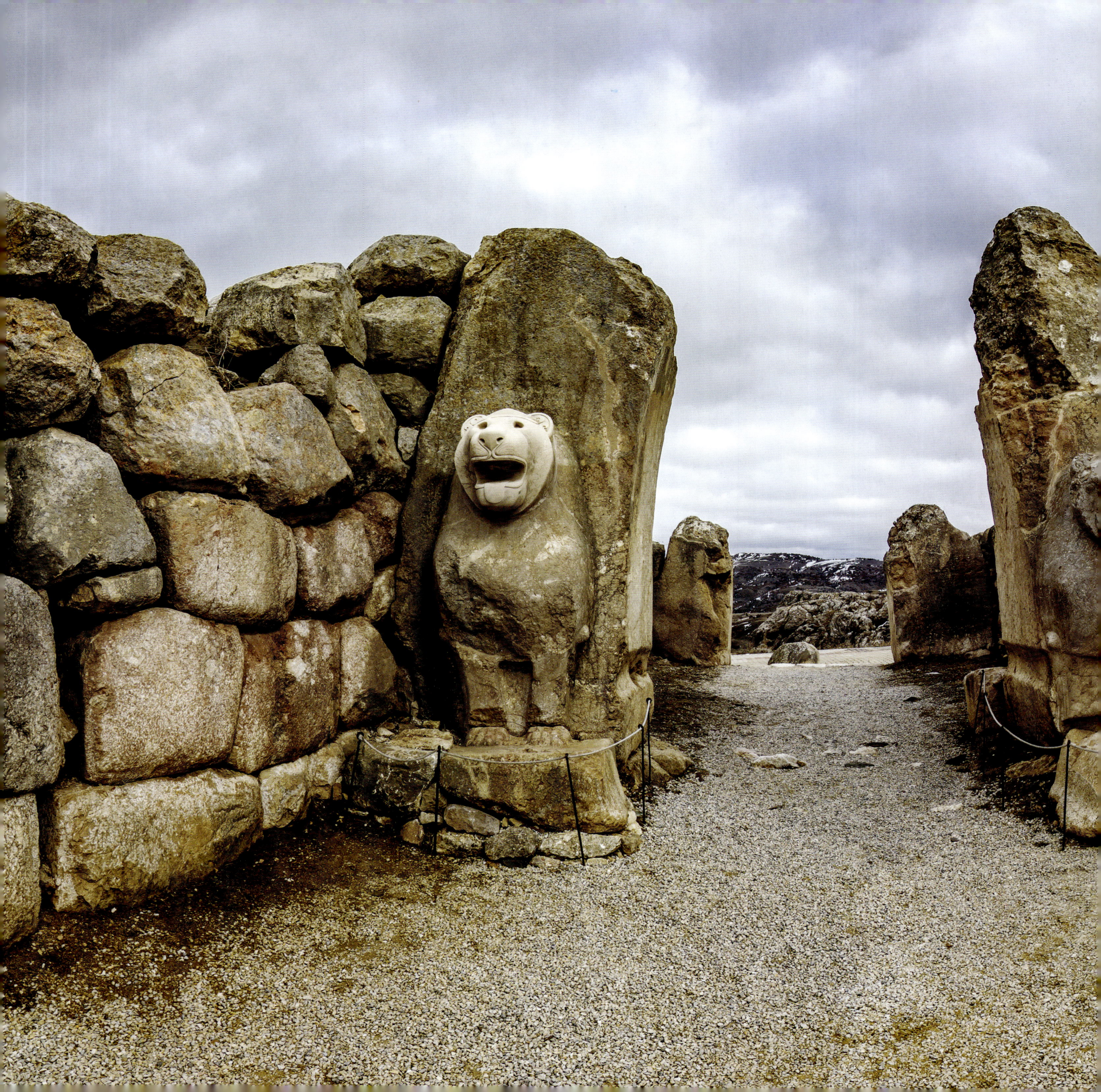

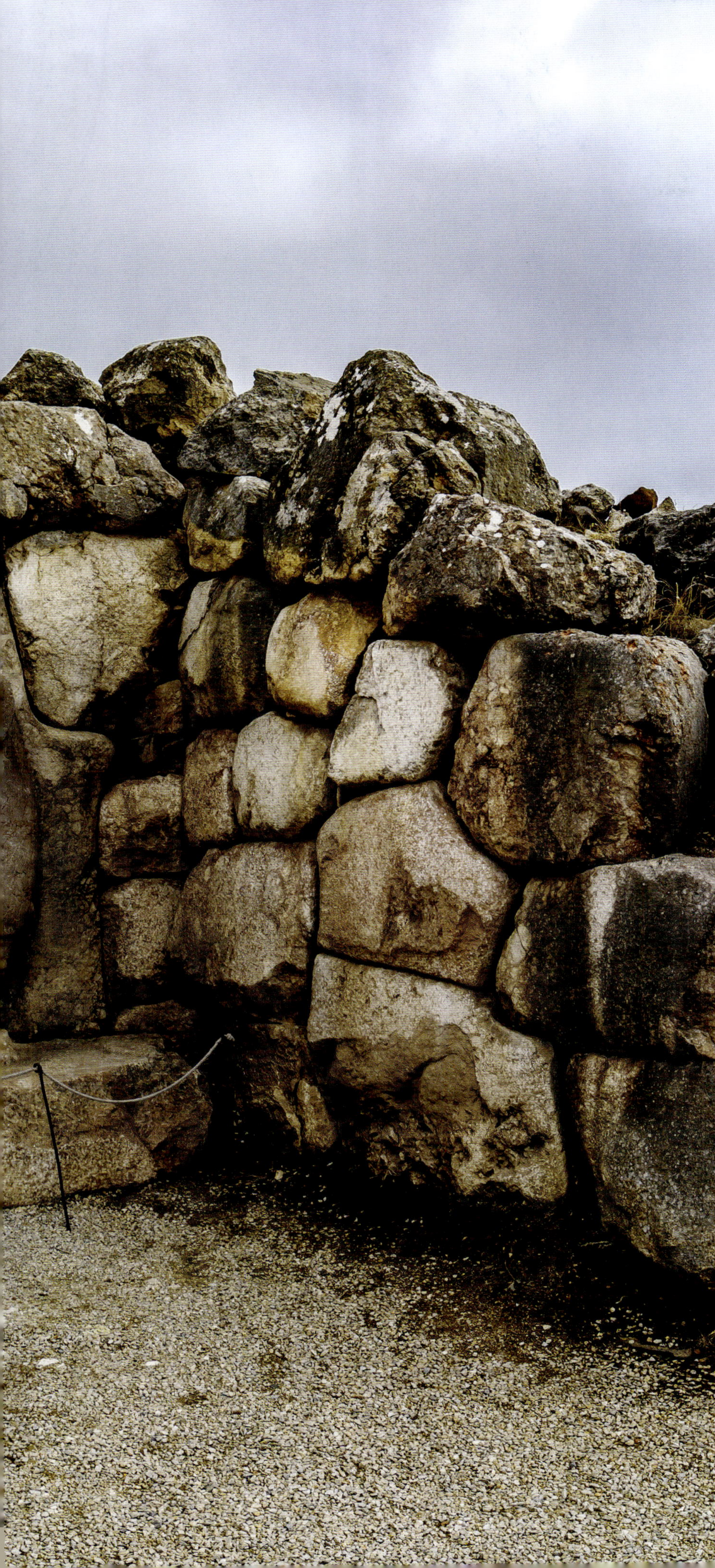

Life Among the Ruins

Ever since our species began to build, we have been haunted by visible remnants of a past whose magnificence puts our own achievements into much-needed context. For almost two millennia in Europe, the Near East and North Africa, imposing ruins have reminded those living among them of the astounding cities of the Roman Empire, while the achievements of Ancient Greece, whose ideas the Romans adopted, are in some ways even finer. In Egypt, the temple complexes of Luxor and Karnak in ancient Thebes bear witness to a civilization in its own way still more splendid. Elsewhere across the world, the many extraordinary ruins that were known of have long pointed to cultures of equal vision, with a sense of the cosmos, and our place in it, as rich in meaning for those who built them as the cumulative revelations of the many branches of science are for the modern mind today.

Rising from the Ashes

But if people had lived since antiquity among these daunting relics of abandoned cities and the abandoned ways of thinking and being they implied, in the first half of the eighteenth century, in southern Italy close to Naples, the first systematic excavation of a suspected ancient site made startling discoveries that led gradually to the birth of a new scientific discipline. Dreams of lost cities tug at our imagination, stirring unfulfilled longings for wonder or wealth. But since the unearthing of Herculaneum in 1738, and the even more remarkable finds at nearby Pompeii a decade later, the increasingly sophisticated methods of what we now know as

Previous page: *Mosque at Kilwa Kisiwani, Tanzania.*
Left: *The capital of the Hittite Empire, Hattusha in modern central Turkey was home to as many as 50,000 people at the peak of Hittite civilization, around 1400 BC.*

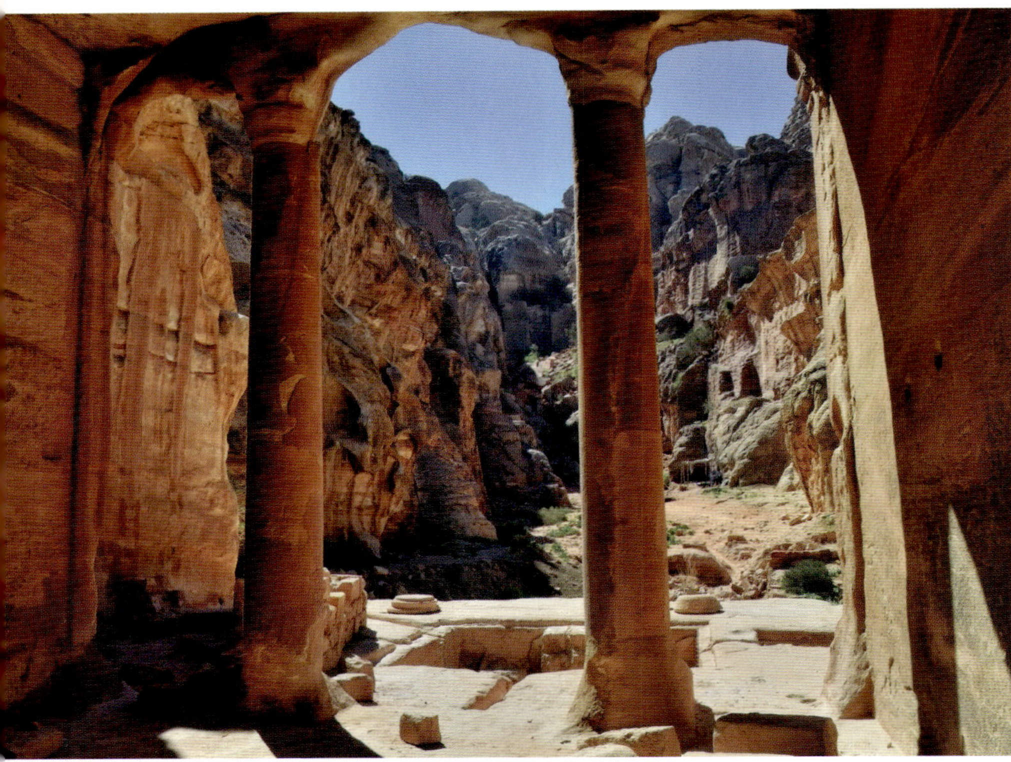

Above: *Petra is one of the most famous of all lost cities. The Garden Hall or Triclinium looks out on to what was once a processional route called the Wadi al-Farasa.*

archaeology have piled one astonishing find upon another. Pompeii remains one of the most compelling of all lost cities, for the quality of what was found and for the tragic circumstances in which it was preserved. The plaster casts in situ of bodies petrified by hot ash at the moment of agonizing death is a sight more vivid than we might wish to see, filling the empty streets with the imagined ghosts of those who were killed.

One of those who witnessed the terrible eruption of Mount Vesuvius that day, 24 August AD 79, was the Roman writer Pliny the Younger, whose uncle and namesake Pliny the Elder died in heroic circumstances trying to rescue a friend and his family from the nearby port of Stabiae. The ruins of this affluent resort town were discovered, and excavations begun, the year after work started at Pompeii, but were later reburied and forgotten about for

Right: *The Al Khazneh (The Treasury) at Petra, Jordan.*

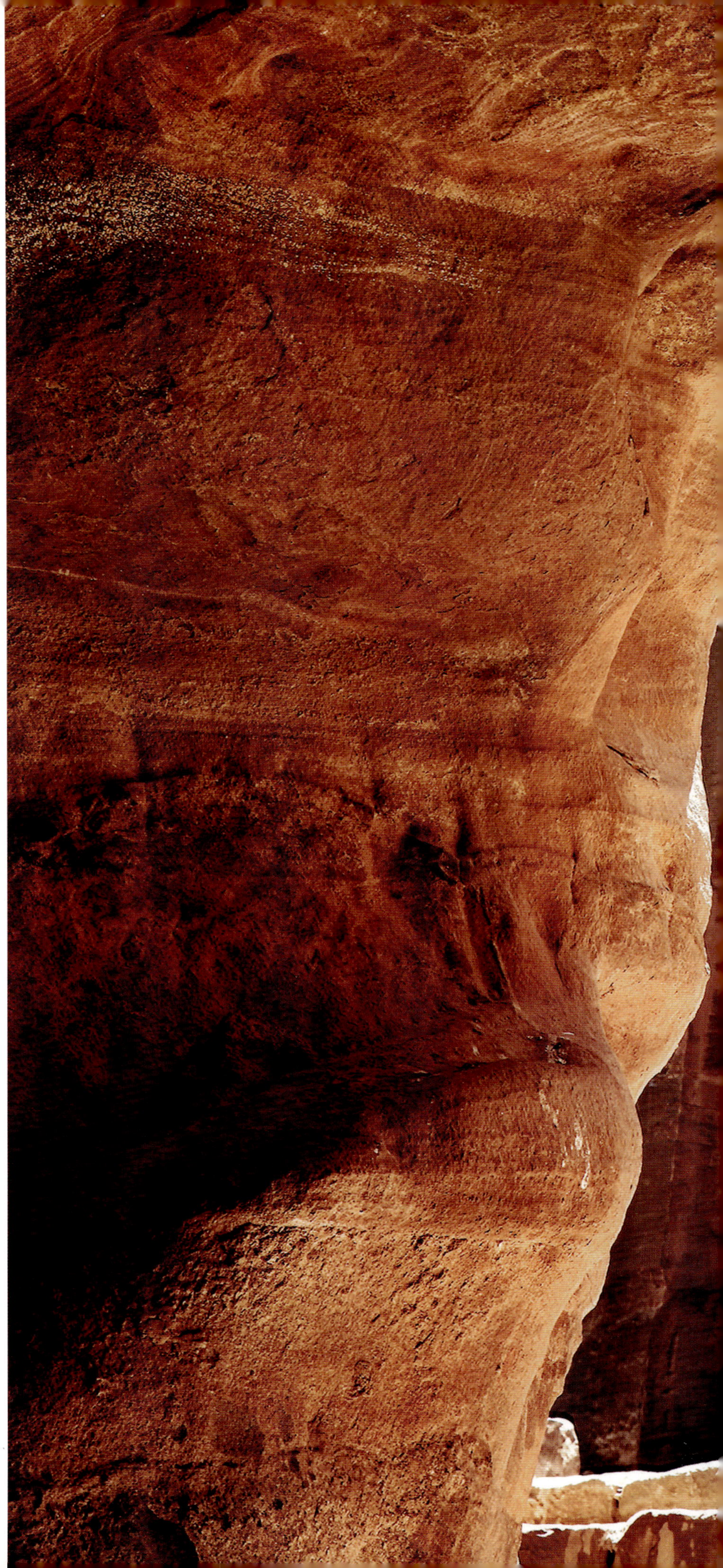

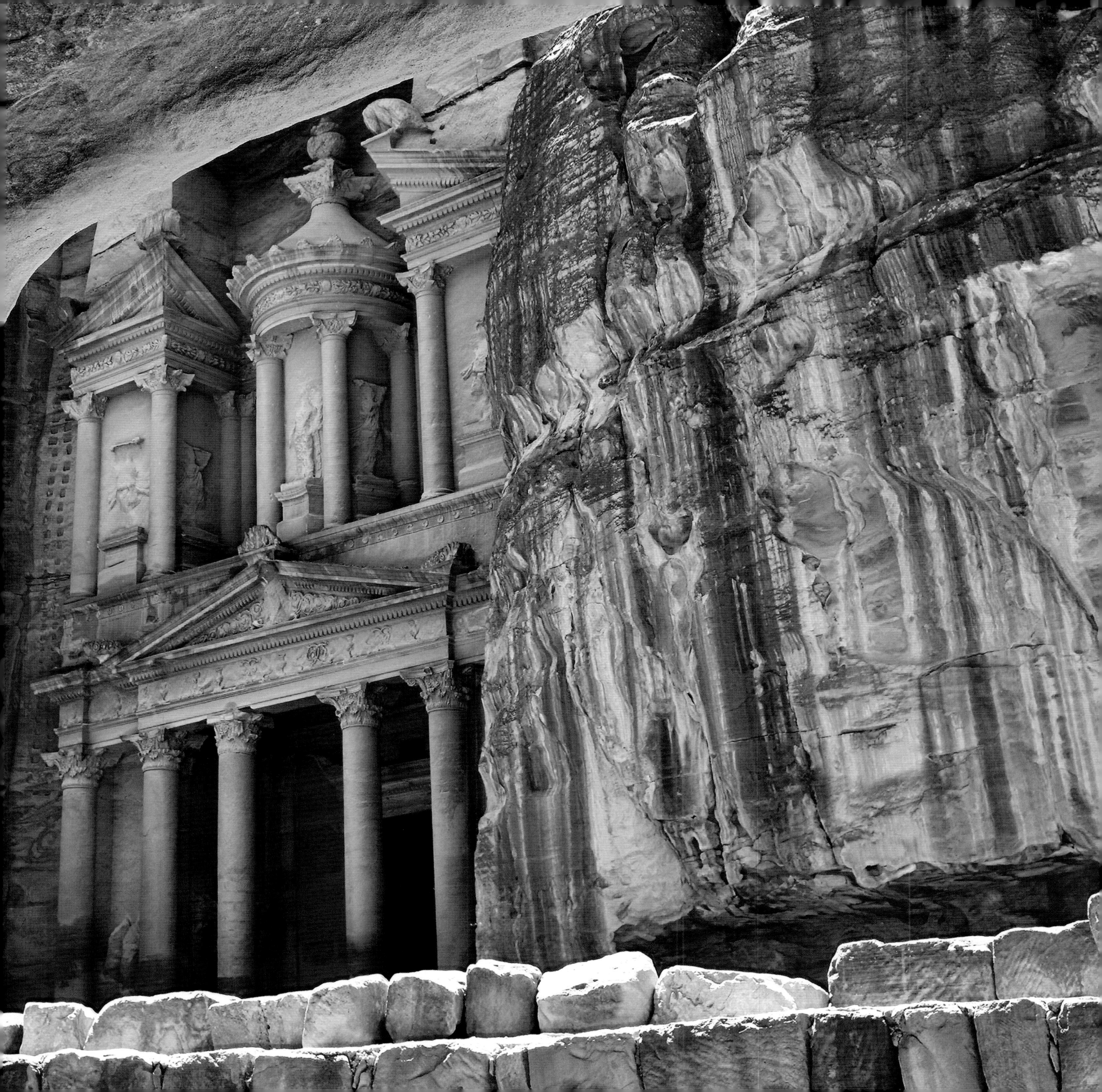

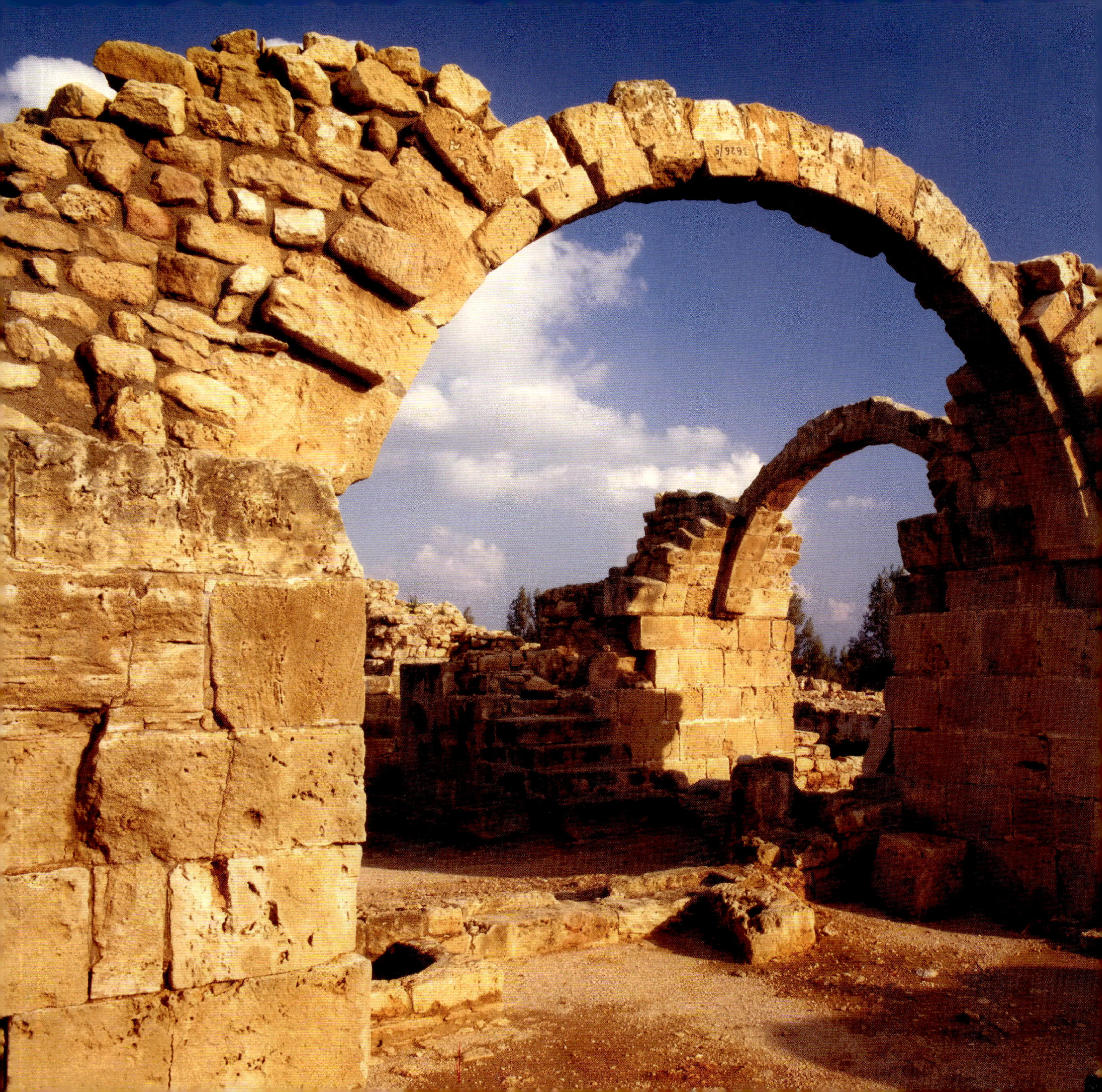

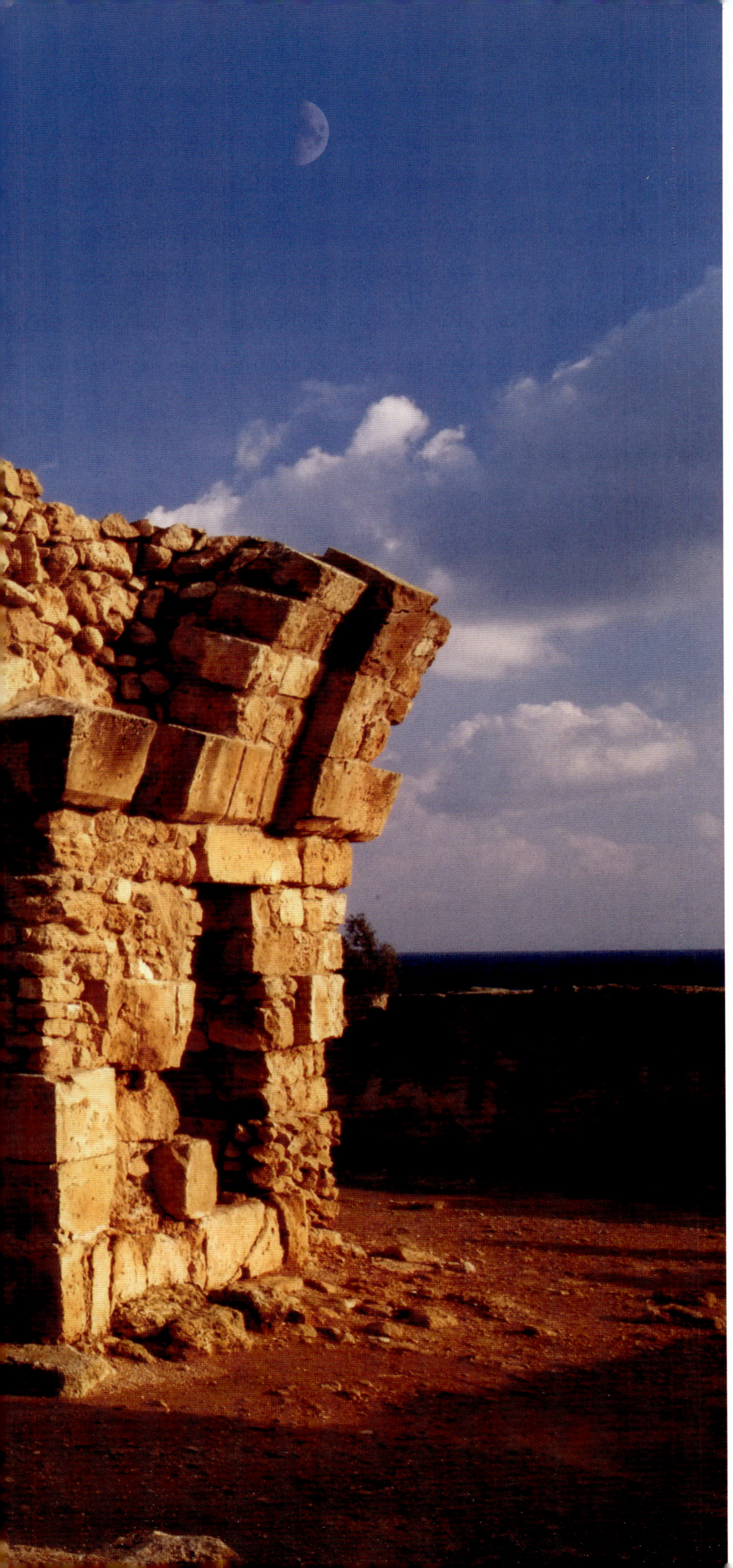

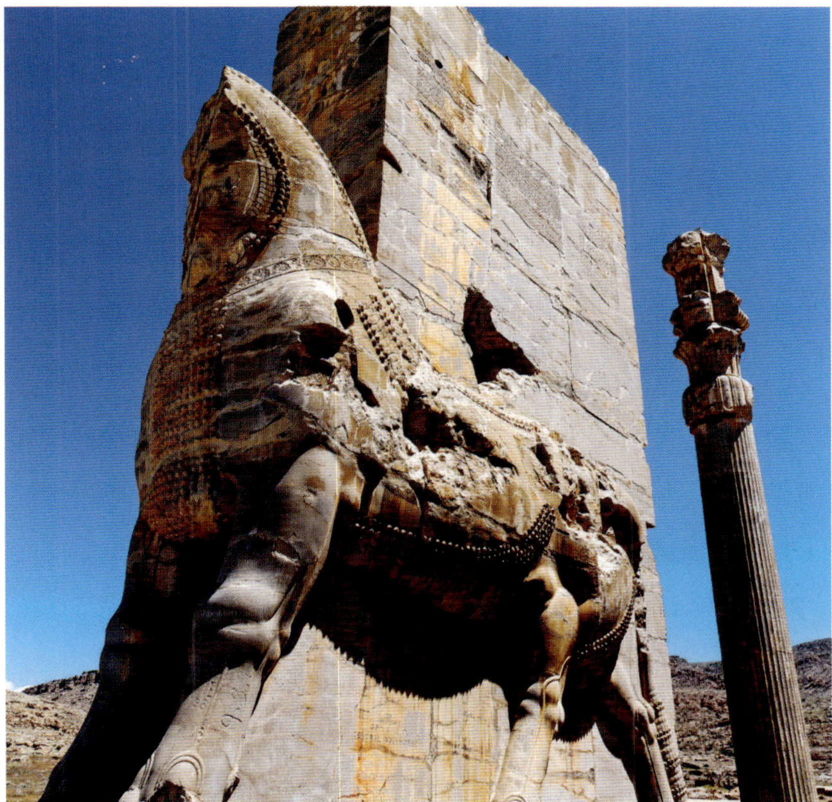

Above: *Persepolis in modern Iran, ancient Persia, was the ceremonial capital of the Achaemenid Empire, until it was sacked and looted by the army of Alexander the Great in 330 BC.*

another two centuries. Re-excavation in the late 1950s revealed remnants of a number of villas, which, added to the detail of Pompeii and Herculaneum, have illuminated the lives of ordinary Roman citizens with remarkable clarity.

The Rose Red City

By the time of the eruption, the older Pliny was one of the most celebrated writers of his day, famous above all for his compendious *Natural History*, which among many other subjects includes reference to the city of Petra in the southwestern desert of Jordan, identified by Pliny and other writers as the capital of a trading people called the Nabateans. Like many places mentioned in the texts of Classical writers or in the Bible, Petra was thought lost, forgotten – by Westerners, at least

Left: *Byzantine castle ruins at Paphos, Cyprus.*

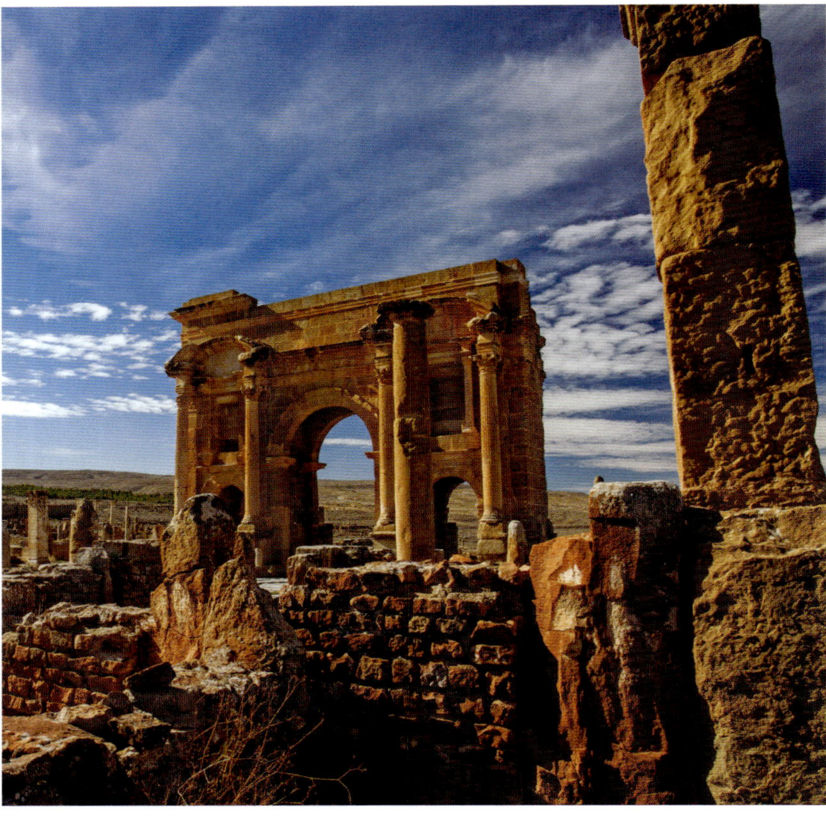

Above: *Like so many ancient cities we know about today, the extensive ruins of the Roman-Berber town of Timgad in modern Algeria were only discovered following extensive excavation in 1881.*

– since the time of the Crusades. But to the nomadic traders of the Levant and Arabia, it had been an important stop for much of the previous two millennia, along the many routes that crisscrossed the region; though by the time in 1812 when the Swiss explorer Johann Ludwig Burkhardt first set on eyes on the city, it had lain deserted for hundreds of years. Large parts of the complex, including a large number of tombs, but also a treasury (*see* page 15) and monastery, were fashioned like manmade caves directly from the red sandstone mountains that tower above the valley of Wadi Musa. But the carved facades of buildings like the treasury and the monastery are of a quality that rivals similar structures in Egypt's Valley of the Kings, though for centuries, until the arrival of Burkhardt, the secrets of Petra lay hidden, forgotten, behind a natural barrier of the same imposing rocks from which they were formed.

Right: *Amphitheatre at Termessos in Antalya, Turkey.*

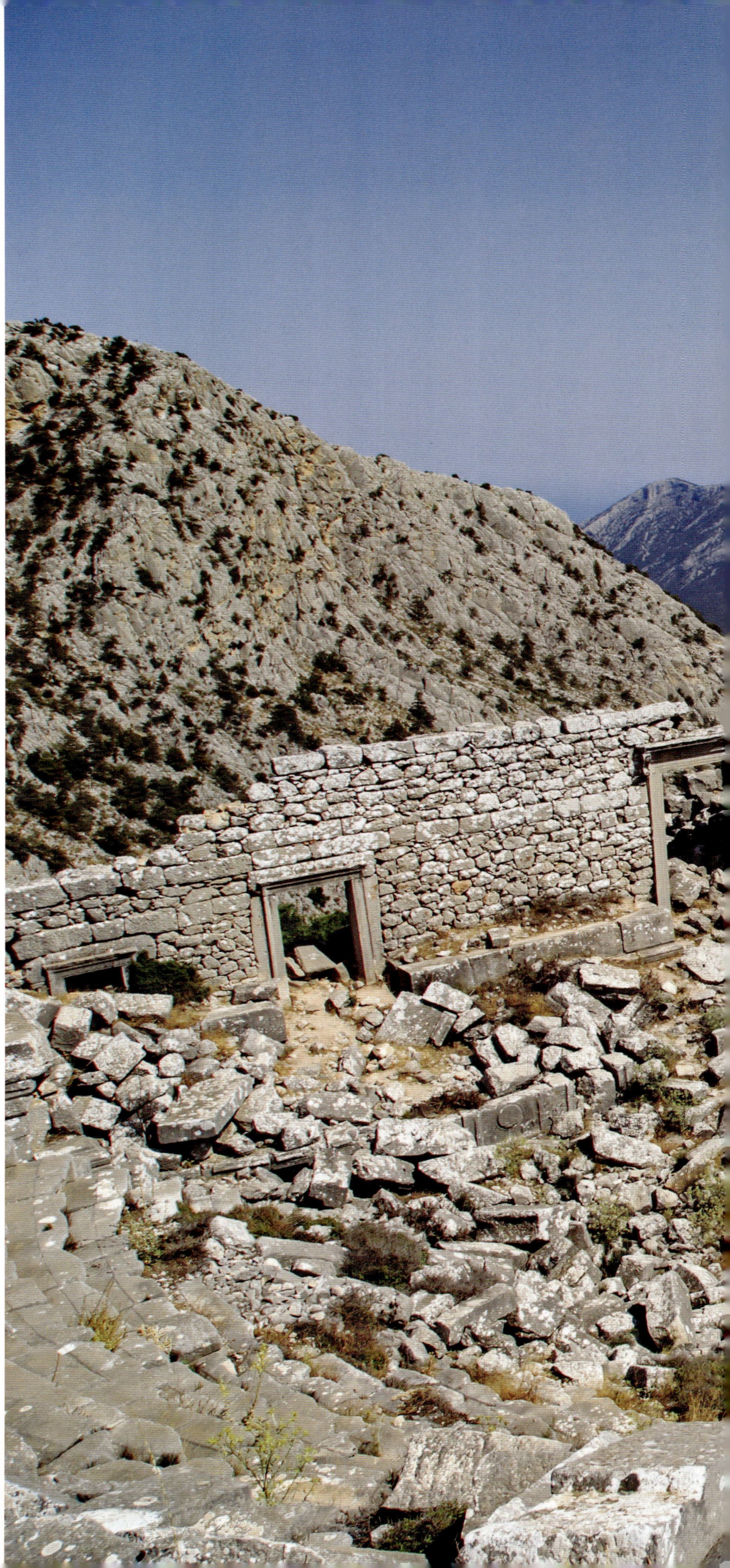

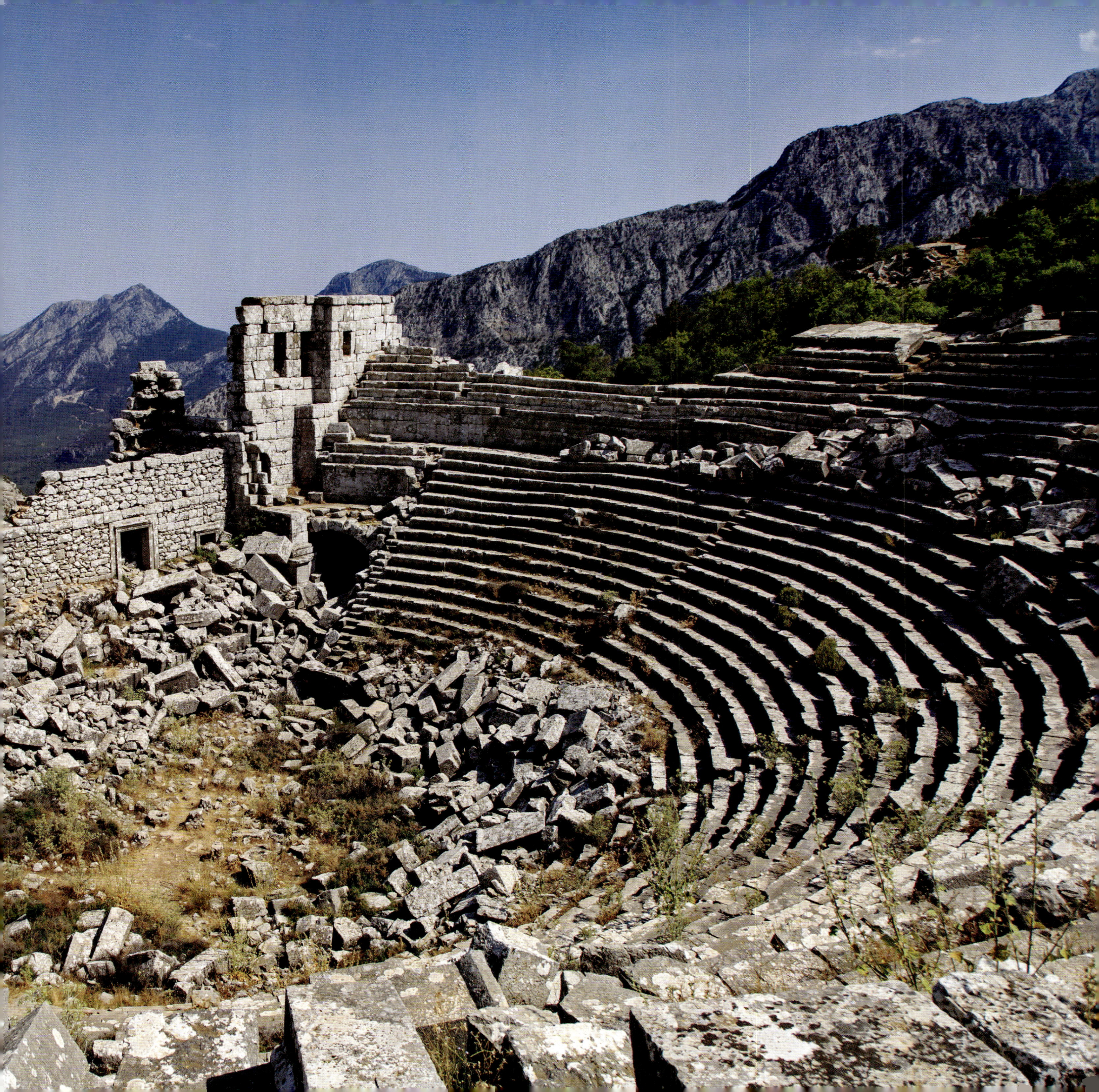

Natural Materials

Humans first took refuge in caves when our species was in its infancy, and early Europeans – some tens of thousands of years ago – are known to have kept the same domestic arrangement, as the caves discovered since the 1870s at Lascaux and Chauvet in France, and Altamira in Spain, have conclusively proved. But cave dwelling persisted until much more recently in Cappadocia in central Turkey (*see* right), attaining a level of complexity and organization that quite beggars belief.

Troglodyte Cities

Above ground at Derinkuyu, where the first discovery was made in 1963, is a series of natural rock pillars – bizarre geological features, which have themselves been hollowed out to serve as dwellings at some time in the past. But below the surface, a vast subterranean city descends through more than five levels of caves that could once have accommodated up to 20,000 people.

Begun in the centuries before the Common Era, most likely by the Phrygians who once inhabited this region, the cave cities were later expanded by the Christians who followed them, and among the chambers they created are chapels decorated with exquisite Byzantine frescoes. Throughout the centuries, when the people of this region were threatened by war, they sought refuge in these troglodyte warrens, which were only finally abandoned in 1923 when the Christians of Turkey were exchanged for Muslims in Greece after the breakup of the Ottoman Empire. With those inhabitants went knowledge of the existence of these dwellings until the accidental discovery 40 years later – since when up to 200 similar, if smaller cave cities have been found in the region, the latest in Nevşehir as recently as 2014.

__Right:__ For centuries until the end of the Ottoman Empire, the cave town of Zelve in central Turkey was home to a mixed and harmonious community of Christians and Muslims.

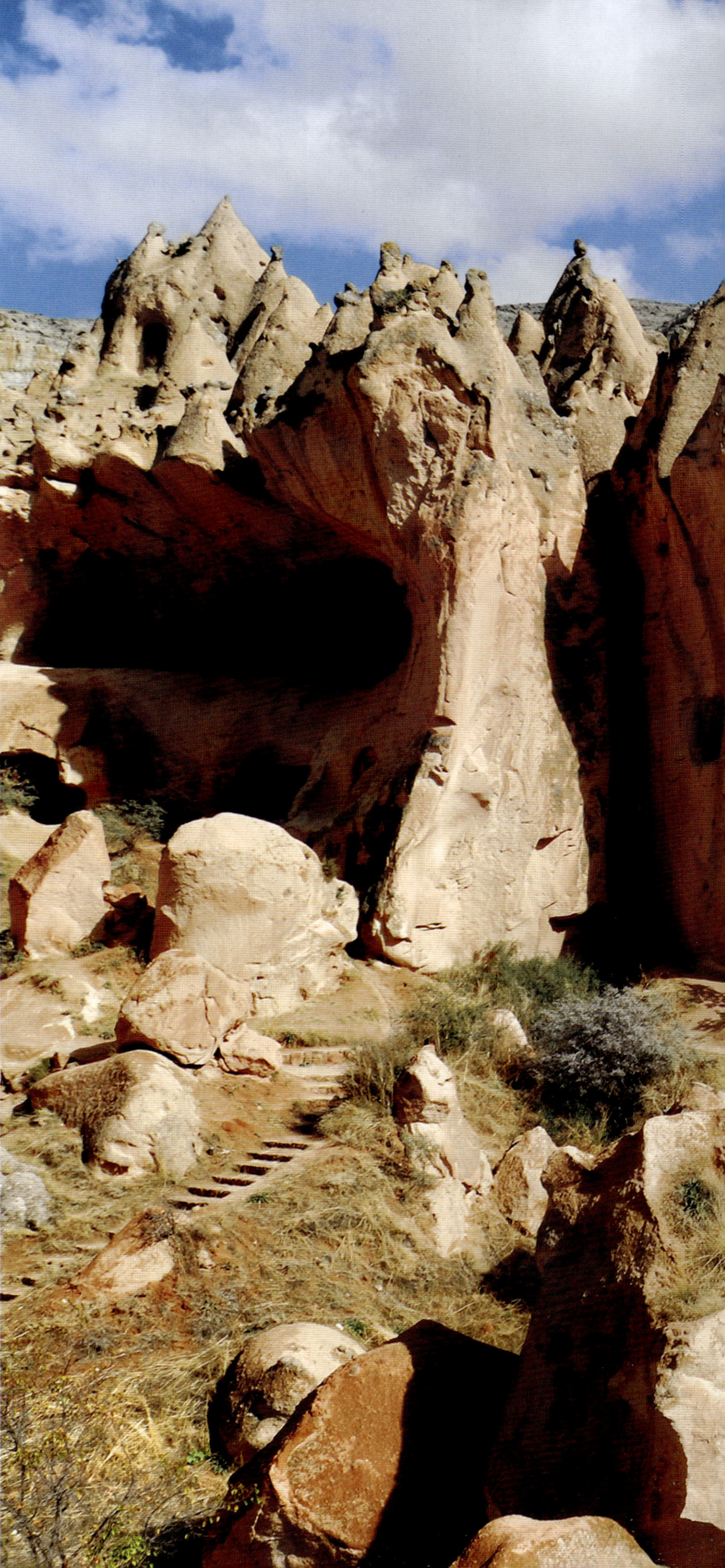

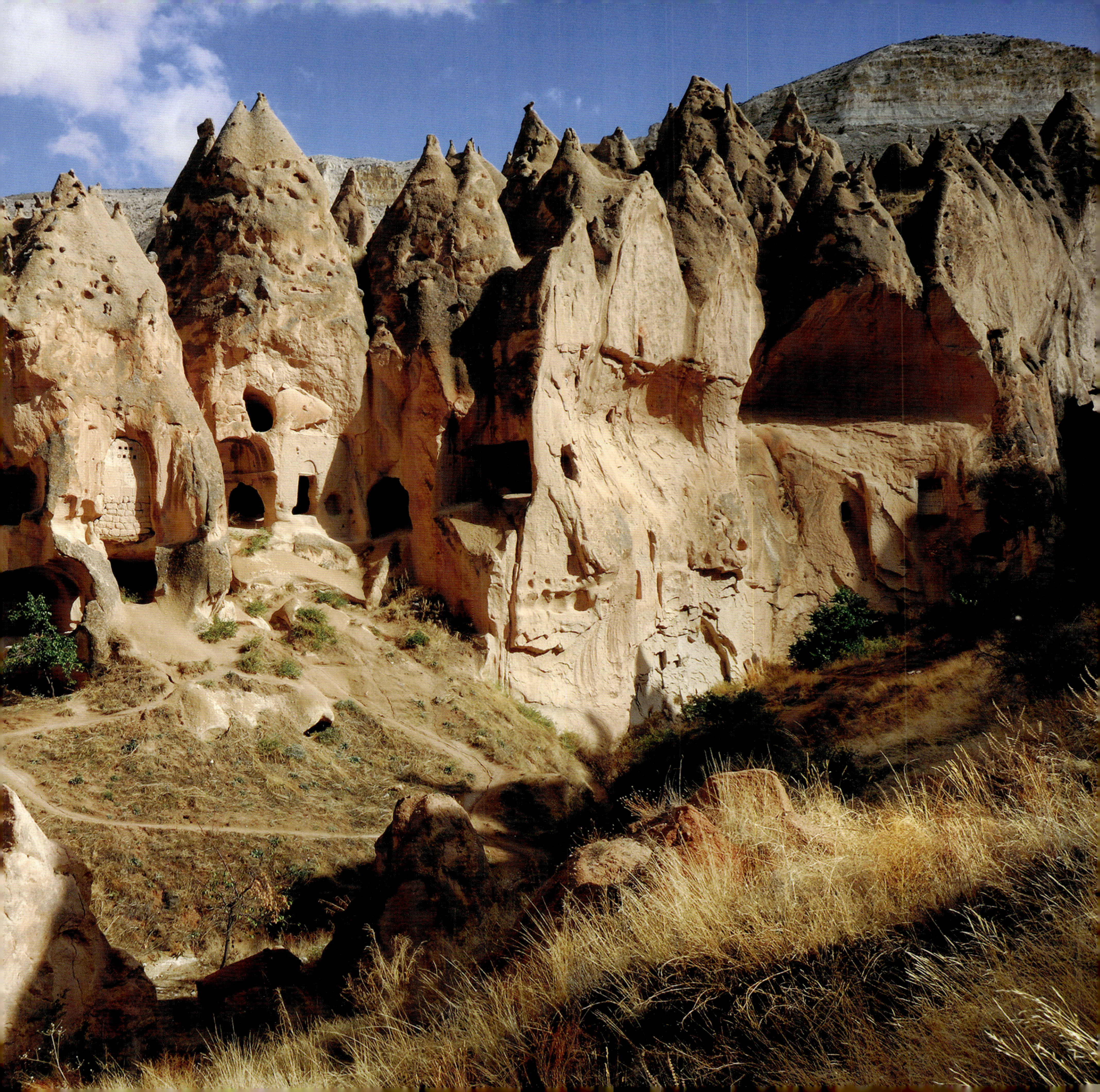

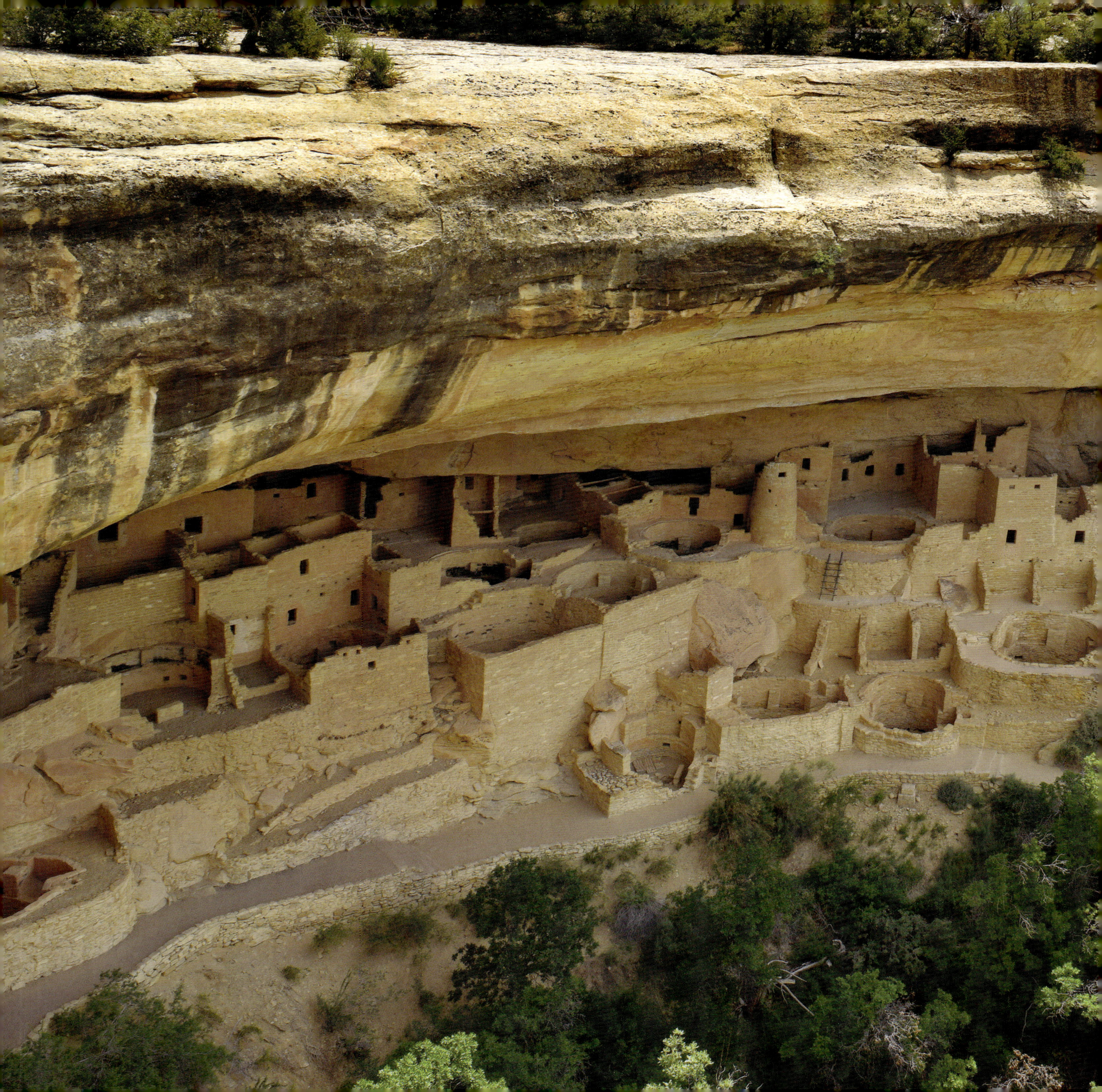

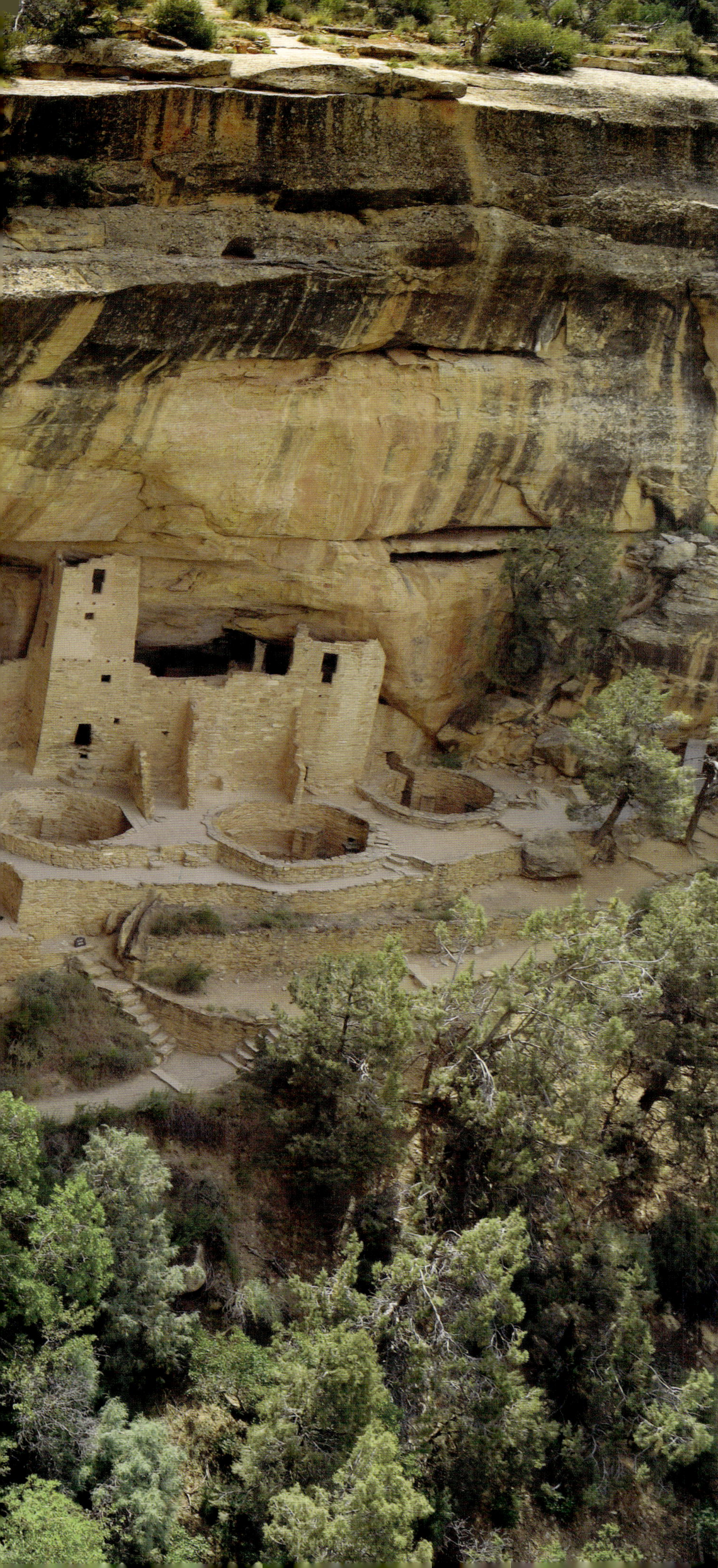

Mesa Verde

Another group to seek the protection of rocks was the Ancestral Puebloan people who lived on the Mesa Verde in southwest Colorado. After many centuries of hunting, gathering and farming in the area, around 1150 the Mesa Verdeans began building highly complex dwellings made of sandstone blocks beneath overhanging cliffs. The move to these more defendable cliff houses from villages in open areas earlier in their history, close to the land they farmed, seems to have stemmed from increasing threats from other peoples, indigenous to the wider region.

By then, the Ancient Puebloans had occupied this area for thousands of years, but they were perhaps more vulnerable to the vagaries of climate – changes that several centuries earlier had forced them to move from the Mesa Verde area to Chaco Canyon in northern Arizona, a hundred miles or so to the south. Here they had built great houses that feature aspects of the later cliff houses, but recessed into the ground in the form of pit-houses, often with many rooms. But here too, prolonged drought in the middle of the twelfth century forced the Puebloans north again to Mesa Verde, where over the following century they built the great cliff dwellings in which large groups now lived – including Cliff Palace (*see* left), the largest and most impressive of them all.

That these unique habitations have survived in various states of preservation into the present century might have surprised the people who built them, as it seems they were not intended to last more than a few decades. But in any case, in the last quarter of the thirteenth century, the region was once again beset by drought – worse than before – and by 1285 the cliff dwellings had all been abandoned.

Left: *This complex structure, known as Cliff Palace, represents the pinnacle of the architectural achievements of the Ancestral Puebloan people of Colorado and New Mexico.*
Next page: *Fasil Ghebbi, a fortress in Gondar, Ethiopia.*

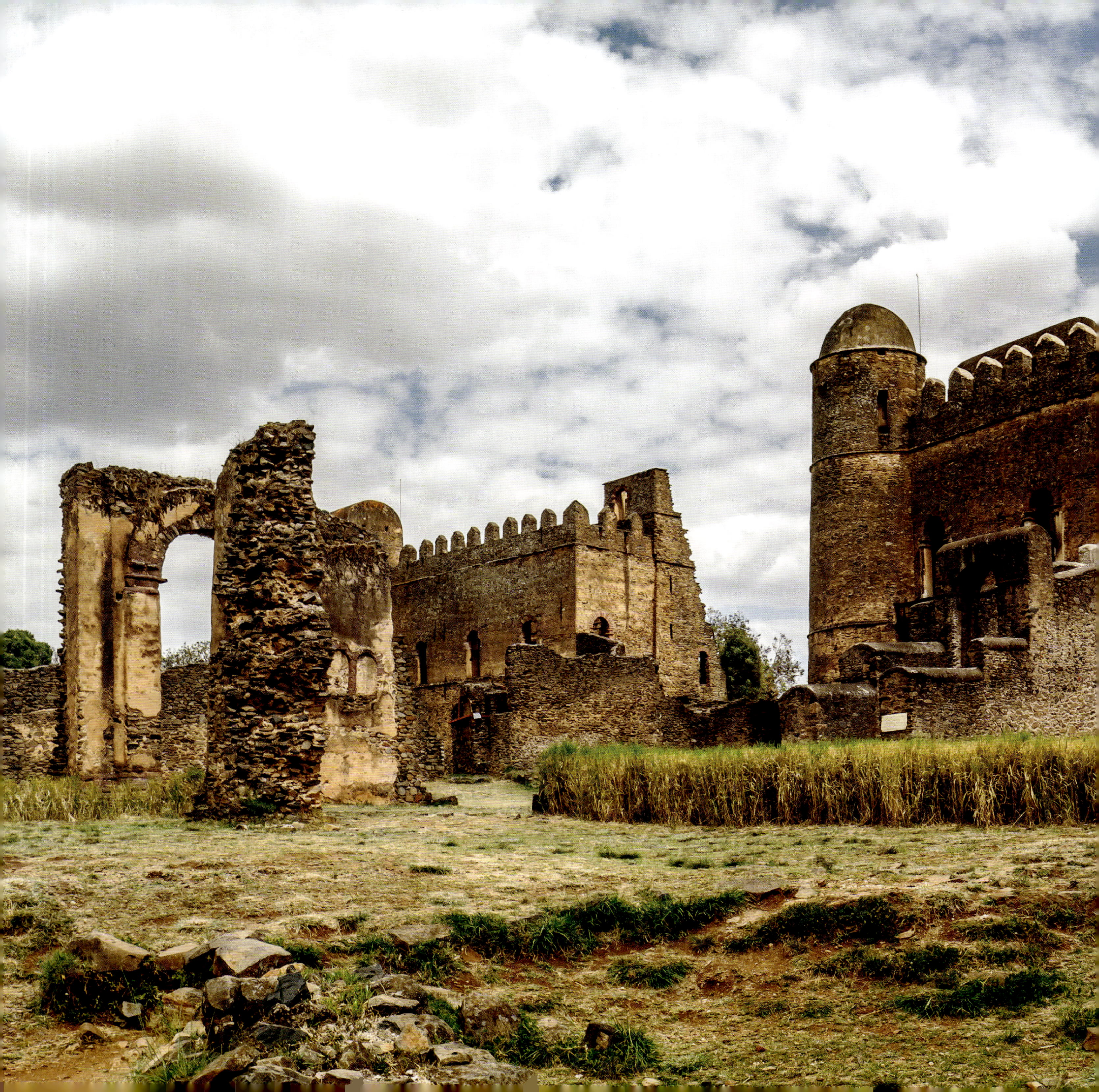

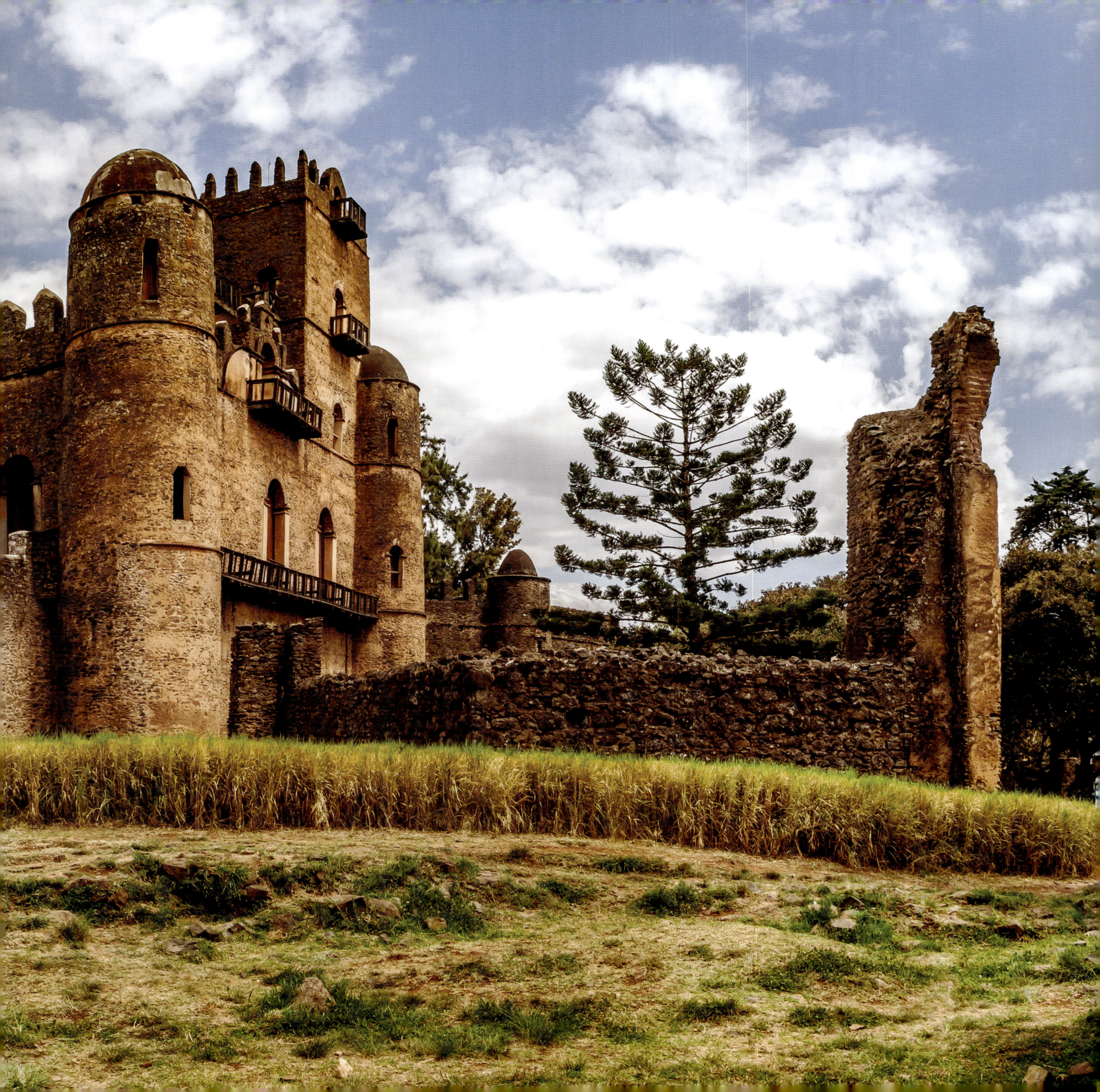

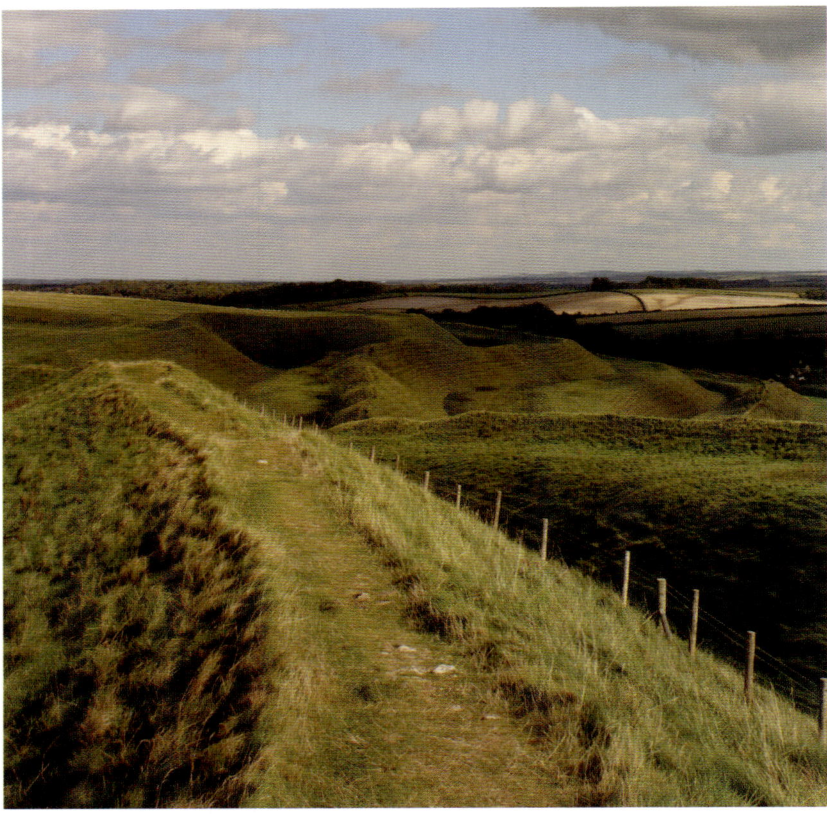

Above: *Construction of the earthwork ramparts of Maiden Castle in England in around 450 BC would have been a huge undertaking for the Iron Age tribespeople who lived there.*

Cahokia

The Mesa Verde dwellings remained unknown to non-indigenous Americans for another 40 years until cattle rancher Richard Wetherill found the great Cliff Palace of Mesa Verde, having been told of it by a member of the local Ute tribe. Over the course of the previous century, the autonomy and dignity – and, of course, the land – of indigenous people in the United States had been slowly taken away, even as archaeological investigation of indigenous sites had been going on in various places since Thomas Jefferson had first dug into a burial mound on his own Virginia property in 1784. Several hundred miles west, in the village of Cahokia, Illinois is a huge consortium of similar mounds –

Right: *Looking down on the village of Child Okeford from the Iron Age hillfort at Hambledon Hill, Dorset.*

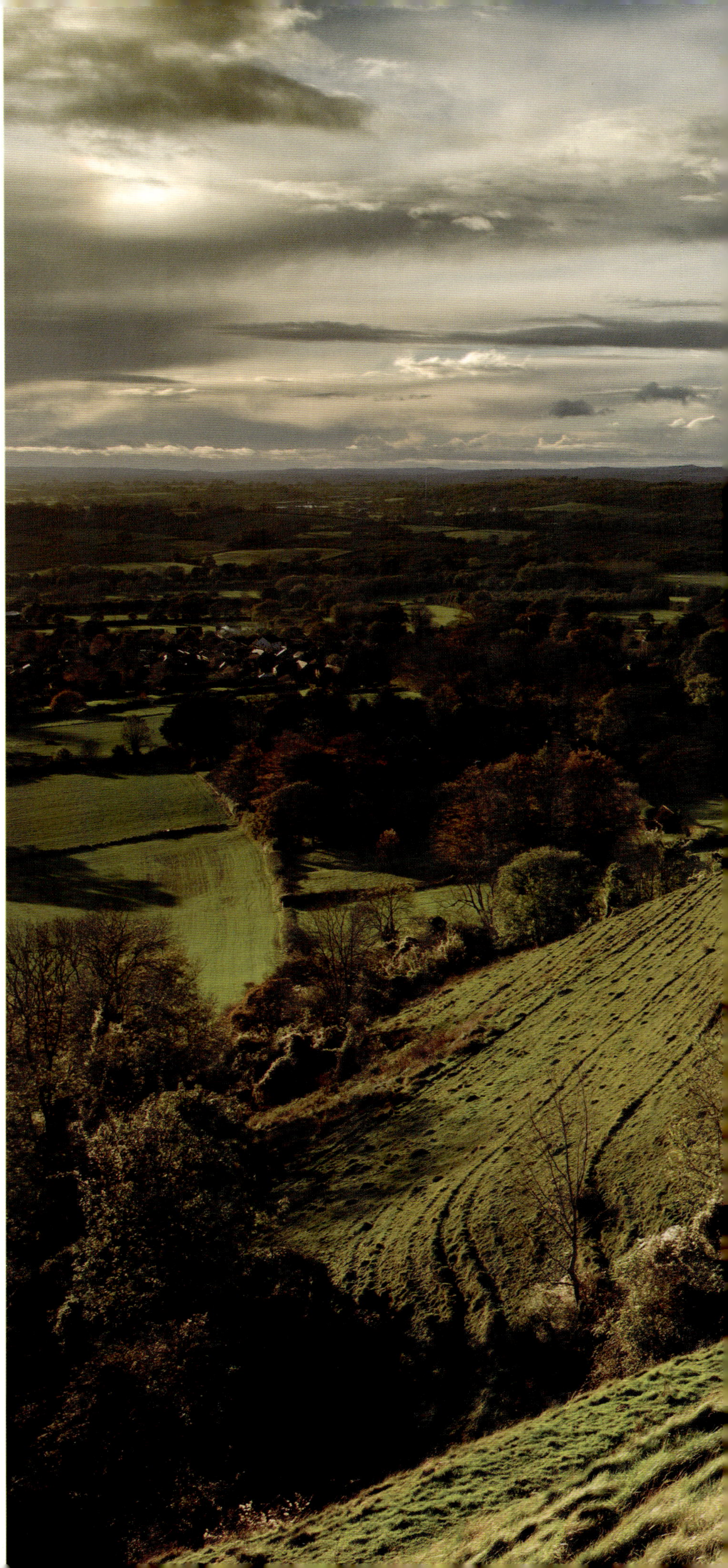

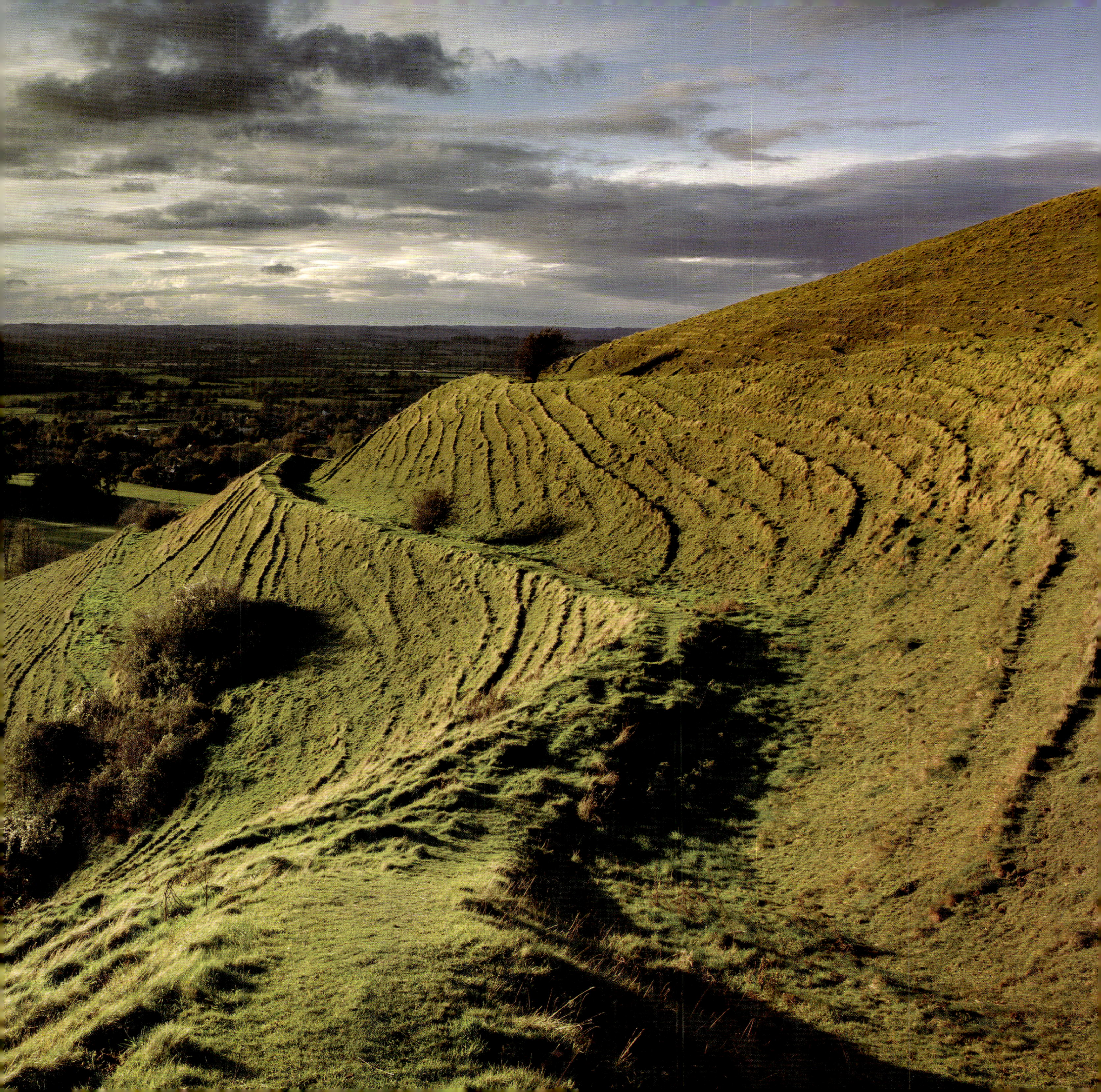

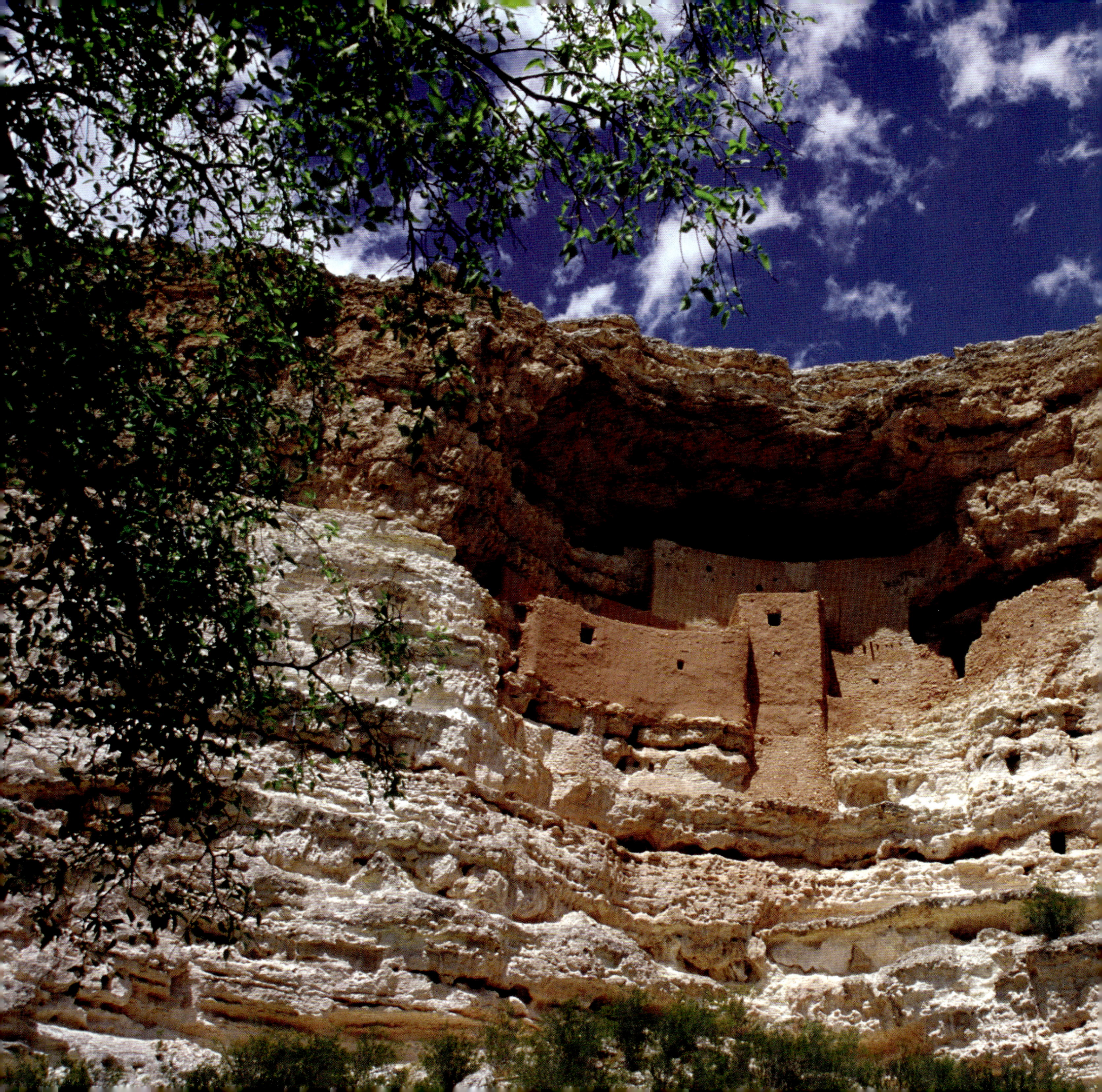

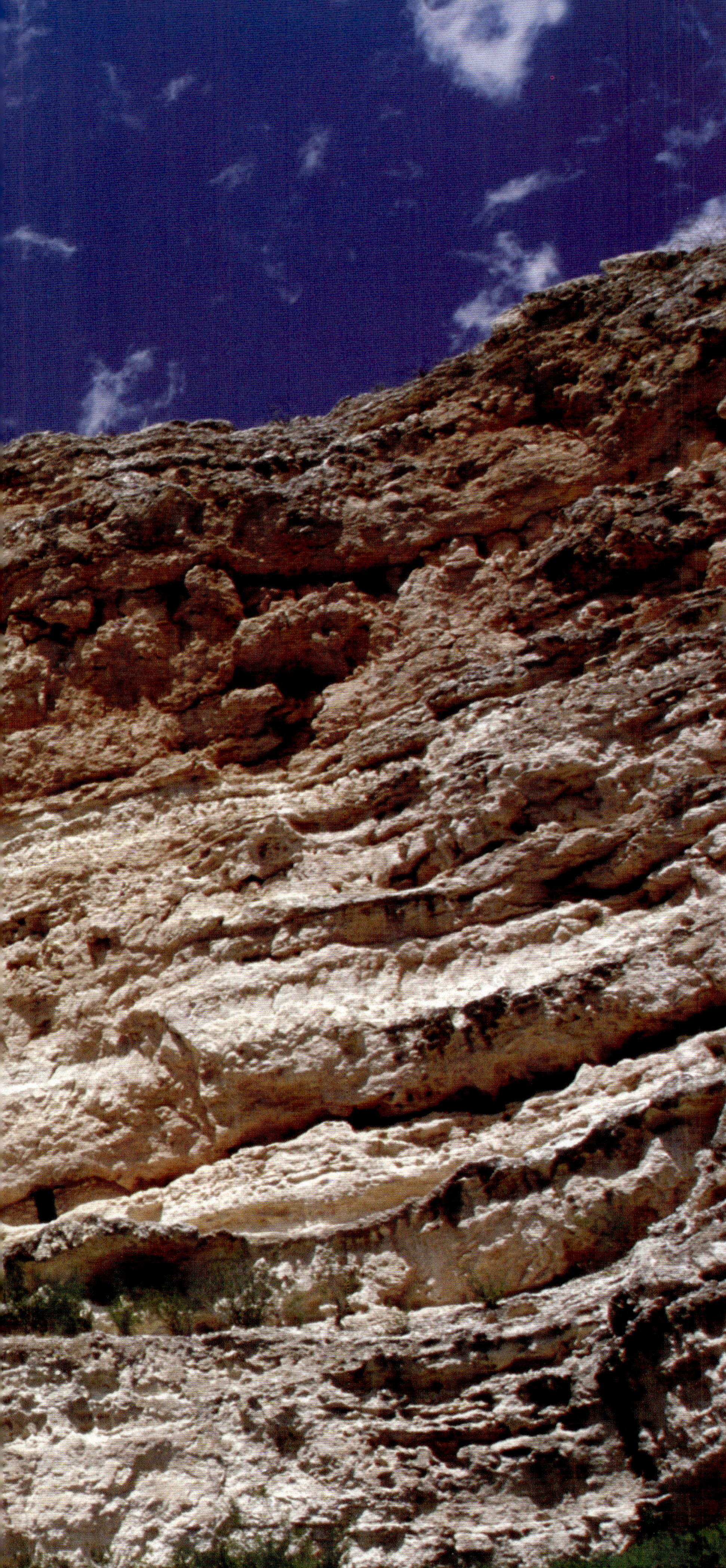

some 80 in all – covering a site measuring more than three square miles. These monumental earthworks are now believed to be the extant, visible signs of a great city known as Cahokia, which at one time had been the largest in North America. Inhabited by the Mississippian people for around seven centuries up to 1300, at the height of its influence some two centuries earlier, as many as 15,000 people, perhaps more, lived in what is thought to have been a site of spiritual significance as well as one of the great centres in the complex networks of trade that spanned the continent in all directions.

As is often the case with these great monuments of past cultures that left no written evidence, there are numerous theories as to why Cahokia was abandoned – from collapse of the local ecology caused by a rapidly growing population to catastrophic defeat in war. But artefacts, such as the exquisite repoussé copper plate figures produced by the Mississippians, paint a compelling picture of an advanced society equal in sophistication to those of their Mesoamerican contemporaries to the south.

Maiden Castle

If there is less to see in Cahokia and other similar sites in North America than in, say, the Yucatán Peninsula in Mexico, it may be simply because the most abundant building material to hand was not stone but the more perishable wood and a soil that was malleable enough to build with. This was also the case with the large number of Iron Age hill forts in Britain – defendable earthwork sites such as Maiden Castle in Dorset in southern England, whose earthwork ramparts and ditches formed a formidable series of barriers and which, at its height, around 450 BC, was possibly the largest such structure in Europe, and home to a sizeable community by the standards of the day.

Left: *Montezuma Castle National Monument, a cave dwelling in Arizona, USA.*

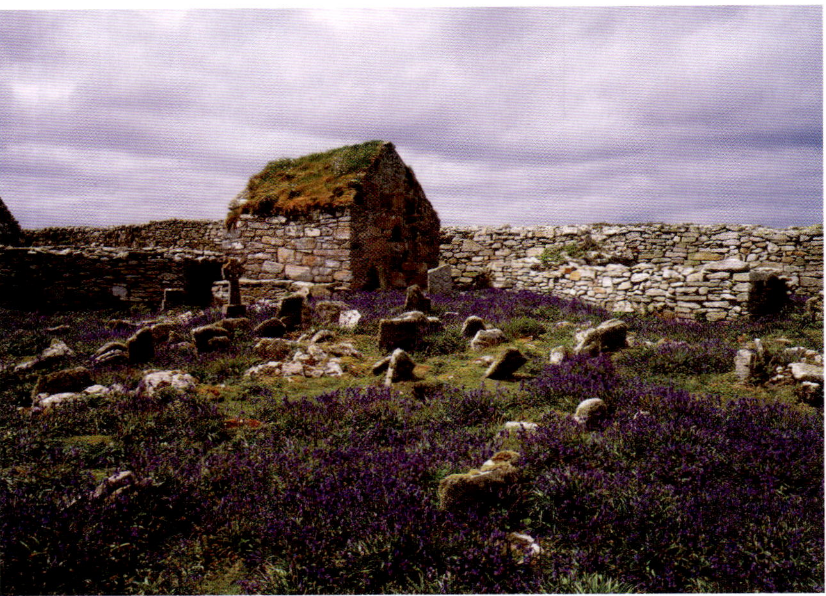

Above: *Monastic ruins on Inishmurray Island, Ireland.*

The regions of southern and southwest England are replete with Iron Age and Neolithic structures, and Stonehenge itself, a site first occupied around 3100 BC, was in its heyday one of the great cosmopolitan centres of Neolithic Europe. It was also a site of sacral importance whose primary axes, famously, seem to have been deliberately placed to line up with sunrise at the winter solstice. This profound knowledge of astronomy was widespread across the ancient world, as we see in structures elsewhere in the British Isles, such as the chambered cairn and passage grave of Maeshowe in the Orkney Islands, built around 2800 BC, or the even older Newgrange passage grave in Ireland, both of whose passages are aligned with the same exacting accuracy to the same day as Stonehenge. And the Great Temple of Abu Simbel in Egypt's Valley of the Kings was constructed with similar precision, if in this case to different astronomical priorities: for more than 3,000 years the setting sun has flooded the inner sanctum of the tomb of Ramesses II on the same two days – the pharaoh's birthday and coronation day – in February and October every year.

Right: *Ruins of the Castle of Kabaw, Libya.*

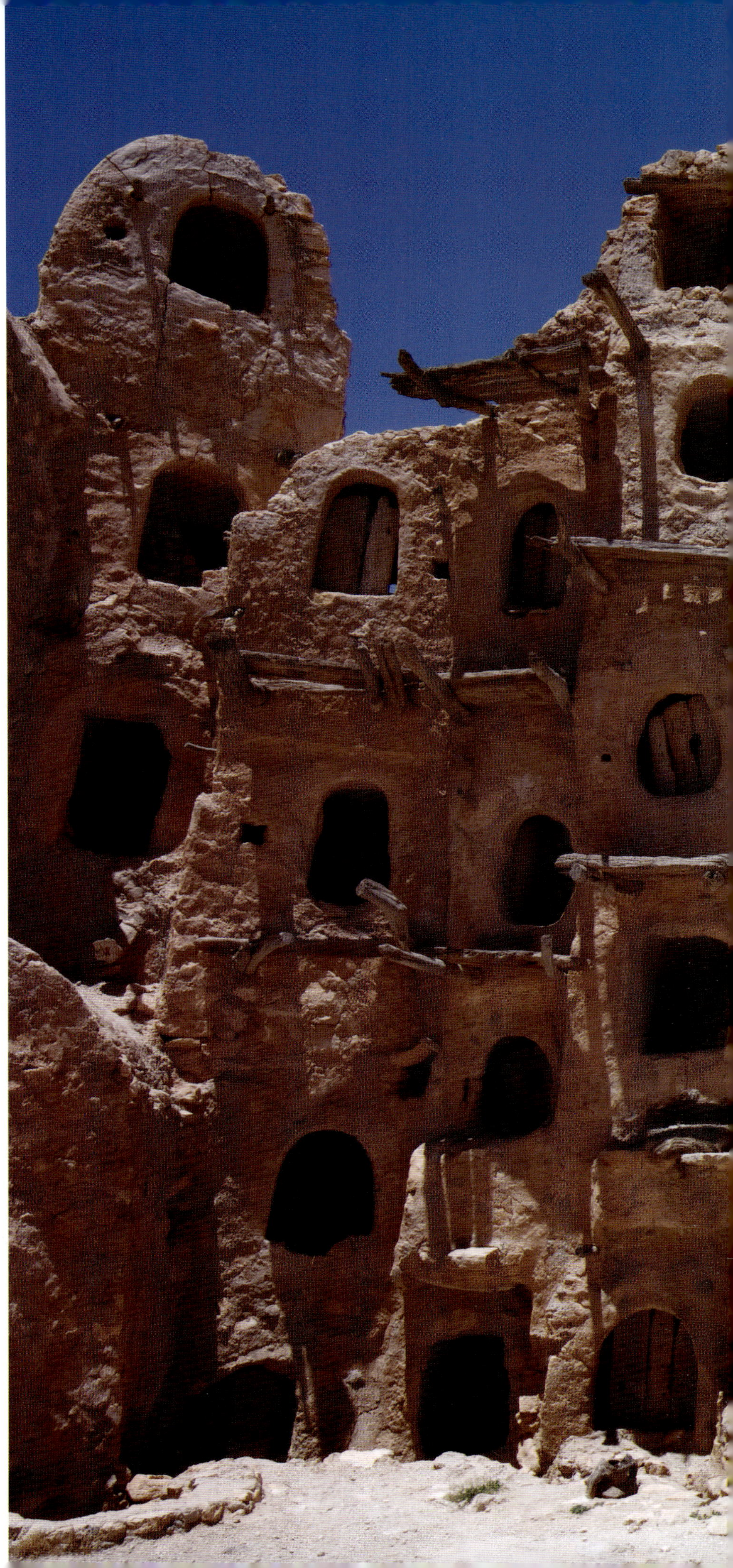

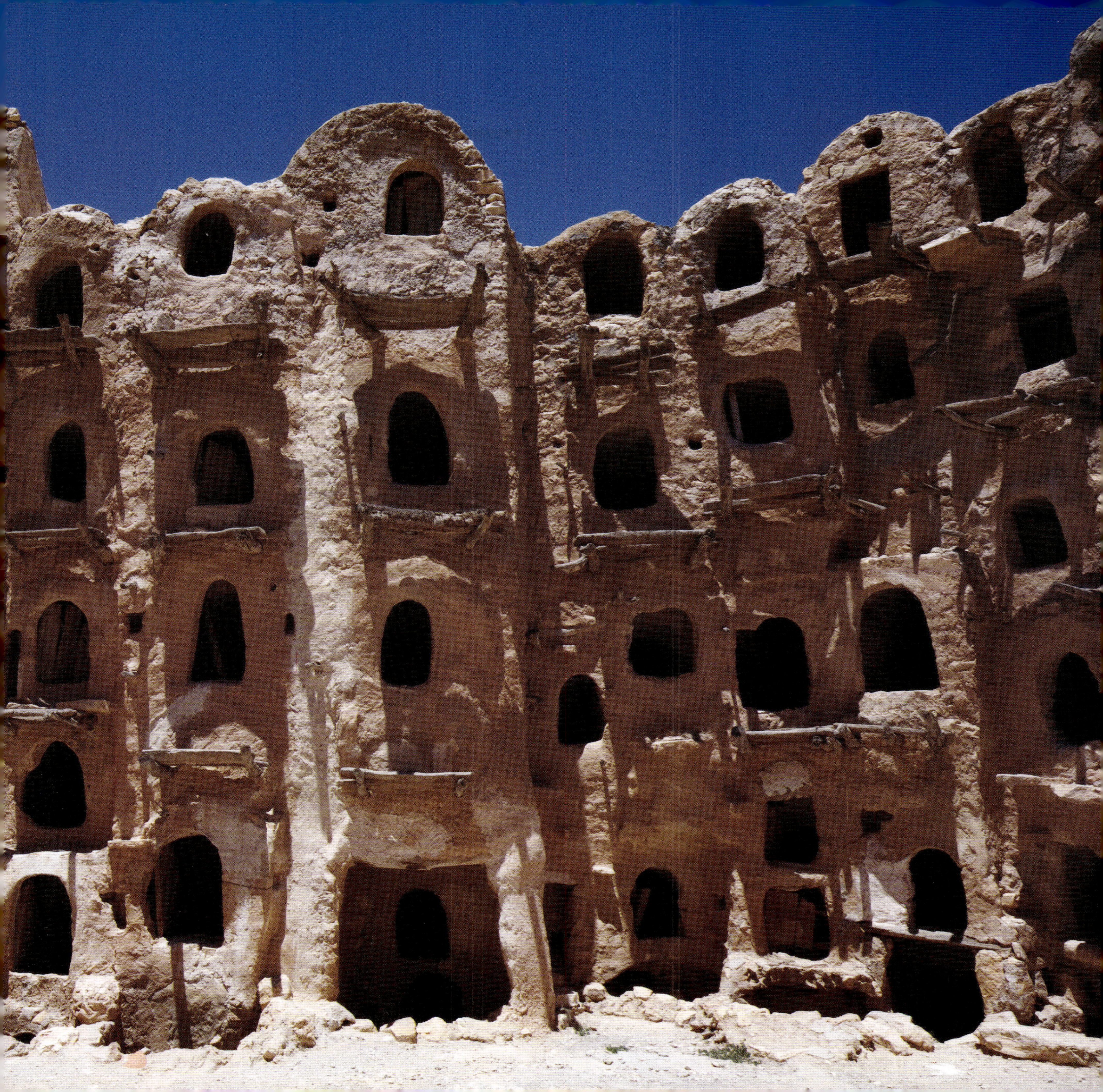

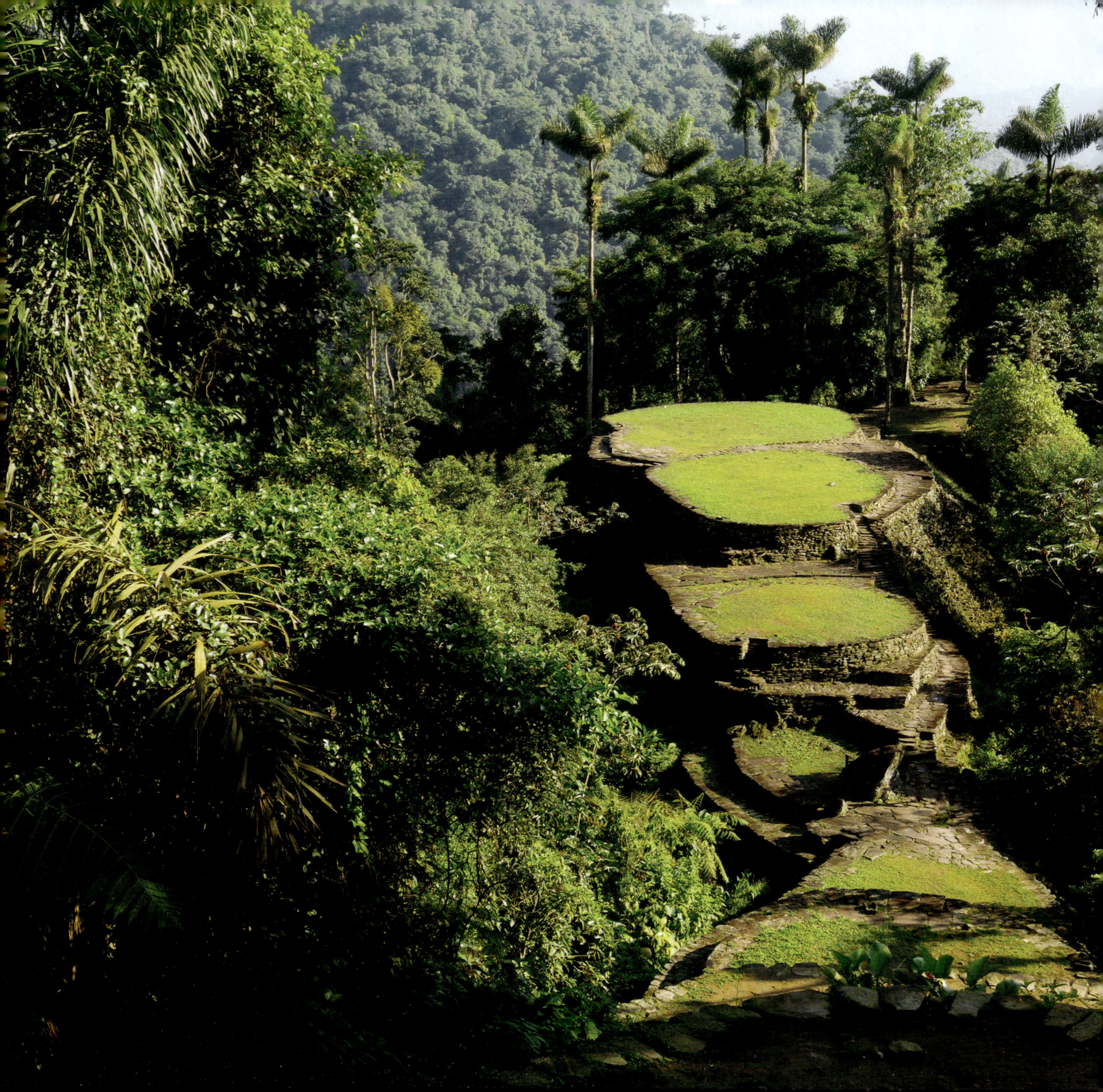

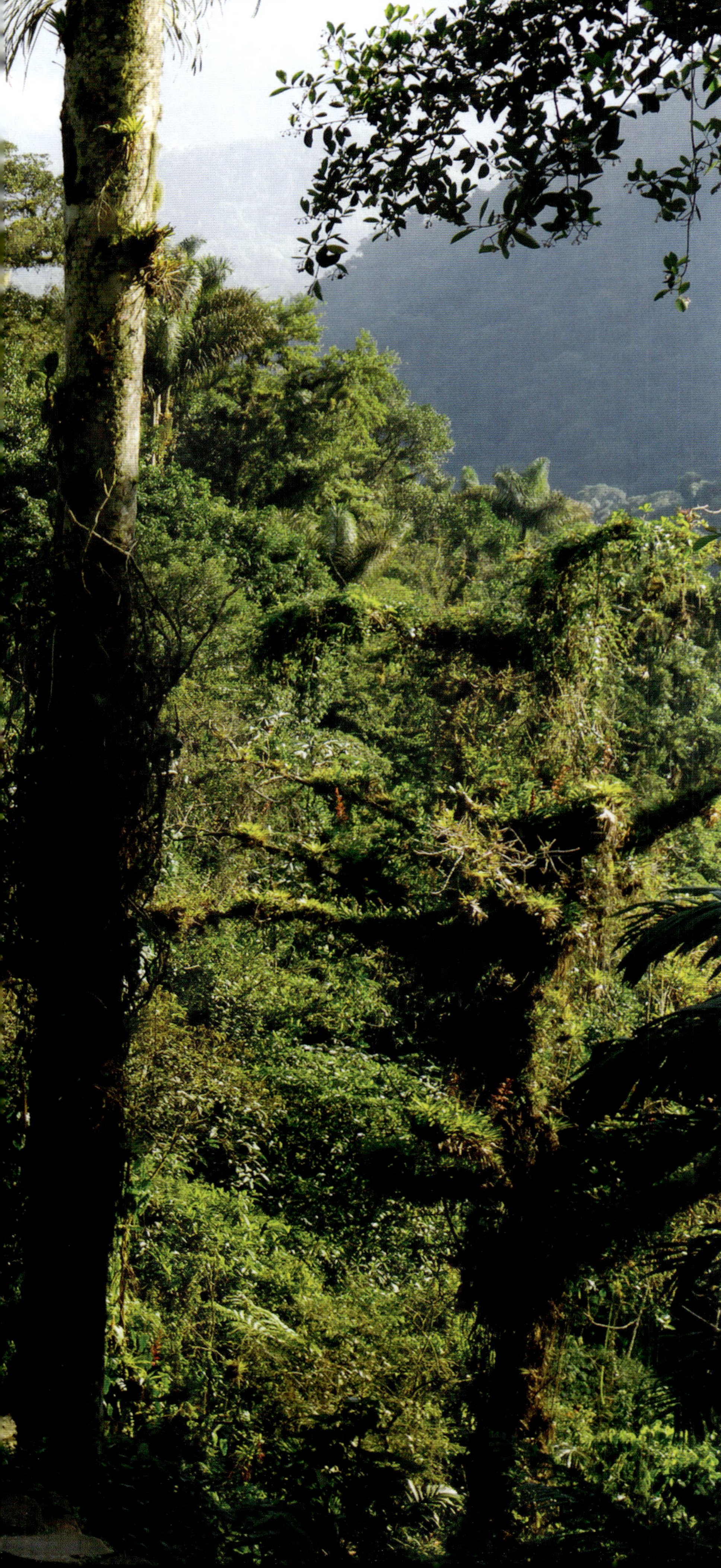

Central & South America

The ancient civilizations of the Americas were at least as curious about the universe – and as highly attuned to it – as those other great peoples.

Mayan City-States

Given the remoteness of the Americas in the pre-Columbian period, the detailed astronomical knowledge of the Mayan culture of Mesoamerica must have arisen independently of traditions in Neolithic Europe, North Africa and the development of the discipline in India, China, Greece and the early Muslim world. Nonetheless, important pyramids and other buildings such as temples and observatories in Mayan cities across the lowlands of Central America, laid out in accordance with observations they had made, are as closely aligned with celestial bodies as any of the pyramids of Egypt, which were themselves conceived along similar astronomical lines. In the great city of Chichén Itzá in the Yucatán Peninsula in Mexico, the great pyramid temple known as El Castillo was laid out so that the setting sun at the spring and autumn equinoxes casts a shadow of the pyramid's northwest corner on the ground, resembling the serpent deity Kulkulkan to whose worship the temple was pledged.

Mayan civilization of the Classic and Postclassic periods – from AD 250 to the coming of the Spanish from 1519 onwards – resembled the Italian Renaissance or Ancient Greece, with great city-states, such as Tikal in

Left: *Ciudad Perdida (literally 'lost city') in Colombia's Sierra Nevada was rediscovered in 1972 by two treasure hunters. It pre-dates the more famous Inca city of Machu Picchu by 650 years.*
Next page: *Machu Picchu in Peru.*

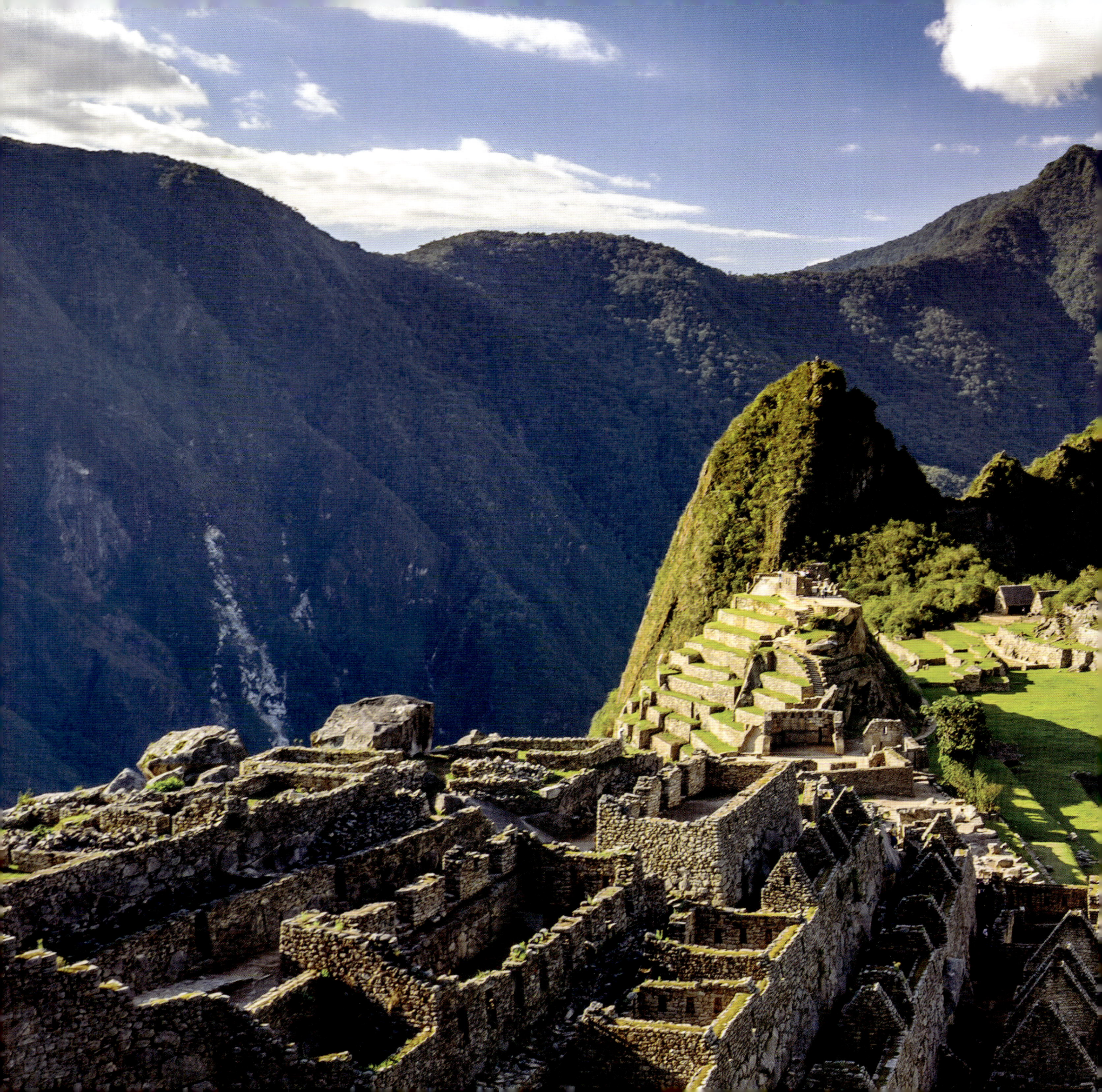

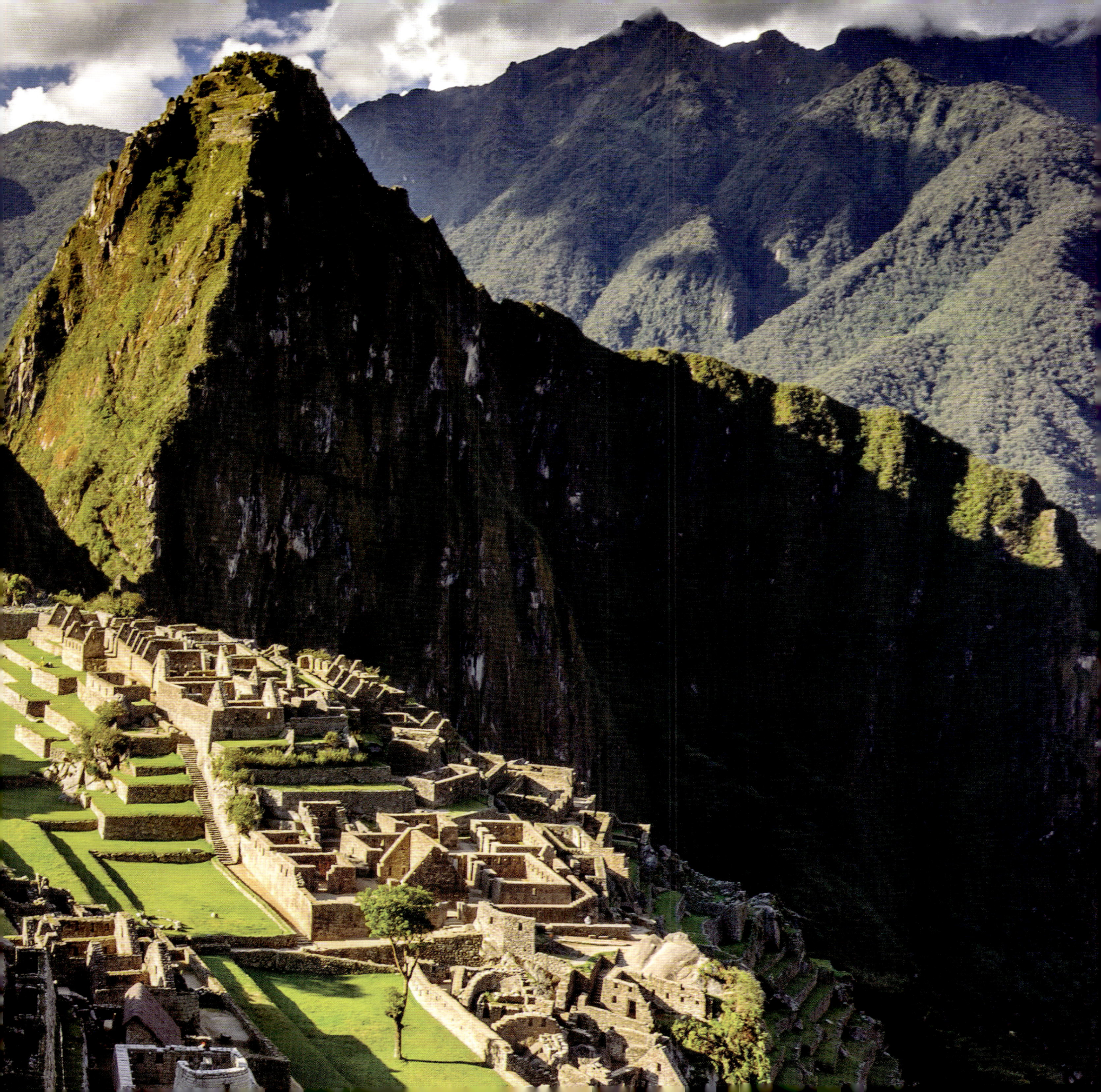

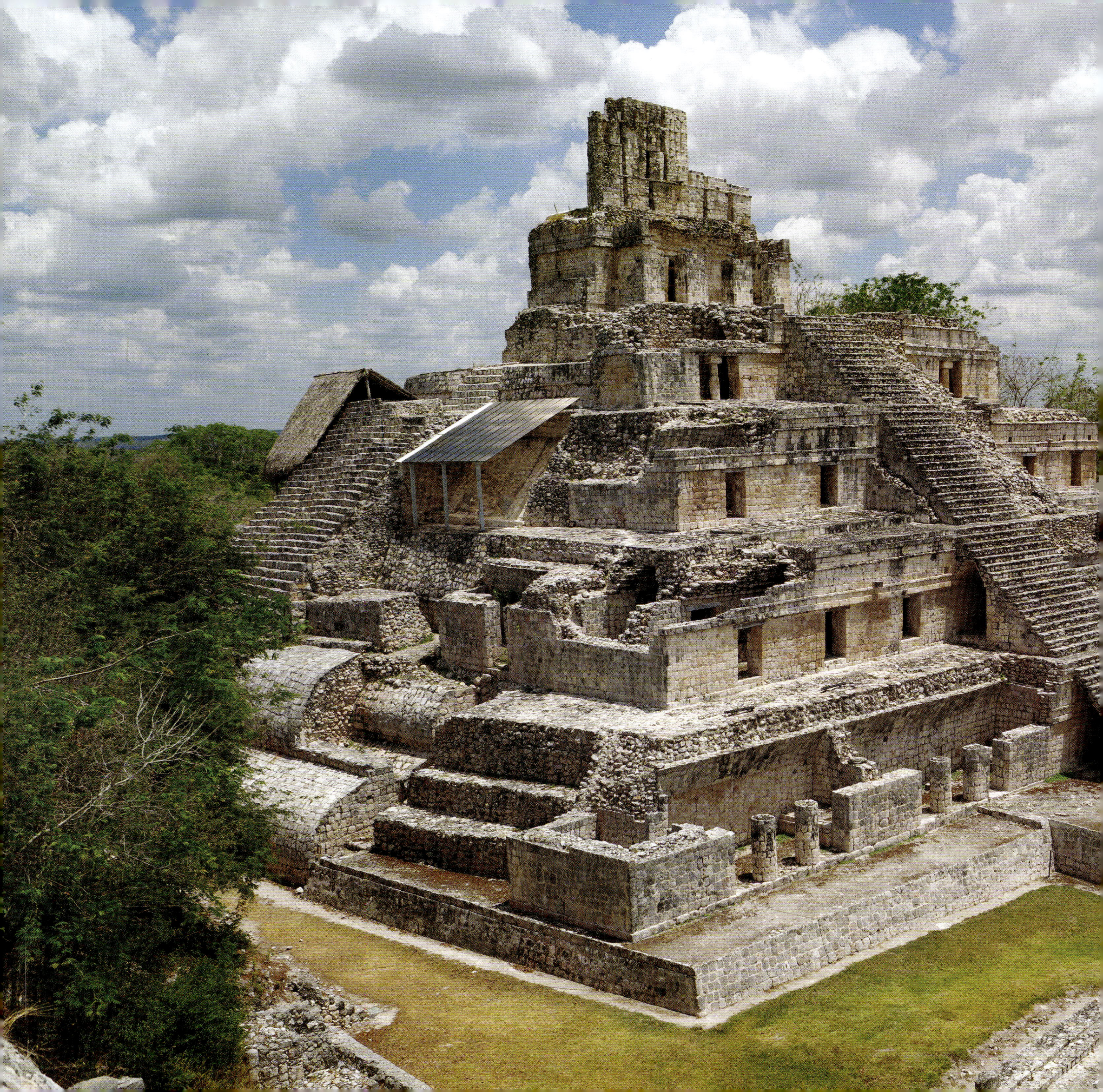

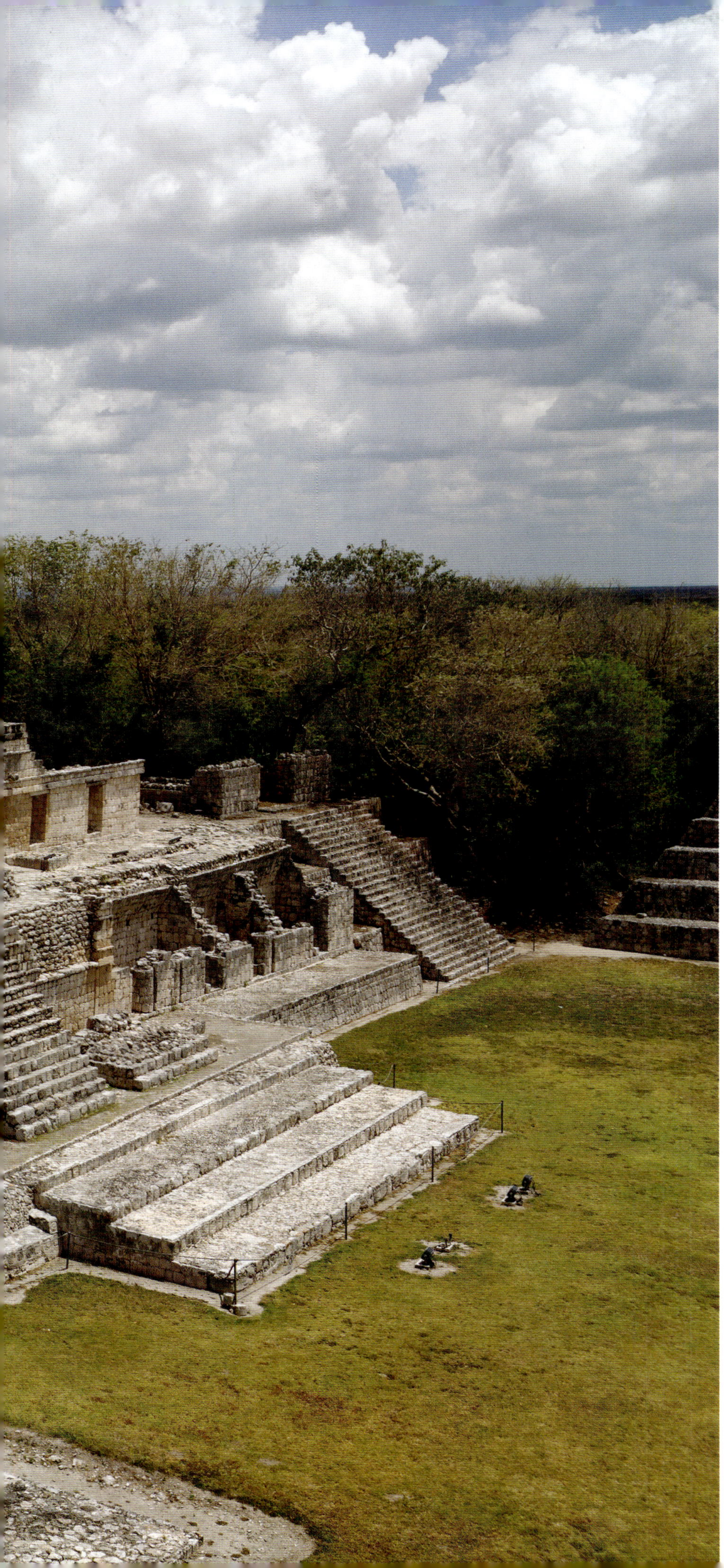

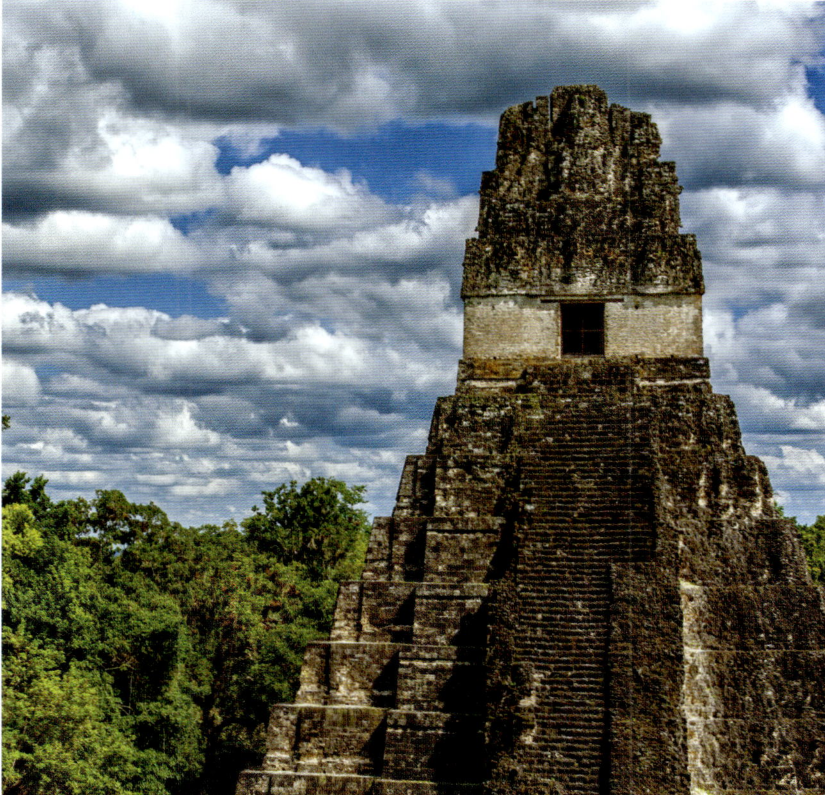

Above: *Mayan temple at Tikal, Guatemala.*

modern Guatemala (*see* above), Copán in Honduras (*see* page 38) and Calakmul in Mexico, commanding the resources and the loyalty of large surrounding regions. A considerable number of these competing cities existed throughout the Central American isthmus, with populations in some cases thought to have been well in excess of 100,000 people, as was the case at Caracol (*see* page 45), in what is now modern Belize. And despite the hundreds of Mayan archaeological sites that are known throughout the subcontinent, including some 40 cities, there are estimated to be still hundreds more yet to emerge from the dense tropical jungle that guards their secrets, with the latest major discoveries, the cities of Lagunita and Tamchen, being identified among the dense jungle cover of Yucatán from aerial photographs taken as recently as 2014.

Left: *The spectacular Mayan ruins of Edzná, at one time part of the Calakmul polity, lie in the state of Campeche in modern Mexico.*

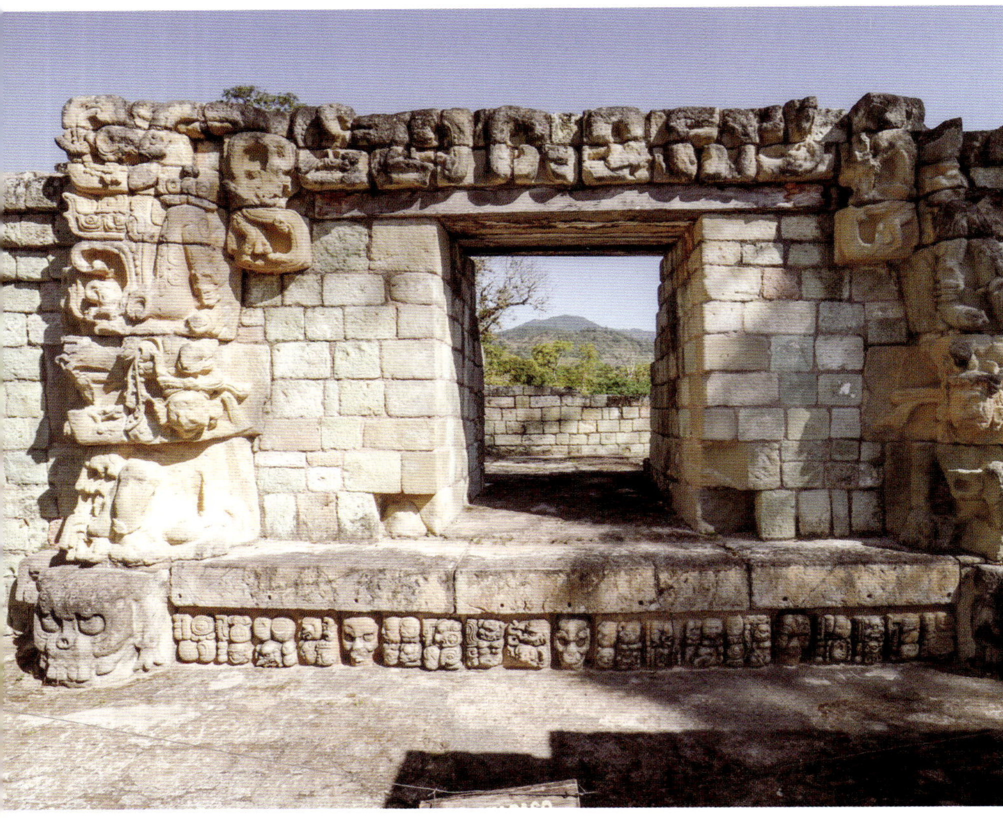

Above: *Copán in modern Honduras was one of the most important of all Mayan cities. Covering an area of 250 square miles, at its height it was home to 20,000 people.*

Teotihuacán

Mayan descendancy is widespread among the peoples of modern Central America, with as many as 70 Mayan languages still spoken by some 5 million people across the region. But they were far from the only builders of monumental cities in this continental area. The later Aztecs were the first Mesoamerican people to have dealings with the Conquistadors, whose desire for gold and whose religious convictions emboldened them to treat the indigenous culture and people with unconscionable cruelty.

Modern Mexico City, like other later Spanish colonial cities in the Americas, such as Cusco in Peru, was built directly on the ruins of Tenochtitlán, the

Right: *Ancient Incan ruins.*
Next page: *Mayan ruins in Tulum, Mexico.*

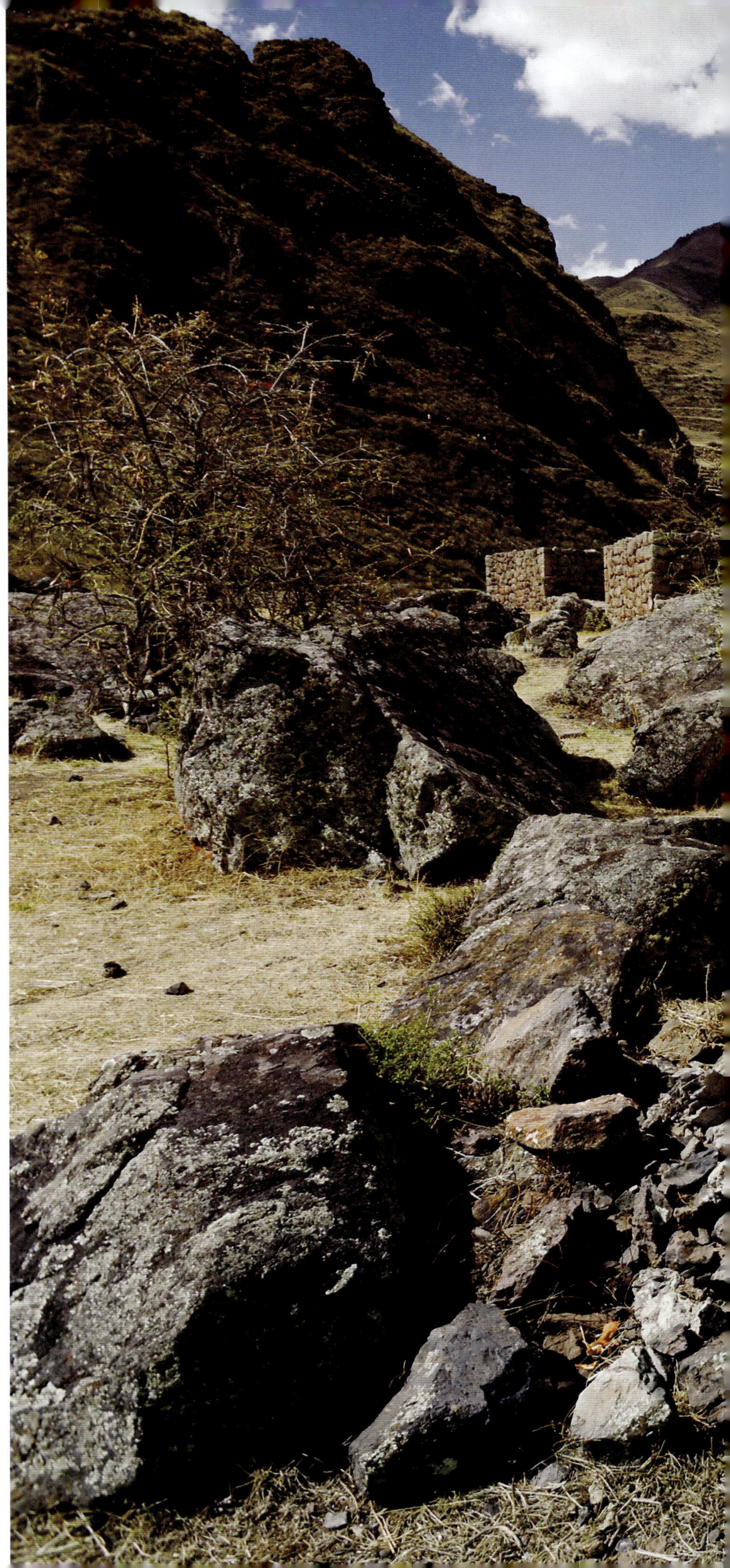

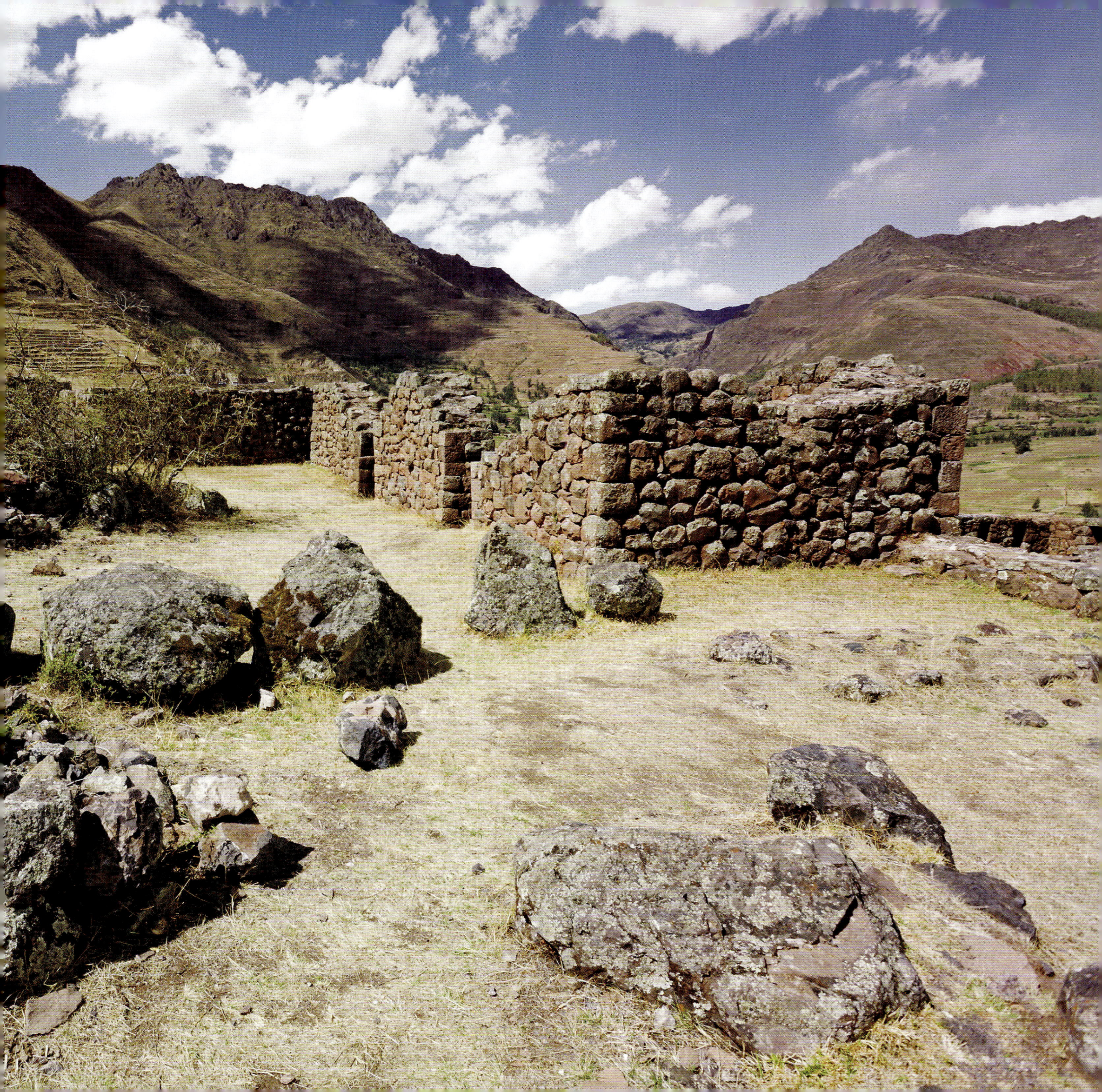

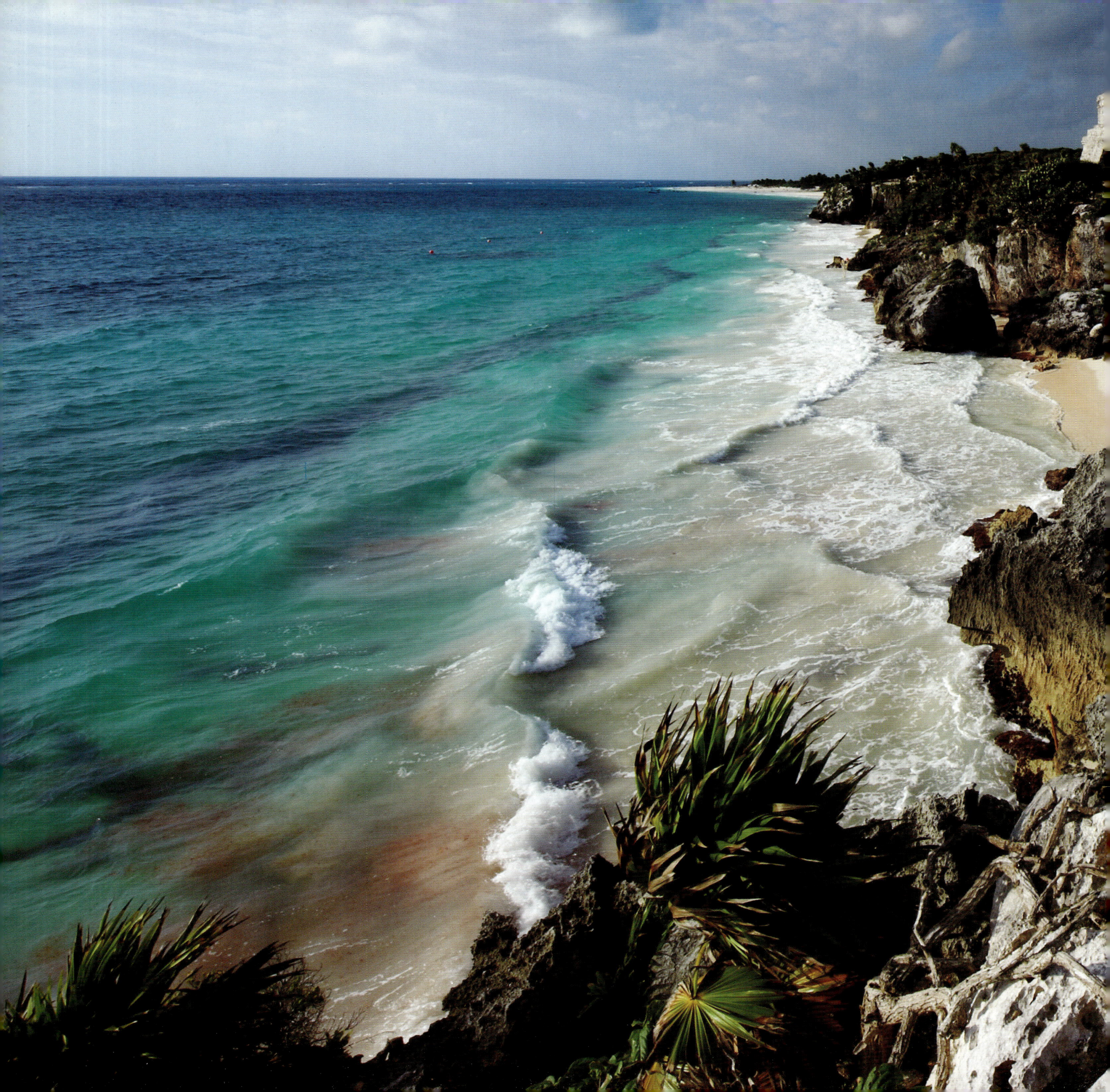

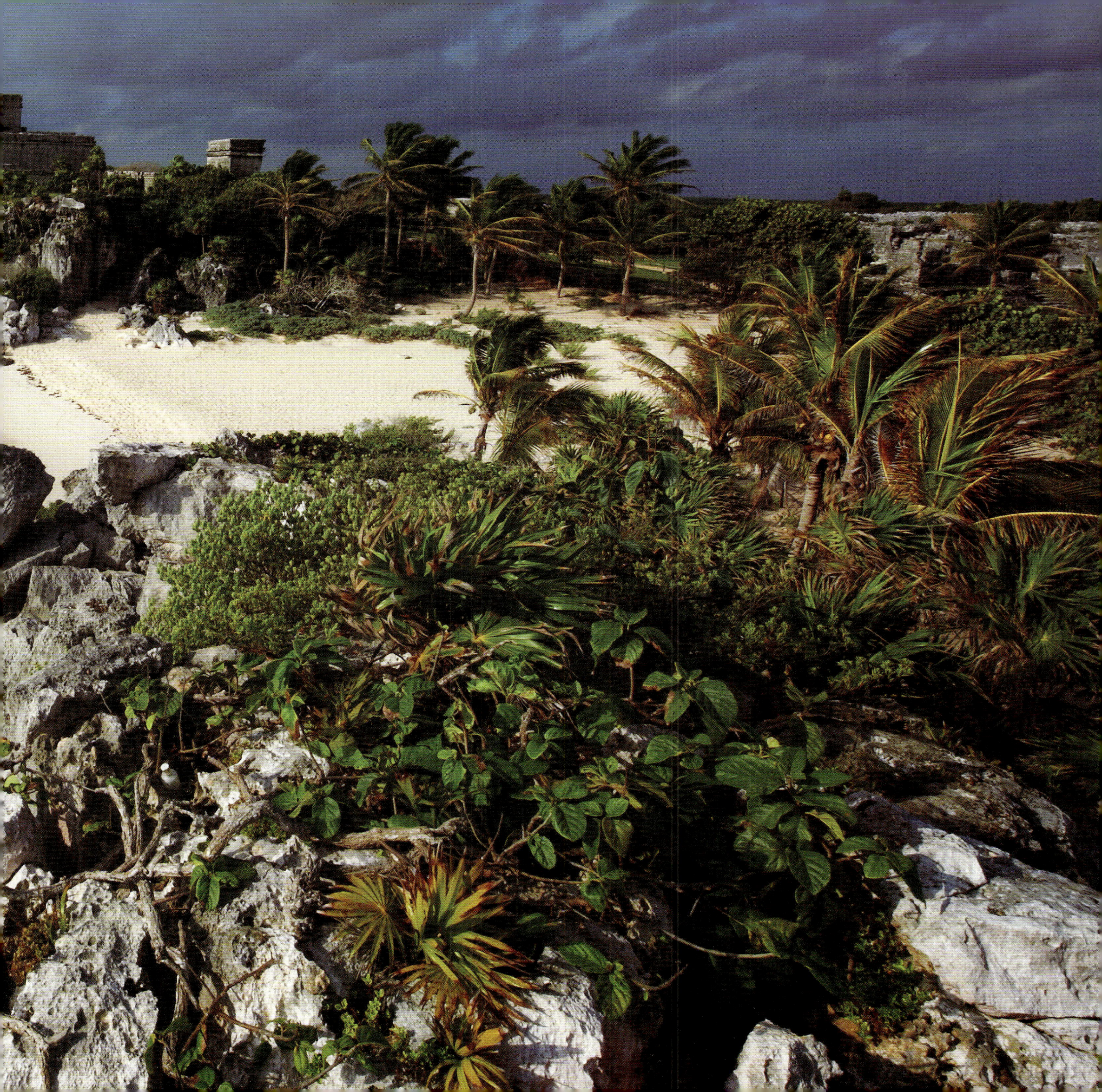

capital of the empire ruled by Moctezuma II; remnants of the main temple of the Aztec city, the Templo Mayor, can still be seen in the heart of Mexico City today. But for some reason, the great city of Teotihuacán, just a few dozen miles northwest of Tenochtitlán, was left untouched by Hernan Cortés and his ruthless band of men.

By then, Teotihuacán had been more or less deserted for many centuries, a lost city even for the Aztecs, who were so impressed by its vacant ruins when they took over this region just a century or so before the Spanish arrived. But it was once the epicentre of another great civilization, the highland Teotihuacanos, who had rivalled the lowland Mayans during their own extraordinary rise. At the height of its power, in the centuries up to AD 500, Teotihuacán had a population of 125,000 and was the largest city in the Americas, and one of the largest in the world at that time. And as with the settlements of Mesa Verde to the north, the city's collapse seems to have resulted from changes in climate, bringing severe drought, from the effects of which it is estimated many thousands would have died.

The Lost City of the Incas

The Spanish may have begun their conquest in Central America, but they did not stop there. Little more than a decade after the Aztecs were defeated by arms and then decimated by smallpox and other European viruses the invaders brought with them, the Spanish were fighting another decisive battle, in Cajamarca in what is now Peru, thousands of miles to the south. Trekking further south still, the small Spanish army, under Francisco Pizarro, eventually took Cusco, the capital of the Incan Empire, and largely destroyed the great citadel of Sacsaywaman, removing all the smaller stones for buildings of their own and leaving only the monumental walls that are still such an imposing presence there today.

Right: *Temple in Palenque, Mexico.*

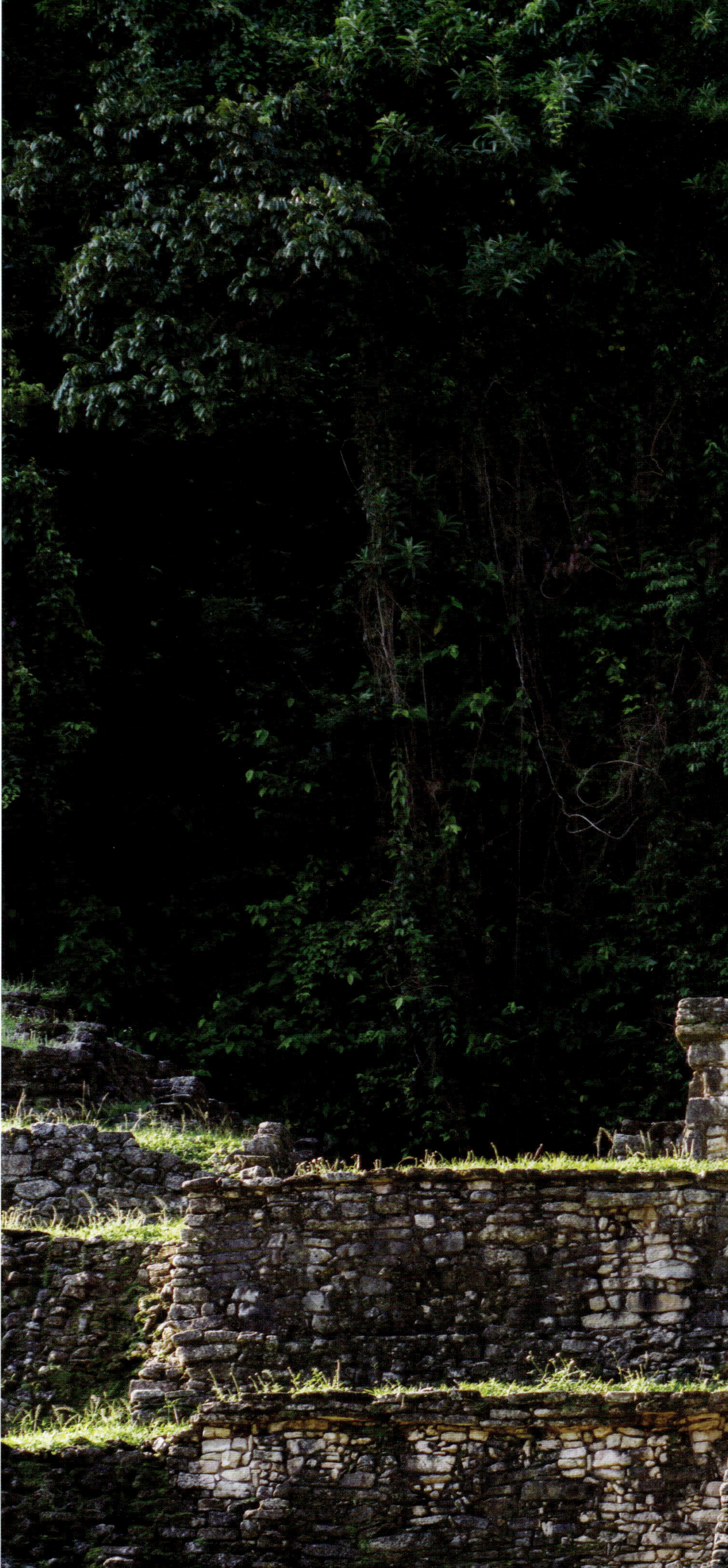

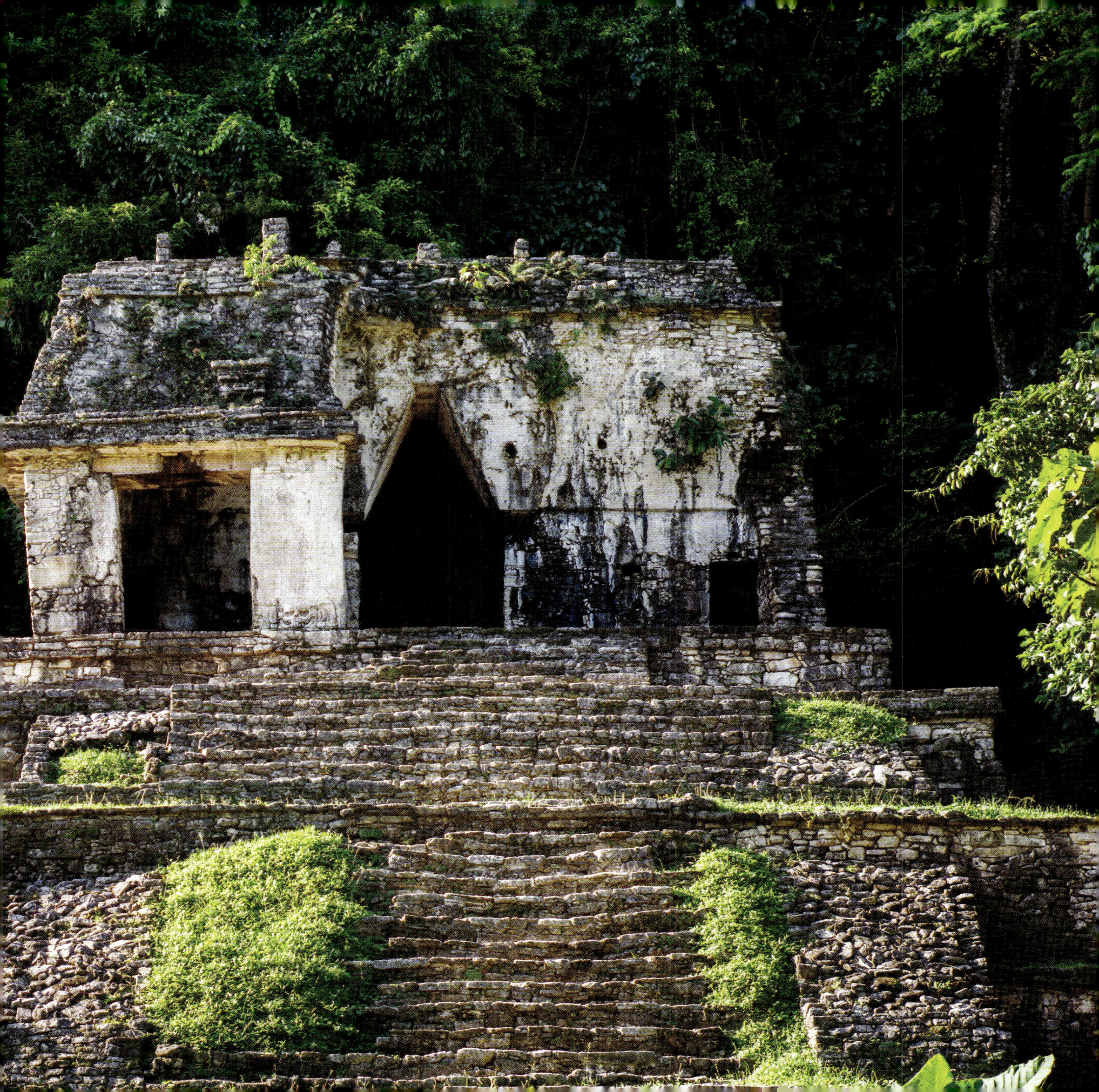

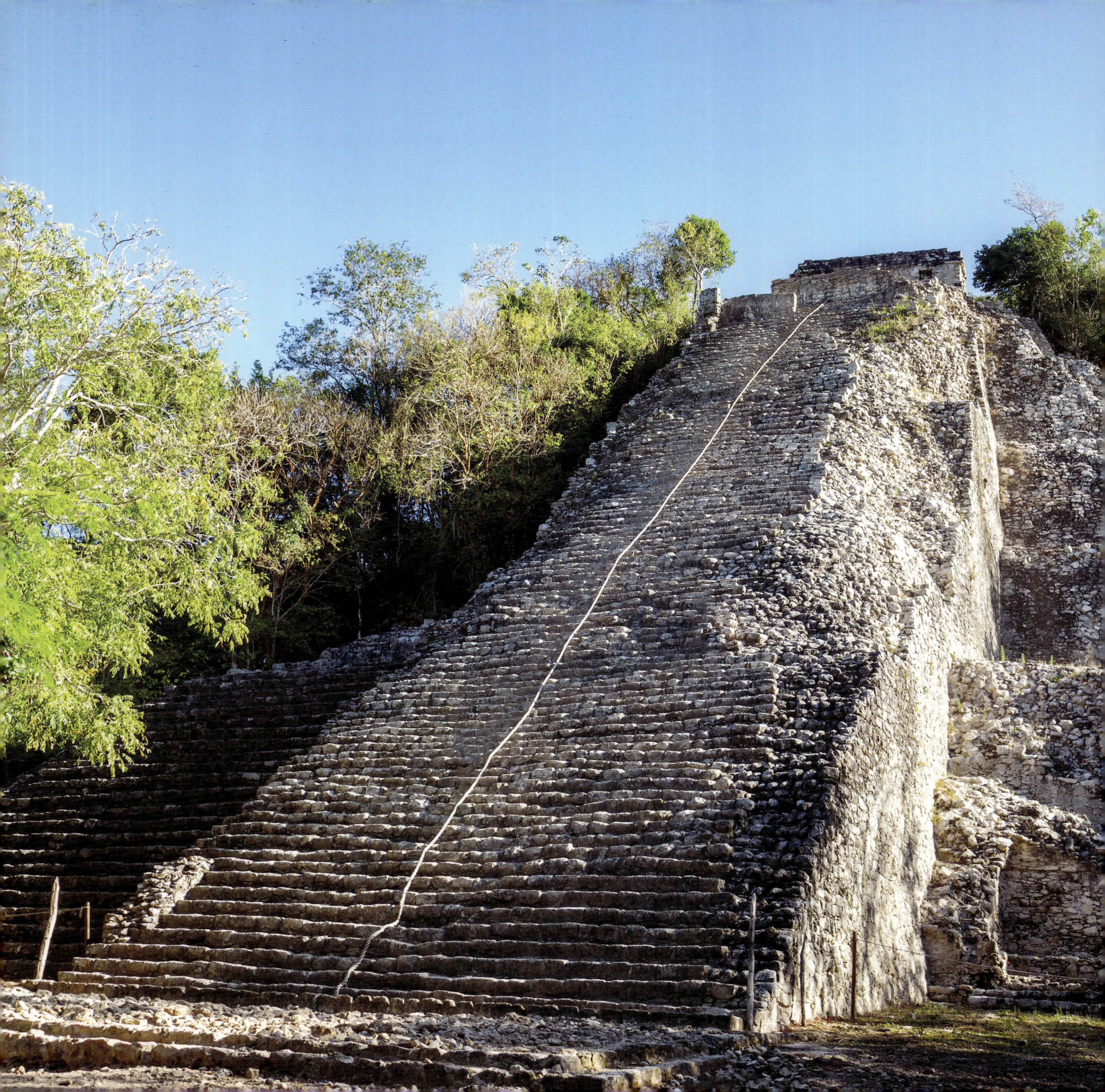

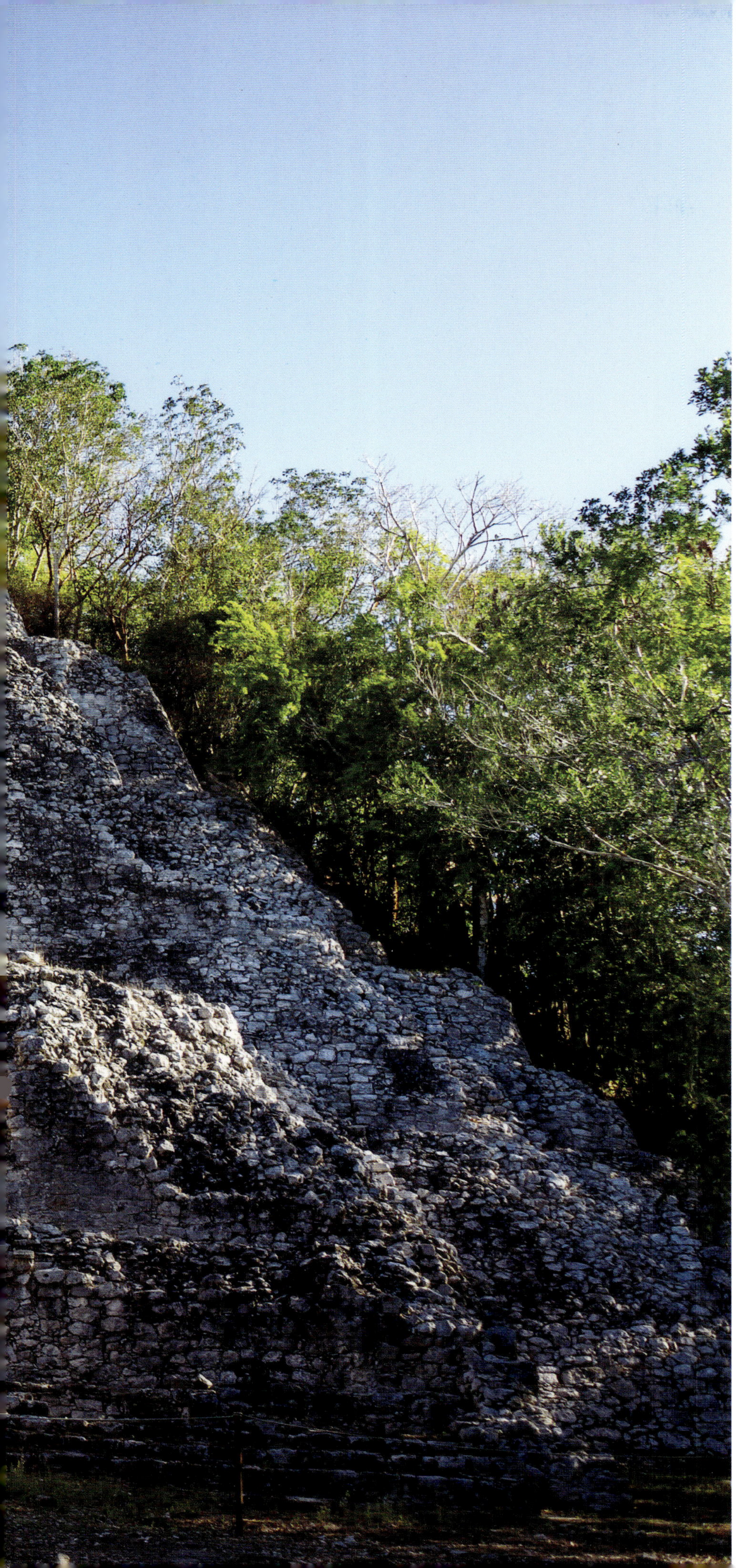

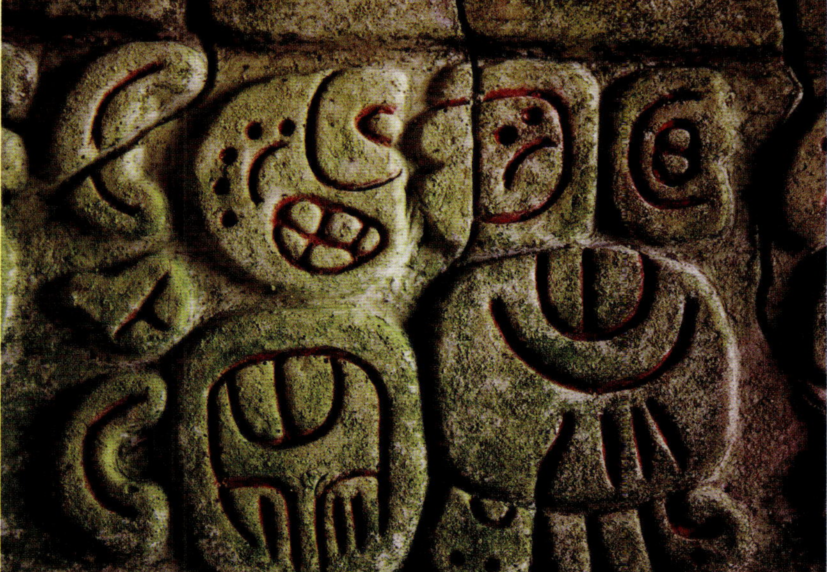

Above: *Ancient Mayan hieroglyphics in stone at the ruins at Caracol, Belize.*

The Inca continued to resist, withdrawing to the fortress of Ollantaytambo in the Sacred Valley close to Cusco, but were eventually forced to flee far to the north in an attempt to survive. It is possible that some retreated to the mountains above the Sacred Valley, to a citadel in the most spectacular location imaginable, known to us as Machu Picchu (*see* page 34). The Spanish never found it, though driven by their greed for gold, encouraged by the riches they had already plundered, they continued to be haunted by rumours of Paititi, the fabled Lost City of the Incas.

The True Lost City

Four centuries later, it was the same myth that drew the American explorer Hiram Bingham back to southern Peru in 1911, having already been taken to Choquequirao, another Inca mountain settlement, on a visit to the region three years earlier. On the return trip, he sought the help of local people, who guided him through the mountains to Machu Picchu, a deserted site he was

Left: *Nohoch Mul Pyramid of the Mayan ruins of Coba, Mexico.*

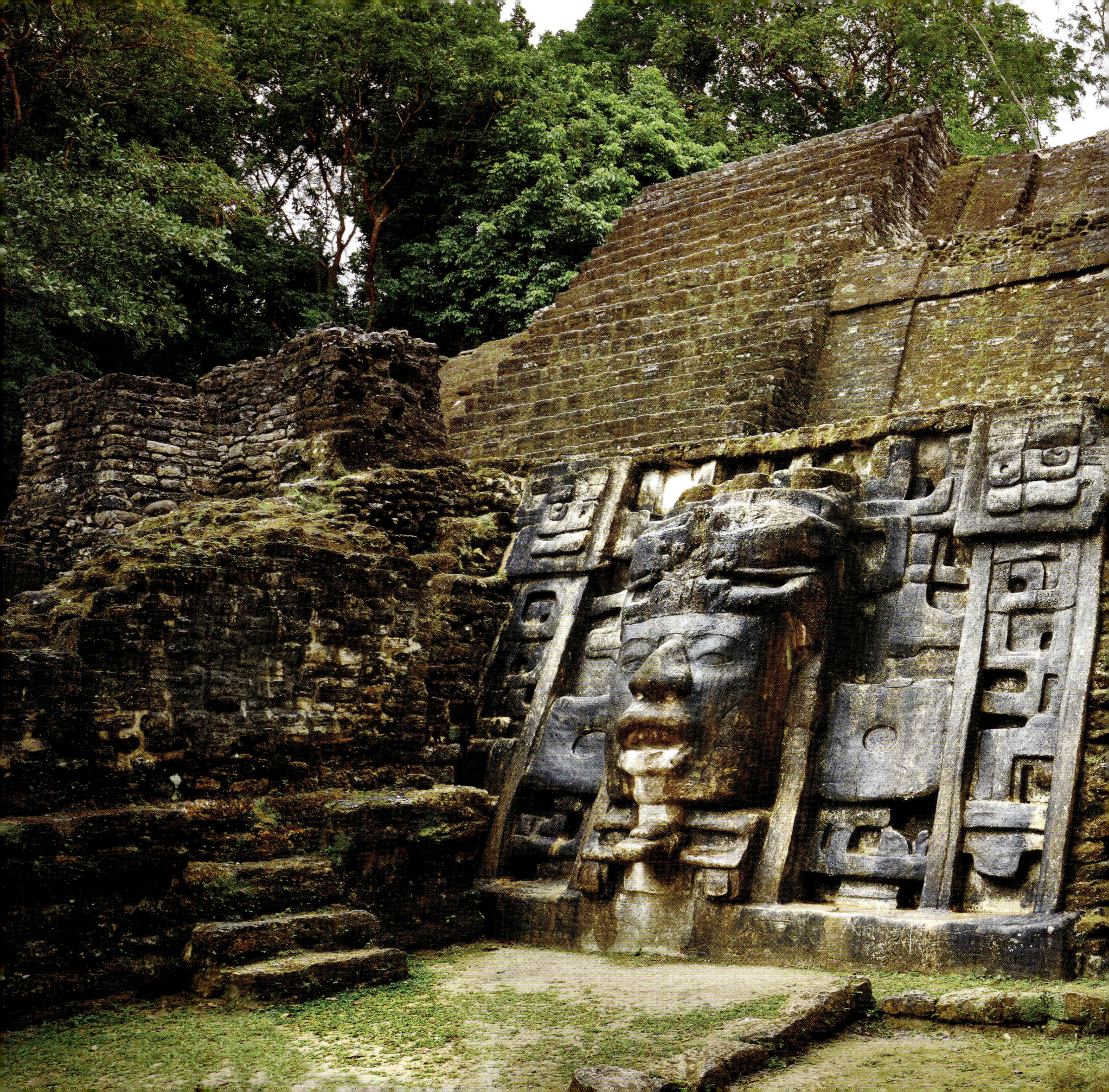

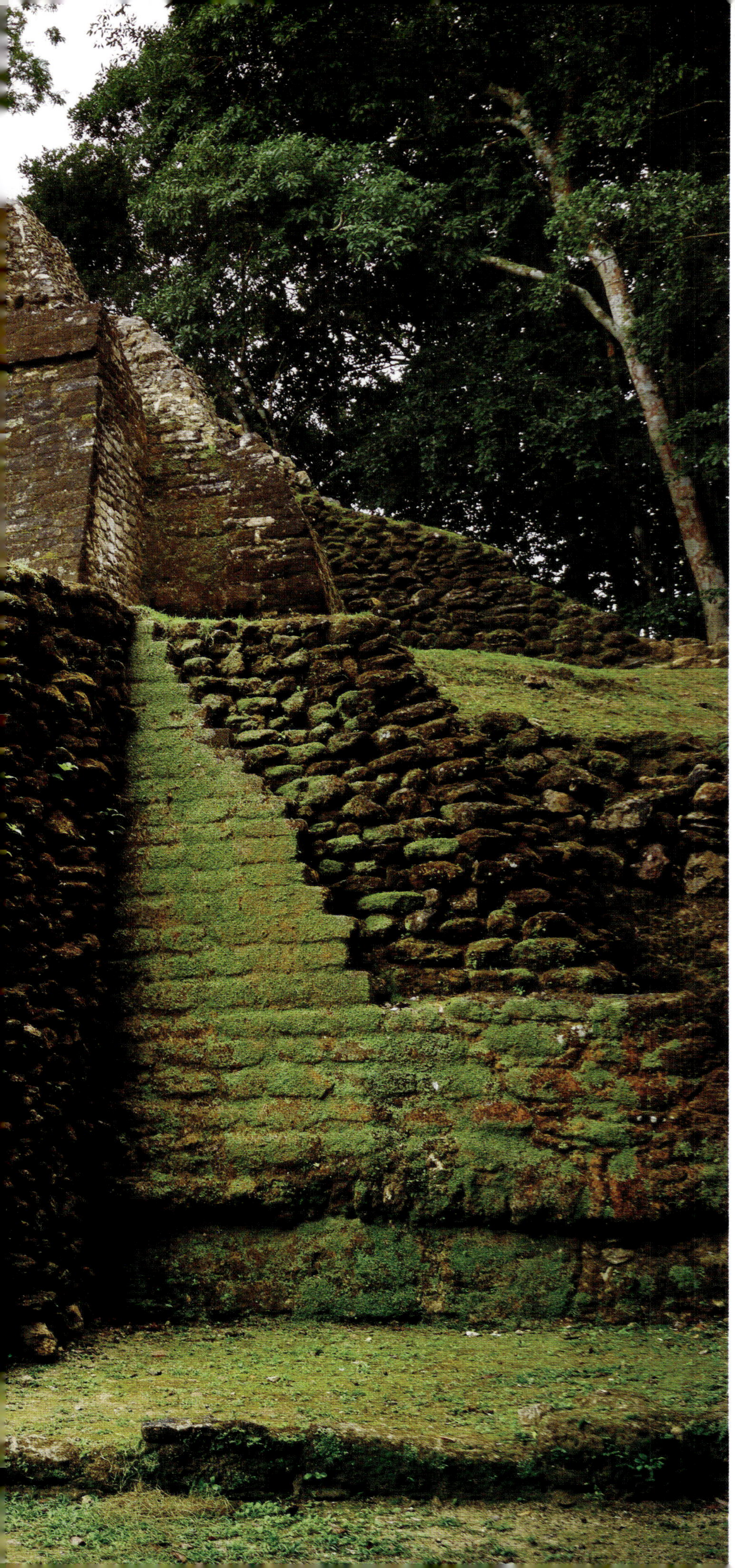

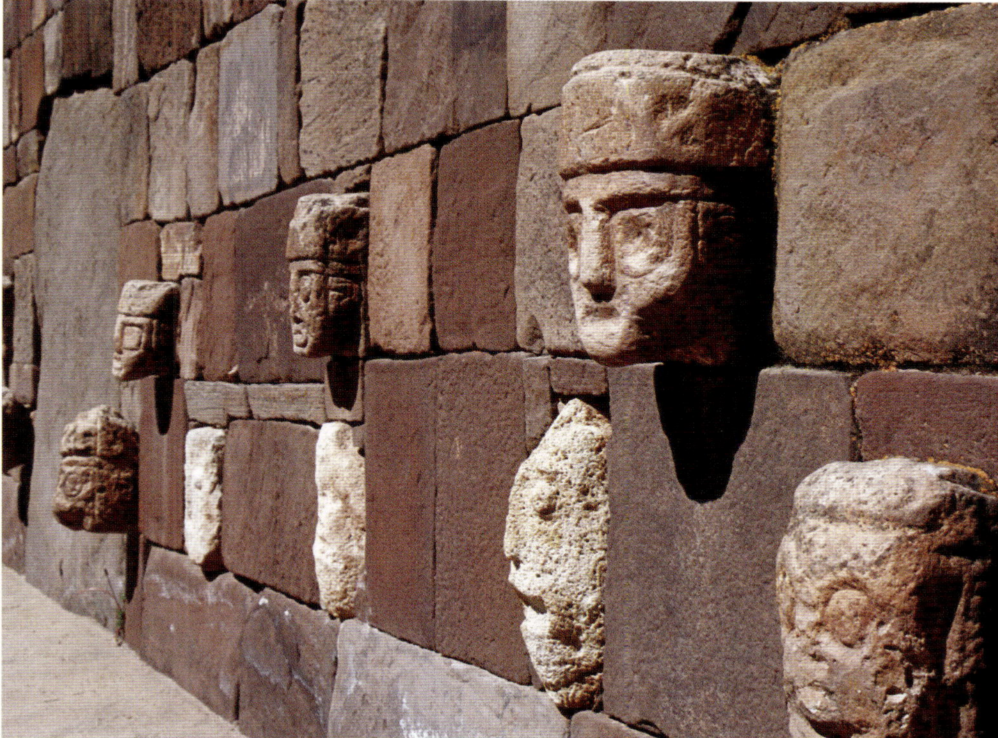

Above: *Stone carvings of heads at Tiwanaku, Bolivia.*

convinced was the legendary lost city, given its forbiddingly remote location. His subsequent bestselling book, *The Lost City of the Incas*, was written on that assumption, pushing an idea that contributes to the citadel's continuing mystique.

Expert opinion today posits another candidate, which Bingham himself also brought to the world's attention in his famous book. Later in the same expedition, having travelled far to the north of Peru, as the remaining Inca had done in flight from the Spanish, he came upon the ruins of Vilcabamba, the city that became the capital of the Neo-Inca state for the three decades or so it evaded Spanish attention after the calamitous defeats in the south. But in 1572, this was also captured, and with it the civilization of the Incas passed into history, leaving behind it their many haunting mountain ruins.

Left: *Mayan Mask Temple at Lamani, Belize.*

Golden Age of Archaeology

Myths such as the Incan Lost City or El Dorado, another South American legend with far less basis in fact, exert a powerful hold on the mind even when evidence seems to dismiss them as make-believe.

Troy

One place which fitted that description despite being at the heart of a seminal work of European literature, Homer's epic poem *The Iliad*, was ancient Troy. Before the advent of archaeology, the city of the Trojans had been thought by some to be the poet's brilliant creation, so the discovery of the real Troy (*see* right) by Heinrich Schliemann, at a place called Hisarlik in Anatolia in western Turkey in 1870, is rightly regarded as one of the most sensational finds in the history of the discipline.

Unfortunately, Schliemann's brutally careless digging methods, which destroyed so much valuable evidence, have damaged his subsequent reputation, as well as priceless physical evidence from the site. But in 1876, this ceaselessly curious antiquarian moved on to further excavations in the Peloponnese region of mainland Greece, where the site of Mycenae was identified and unique treasures, like the fabled golden mask of Agamemnon, the king who started the Trojan War, were retrieved from the dig.

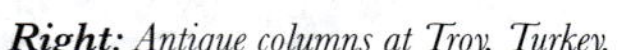

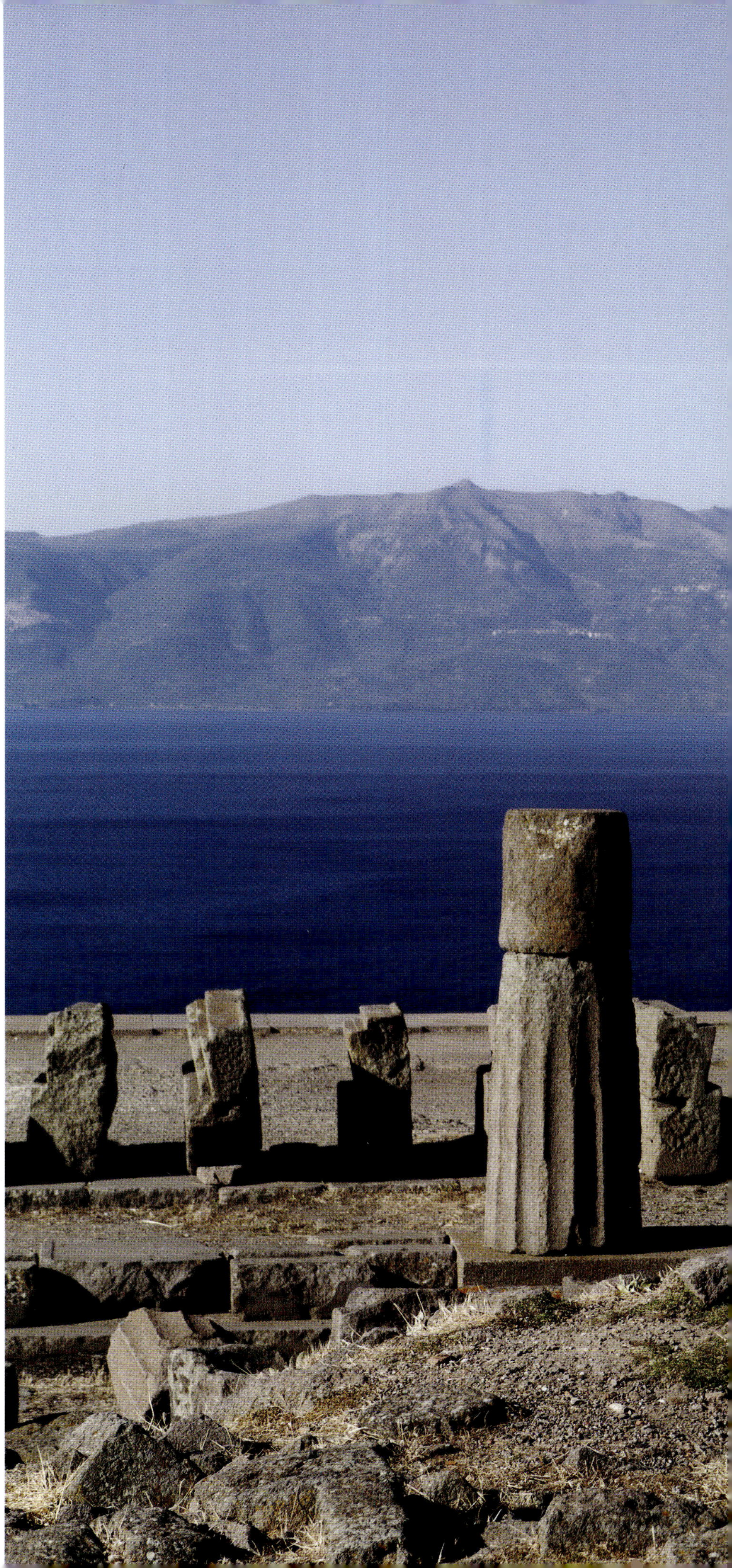

***Right:** Antique columns at Troy, Turkey.*

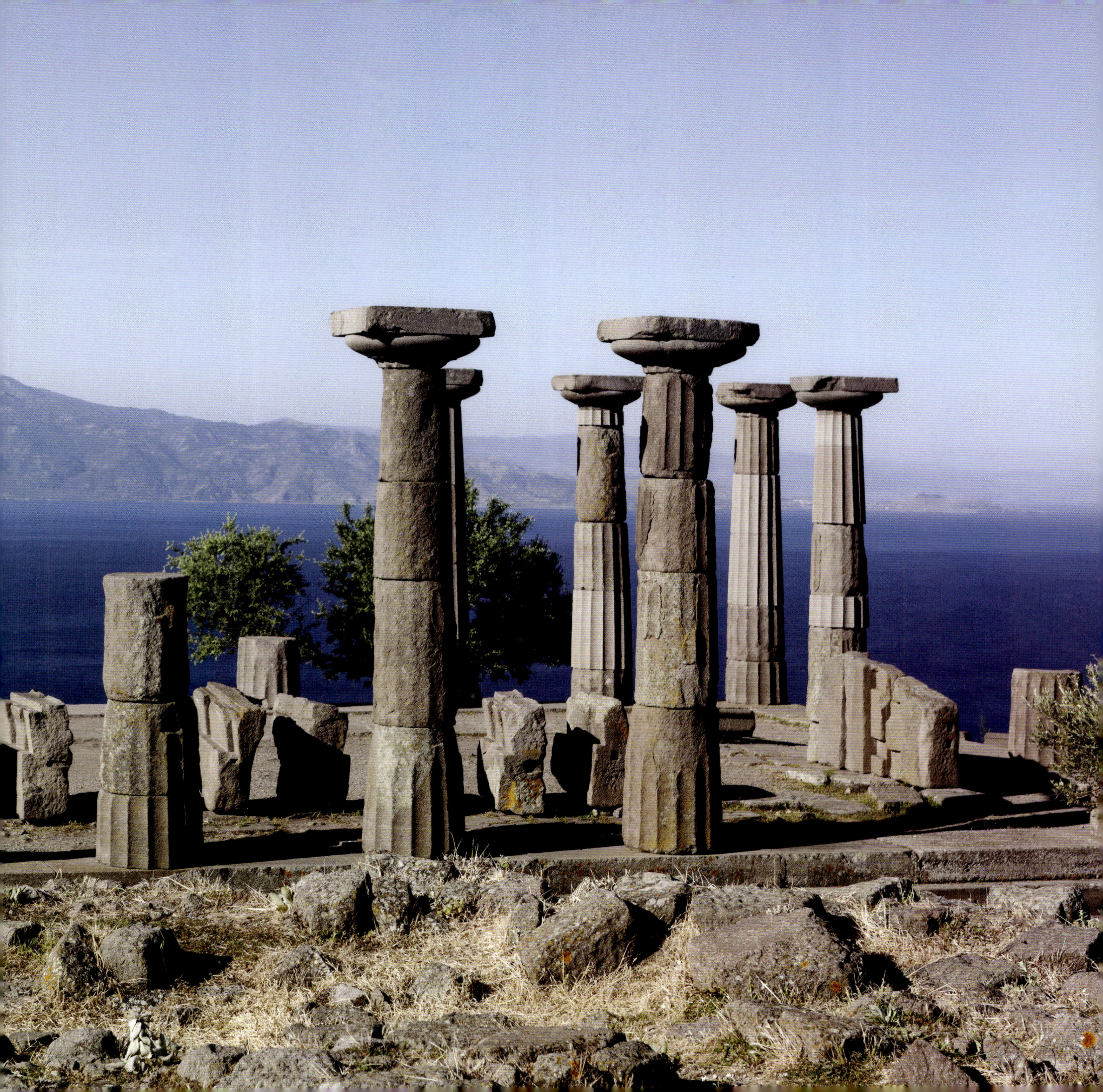

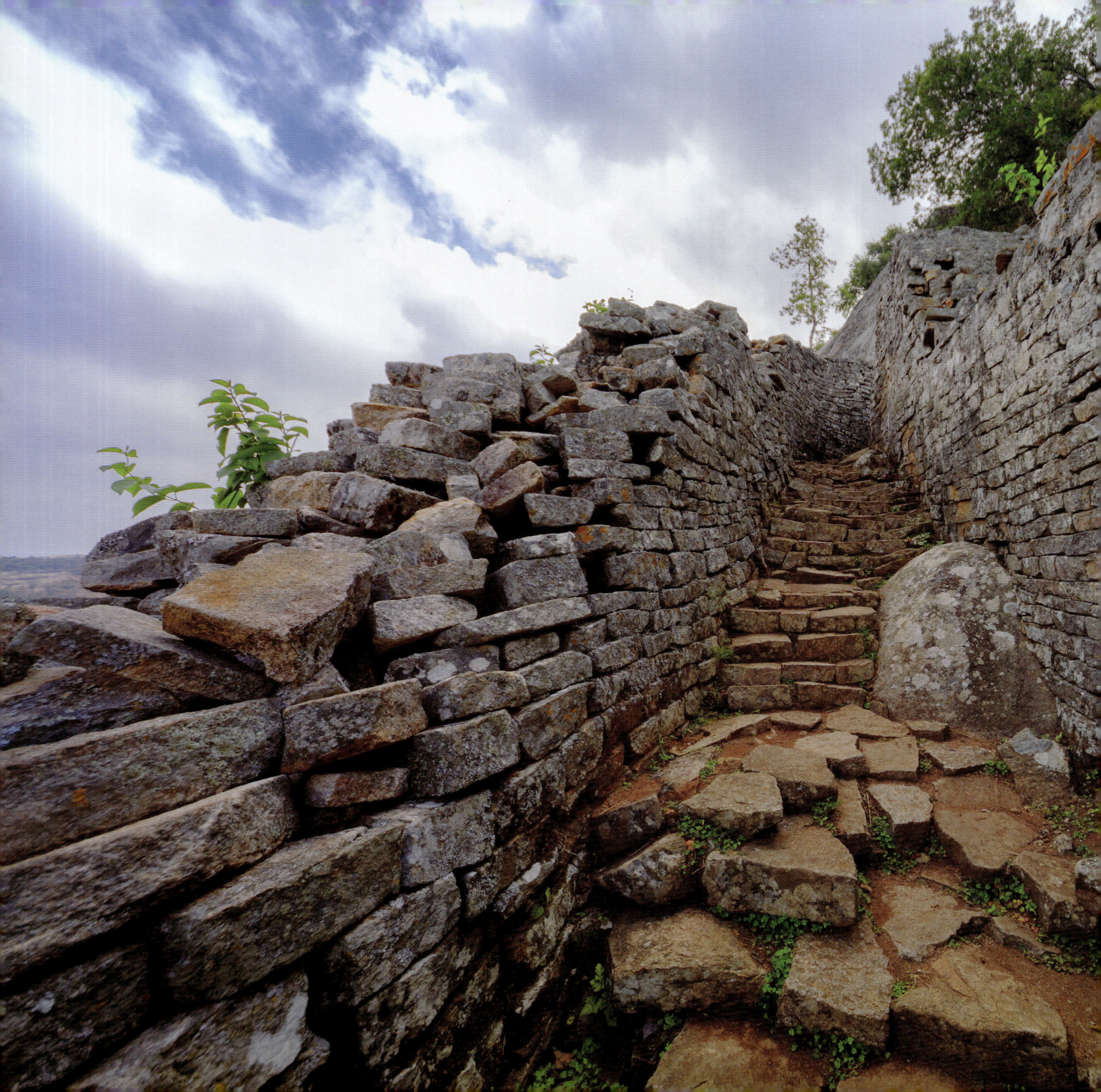

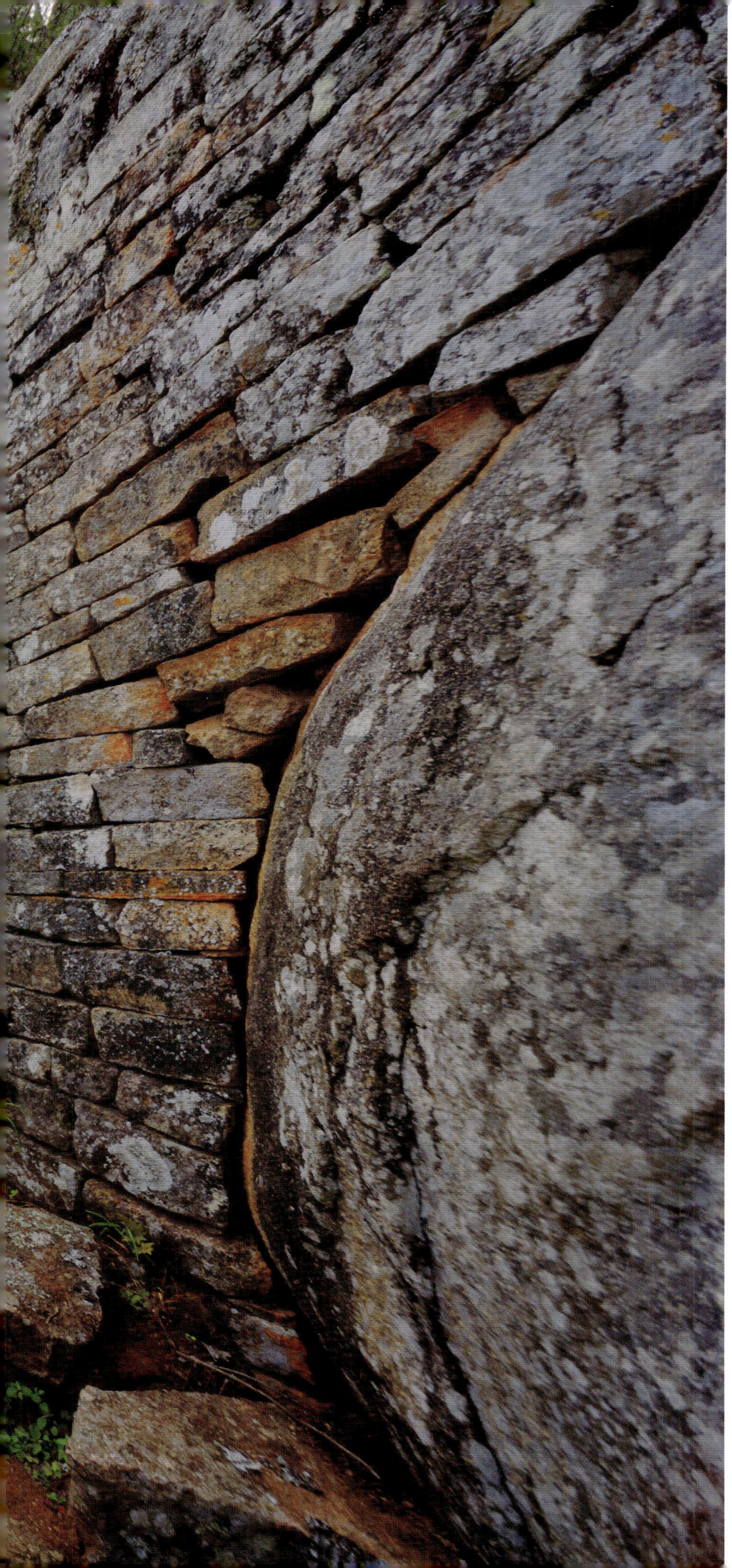

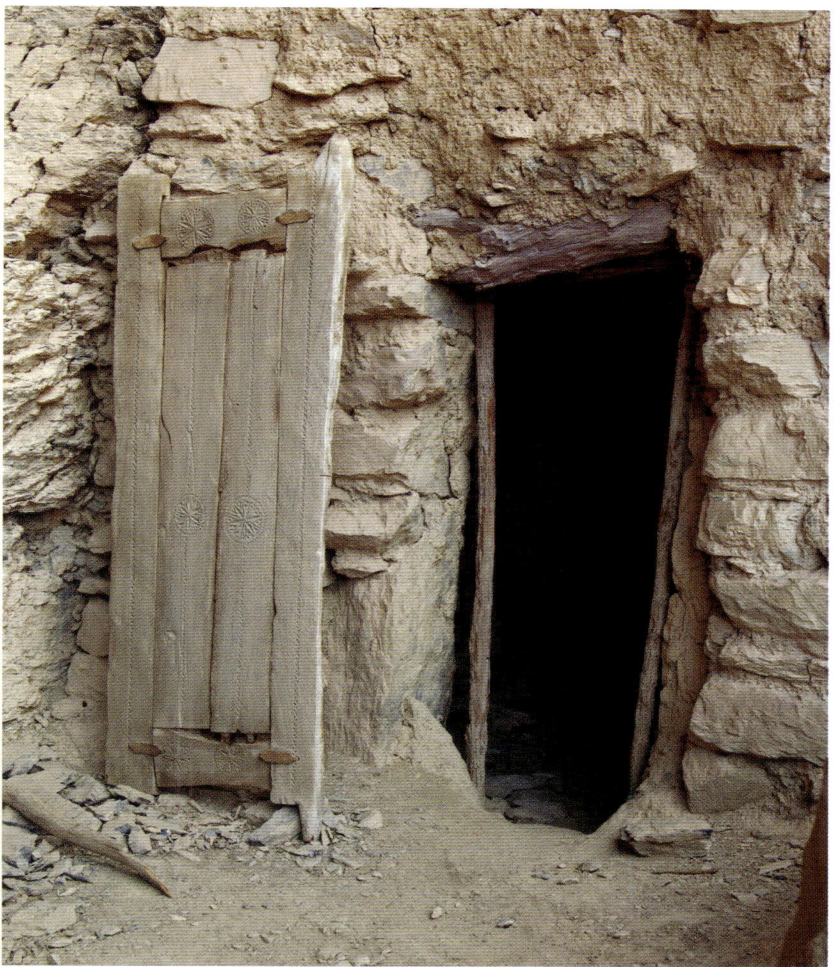

***Above:** Entrance to a stone hut at the abandoned settlement of Sap Bani Khamis, Oman.*

Great Zimbabwe

This golden age of archaeology was enabled by ready access to so many parts of the world that were then coming under colonial rule. The ruins of Great Zimbabwe (*see* left), at the heart of the medieval Kingdom of Zimbabwe, had been known about by Portuguese traders in earlier centuries, but were then forgotten by anyone outside the immediate region until renewed European interest in Africa during the late colonial period brought explorers such as the German geographer Karl Mauch,

***Left:** The citadel of Great Zimbabwe.*

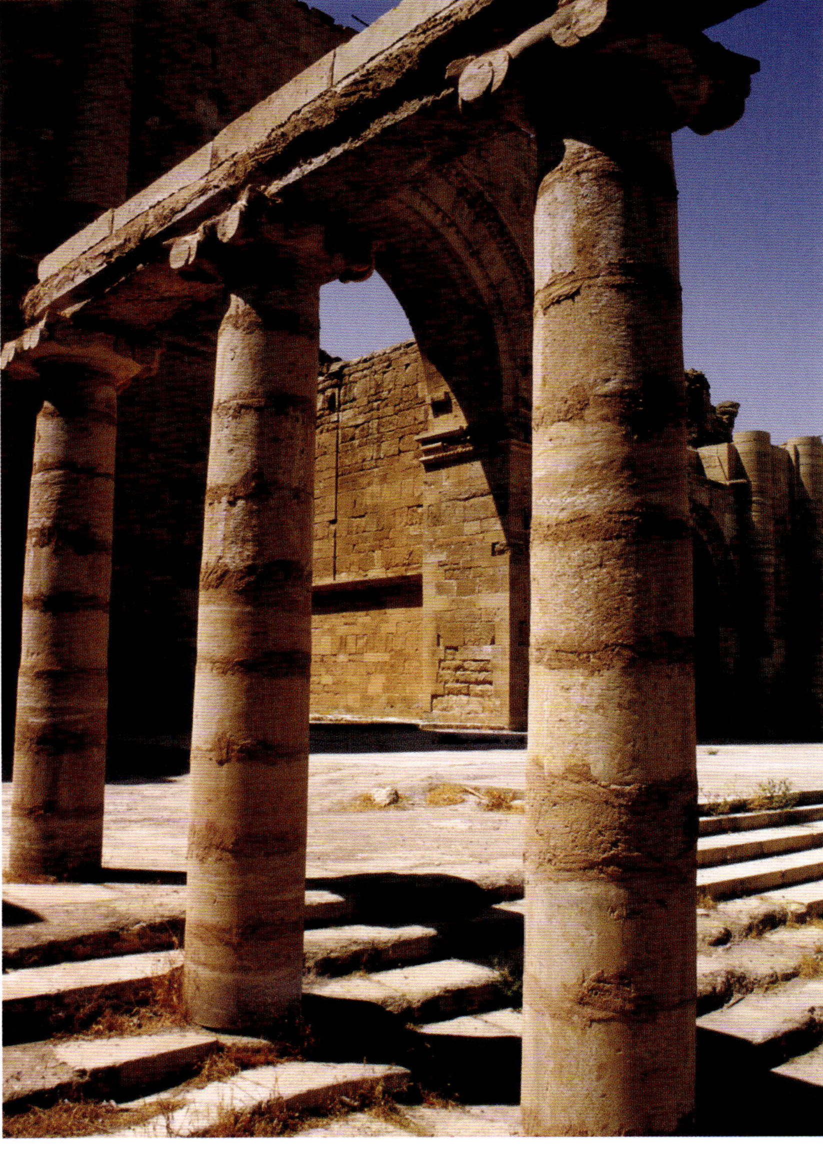

***Above:** The ancient site of Hatra, Iraq.*

who in 1871 was able to make the first detailed observations of this once significant city. Originally constructed by the ancestral Shona, by then it had been abandoned for almost 400 years, but in the previous three centuries the massive stone walls of the Great Enclosure, along with the various other compounds whose footings can still be seen, had comprised a city of some 18,000 people.

***Right:** The Minoan was the earliest European civilization, beginning around 3650 BC and lasting over two millennia. Knossos, on the edge of modern Heraklion in Crete, was its greatest city.*

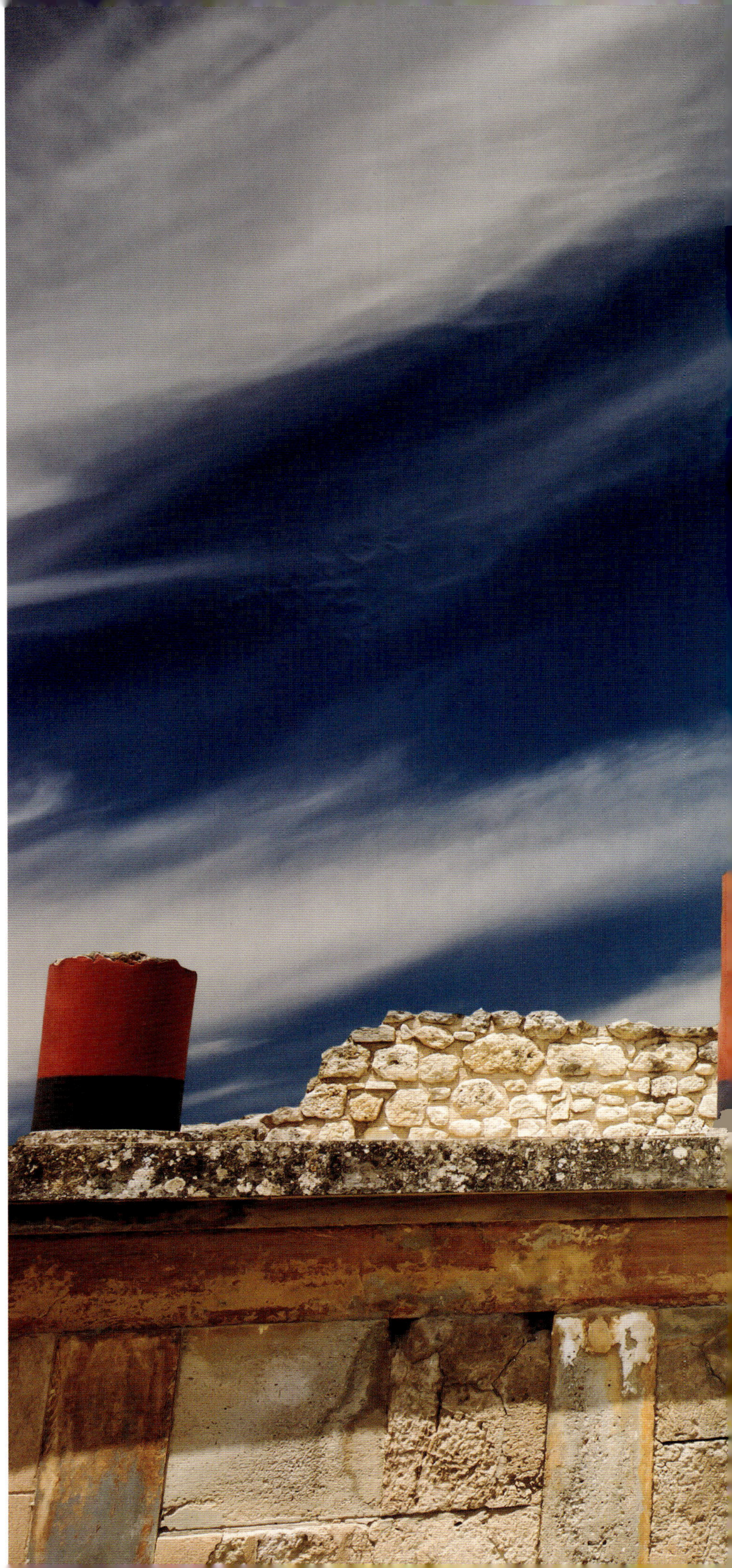

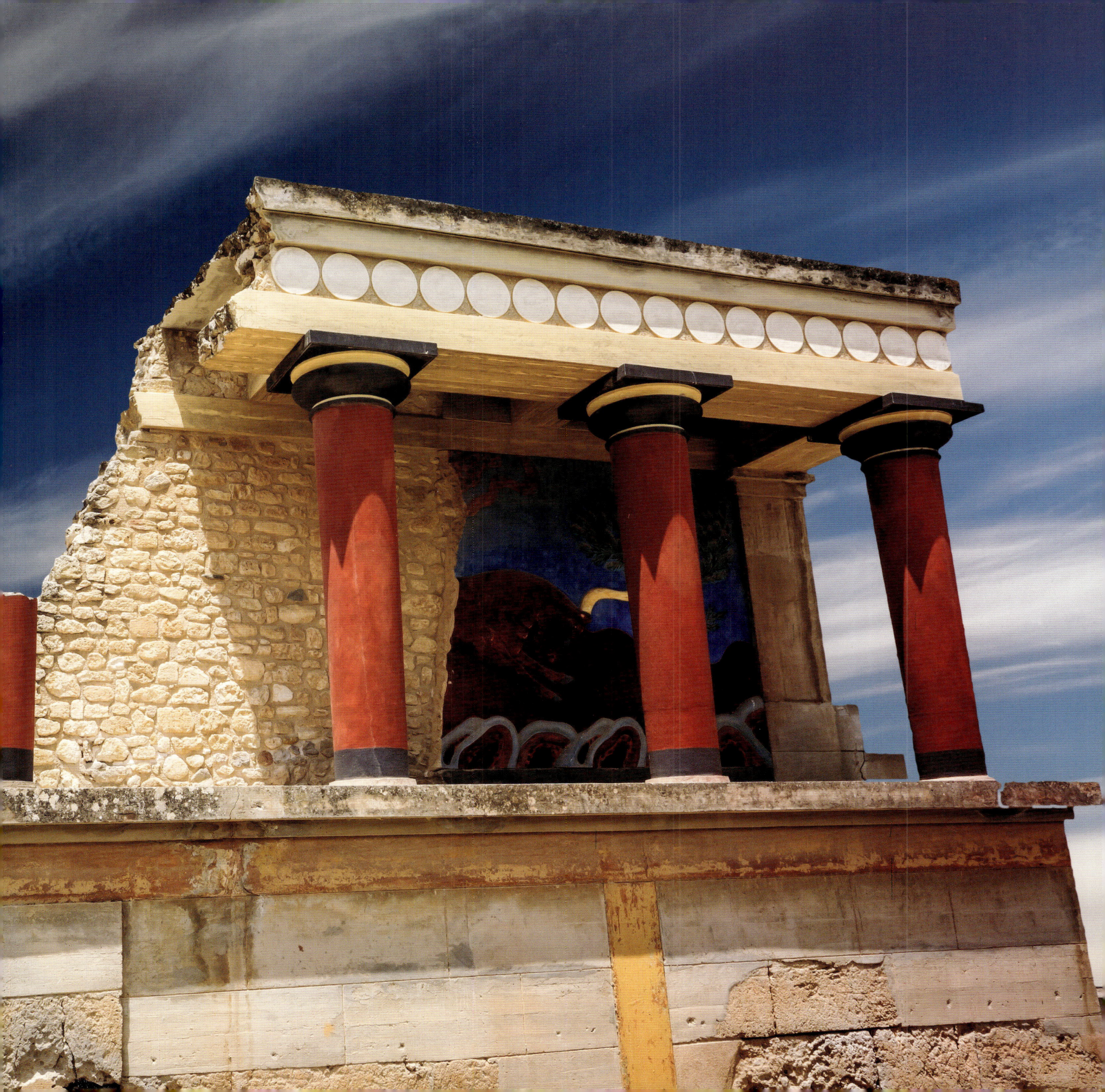

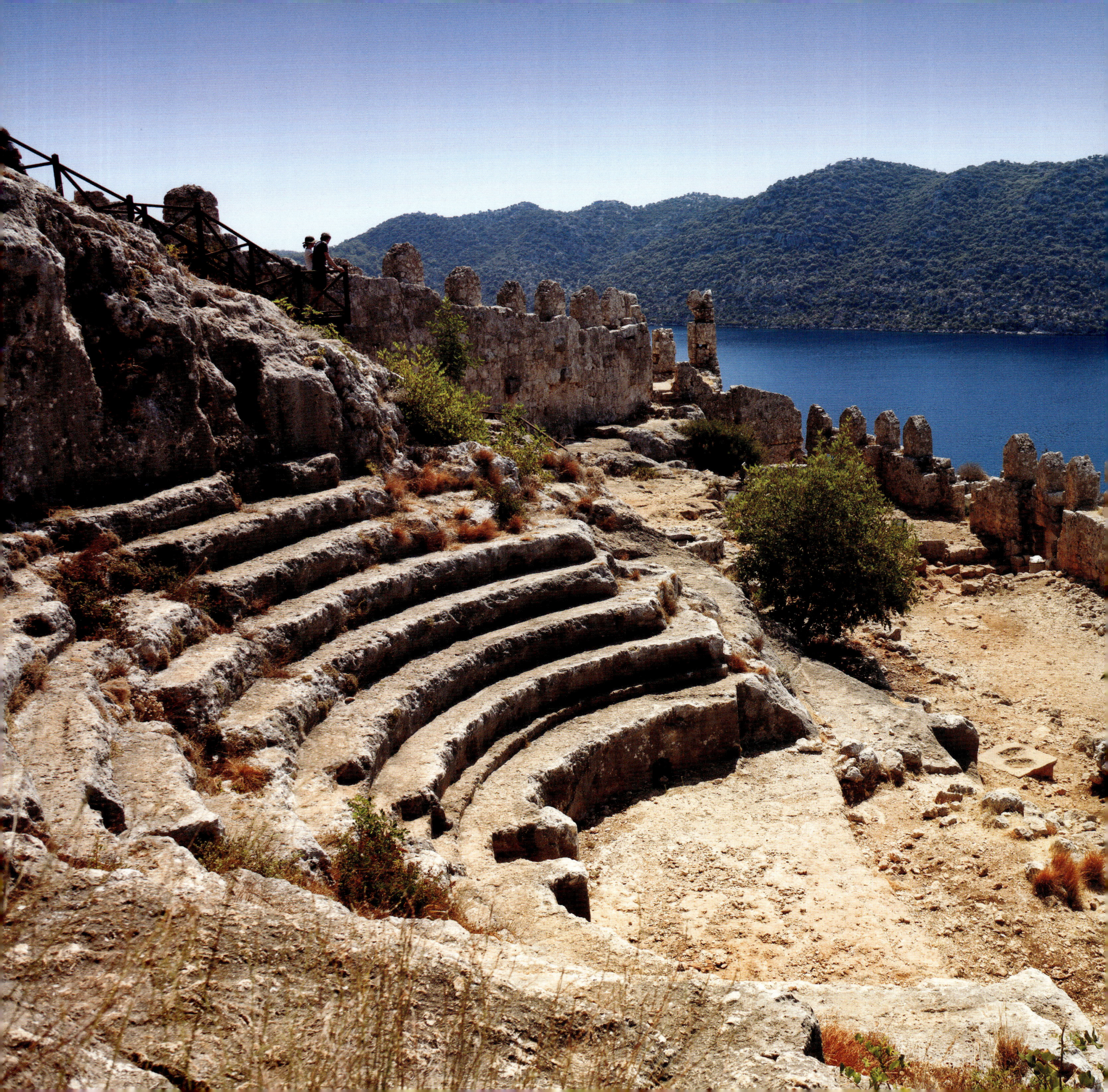

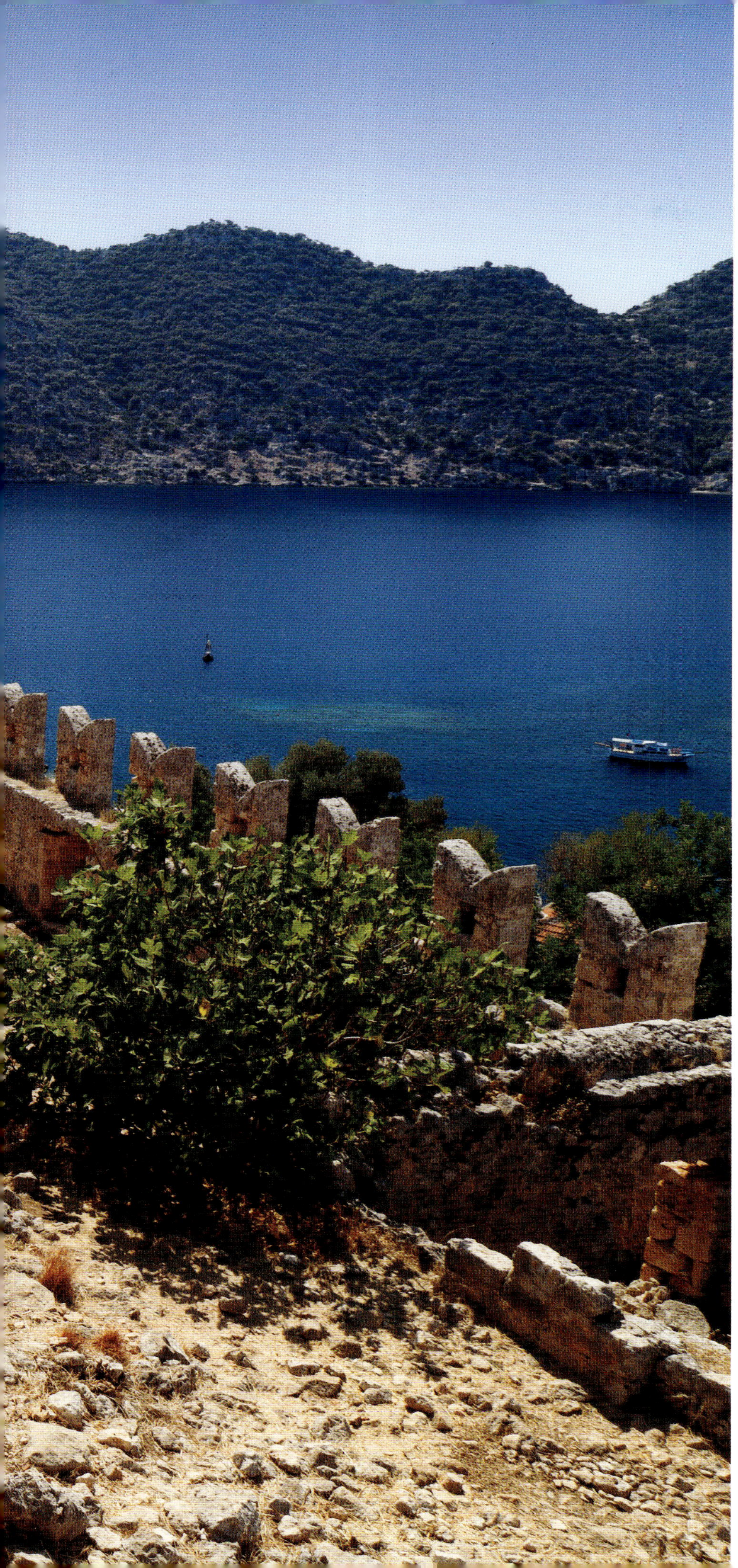

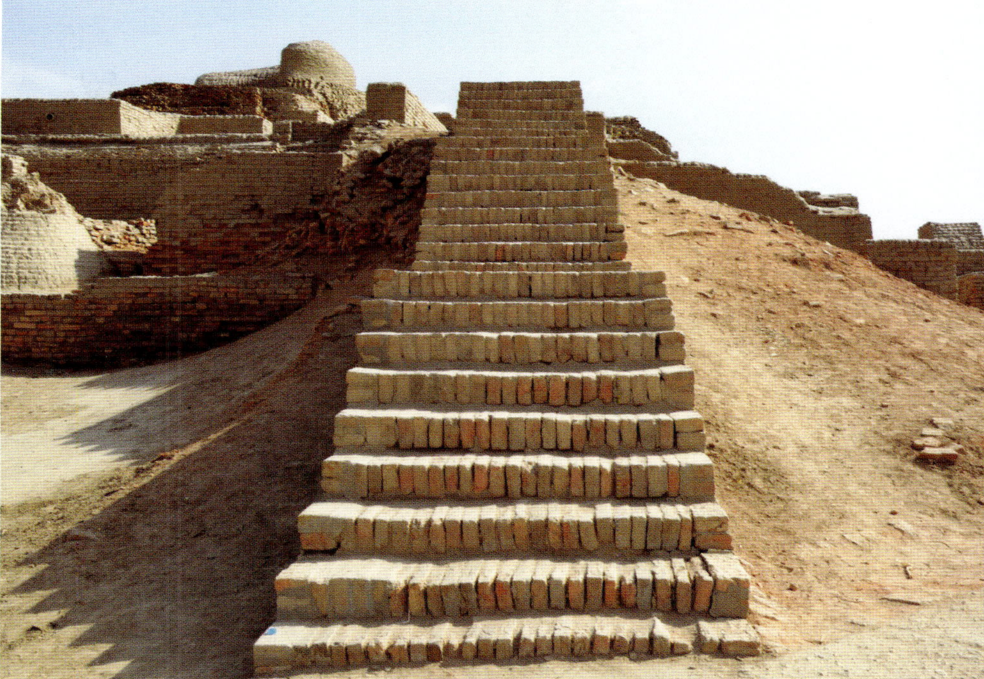

Above: *Mohenjo-daro, whose ruins are found in Sindh province in modern Pakistan, was a city of the Indus Valley civilization, and contemporaneous with both the ancient Egyptian and Mesopotamian civilizations.*

Knossos

In another part of the British Empire, just a few years later, in 1878 on the Greek island of Crete, the Greek archaeologist Milos Kalokairinos found what was later assumed to be the ancient capital of a Bronze Age civilization that pre-dates those of Classical Greece by a thousand years (*see* page 53). Following a reference in Homer's *Odyssey*, Europe's oldest city was named Knossos and its people Minoans by Sir Arthur Evans, the British archaeologist whose own extensive excavations at the site began in 1900. Evans took the now rather controversial step of reconstructing parts of the palace using modern building materials, but the vivid colour of the frescoes in the palace, the result of restoration in the early twentieth century, offer compelling evidence of a sophisticated culture and a city which at its height, around 1700 BC, numbered as many as 100,000 souls.

Left: *Amphitheatre in the castle at Kaleköy, Turkey.*

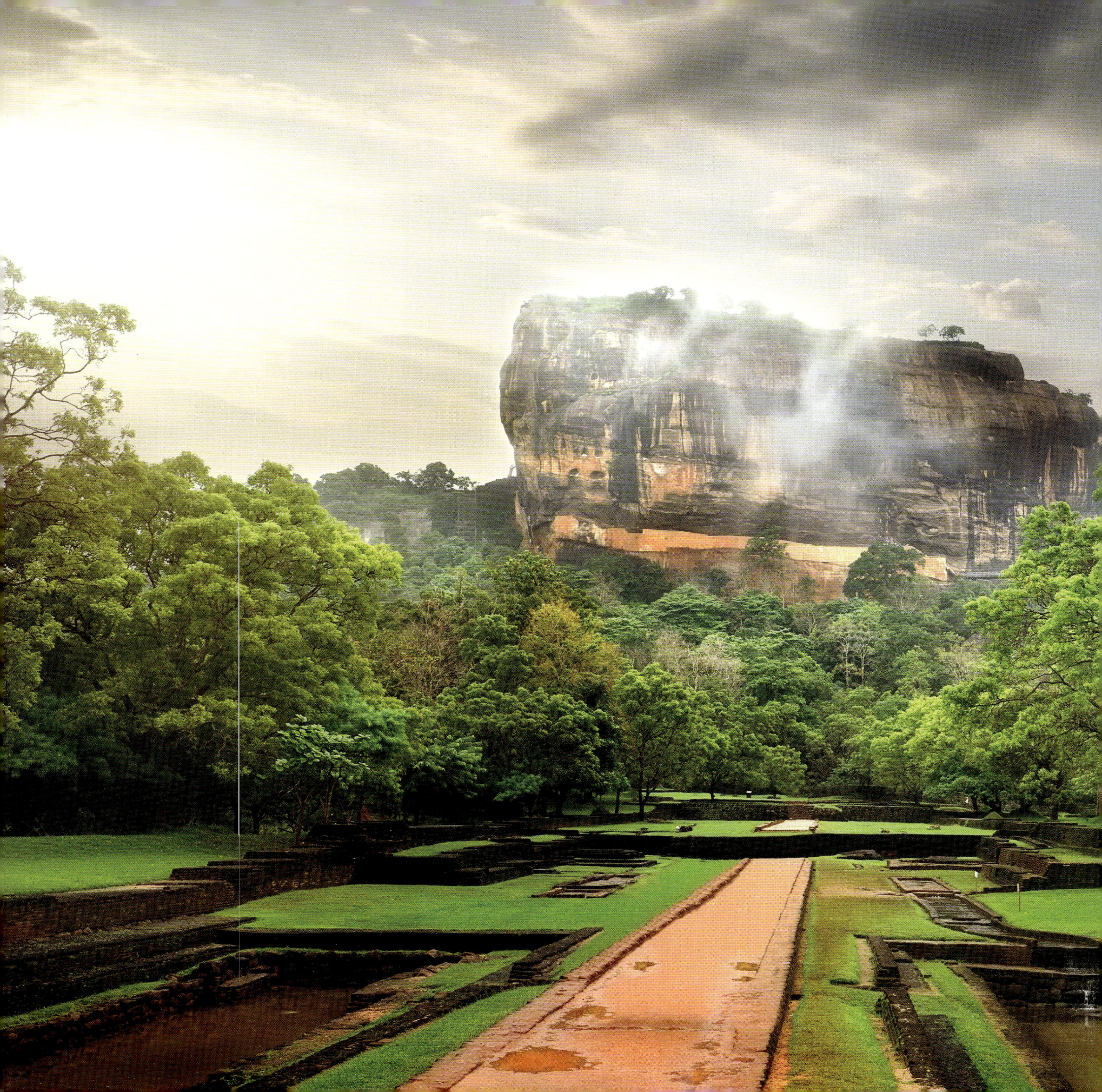

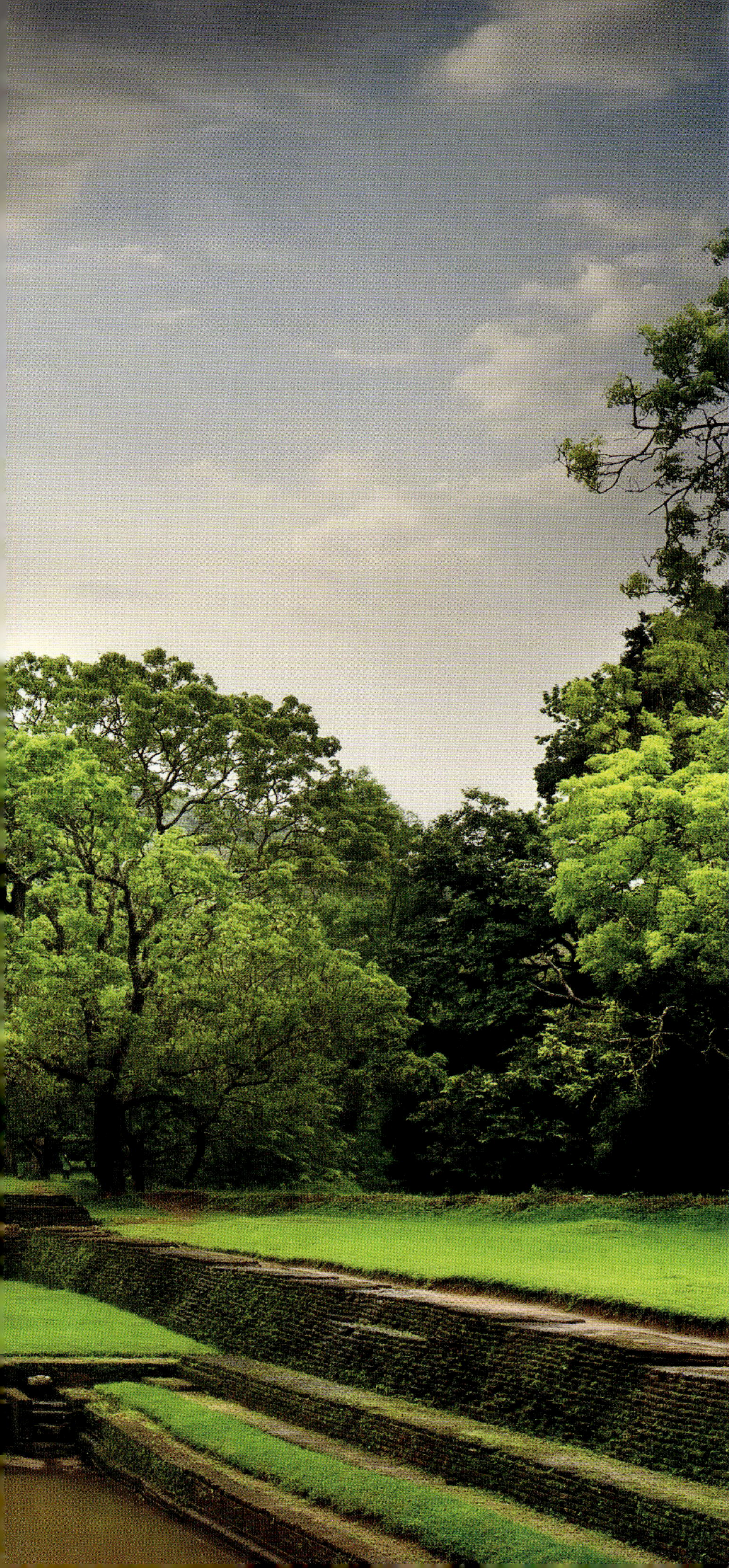

The Indian Subcontinent

The country which, above all others, has come to be associated with the British Empire is India, a source of so many of the world's great religions since the earliest times.

Pakistan

Here, in the northern part of modern-day Pakistan close to the city of Rawalpindi, evidence was uncovered in the late nineteenth century of the city of Taxila, a great centre of Buddhist learning and, as somewhere mentioned in the *Mahabharata*, a place of equal importance to Hindus.

Excavations of this 3,000-year-old site continued well into the twentieth century, while in southern Pakistan, a city some 4,500 years old, named Mohenjo-daro (*see* page 55), was unearthed in the 1920s and 1930s by Indian and British officials. This offered evidence of the Indus Valley civilization, which once thrived in this region, as far to the north as ancient Harappa, near modern Faisalabad, the site of another city excavated around the same time.

India

There are also many abandoned ancient and not-so-ancient city sites in modern India itself, from the eerily intact and fairly recent ruined city of Mandu (*see* page 61) in the northern state of Madhya Pradesh, to Vijayanagara in Karnataka in the south, abandoned around the same

Left: *Among the most spectacular cities of all, Sigiriya in Sri Lanka was both an impregnable fortress, built on top of a huge rock, and a garden city to rival Babylon.*
Next page: *Ruins of a Buddhist temple at Anuradhapura, Sri Lanka.*

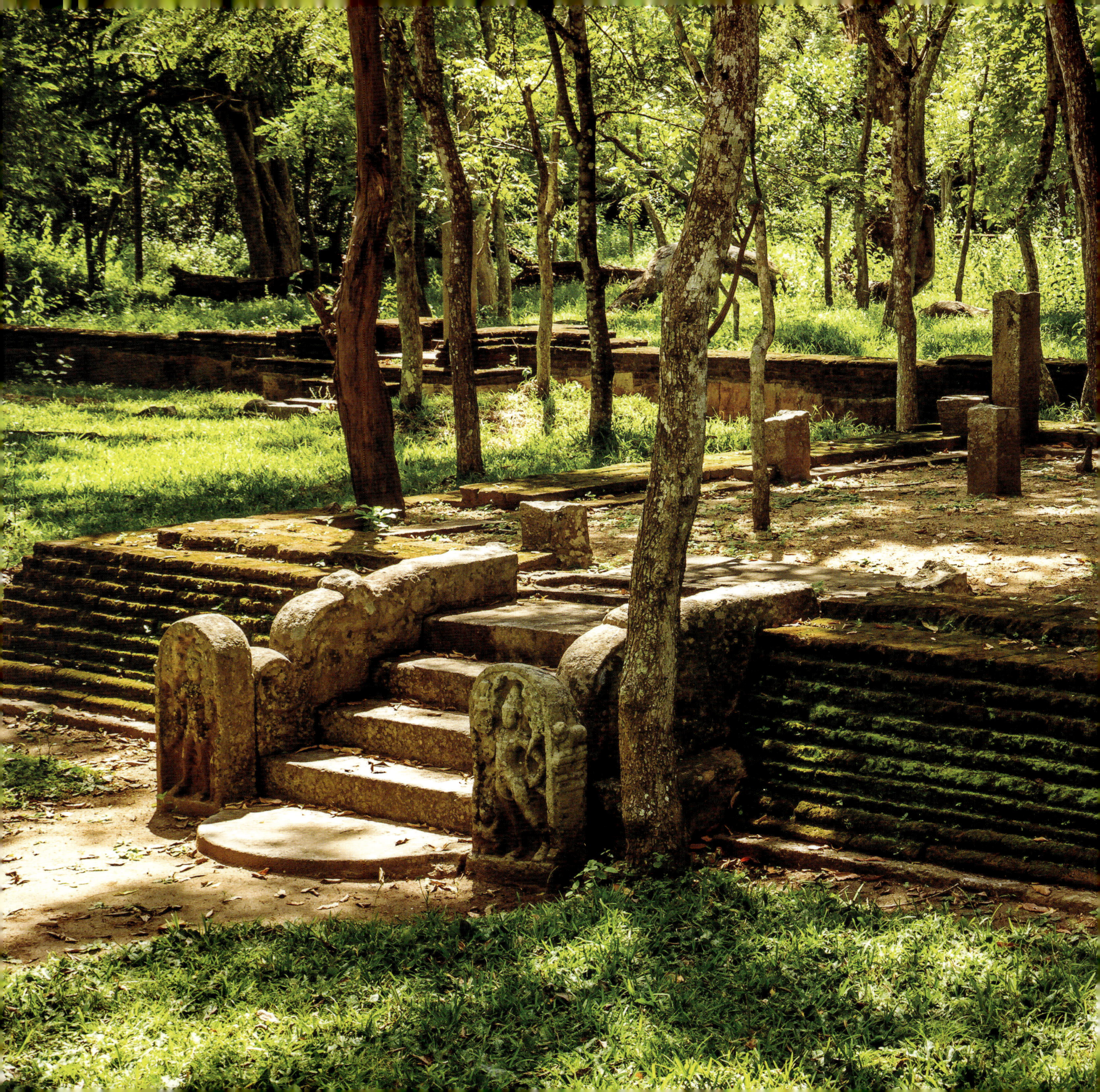

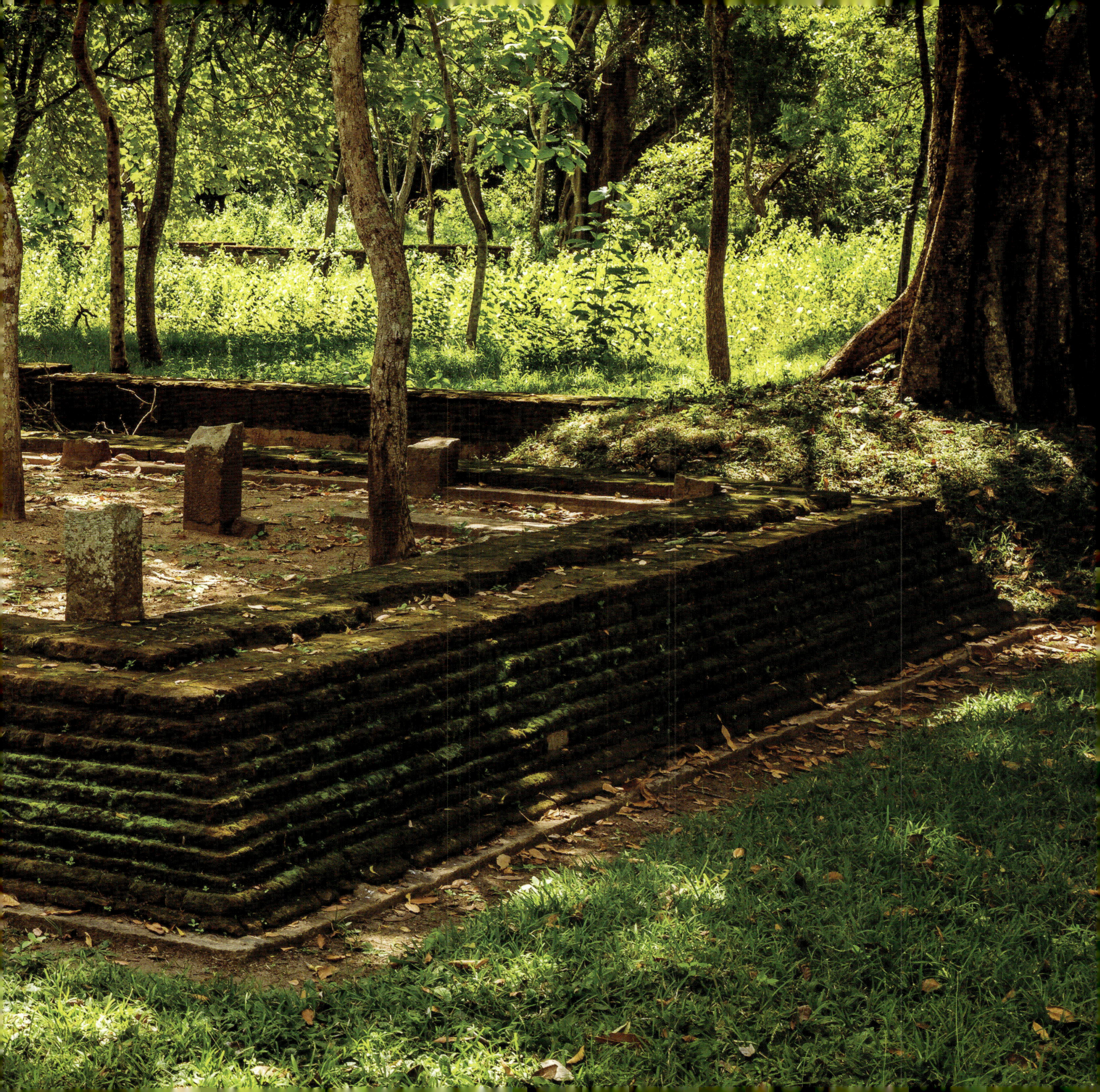

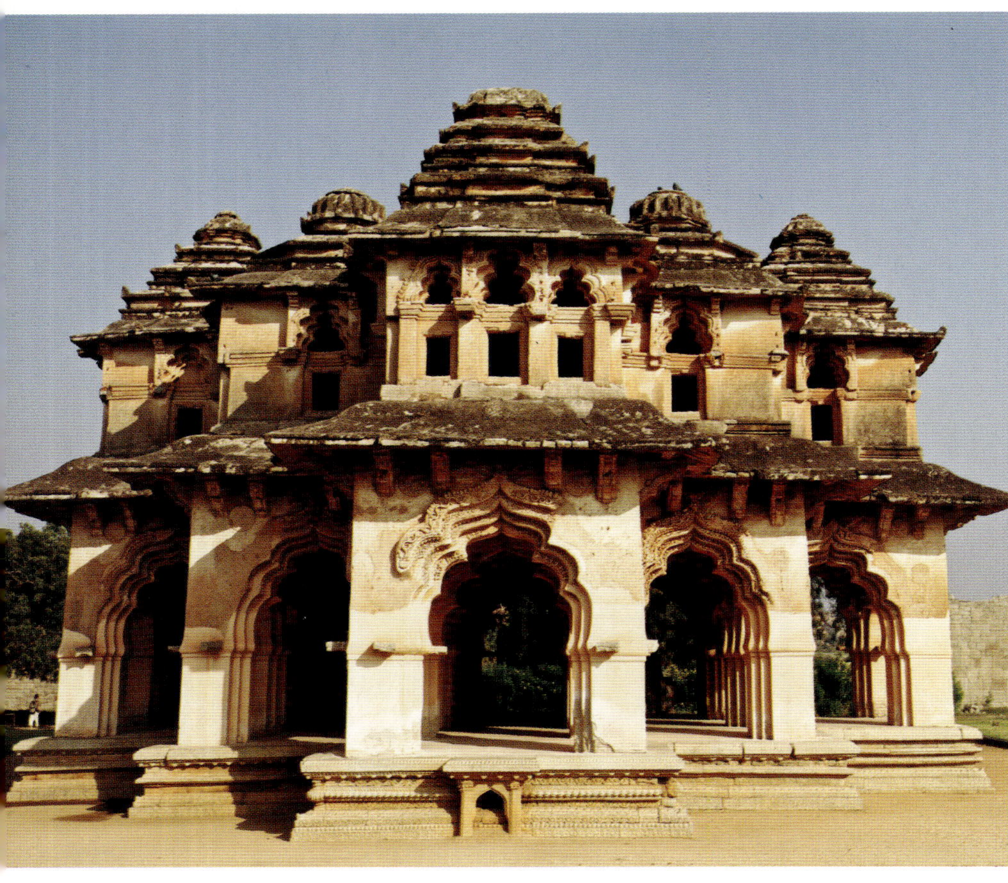

Above: *Lotus Mahal at the ruins of the city of Vijayanagara, Hampi, India.*

period but which from the fourteenth to the sixteenth centuries had been the capital of a great empire. But perhaps the most intriguing find of recent decades has been the ruins of an ancient city discovered in 70 feet of water off the coast of the state of Gujarat at Dwarka in India's northwest corner. Investigations began in 1988, and the submarine city was found to be incredibly well-preserved: a grid of streets, sandstone walls and the remnants of a seaport. Serious scholarship believes these to be ruins of the city the *Mahabharata* tells us Lord Krishna himself once founded at roughly this spot, given that the detailed description of Dwarka in the Hindu epic conforms to what marine archaeologists have found on the ocean floor.

Right: *The abandoned fort of Mandu, known for its exquisite architecture, dates from the golden age of the much older city of the same name, beginning in the fifteenth century.*
Next page: *The Ancient City of Polonnaruwa, Sri Lanka.*

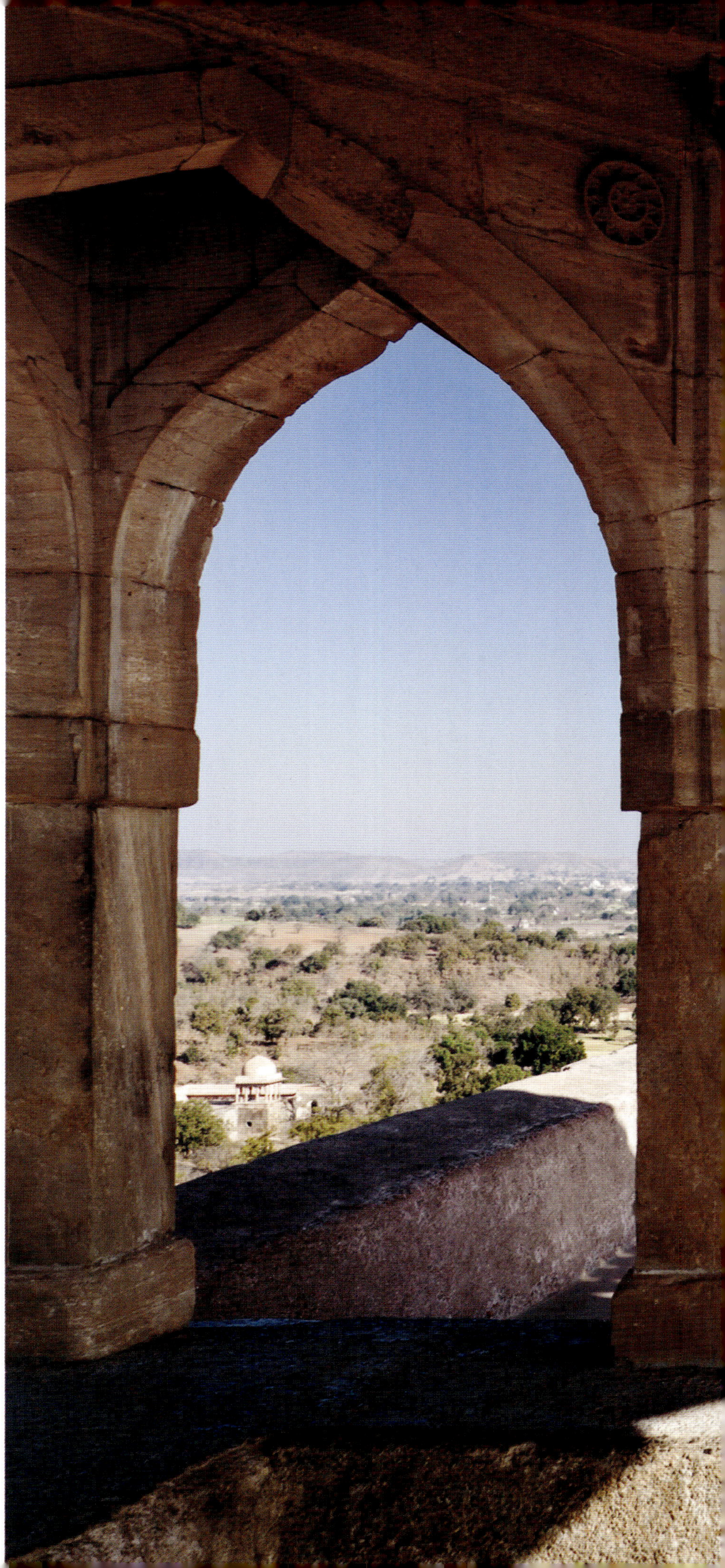

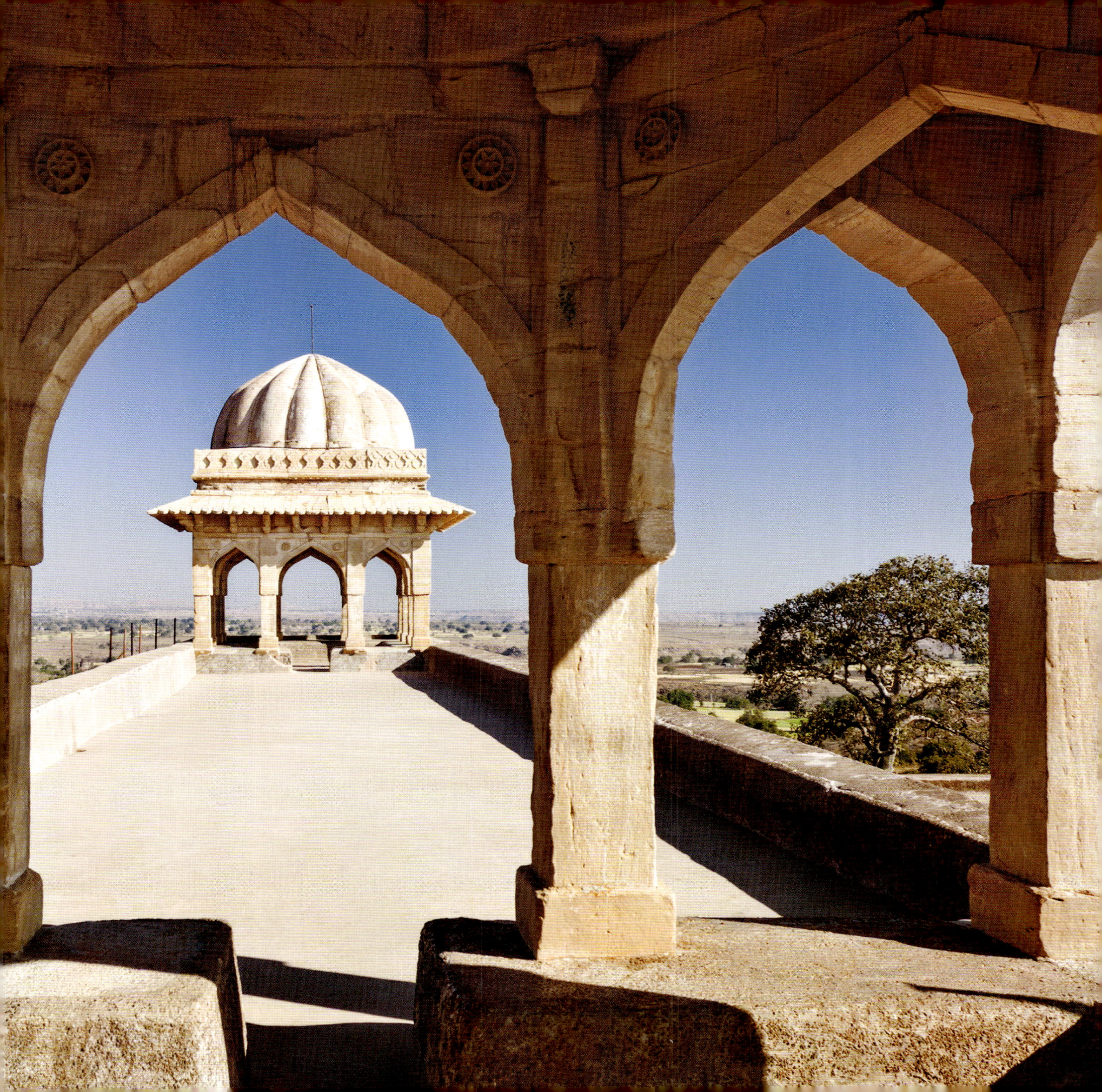

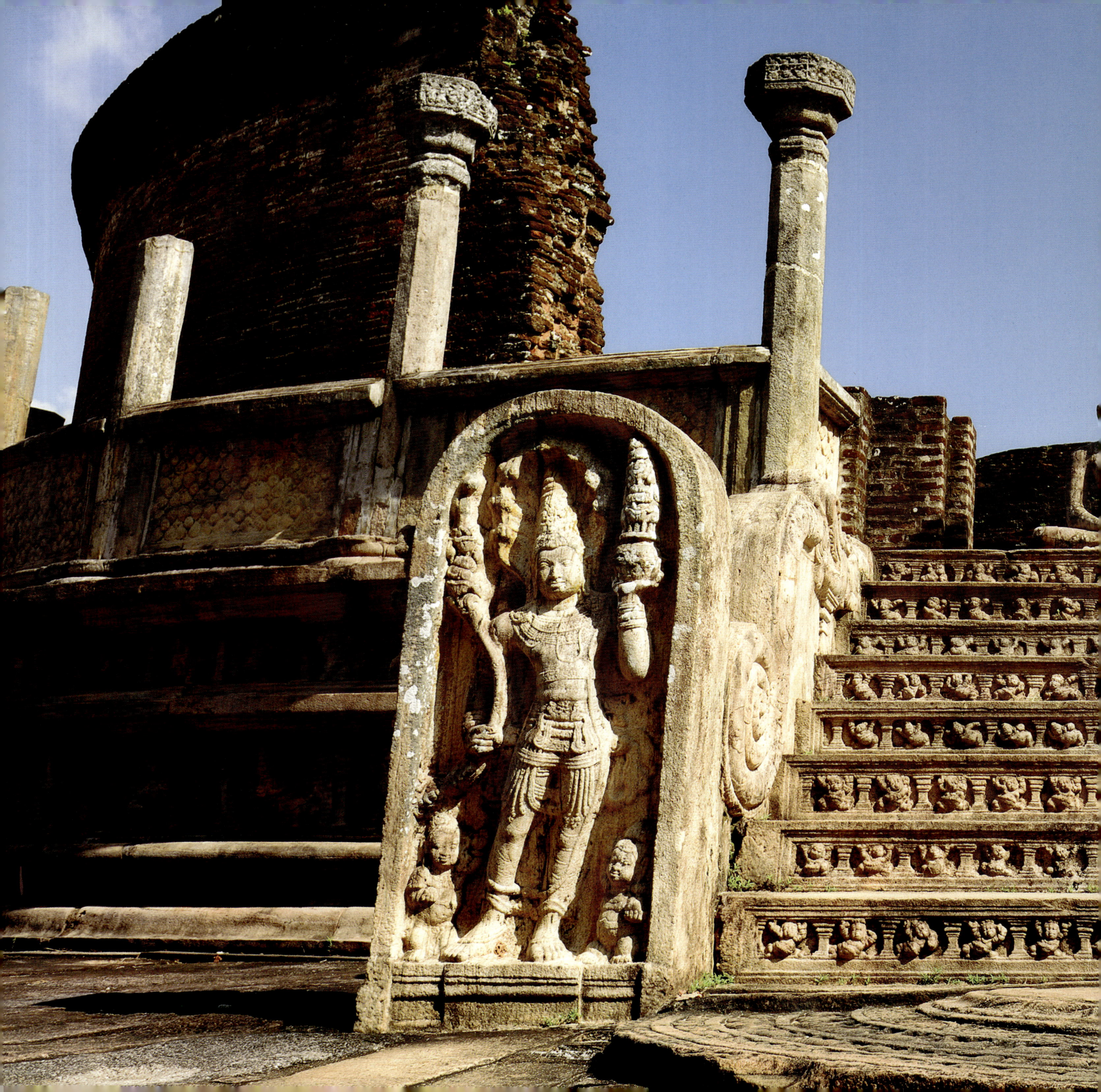

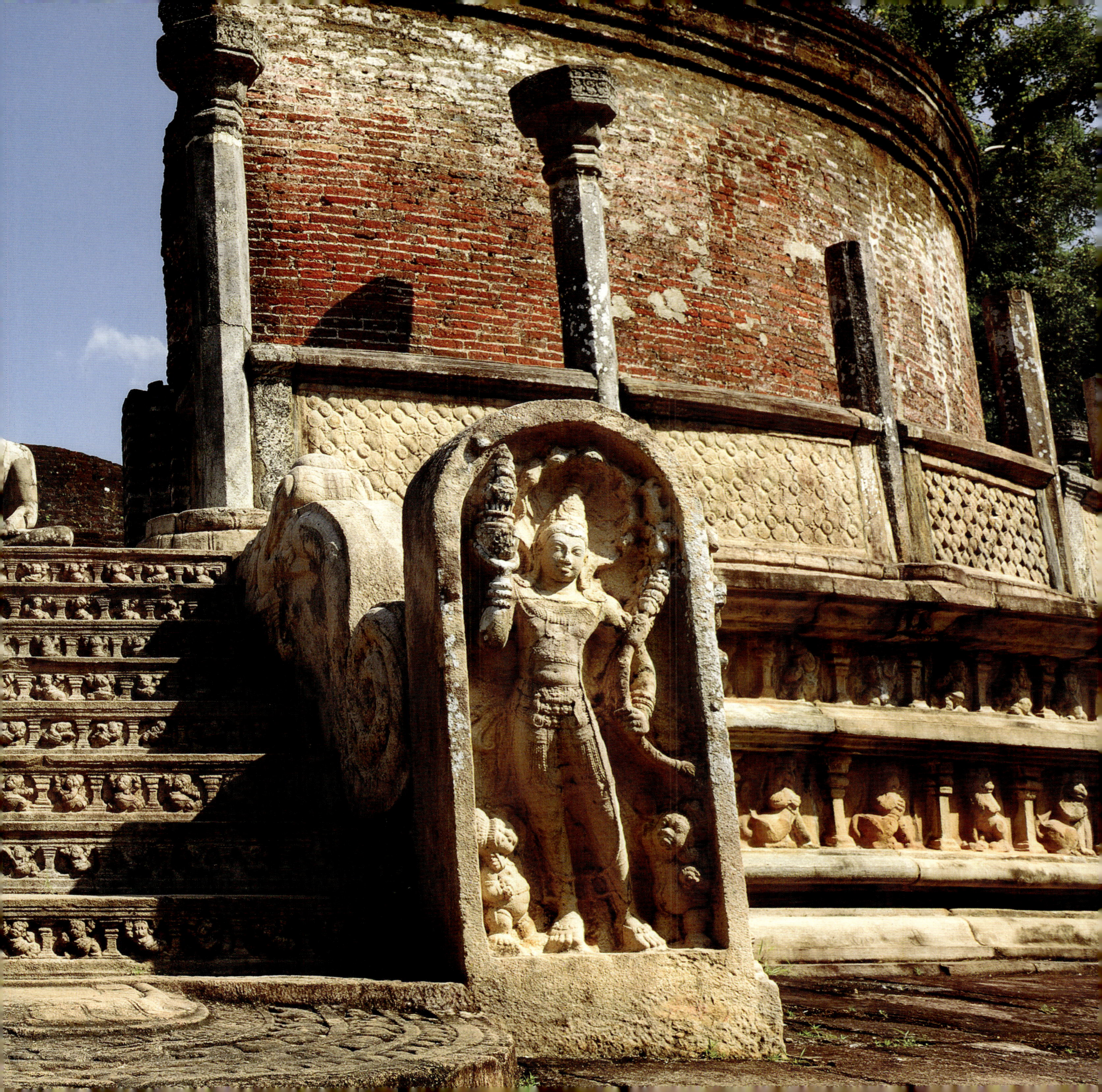

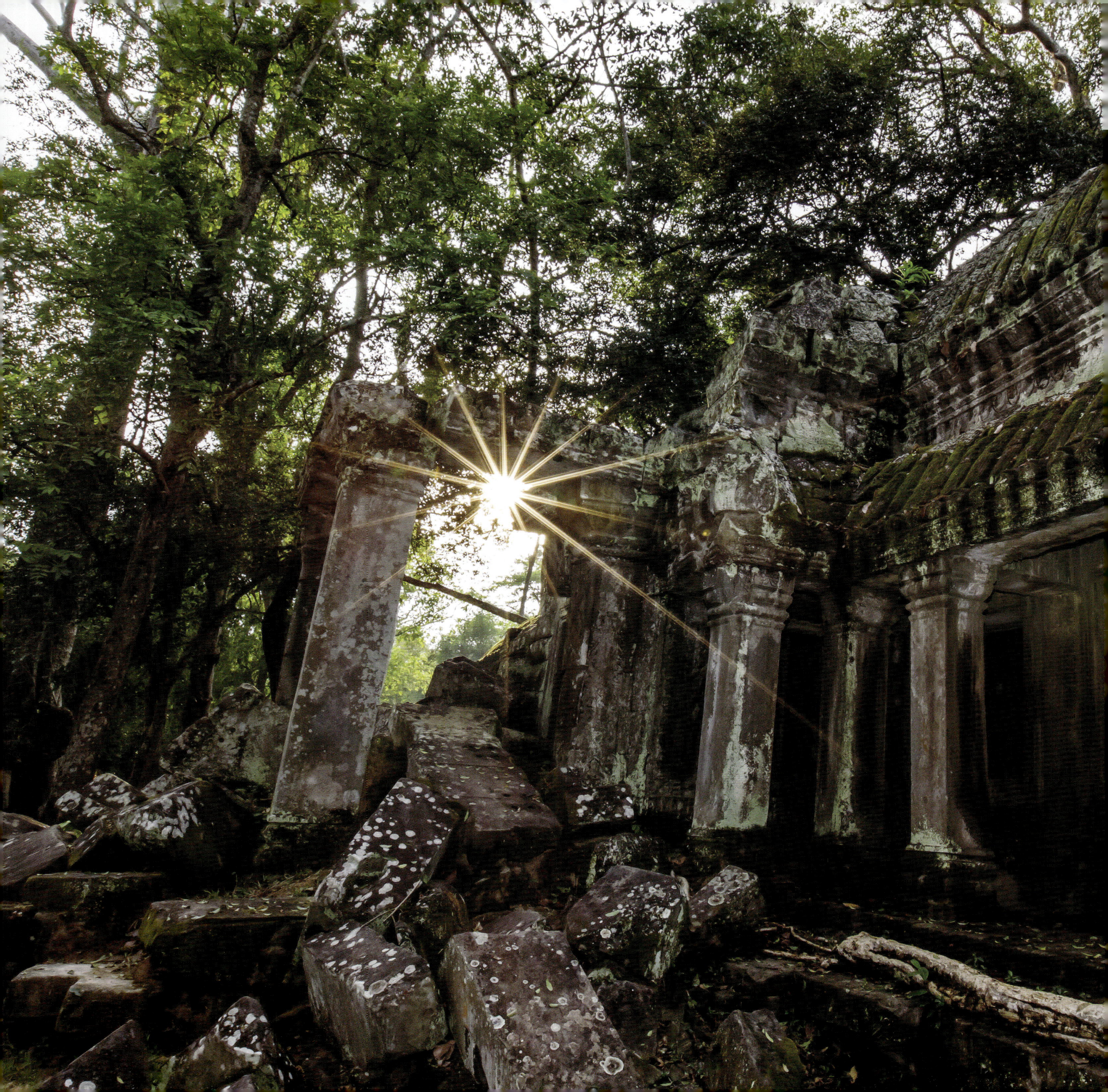

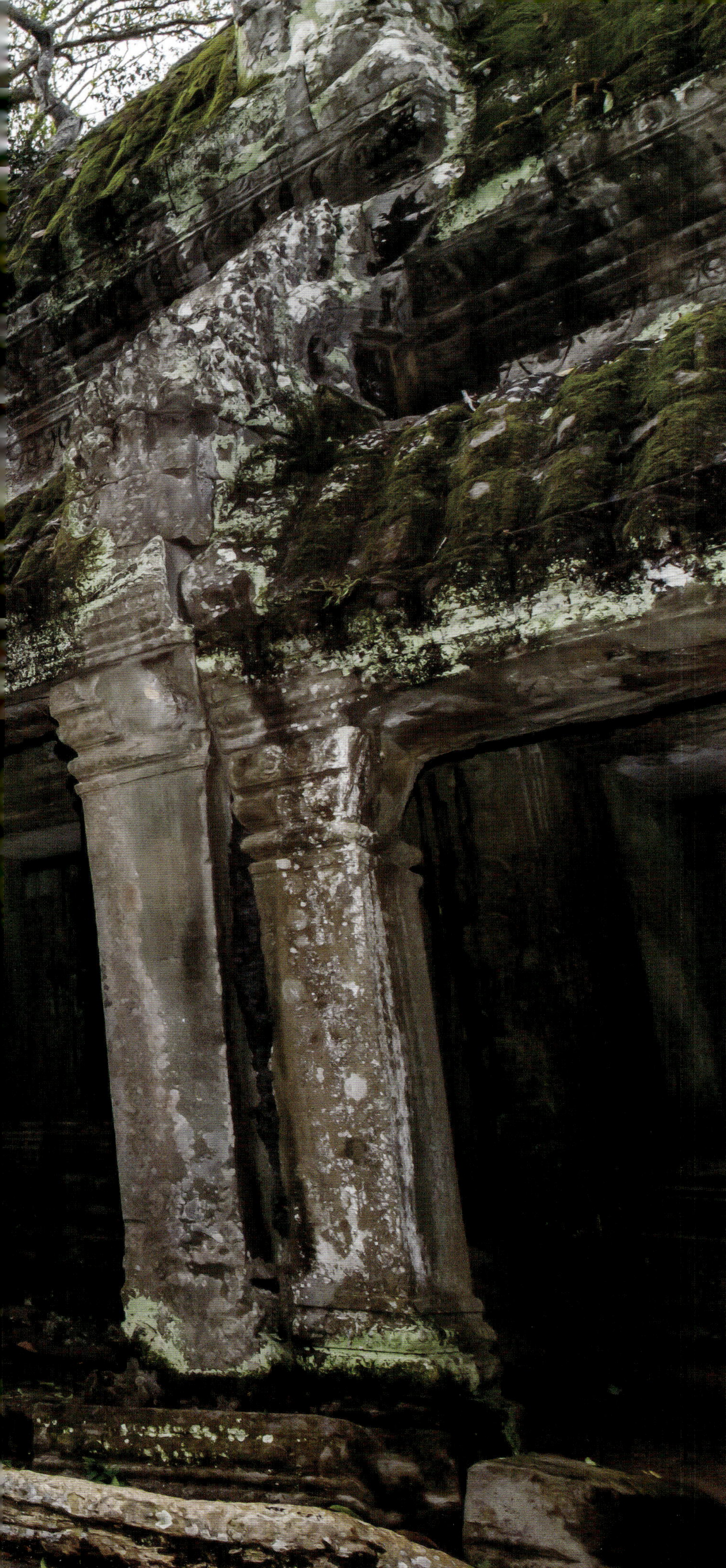

Submerged Cities

Like the song of a siren, stories of sunken cities are perhaps the most alluring of all the ancient urban legends, going back to Plato's detailed description of the island of Atlantis in his dialogue *Critias*.

Full Fathom Five

But more startling still is the real-life discovery of places like Dwarka beneath the waves – or the port city of Thonis-Heracleion, mentioned by Greek authors like Herodotus but lost until divers discovered it in the year 2000, beneath the sandy Mediterranean seabed in the waters close to Alexandria off the Egyptian coast.

These doubly buried ruins – submerged and subterranean – were first glimpsed beneath the waves by an RAF pilot flying along the coast as long ago as 1933. The pilot's report was dismissed at the time, which perhaps was a missed opportunity given that only a few years earlier the ruins of the Roman city of Leptis Magna (*see* page 69) had begun emerging from the sands of Libya after an Italian archaeologist had discovered them in 1926.

Under the reign of Libyan-born emperor Septimus Severus in the late-second century AD, Leptis had risen briefly to prominence as one of the largest cities in North Africa, but a terrible tsunami in 365 saw large parts abandoned by those who survived. The depopulation continued over the next few centuries under pressure of threats from Vandals, Berbers and then the Arab conquerors of the new religion of Islam in the late seventh century,

Left: *Jungle-surrounded ruins at Ta Prohm Temple in Angkor Wat, Cambodia.*
Next page: *The Bayon, a temple at Angkor Thom, Cambodia.*

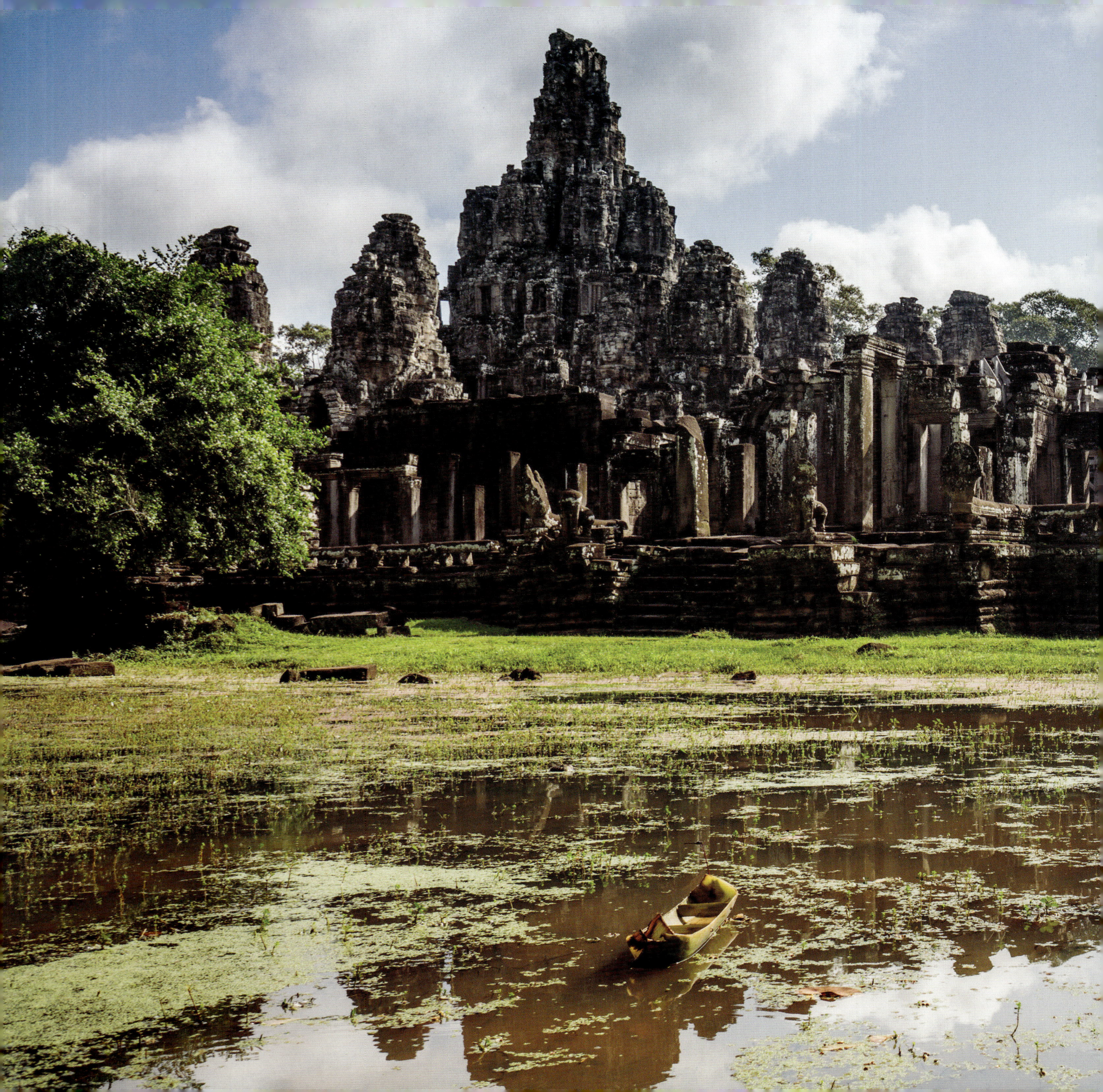

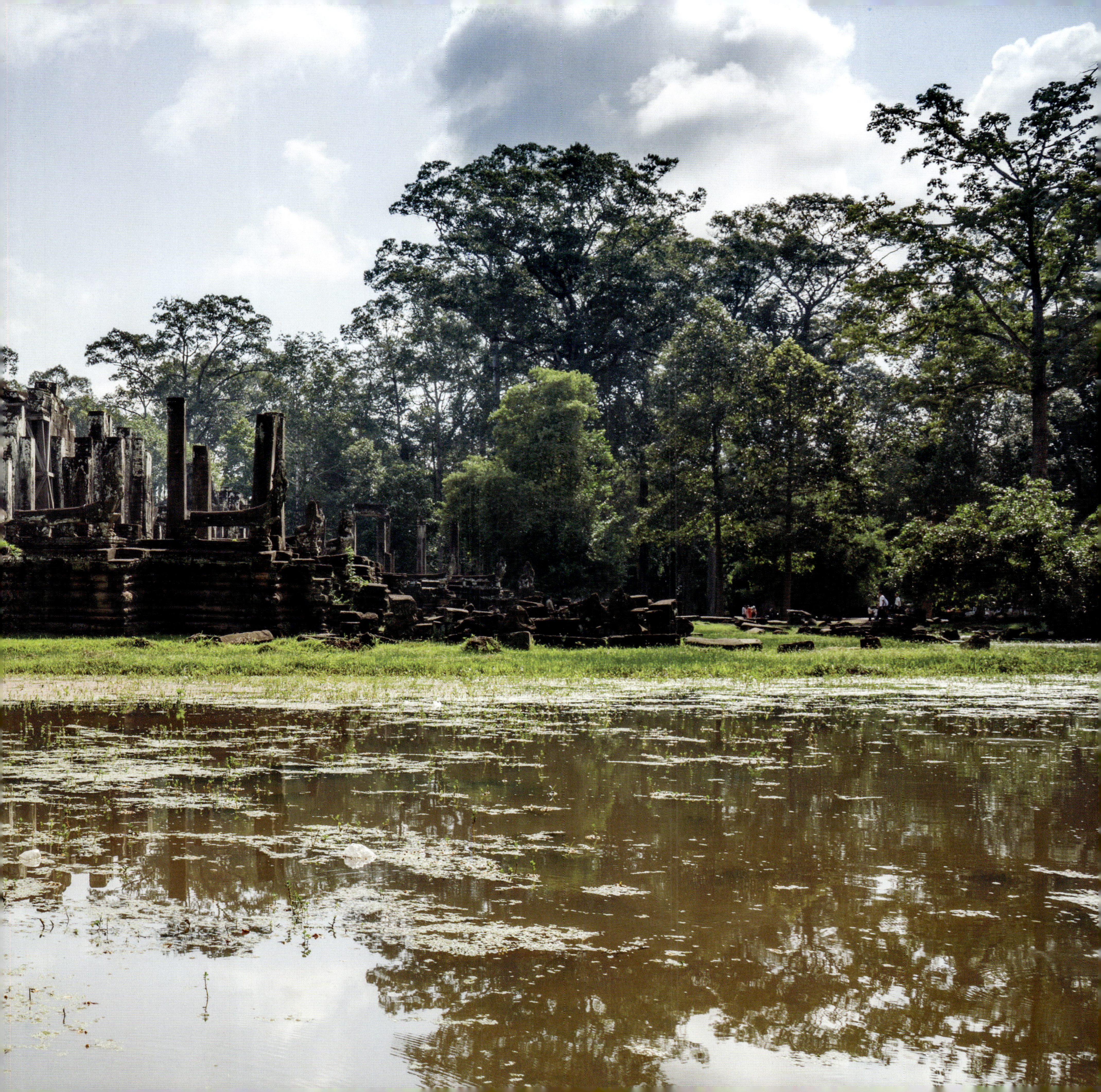

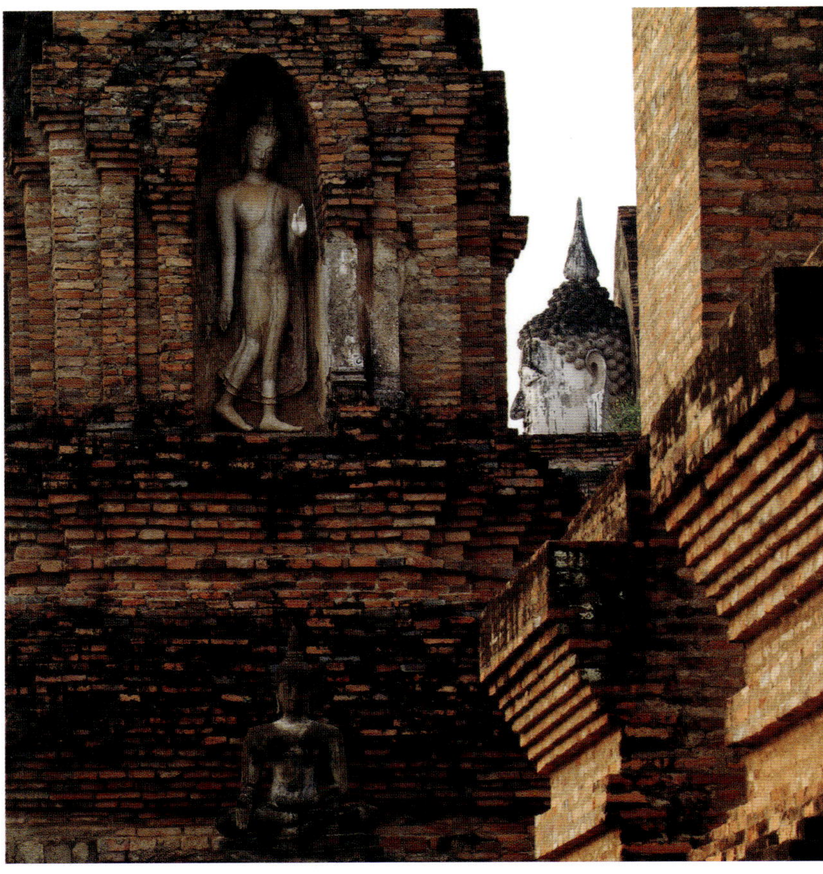

Above: *Sukhothai Historical Park, Thailand.*

after which the city was abandoned once and for all. And as a symbol of how quickly places can be forgotten, within a mere 300 years Leptis had been completely interred in coastal sand.

Angkor

Legends of a similar lost city beneath the sands of the Arabian Desert are almost as old as Leptis Magna and certainly pre-date its demise. The fabled city of Ubar has many names, being referred to in the Qur'an as Iram of the Pillars, and by T.E. Lawrence as an Atlantis of the Sands. Its whereabouts remain unproven, though in 1992 photographs taken by the NASA space shuttle Challenger were claimed by some to show definitive evidence for its existence at a site in southern Oman.

Right: *The market place in the Roman city of Leptis Magna, Libya.*

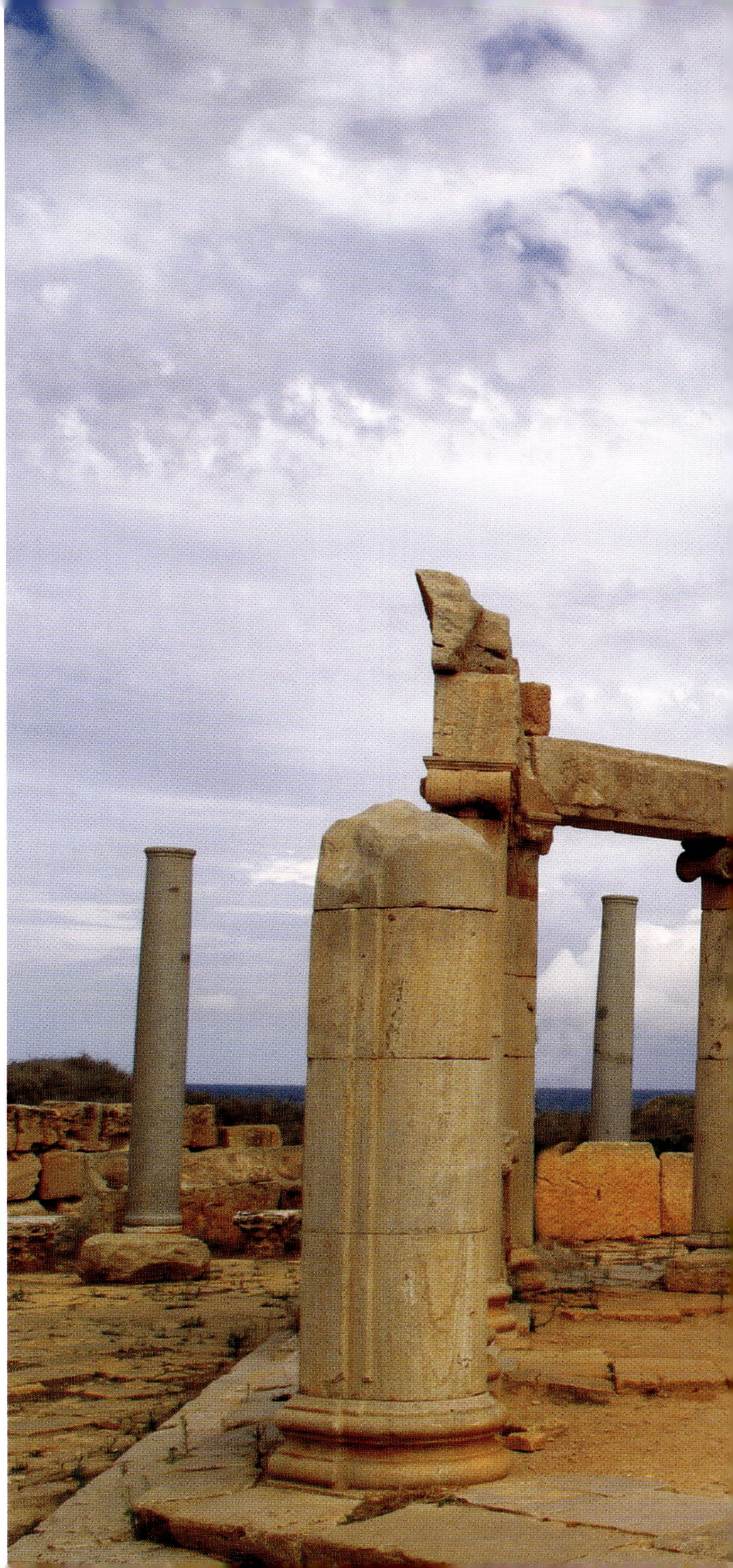

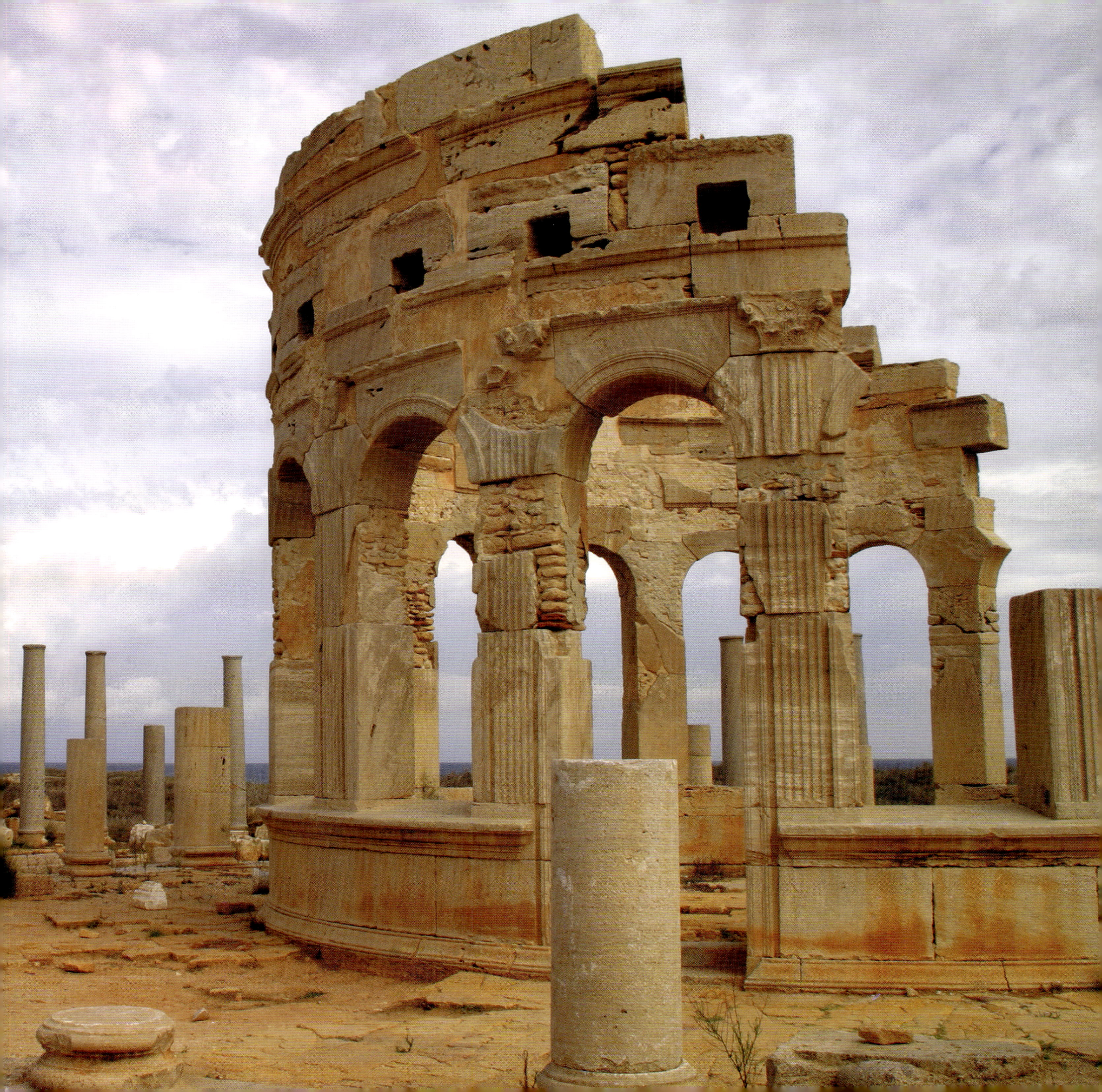

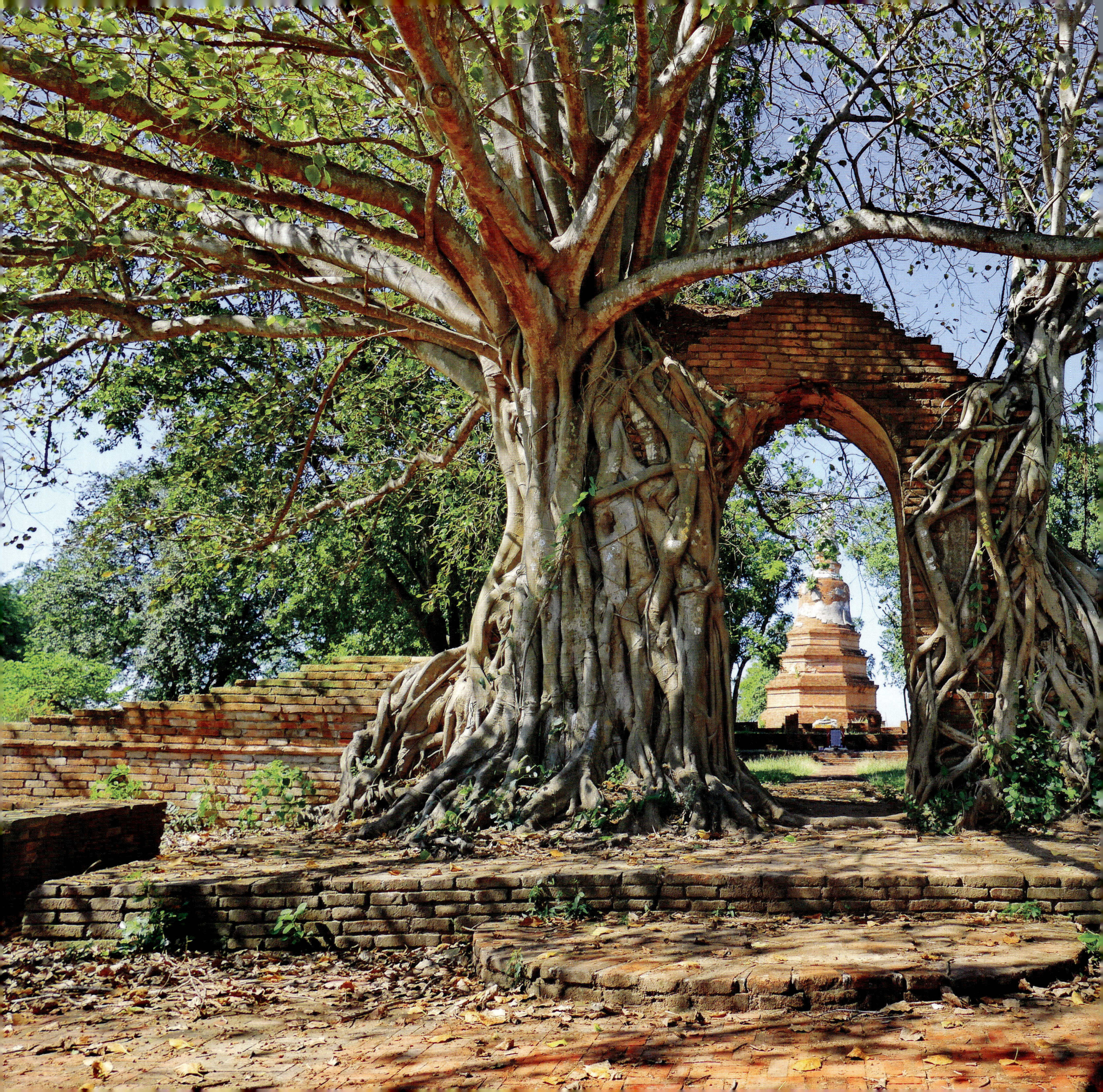

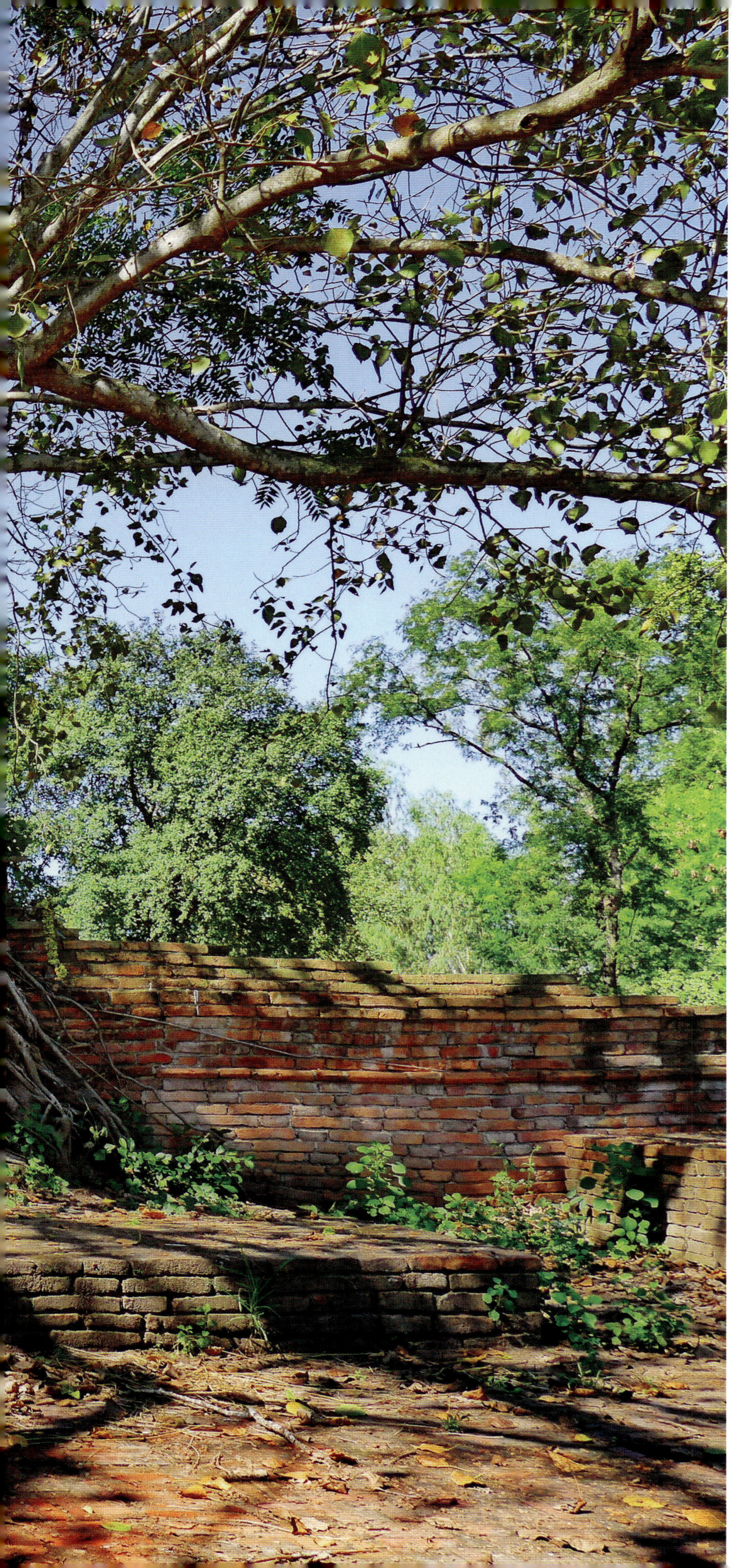

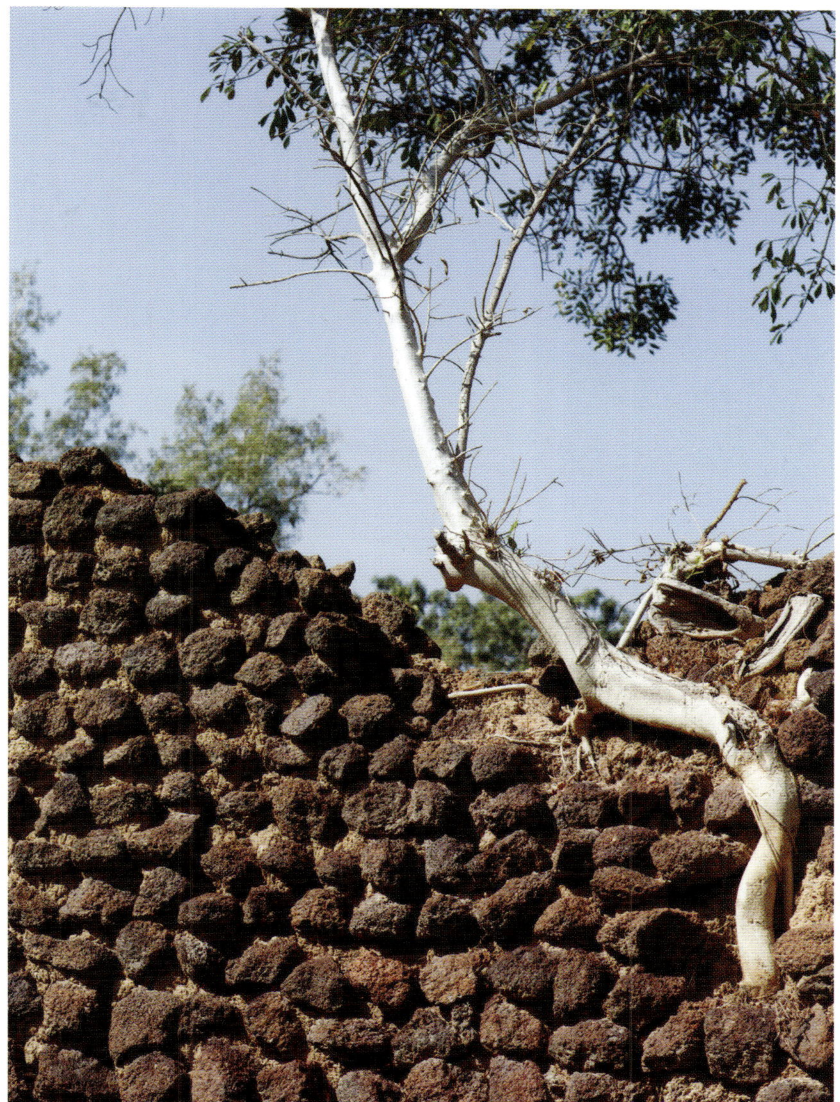

Above: *The Loropeni stone walls, Burkina Faso.*

Since then, aerial photo technology has become increasingly sophisticated, and in 2012 a laser imaging system known as LIDAR identified a lost city known as Mahendraparvata, close to the world-famous ruins of Angkor in modern Cambodia. Angkor's main temple, Angkor Wat (*see* page 64), was built in the early twelfth century and later became a Buddhist shrine, but like Mahendraparvata, 350 years older than Angkor, it was conceived in service to the Hindu faith. Over the course of more than two centuries,

Left: *Ayutthaya in modern Thailand was the capital of the Buddhist Ayutthaya kingdom for 400 years from 1351 until its demise in 1767. Foreign observers referred to the kingdom as Siam.*

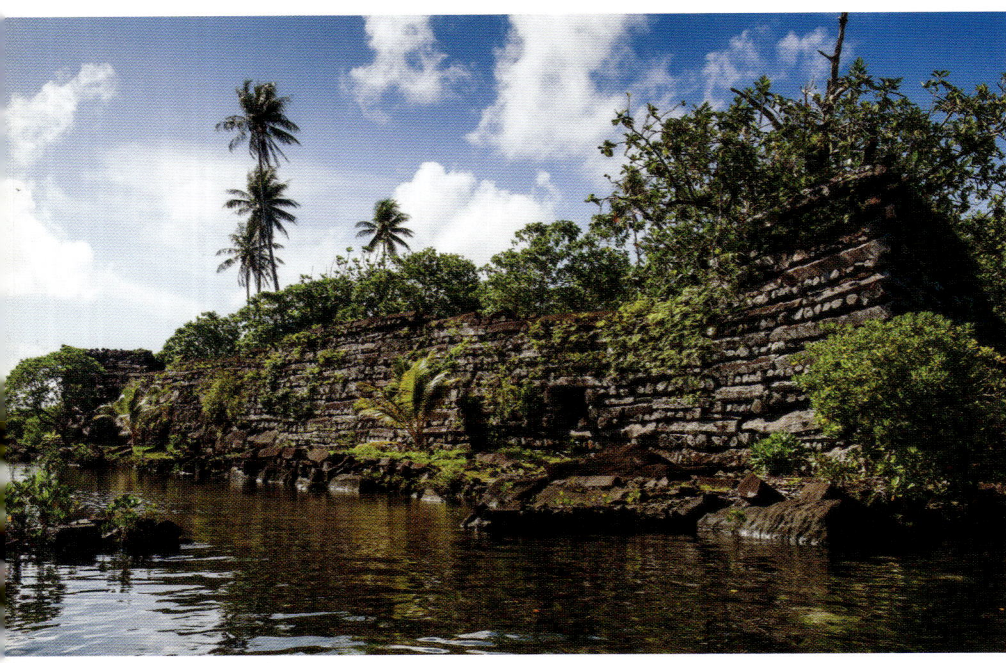

Above: *Ruins of the ancient city Nan Madol at Pohnpei, Caroline Islands, Micronesia.*

the city of Angkor, capital of the Khmer Empire, gradually expanded into a vast agglomeration, its total urban area now regarded as the largest city ever to have existed prior to the Industrial Revolution. Then in 2015, new LIDAR scans revealed further unknown cities across hundreds of miles beneath the forest canopy that covers large parts of Cambodia, evidence of a complex society whose sophistication in its heyday would have rivalled anywhere else on earth.

Angkor became gradually deserted over several centuries, and many causes have been offered for its demise, from natural disasters to disease, to invasion by a foreign power and even a change of official religion. No one can say for sure why the city was abandoned, but that even somewhere as magnificent as this could suffer such a fate confirms the ancient wisdom of the religion of the Khmer – that everything is impermanent and all must one day submit to the same common end.

Right: *Sandstone Buddha head in a tree root at the Wat Mahathat temple in Ayutthaya, Thailand.*

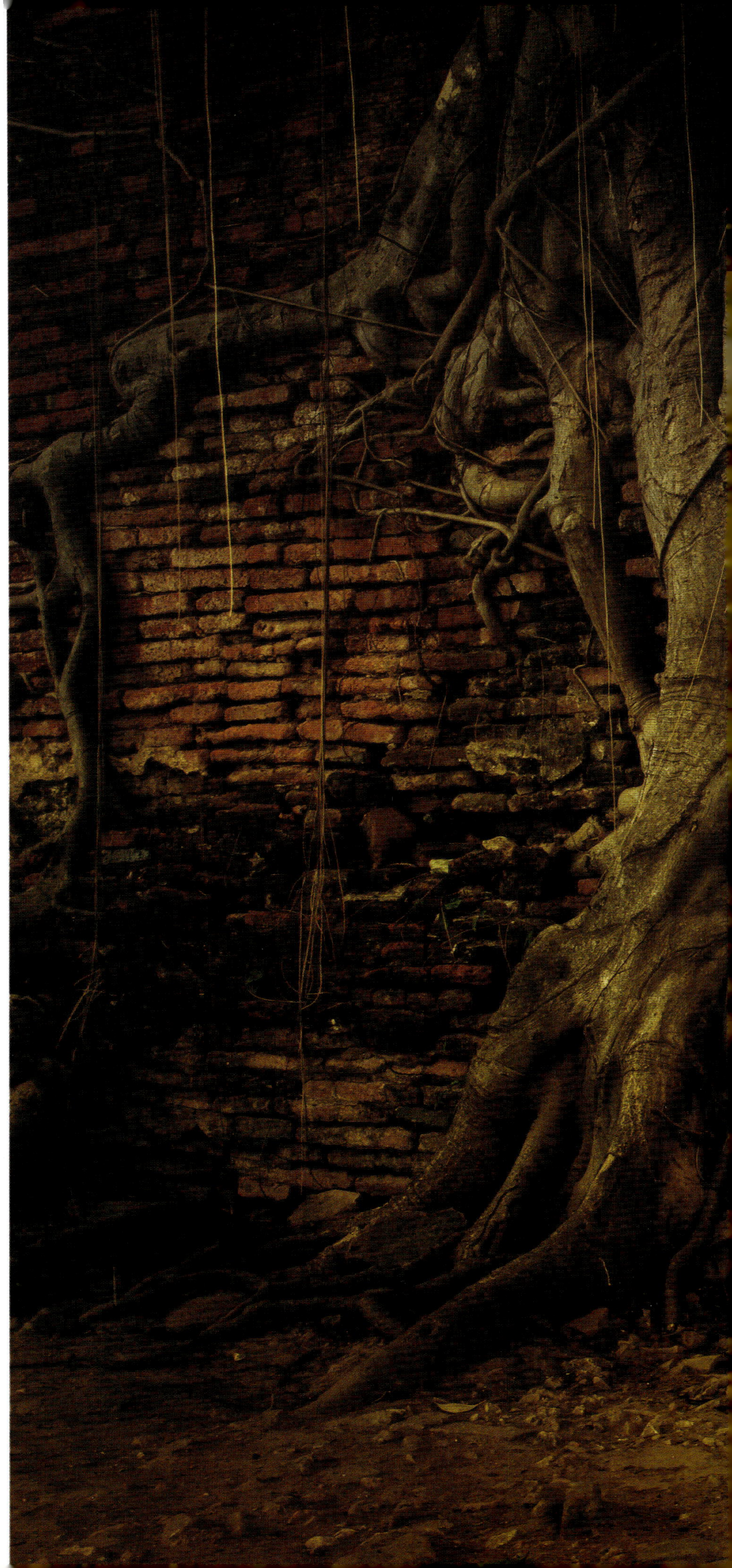

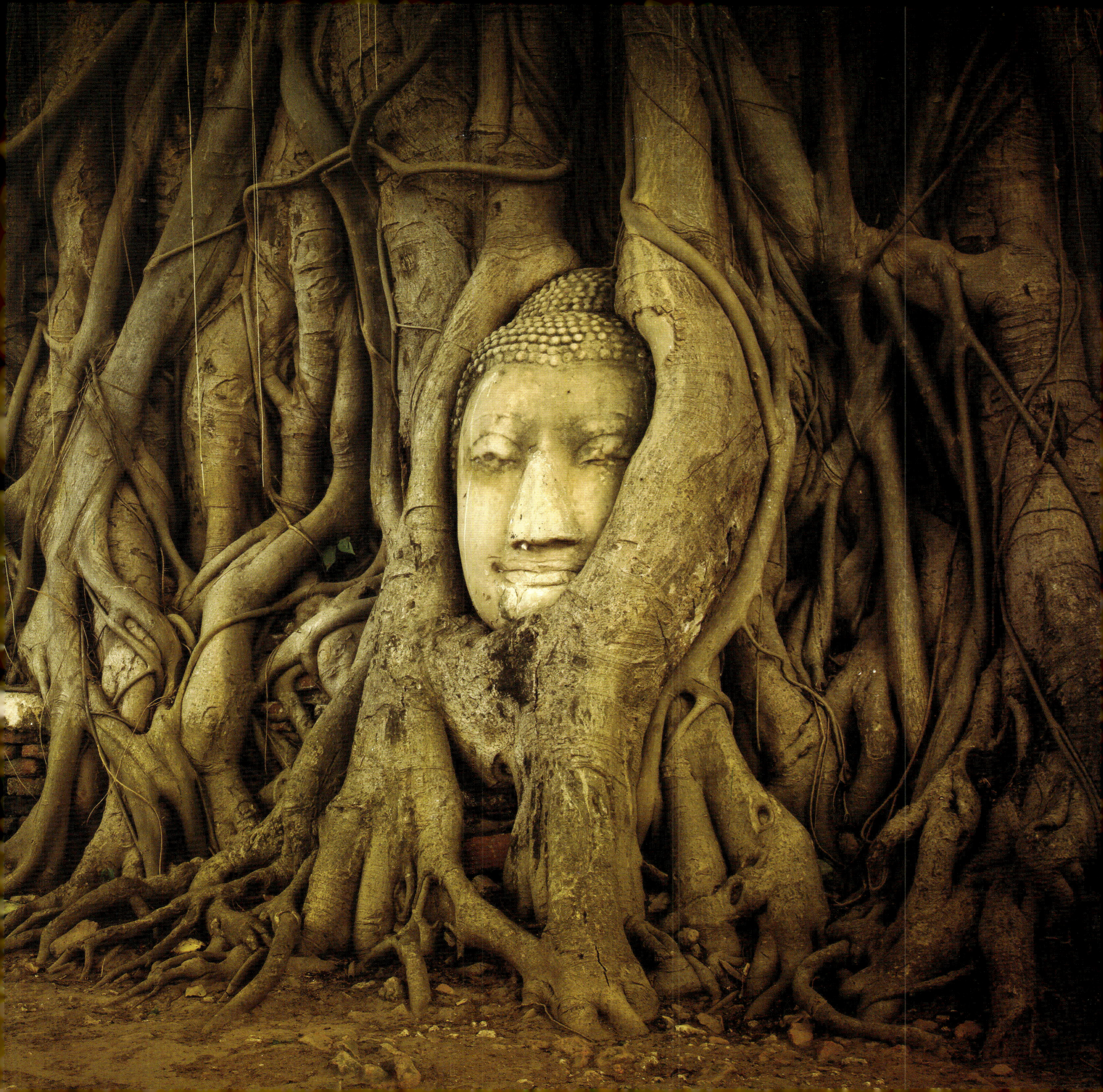

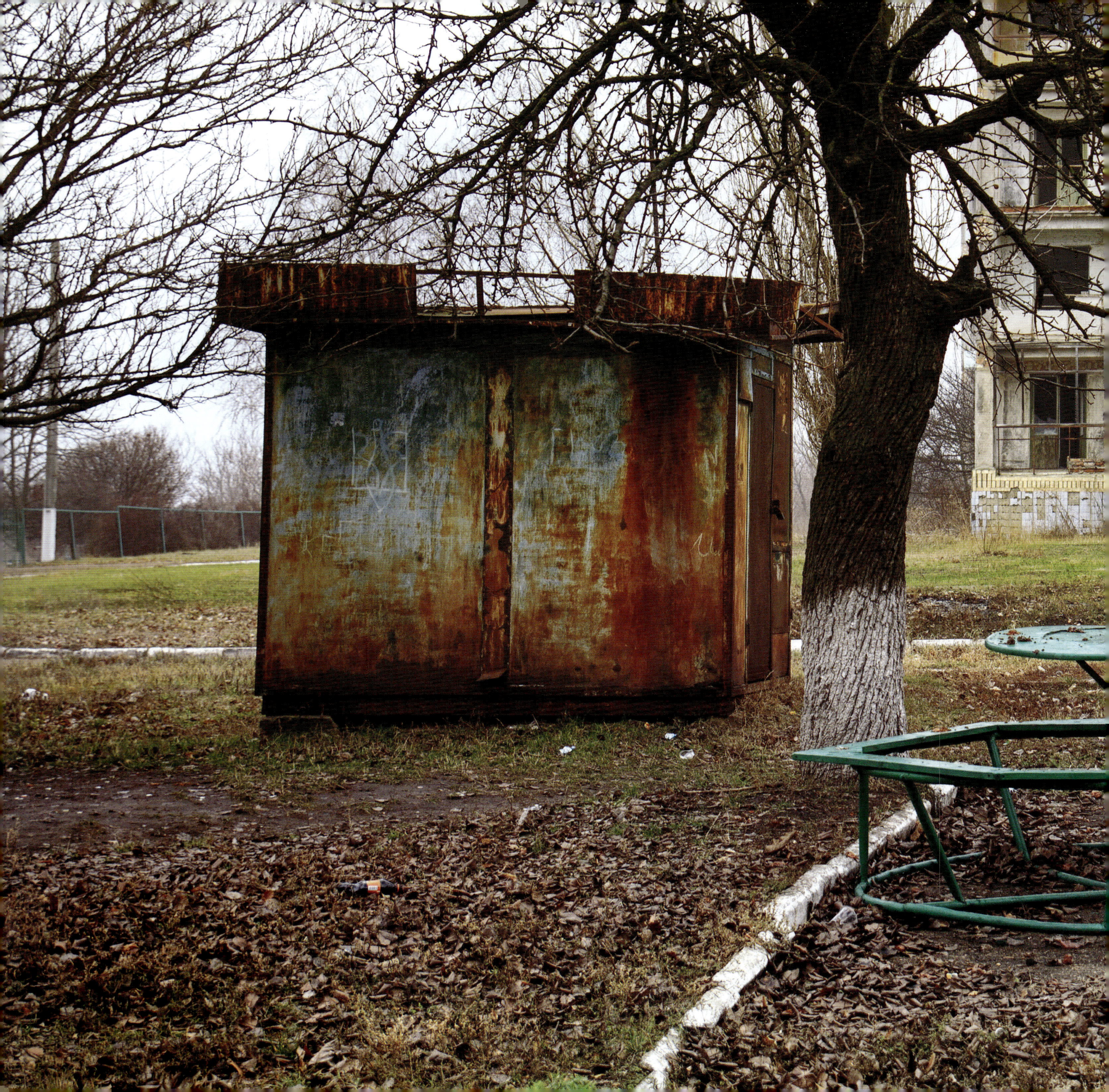

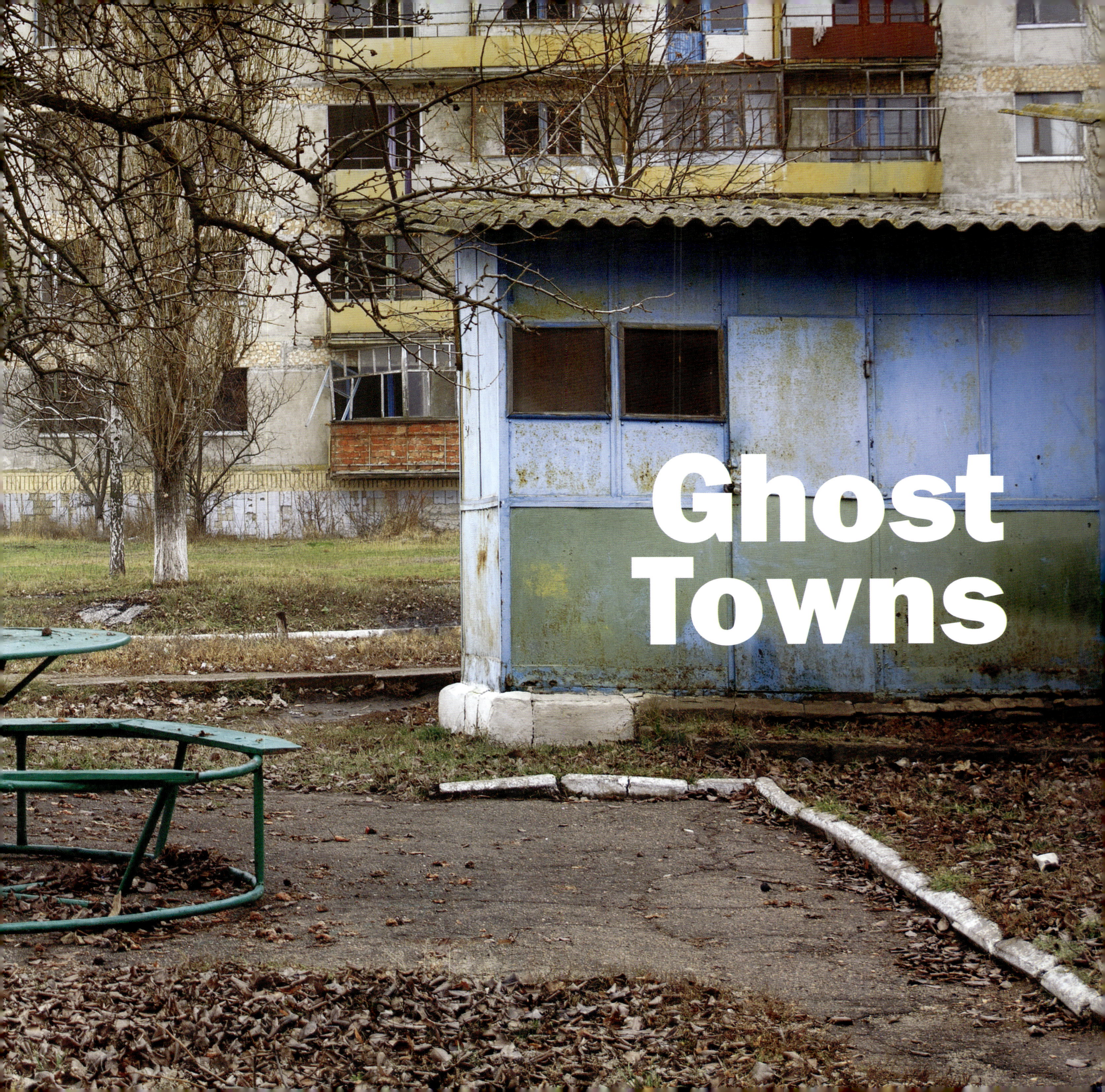

Ghost Towns

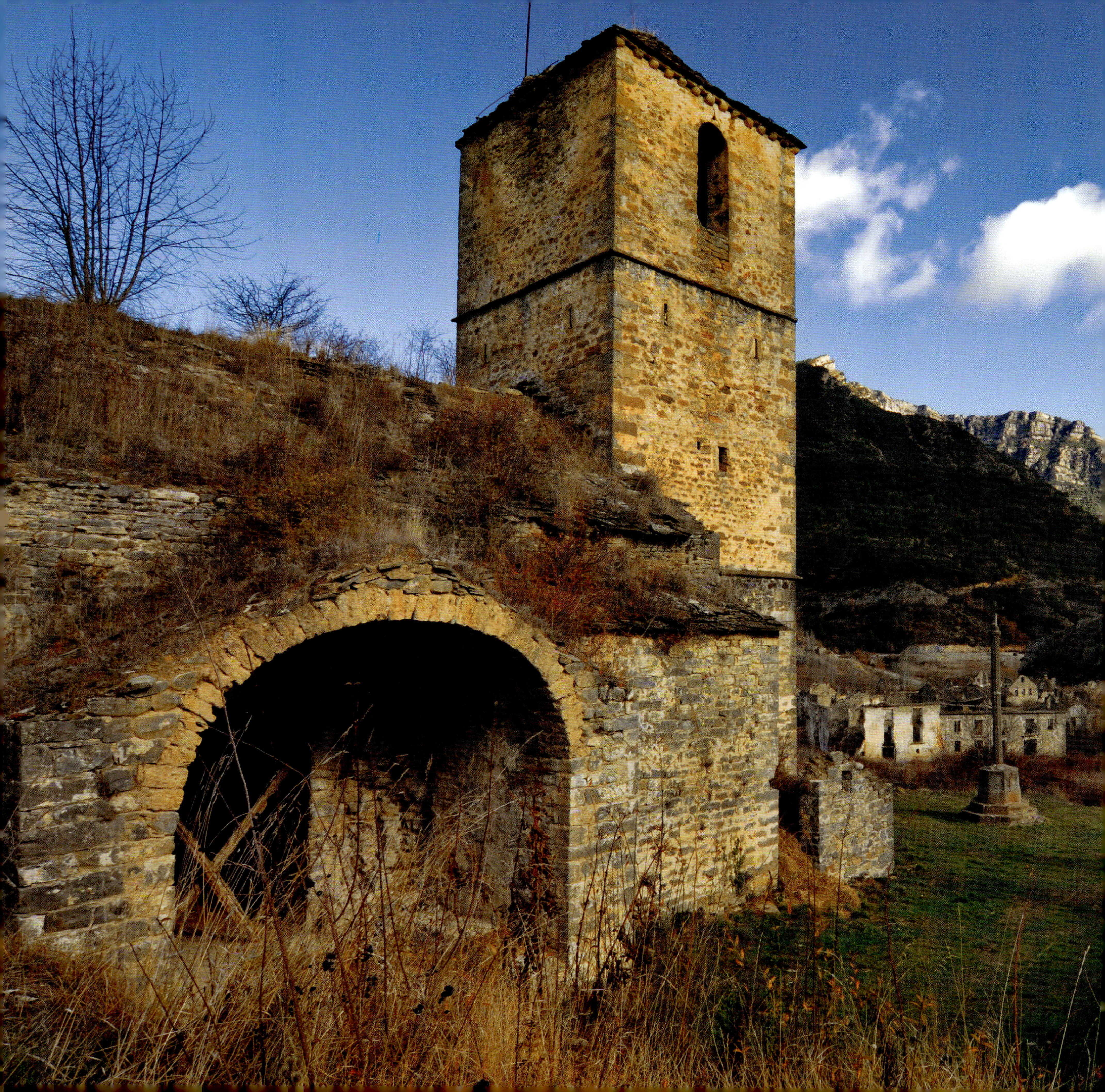

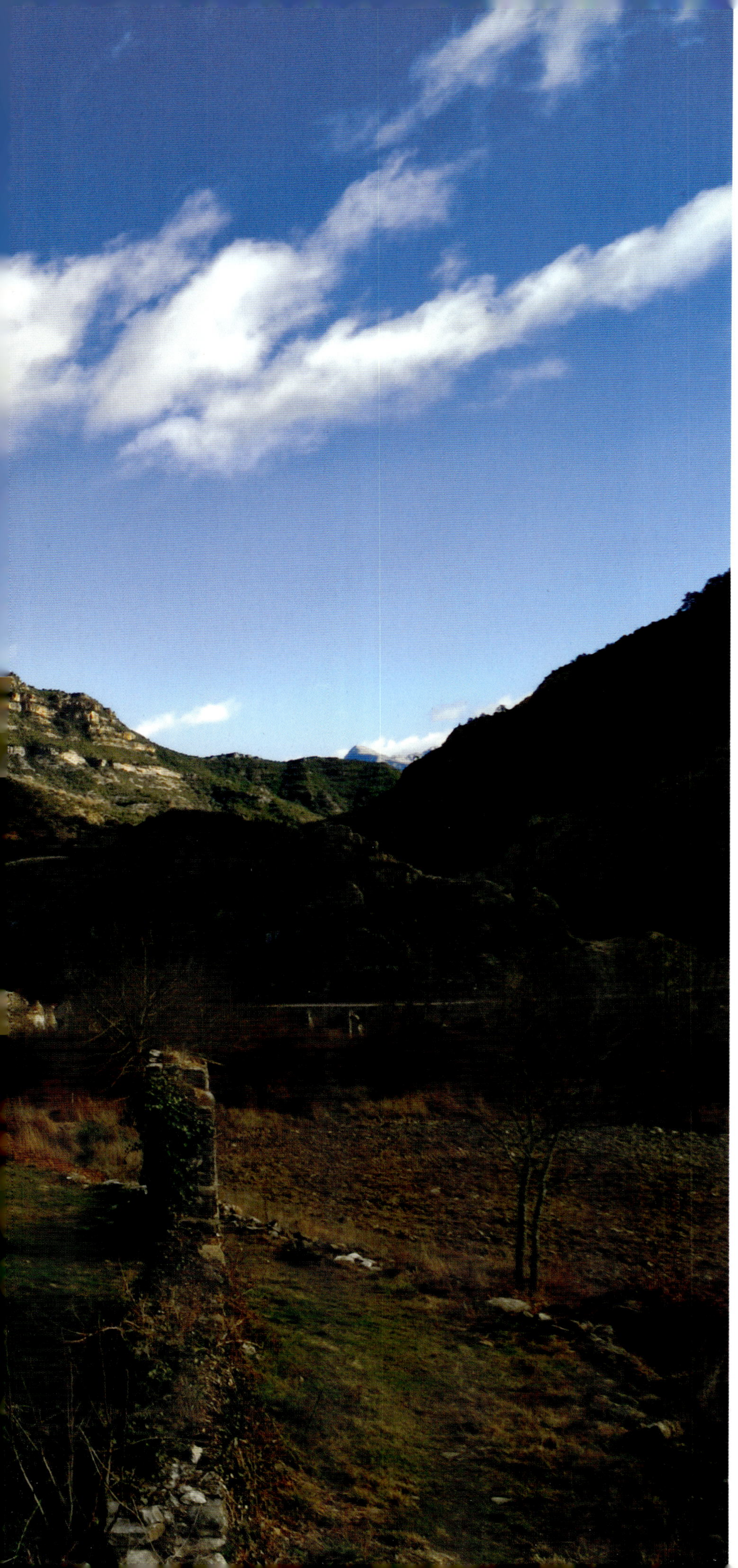

Fragile Hopes

These ancient cities are known to us because they were built to last, with a sense of time that contemporary human cultures have all but lost sight of. Modernity is too often wedded to the short-term vision of immediate gain, epitomized by the numerous towns around the world set up to exploit a newly discovered resource – or more recently to speculate on future economic growth – which have then been left behind as soon as that resource runs out or becomes economically unviable to extract.

Of course, there were ghost towns in the ancient world too – built with the same lack of long-term concern – which have not lasted into the present, but there are perhaps no more poignant reminders of the frailty of fortune and the fickleness of hope than those from our own time whose so recent investment in future prosperity was quickly scattered to the winds.

Previous page: *A ghost town in Ukraine.*
Left: *Remote villages across southern Europe, like this Spanish one, are abandoned due to economic and social factors.*
Below: *Since its depopulation, Doel in Belgium has begun to attract street artists.*

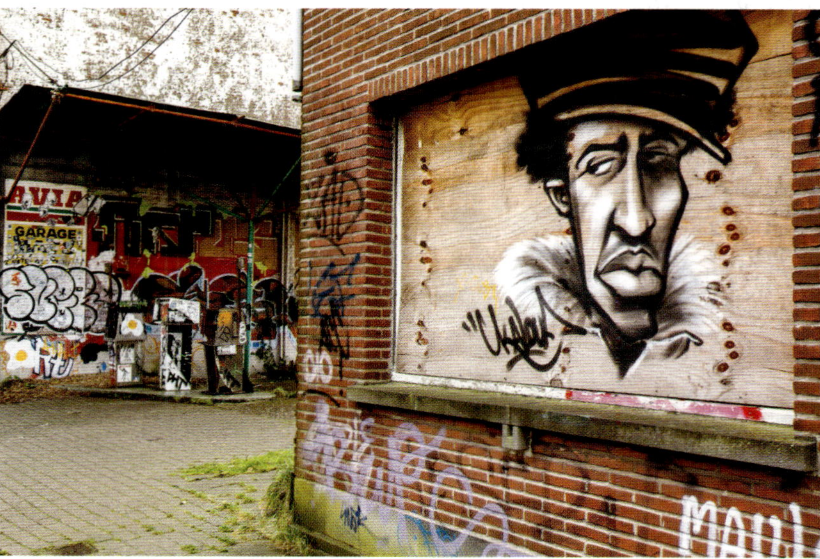

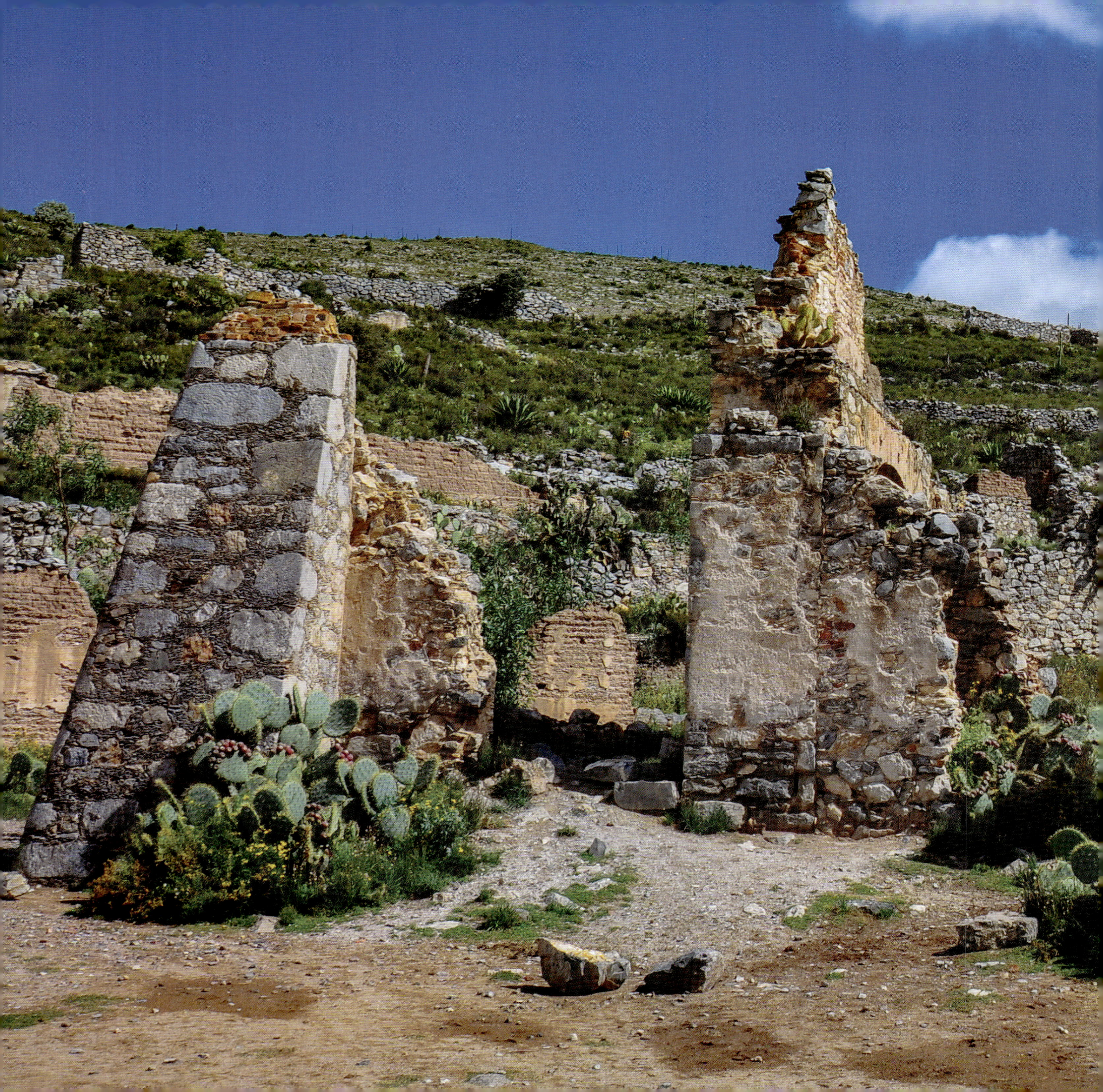

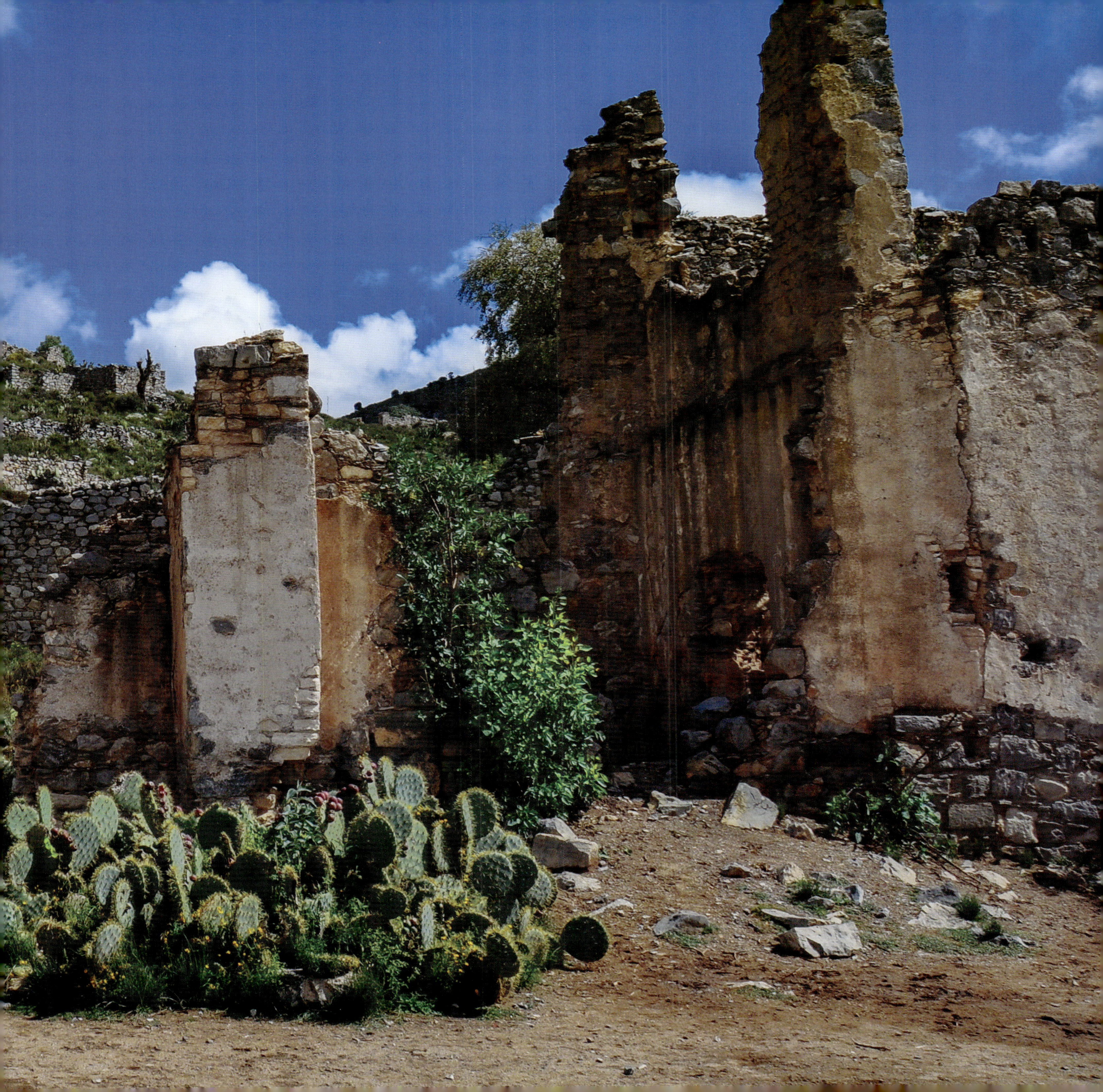

America

Perhaps nowhere on earth has as many ghost towns as the United States. Like so many settler colonies of the 'New World', the USA held deposits of precious metals, and potentially instant wealth, that were long since exhausted in the Old, and the history of the settlement of the west is partly a story of feeding frenzies of prospectors rushing to each new find like flies to a corpse.

The California Gold Rush

After strikes in Carolina and Georgia during the previous 50 years, the first significant gold rush attracting global attention was the California Gold Rush of 1848. Gold rush towns like Auburn and Nevada City, California have survived the decline of prospecting and now stand as testimony to the aspirations and the architecture of that era, but other places have not been so lucky and were long ago left for dead.

Bodie, California

One such place is Bodie, California's official state gold rush ghost town (*see* right), founded in the 1850s but reaching the zenith of its fortunes in the late 1870s, when between 5,000 and 7,000 hopeful souls, drawn by news of a new, much bigger strike, descended on this frontier settlement, which soon numbered some 2,000 buildings in all. As with so many places, the bonanza was short-lived, and the men who had flocked to Bodie were drawn away by rumours of new and bigger deposits discovered elsewhere in the country. The brothels closed down and Chinatown with its opium dens soon went the same way.

Previous page: *Ruins of Real de Catorce, San Luis Potosí, Mexico.*
Right: *Bodie State Historic Park, California, USA.*

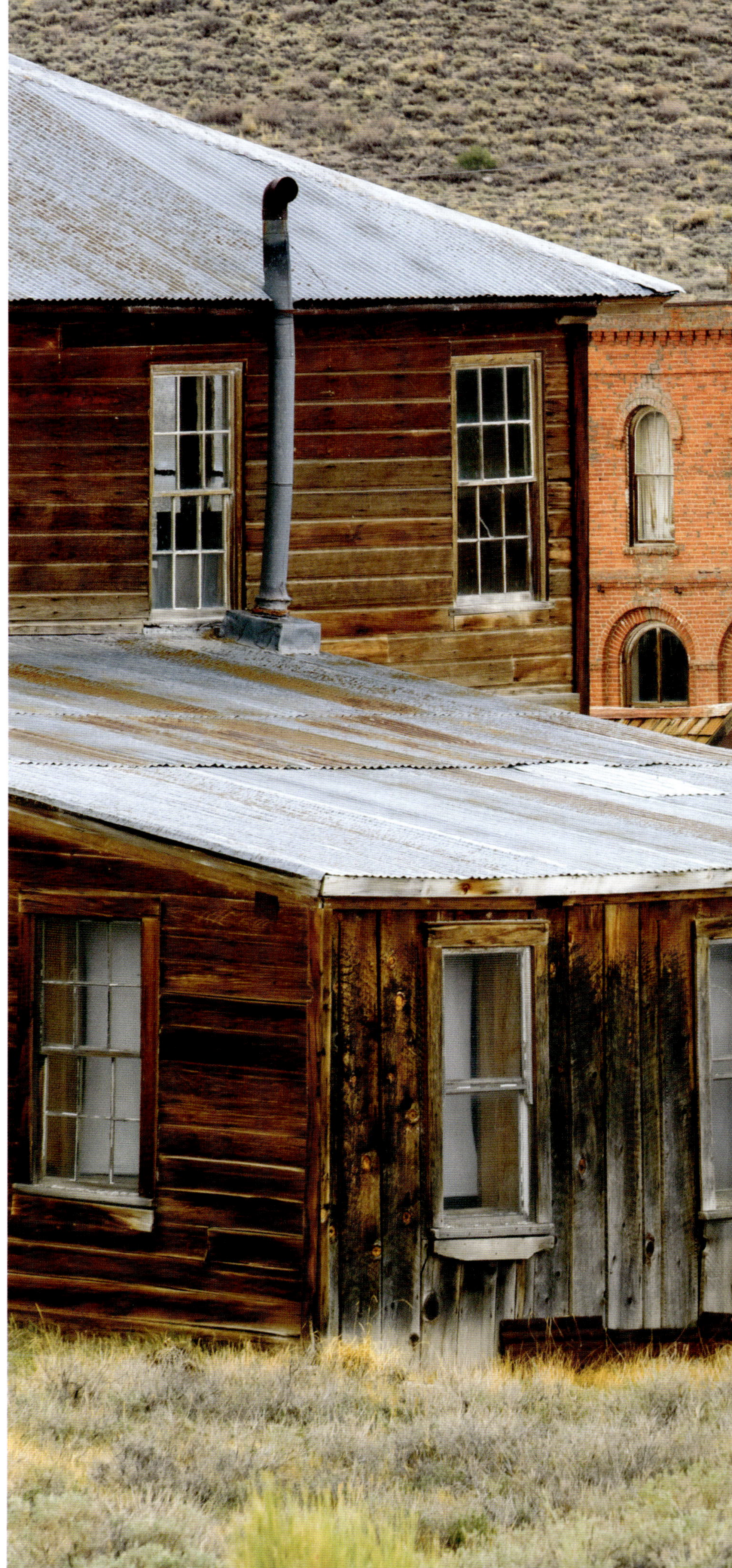

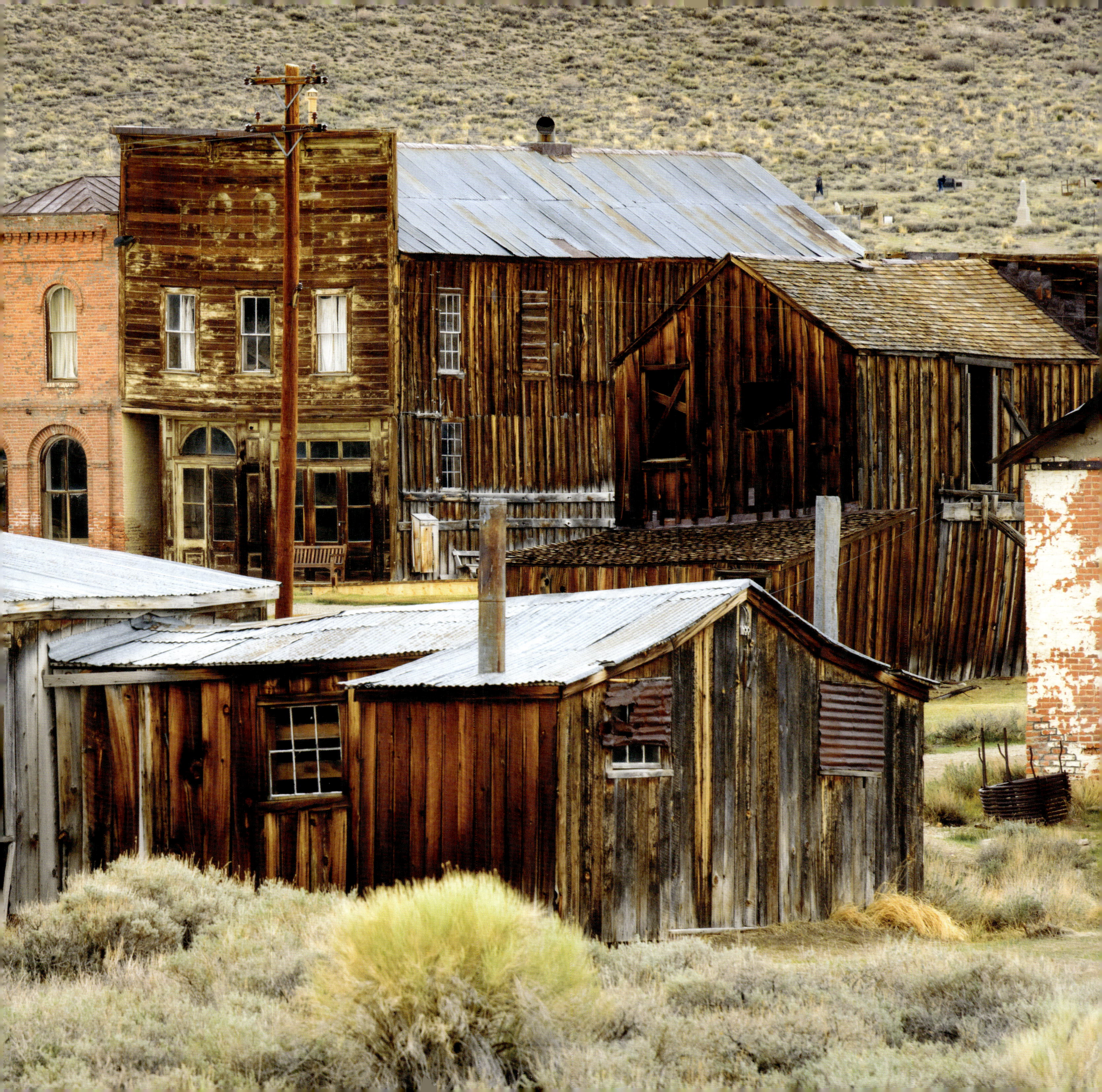

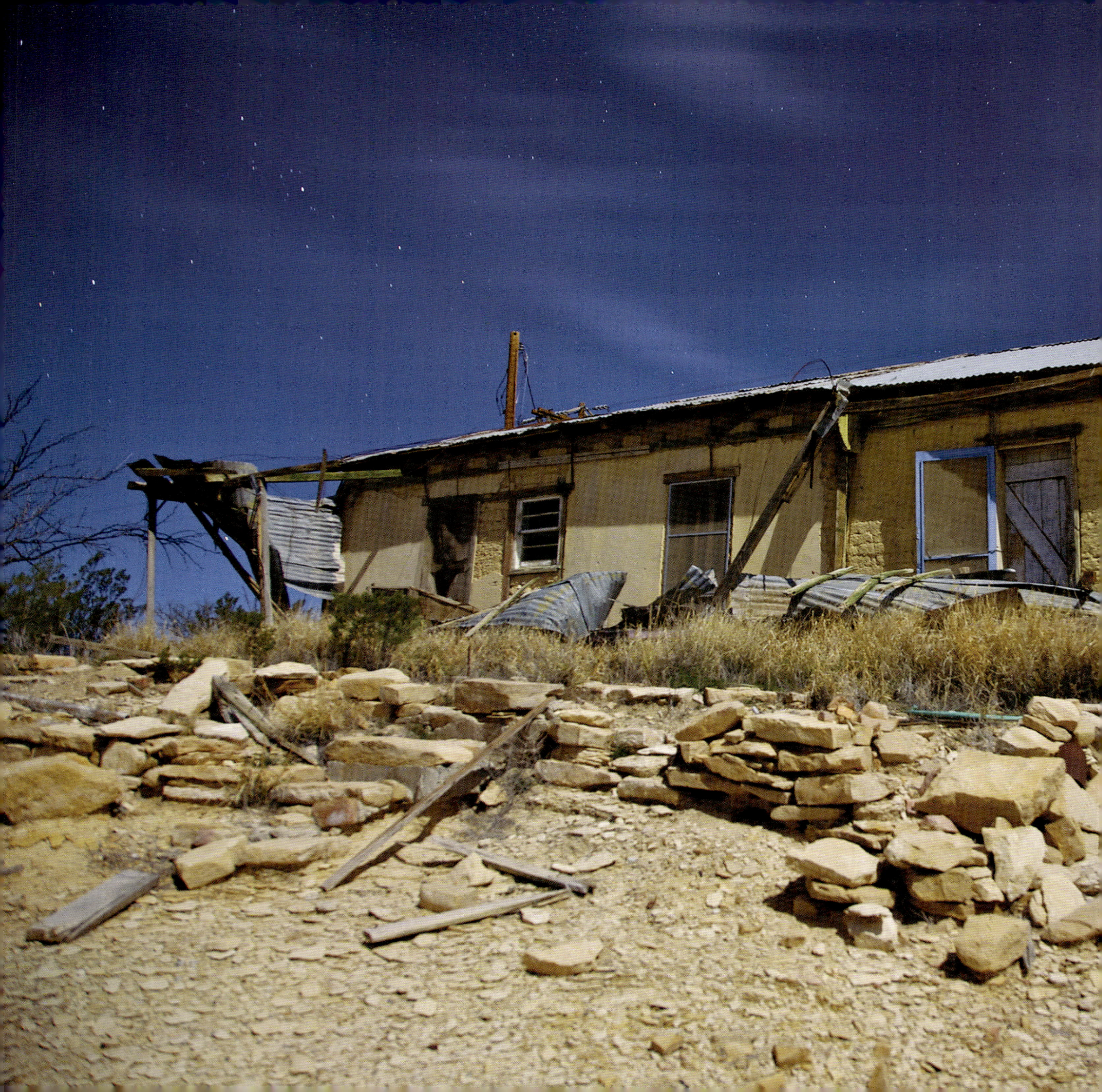

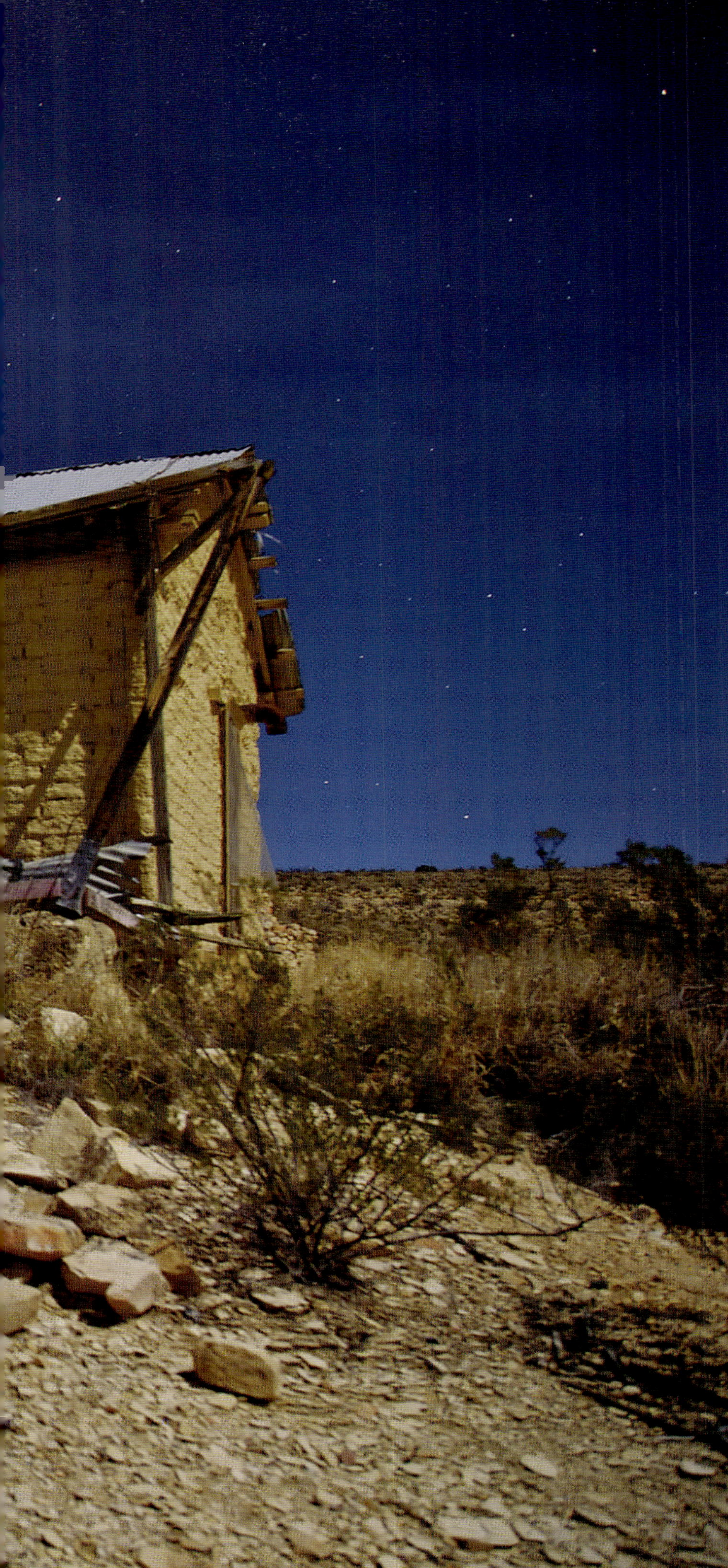

Despite periodic revivals of the mines, as new techniques made more difficult deposits easier to extract, by the 1920s Bodie's population had dwindled to little more than a hundred people, and by 1950 the place had been completely abandoned. It survives today as a symbol of the old Wild West, its restored but empty buildings, some 170 in all, giving the sense of somewhere frozen in time.

The Nevada Silver Rush

Back in the early 1860s, at the same time as gold-hunting hordes were flocking to California or north to Montana, which had a gold rush of its own, another precious metal was being discovered in significant quantities in nearby Nevada. Among those who tried their luck here was one Samuel Clemens, who as Mark Twain would later write about his experiences in his memoir *Roughing It.*

One of the places he lived in, Aurora, is a ghost town today, where almost nothing remains, but whose generous deposits of both silver and gold once supported a lively population of some 10,000 people. The boom lasted until the veins were exhausted and then began the decline, so that by the 1920s the town was all but deserted. But if there is not much left to see in Aurora, elsewhere in Nevada, in the ghost town of Berlin, the remains of mills and other buildings established in the late 1890s offer further reminders of the sudden growth of communities around the discovery of a valuable resource; while the crumbling ruins of Rhyolite, another casualty of that period, are a brutal lesson in the ruthless economics that apply when it's all used up.

Route 66

Not that laissez-faire capitalism alone creates these places. Such reversals can come about through the well-intentioned policies of an active state as readily

Left: *Following the discovery of cinnabar in the vicinity, from which mercury is made, the town, now ghost town, of Terlingua in Texas grew to a population of some 2,000 people.*
Next page: *Glenrio, next to the Texas-New Mexico state line, USA, was once a thriving collection of motels, restaurants and gas stations on Route 66.*

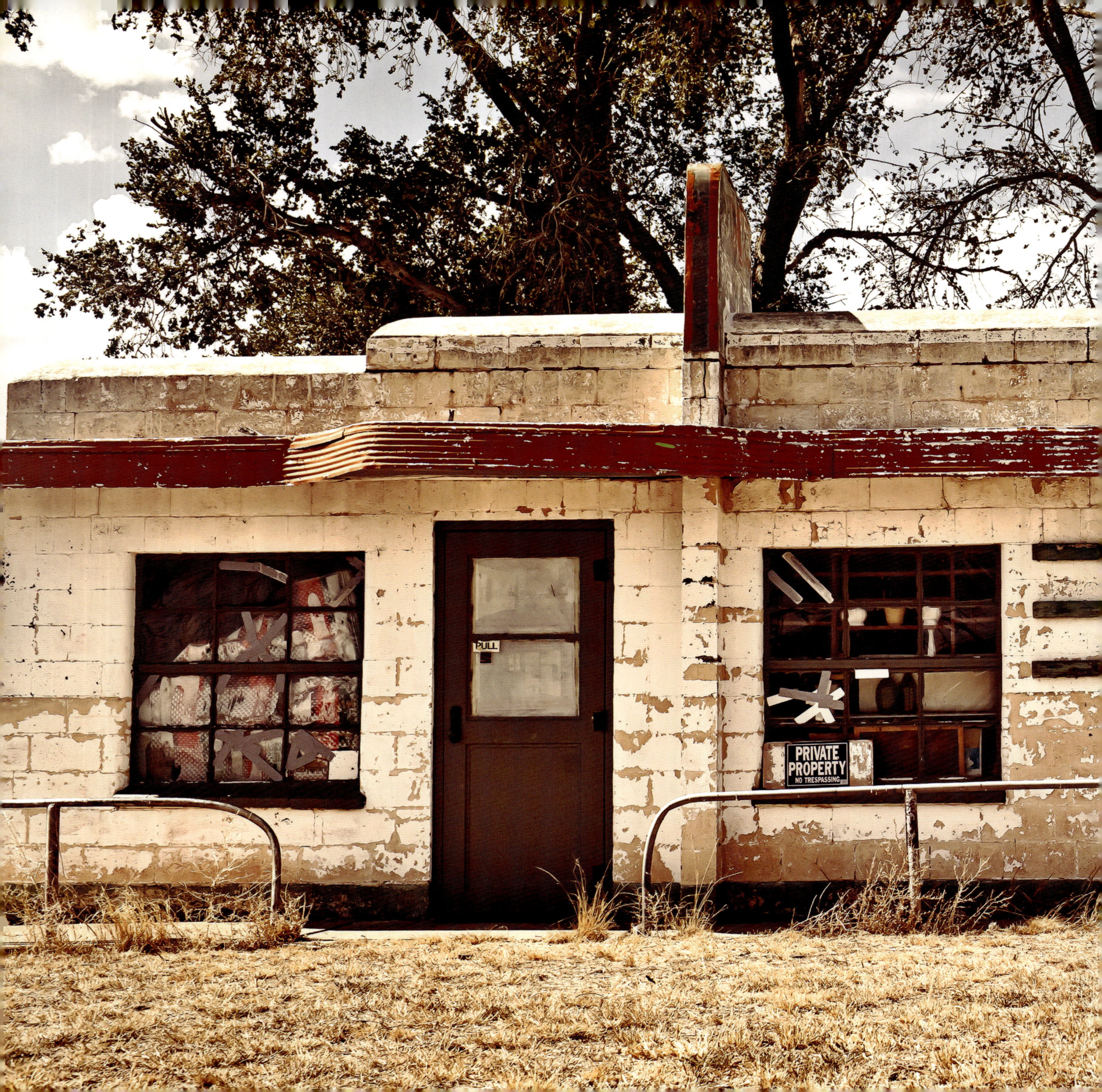
PULL
PRIVATE PROPERTY
NO TRESPASSING

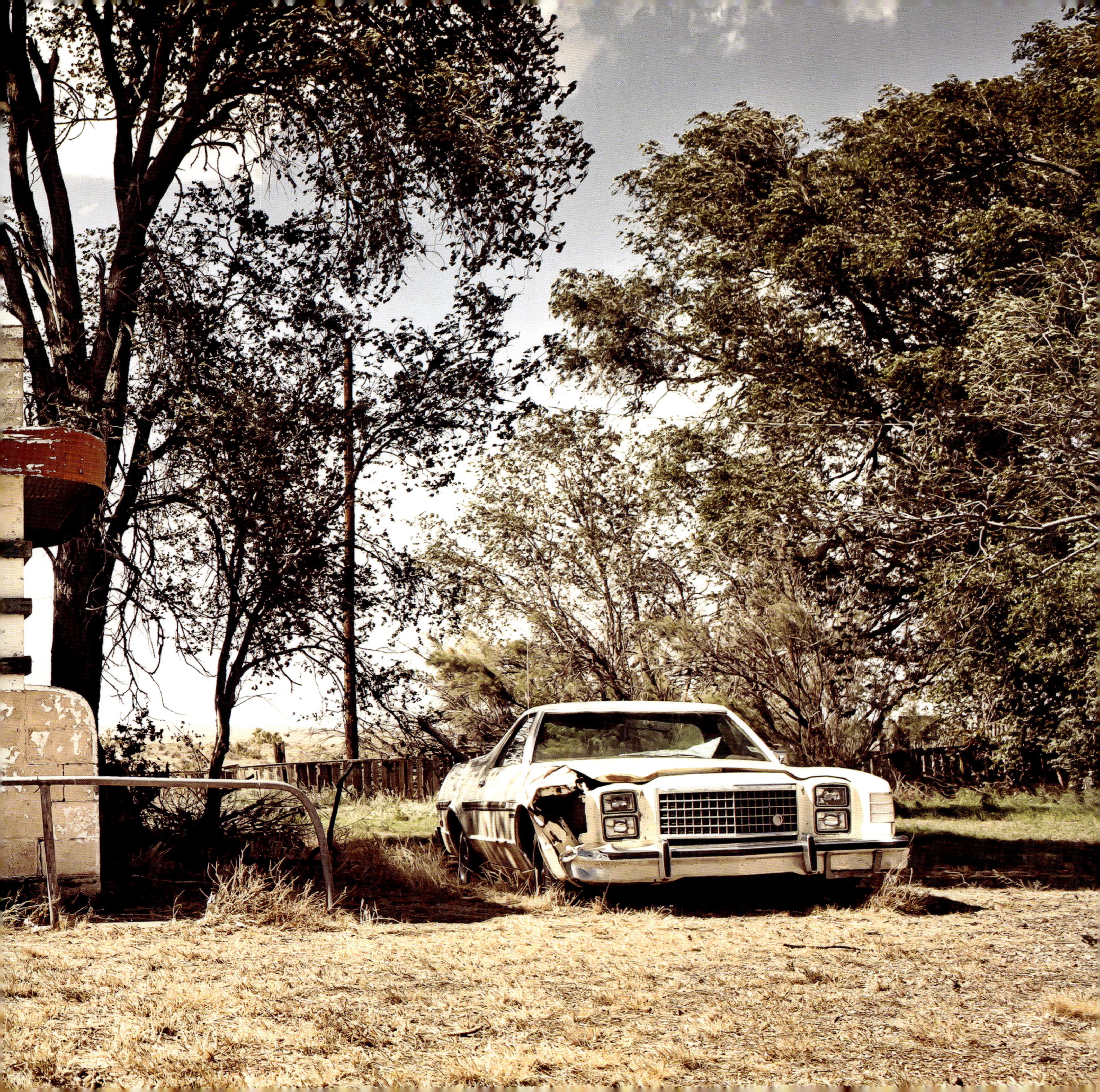

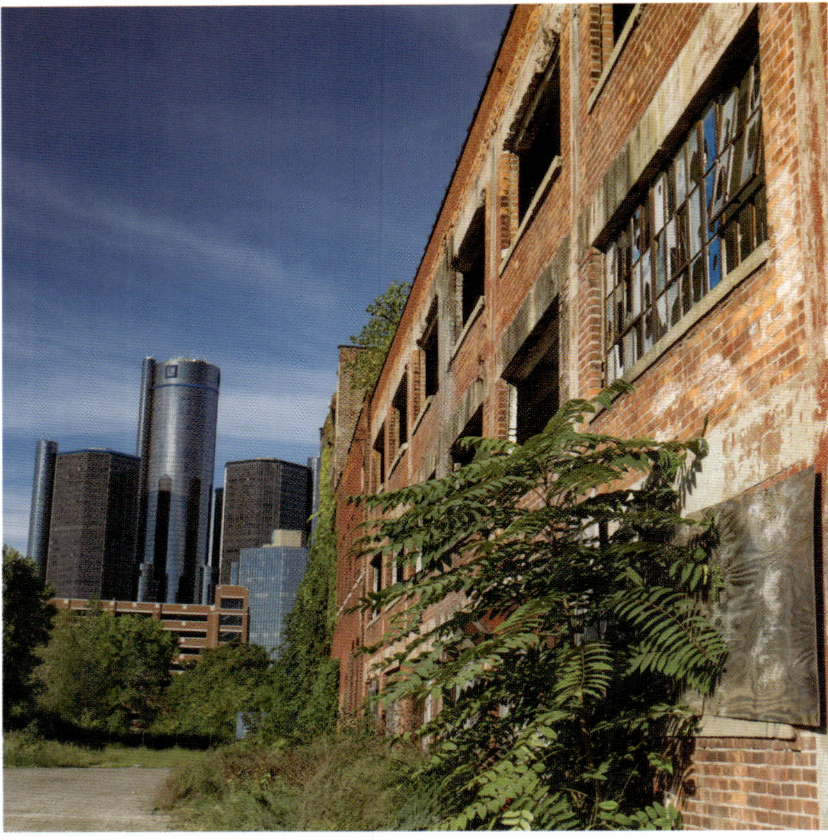

Above: *Abandoned factory building in Detroit, Michigan, USA.*

as from the amorality of an unregulated market, as the ghost towns of one of the most famous roads in the world prove with mournful poetry. Running for almost 2,500 miles from Chicago, Illinois to Santa Monica, California, Route 66 was built in the mid-1920s and made famous through cultural classics such as John Steinbeck's novel *The Grapes of Wrath* and the pop song '(Get Your Kicks on) Route 66'.

America's 'Main Street', the iconic road was built on the footprint of earlier trails to the west, and during the Depression of the 1930s carried thousands of people like the Joad family in Steinbeck's book away from the Dust Bowl of the Midwest towards what they hoped would be a better life. But the building of the Interstate Highway system across America from

Right: *Abandoned buildings at Old Town Mall, Baltimore, Maryland.*

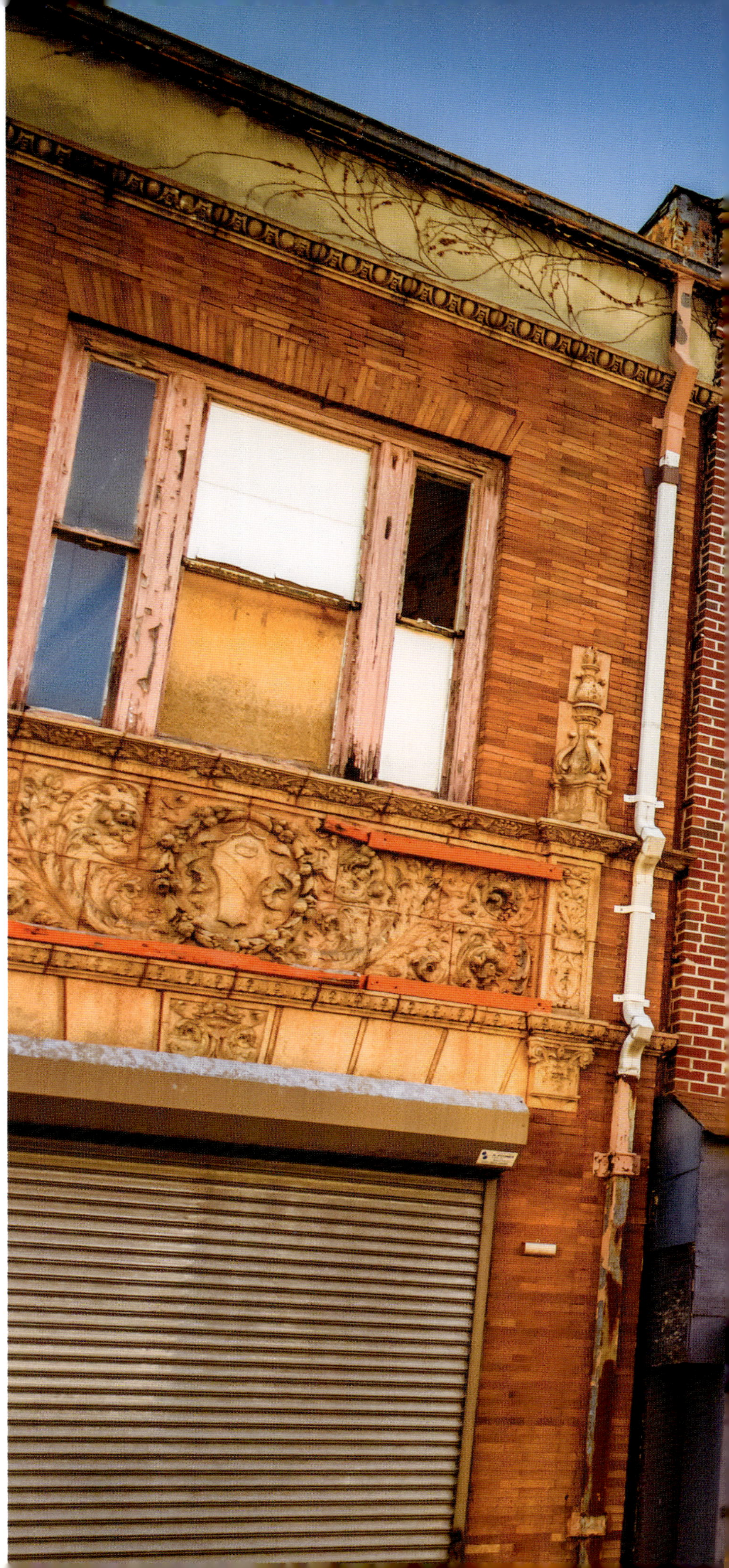

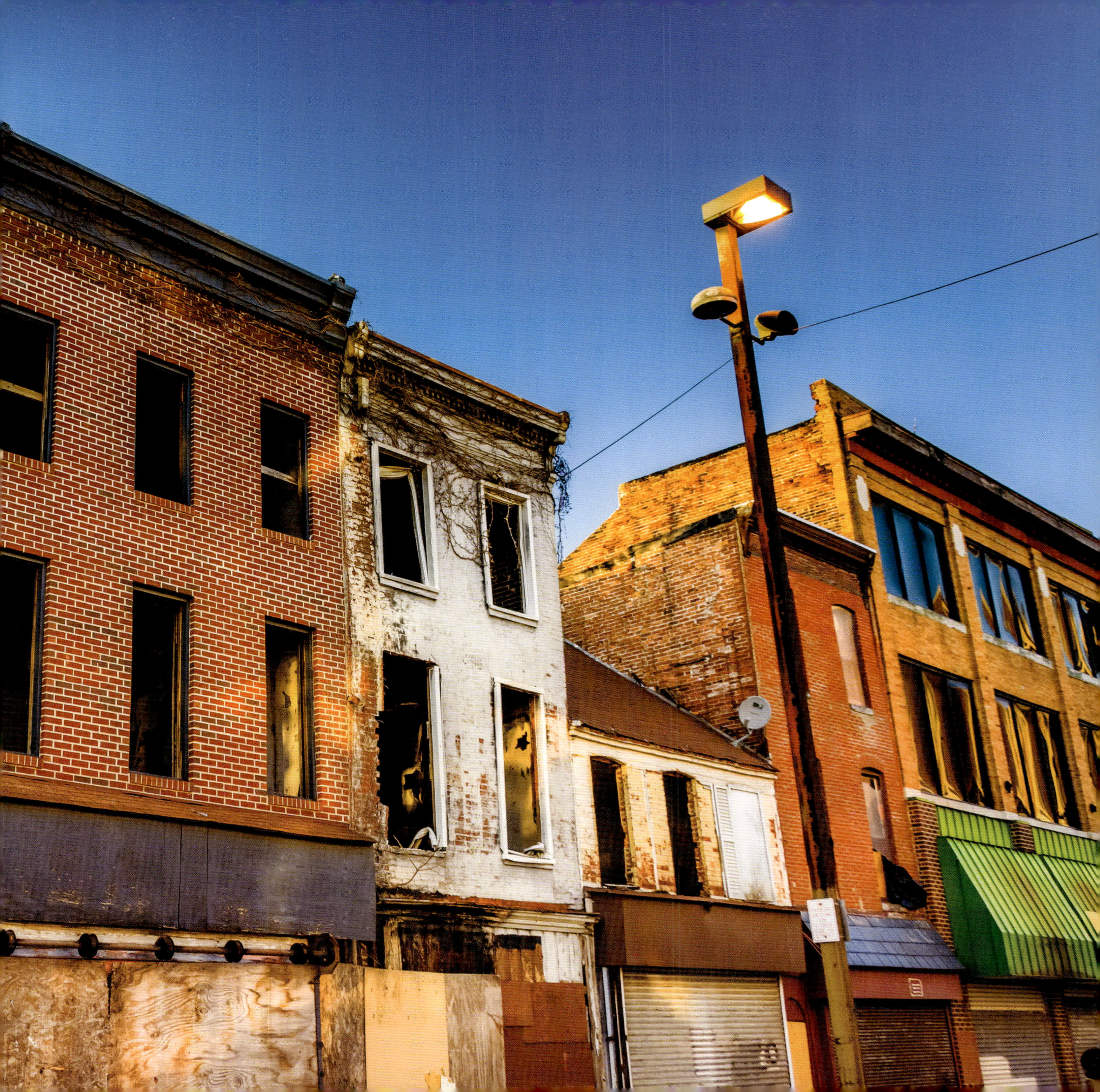

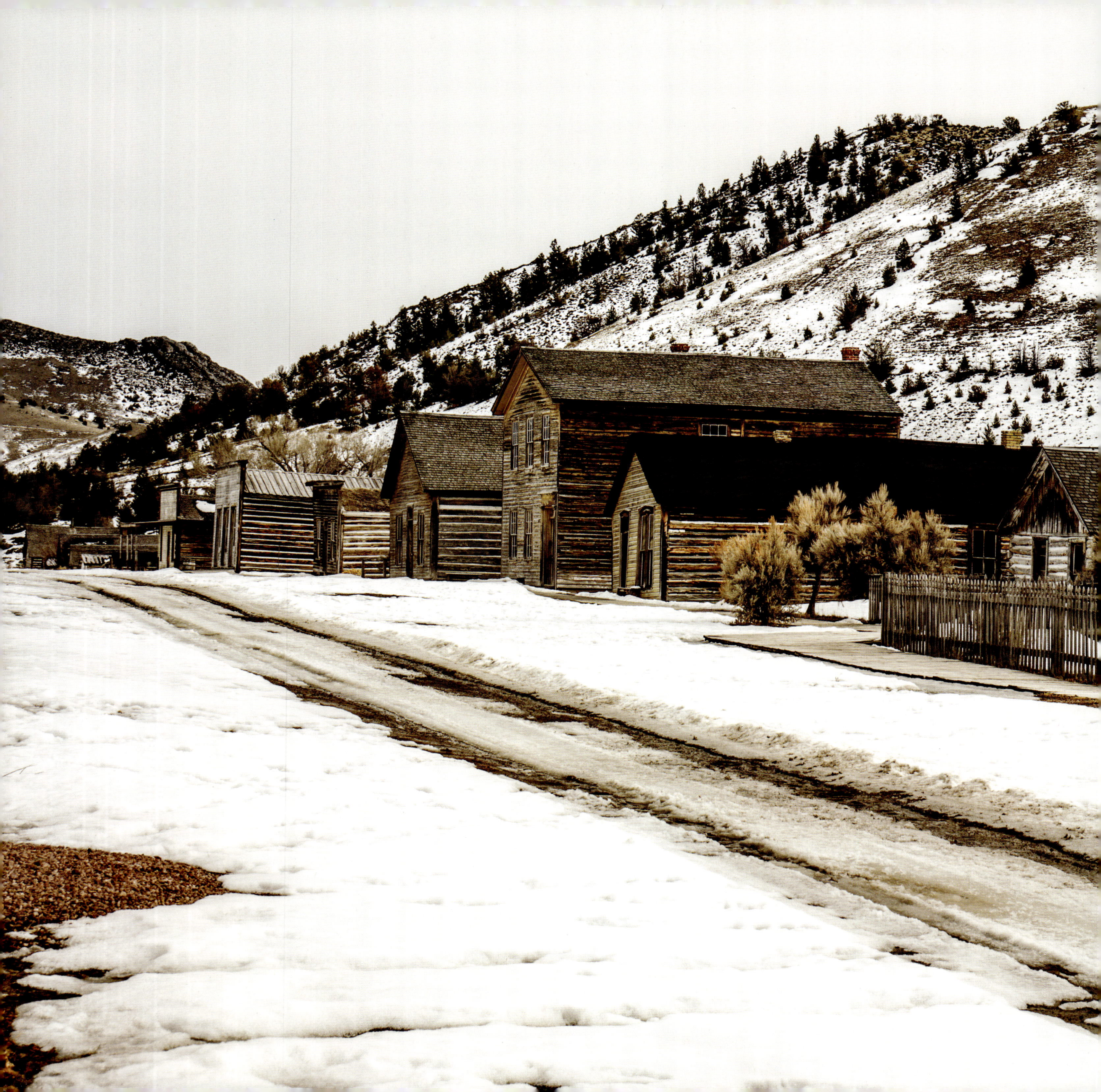

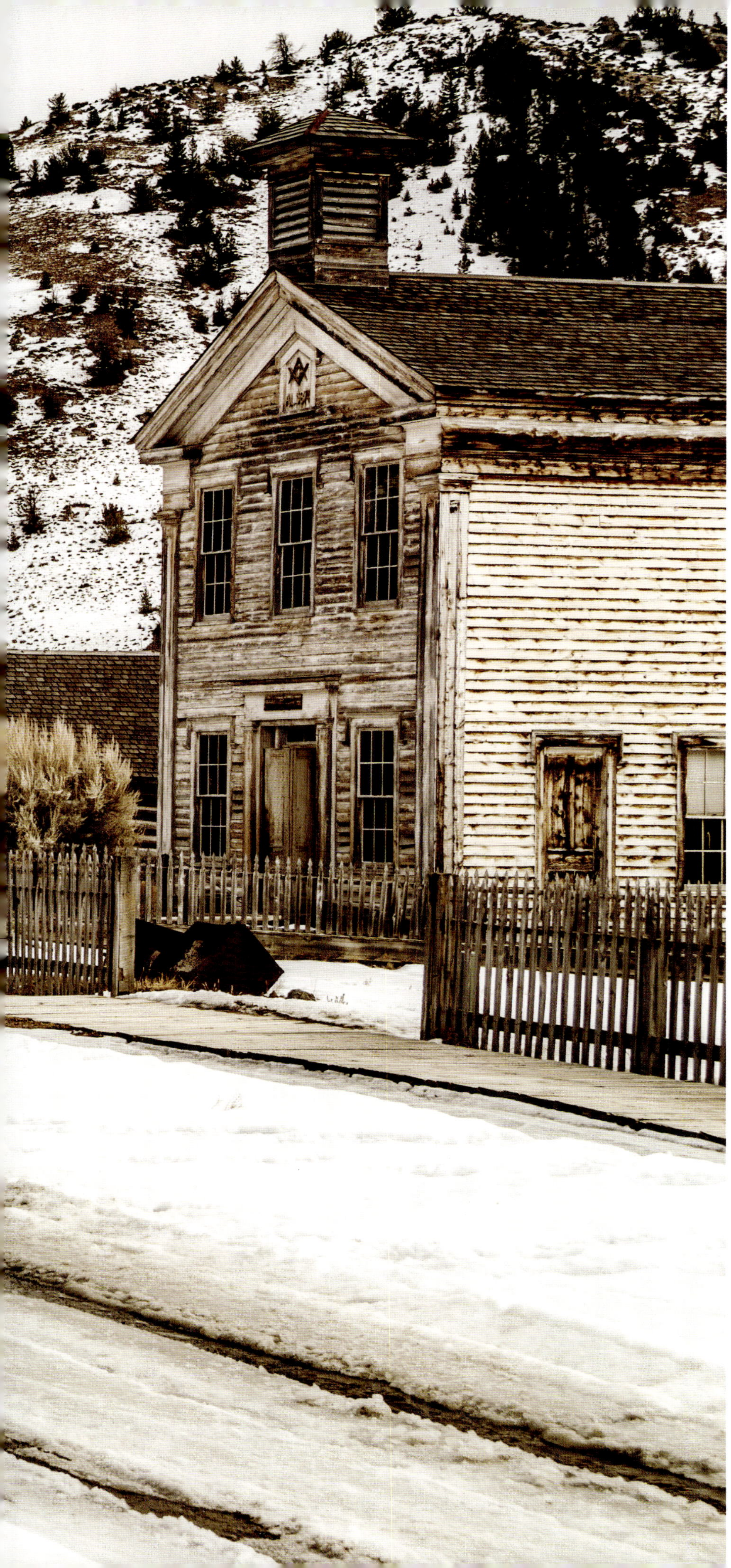

the mid-1950s saw roads like Route 66 – still mostly single-lane highway – rendered surplus to requirements, and over the next few decades, state by state, it was gradually decommissioned from maintenance and use. Though some sections today have been preserved, others are no longer in a driveable condition. With the businesses in many communities along the route relying almost exclusively on passing trade, the effect on numerous places across several states was catastrophic.

In the historic town of Glenrio (*see* page 84), on the border of Texas and New Mexico, where parts of the later film of Steinbeck's novel were shot, only a boarded-up Art Deco café and a few other buildings remain today. Further west, in Arizona, a general store clings on in the almost-deserted hamlet of Hackberry, while in the evocatively named Two Guns (*see* below) – a true tumbleweed town – little more than a closed-down gas station can be found. And reaching California, the flyblown settlements of Bagdad in the Mojave Desert and the crumbling Ludlow a few miles further west confirm the impression that all along the old 'mother road' of America, abandoned towns now line this abandoned highway of dreams.

Left: *The town of Bannack, Montana grew rapidly after a large gold strike in the area in July 1862, but fell dramatically the following year when another strike drew prospectors away.*
Below: *Ruined house along Route 66 in Two Guns, Arizona.*

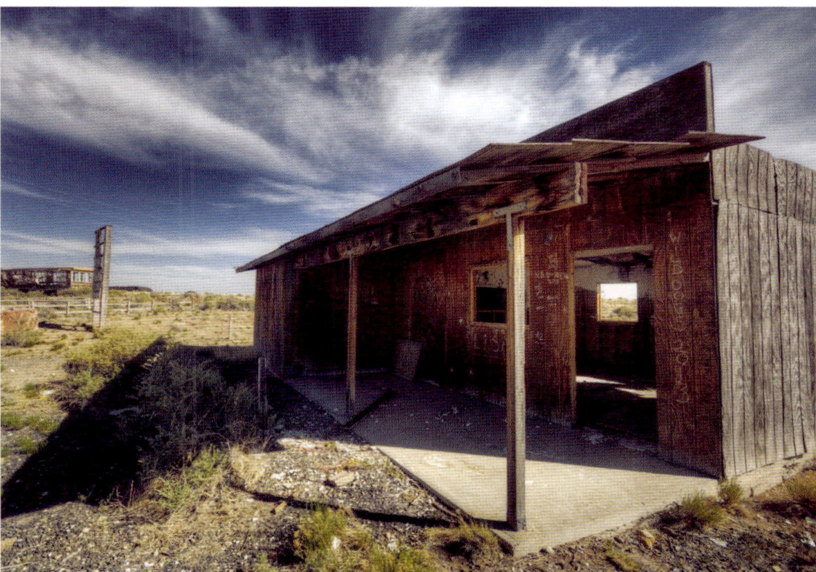

The Frozen North

Perhaps the only country with as many ghost towns as the USA is its northern neighbour, Canada, where the mineral wealth or available land for settlement is as great if not greater than in America, but where the harshness of local conditions have made some communities unsustainable overnight if the economic winds switch suddenly the other way. Similar conditions have affected other locations close to or inside the Arctic Circle.

British Columbia Rushes

Canada has a history of mineral extraction and metallic rushes to rival America's, especially the Cariboo Gold Rush of the mid-1860s, whose main centre at the time, Barkerville in northern British Columbia, is a heritage town and tourist attraction today. But decaying remnants of several settlements surviving from the Kootenay Silver Rush of the late 1890s can still be seen in what is known as the Valley of the Ghosts in the Selkirk Mountains of the Kootenay region of eastern BC. Across a sequence of towns that once thronged with keen-eyed prospectors – Nashton, Retallack, Zincton, Three Forks/Alamo, Cody and especially Sandon – a handful of wooden buildings cling on in various states of dilapidation, their purchase on the former town sites as precarious now as were the chances back then of so many of those hopefuls ever making a fortune worth the name, though a few of them certainly did.

The Canadian Prairies

Canada is large and inaccessible, and the task of binding such a huge expanse of territory into a coherent nation has been a challenge throughout its history.

Right: *Deception Island, Antarctica, is in fact the caldera of an active volcano. The whaling station at Whalers' Bay closed in 1931. It is the southernmost ghost town of all.*

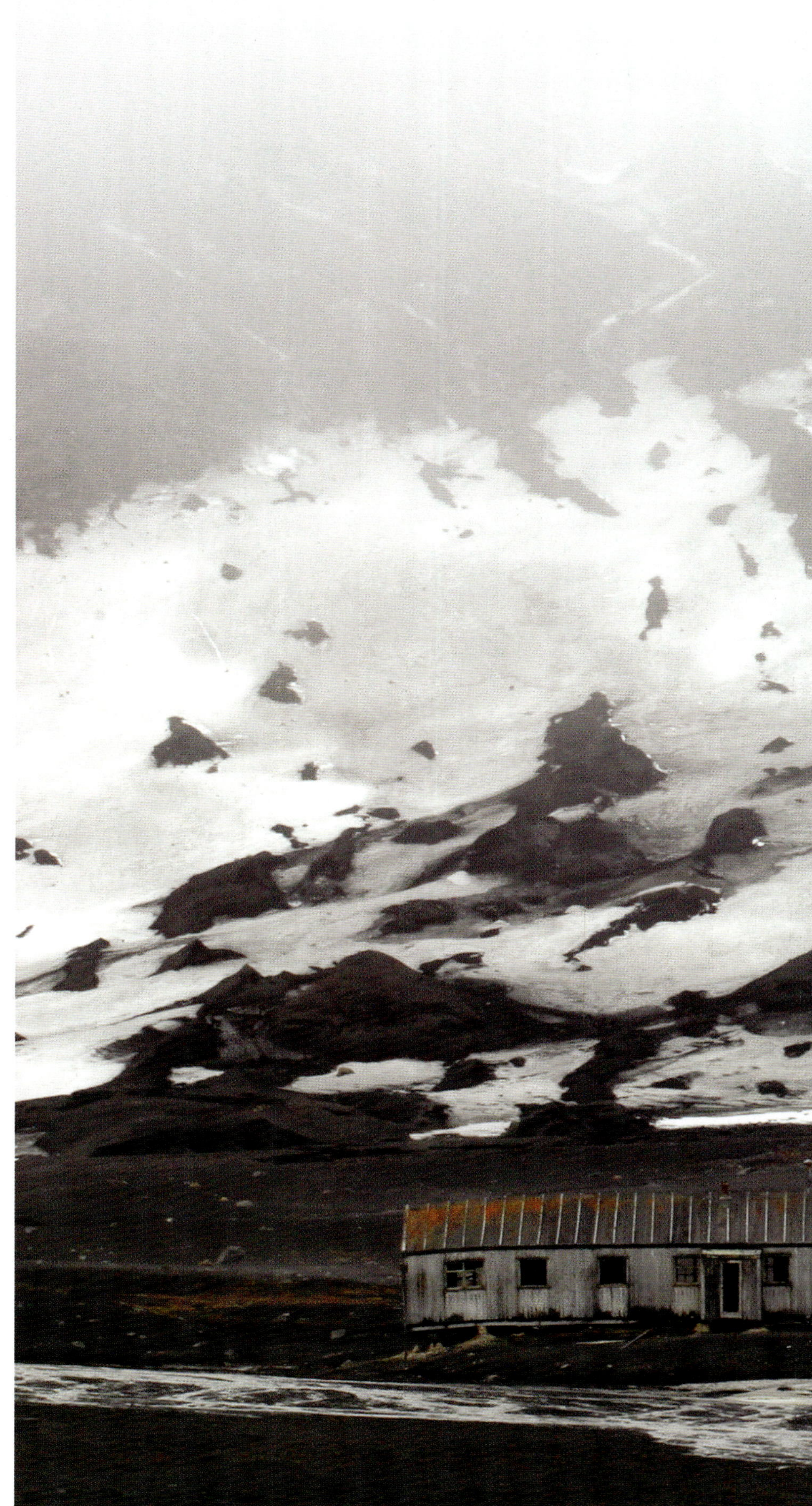

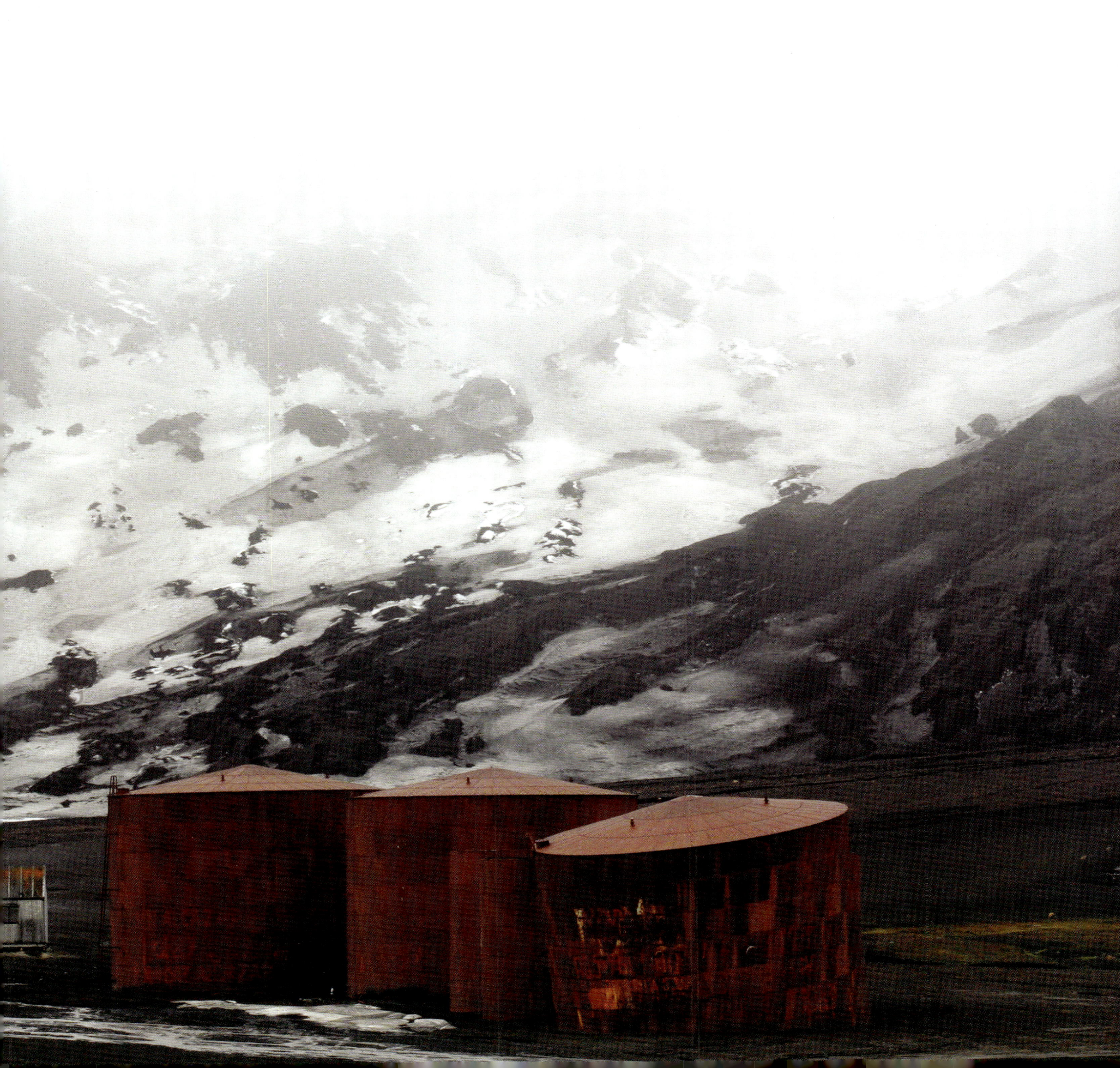

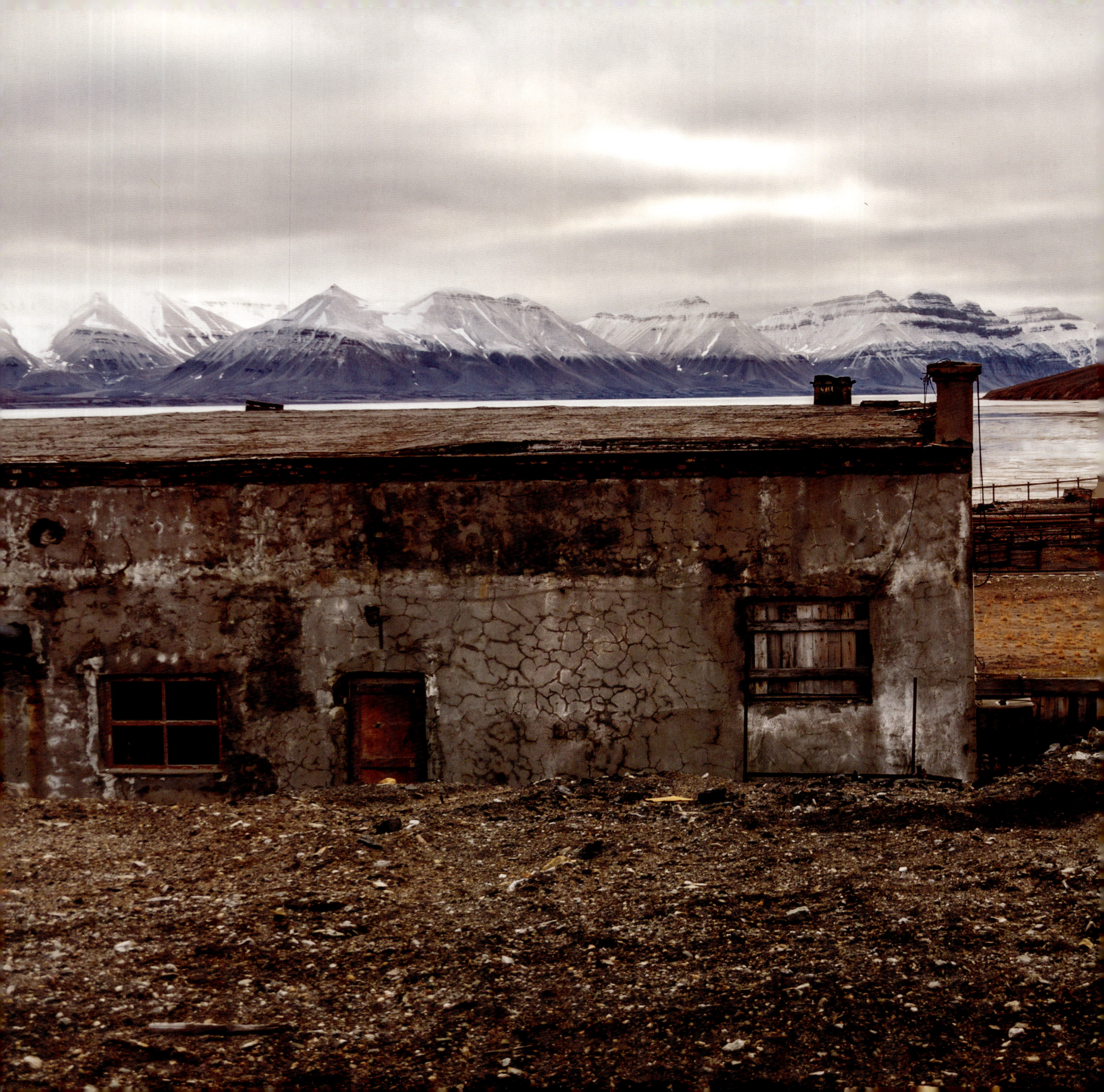

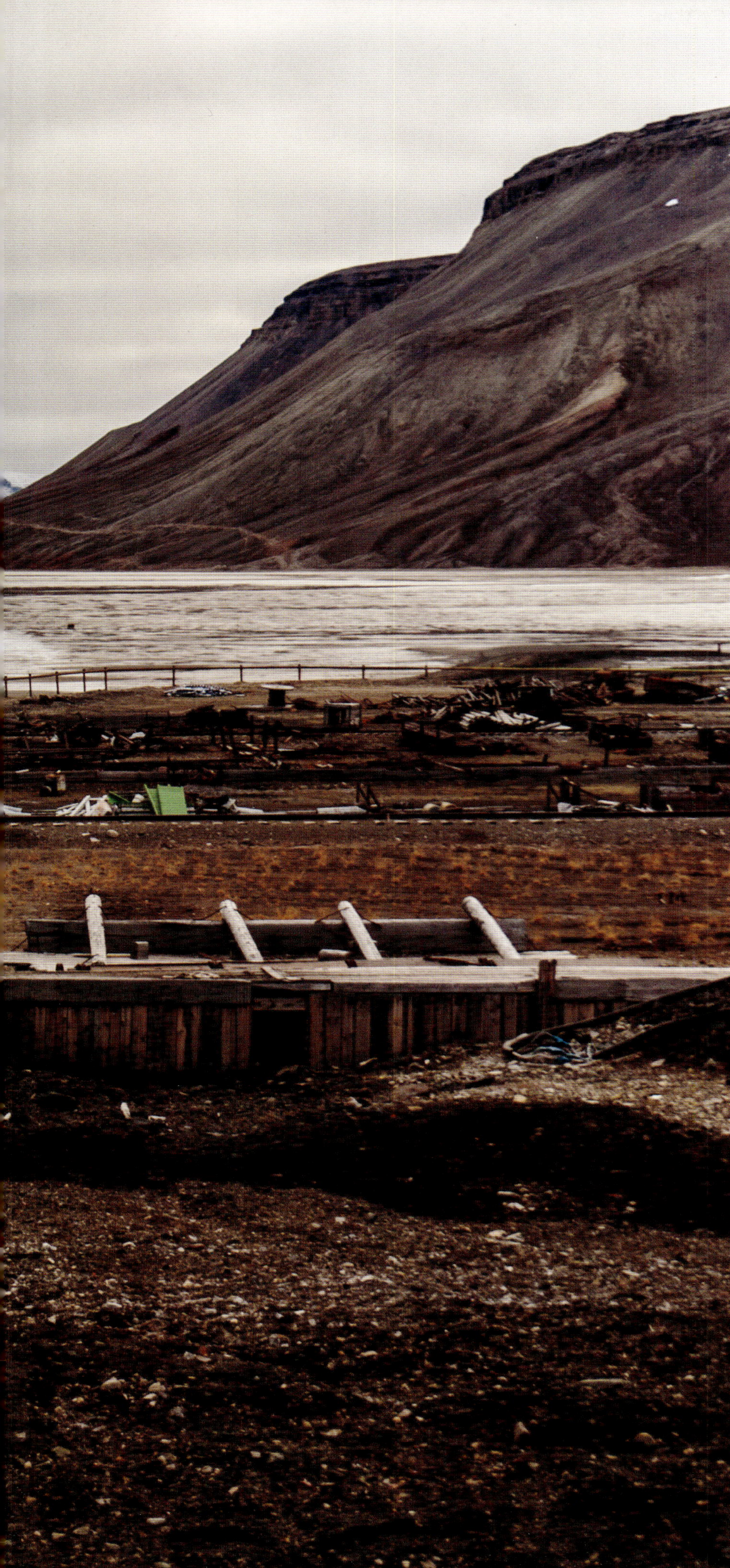

One solution the national government adopted was the building of the Canadian Pacific Railway, linking the east of the country with the Pacific Ocean beyond the Rocky Mountains to the west, and using it to settle places in between with immigrants given generous grants of land.

Communities such as Maybutt and Orion in southern Alberta, and Robsart (*see* page 96) in neighbouring southern Saskatchewan, grew prosperous on the yields of grain that is still a widespread harvest crop in the Prairie provinces, Canada's breadbasket, along with other staples that were sent back east on CPR trains via the 'ribbon of steel' that linked these towns. But the boom of the early twentieth century was followed by a devastating bust as the Great Depression of the 1930s suppressed demand across the world, and then the Dust Bowl of the American Midwest, knowing no borders, swooped like a desiccating angel across the Canadian prairies. Though never large, these once-prosperous communities now clung to a meagre existence, as Robsart still does today through the few hardy souls who live on in the town. The large number of abandoned buildings in these dwindling sites mark them out as relics of a future that died in a cloud of dust.

Ghosts of the Big Water

A thousand miles east along that same railway track, on the north shore of Lake Superior, the community of Jackfish was once a coal stop for the CPR trains that followed this route. The village grew quickly in this remote location after the line was opened in 1885, as the coal, the travellers who stayed in its two hotels, and the bountiful hauls of trout from Lake Superior gave rise to a thriving community in just a few short years. But it's always hard to know what's just down the tracks, and the demise of Jackfish, when it came, was rapid. Beginning in the late 1940s, first the trains switched to diesel and so did not need to stop; then the sea lamprey that had penetrated the Great Lakes system killed all the lake trout in Superior; and finally the building of the Trans-Canada Highway in the early 1960s meant travellers drove straight past the now struggling village.

Left: *Deserted junk yard in the mining village of Pyramiden, Norway.*

The last person to leave was the schoolteacher in 1963, since when bushfires and the passage of time have destroyed all but a few remaining shacks.

Kennecott, Alaska

Ghost towns are the downside of adventure, where the chance of riches or even just a different life once persuaded otherwise sensible people to settle in places that any sane assessment would counsel against – forbidding locations far from the centres of culture where most of us live. This remoteness is part of their appeal to anyone seeking out such abandoned sites today, and perhaps explains why the people who once lived there may have gone there in the first place, but also why they have all since left. Often, the more remote a place is, the more extraordinary the congeries of buildings that arise, such as in the Alaskan mining town of Kennecott (*see* right), which grew quickly following the discovery of copper there in 1900. The deposit was exhausted in less than forty years, and the impressive group of buildings that cluster on the mountain has lain abandoned ever since.

Pyramiden

Even more remote than Kennecott is the town of Pyramiden (*see* page 92) on the Norwegian island of Spitsbergen, part of the Svalbard Archipelago located well inside the Arctic Circle. The most northerly ghost town of them all is a former coal-mining settlement, founded by Sweden in 1910, then sold to the Soviet Union in the late 1920s. Named for the pyramid-shaped mountain in whose shadow it was built, Pyramiden was once home to a community of more than 1,000 people and even outlasted the Soviet Union itself, continuing to extract coal until the mine was closed in March 1998. Owned by the same Russian company as before, but for a small caretaking staff the town has lain empty for 20 years, though is still quite intact on account of the sub-zero temperatures at these latitudes for most of the year – literally frozen in time.

Right: *Abandoned mining town of Kennecott in Alaska, USA.*
Next page: *An overgrown sidewalk in Robsart, Saskatchewan, Canada.*

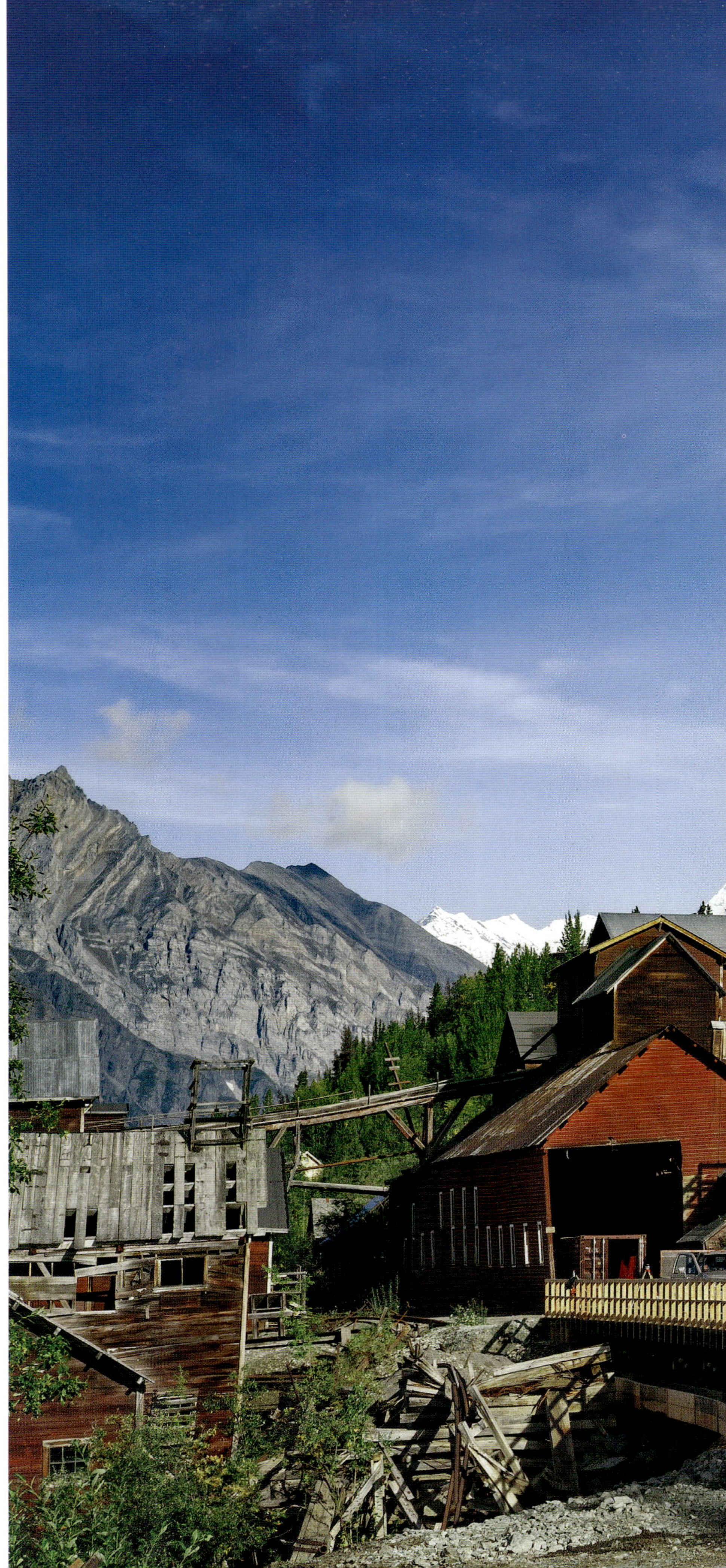

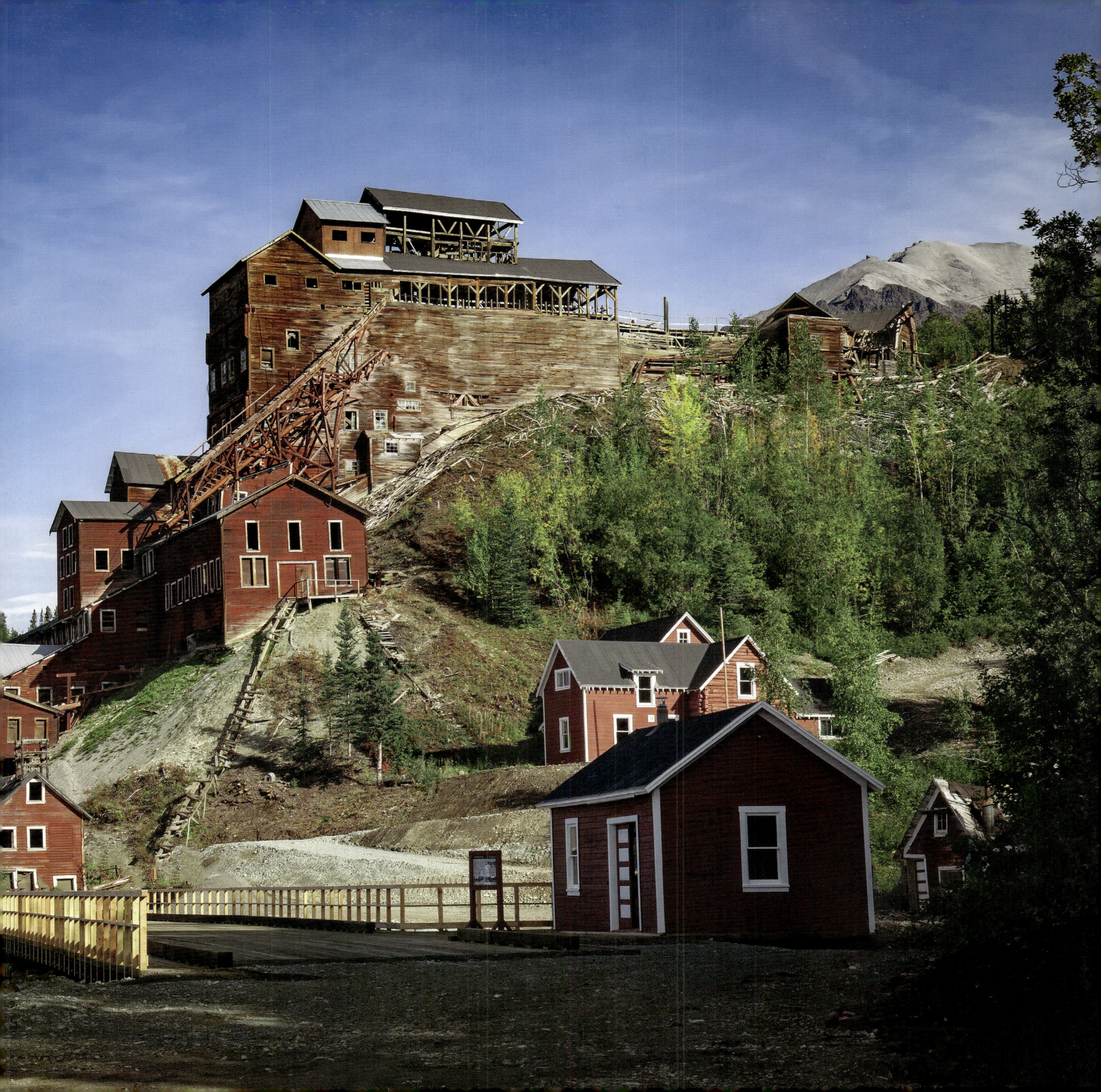

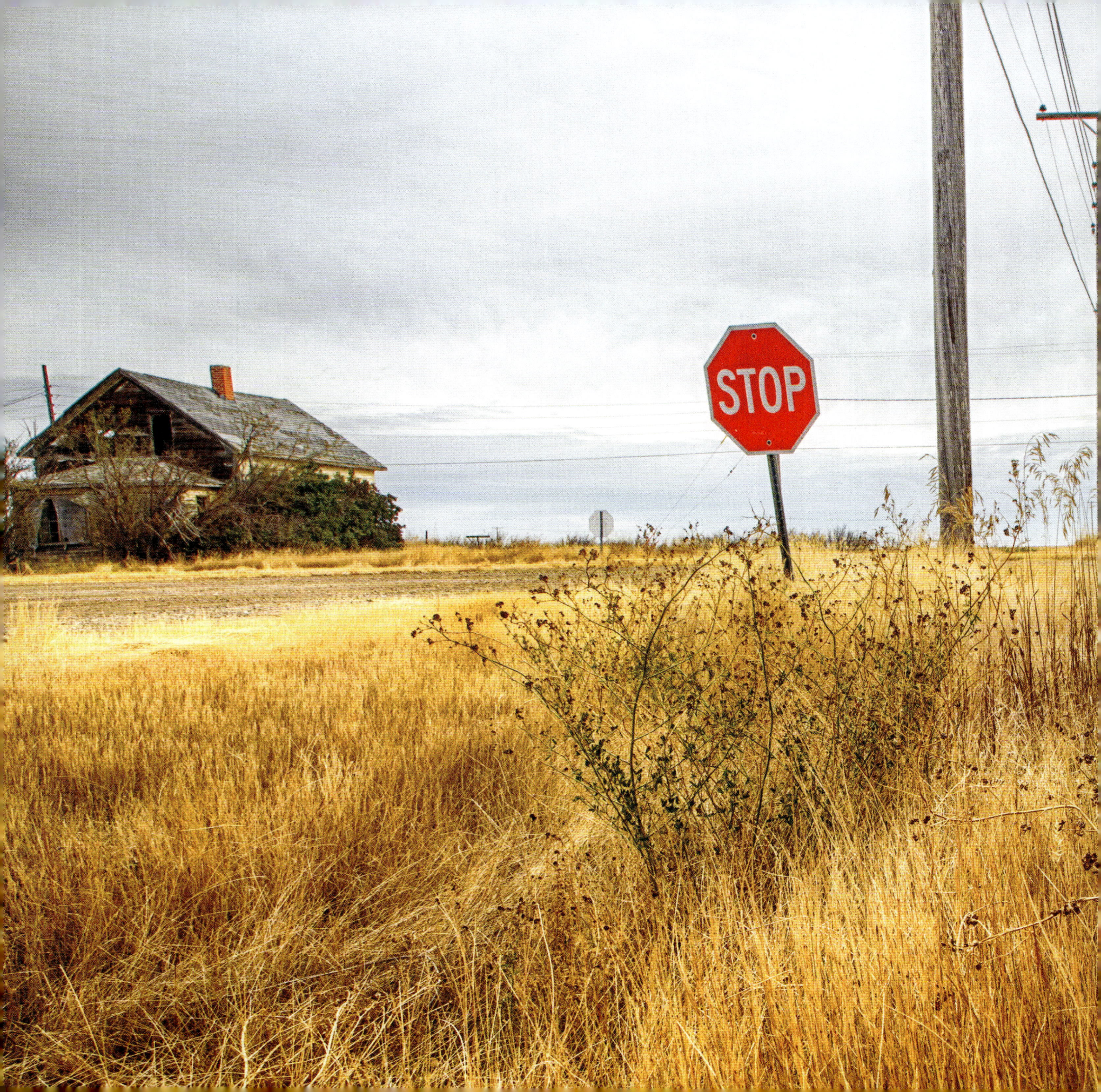
STOP

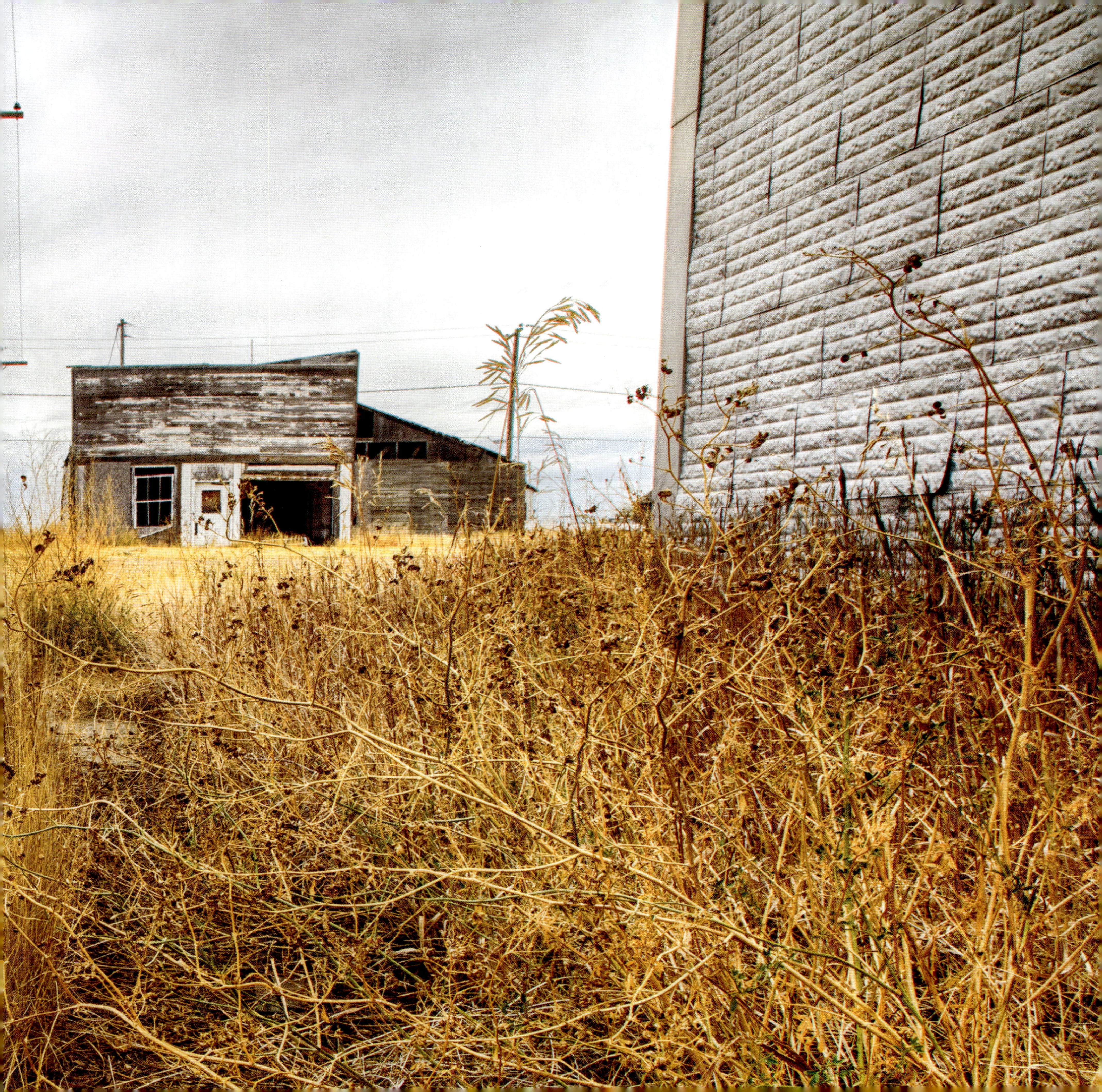

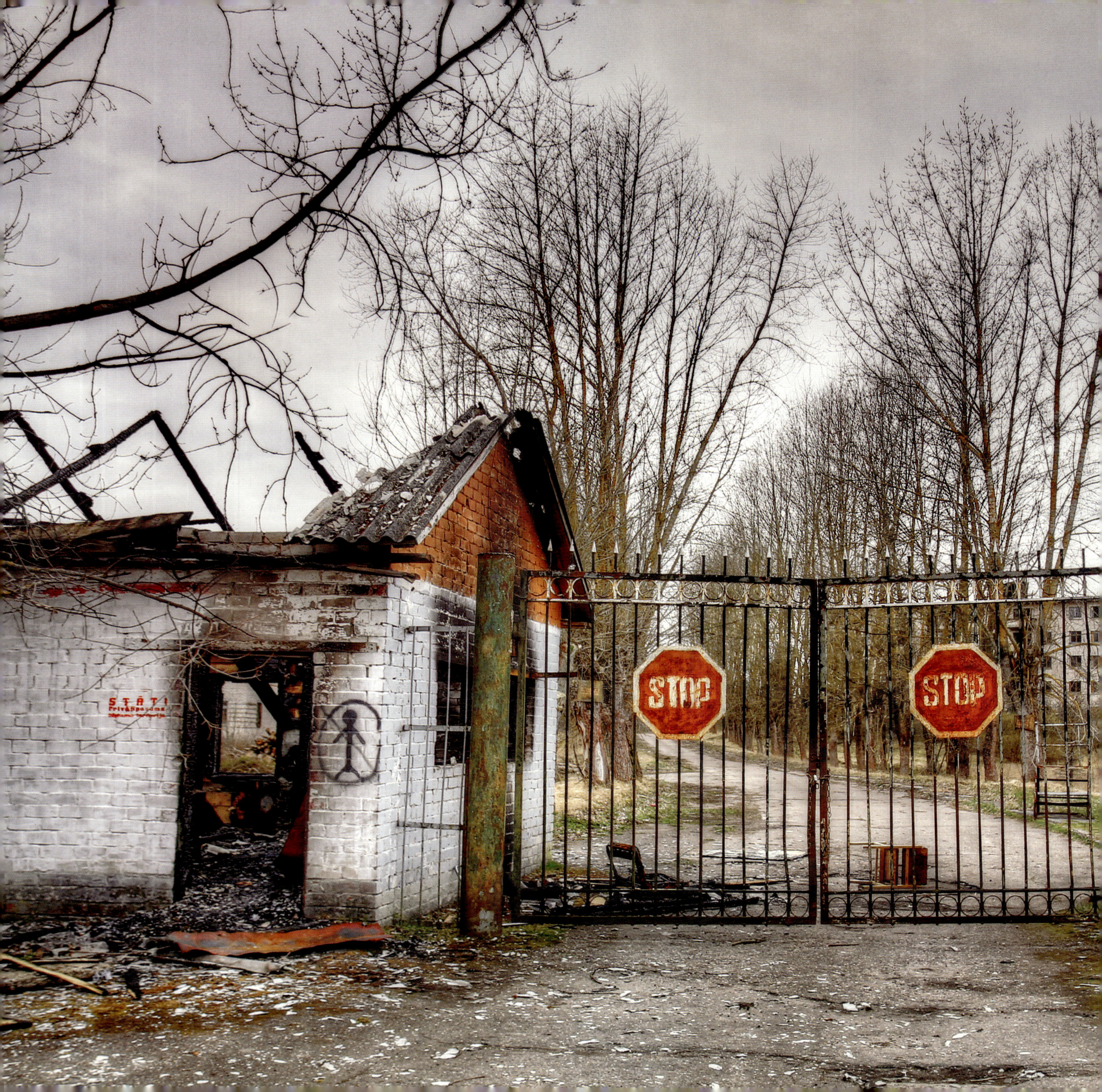
STĂTI!
STOP
STOP

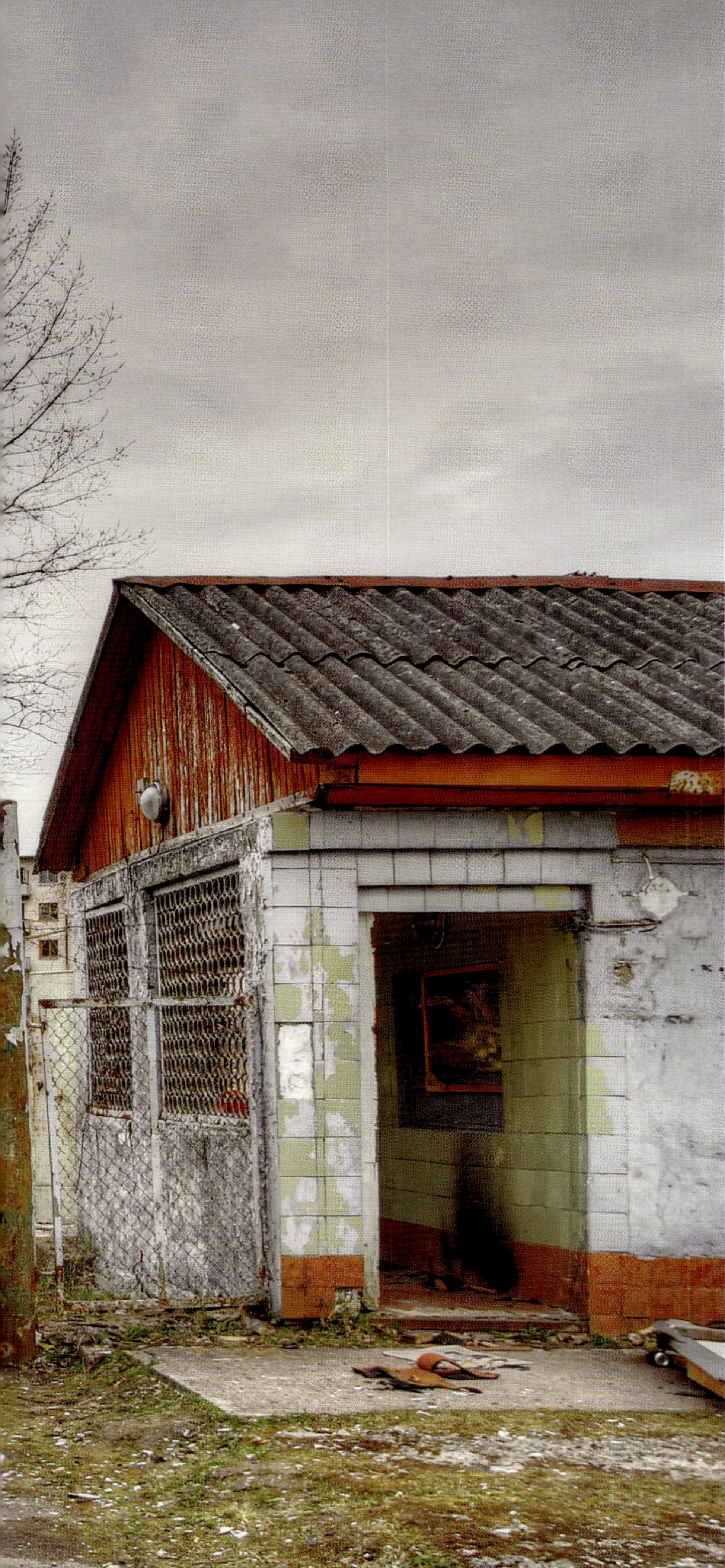

Old Soviet Cities

The Soviet Union was a vast if short-lived empire by most historical standards. Notoriously repressive to its own citizens and those of its satellite states, the crumbling remnants of Soviet paranoia and state control can be found across 10 time zones from the old Iron Curtain countries of Eastern Europe to far north-eastern Siberia.

Troop Towns

At the old empire's western edge was Klomino, then a garrison village for Soviet troops stationed in the country and now Poland's only ghost town. Originally built as a training base for the Wehrmacht in the Second World War, after 1945 it housed some 6,000 Soviet troops but was abandoned in 1993 after the fall of the USSR, since when it has been all but deserted, waiting for a new role that may never come. Of perhaps more strategic importance, a little further east at the heart of a once-secret settlement in the Baltic state and former Soviet republic of Latvia, two early warning radar systems remained on high alert throughout the Cold War for the nuclear missiles the Red Army feared would one day be launched against them. The town that was built around them, known as Skrunda-1, was identical in size to Klomino, its dour apartment blocks built to the same centrally planned design. Skrunda-1 has fared slightly better than its Polish counterpart, with the Latvian government having turned over half the site to the Latvian army, while leaving the rest to rot like the system it once served.

Left: *The ghost town of Skrunda-1, which sounds like something from a science fiction novel, was in fact a Soviet radar station in what is now the democratic state of Latvia.*

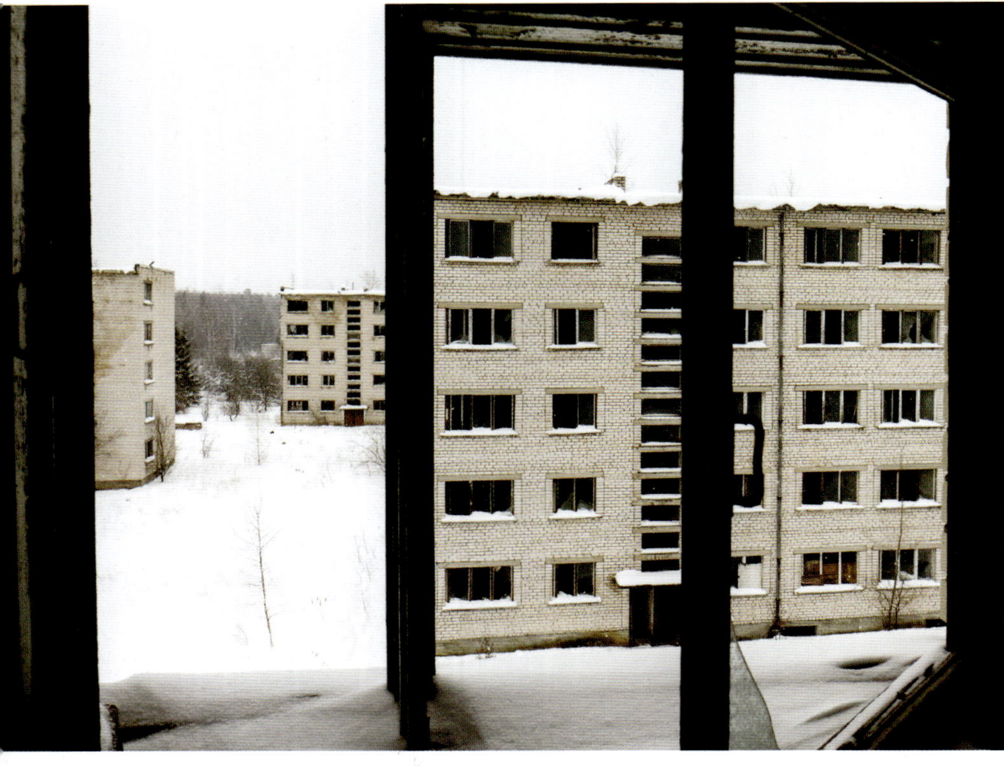

The Stakhanovite Myth

In Russia itself, the disintegrating ghost town of Khalmer-Yu in the Komi Republic in the country's far north was first established in 1940 after coal deposits were discovered in the area. The mines continued to supply domestic need until 1993, whereupon the mine was closed and the town soon abandoned. Now a proving ground for the Russian military, which may include the testing of heavy weapons, this might explain why the derelict buildings of Khalmer-Yu have been ruined quite as quickly as they have.

Another mining town, Kadykchan in far-eastern Siberia, was built by prisoners of the notorious gulag system during the Second World War. After the collapse of the Soviet Union, the Stakhanovite slogans were shown up for what they were, as inefficient working practices allowed to persist under the command economy of the Communist system could not withstand the

Above: *An abandoned former Soviet radar station*
Right: *The coal-mining ghost town of Kadykchan in eastern Siberia did not survive the collapse of the Soviet Union.*

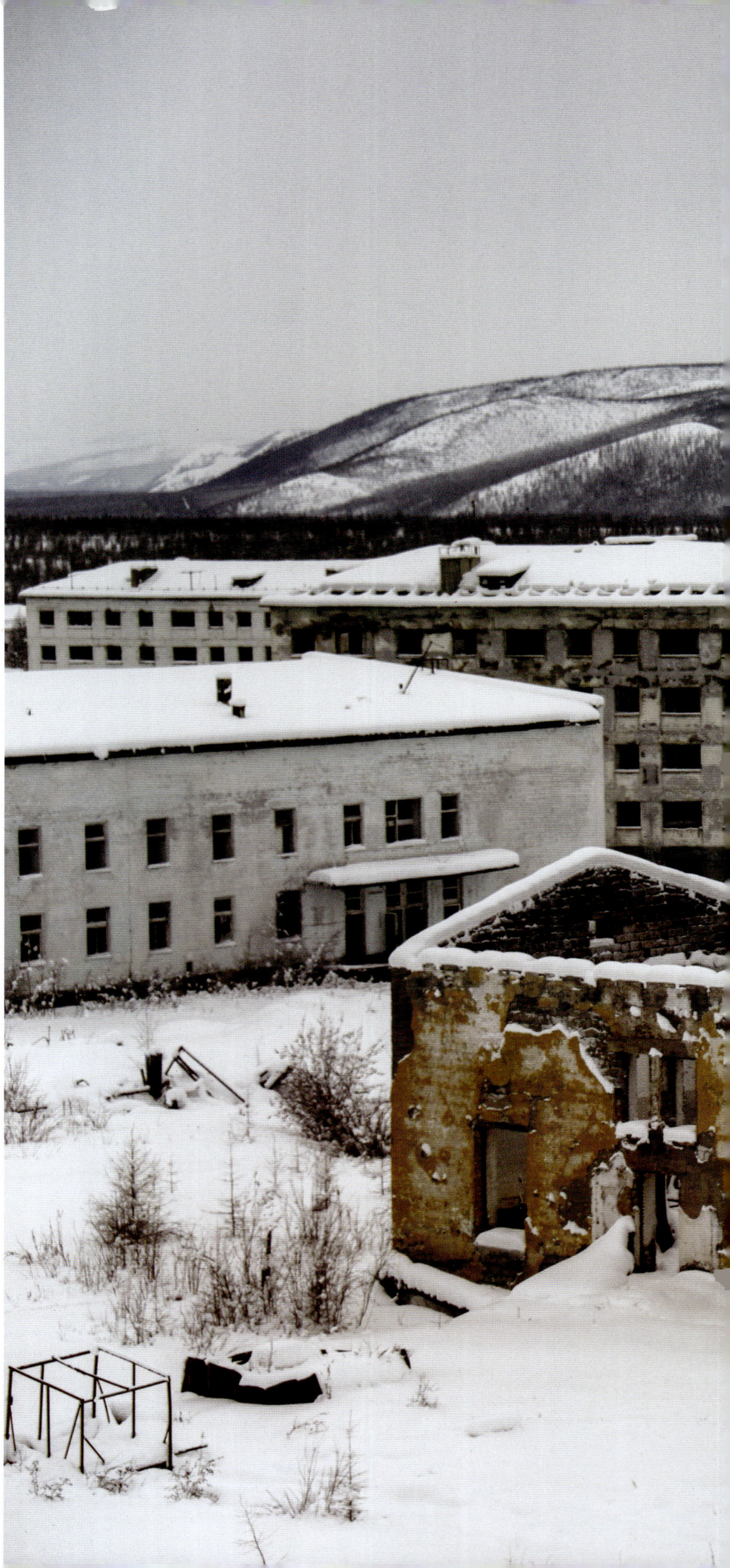

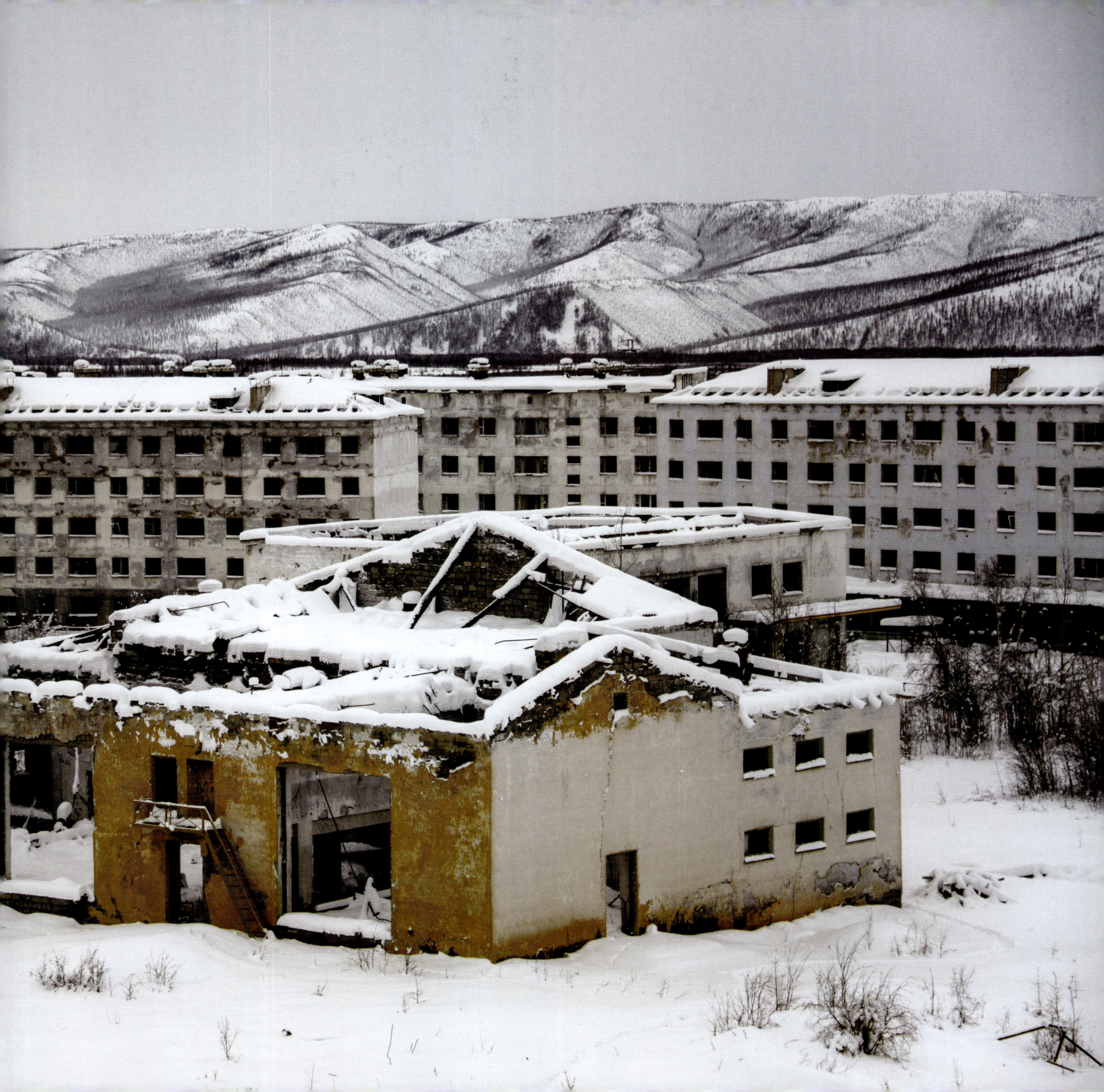

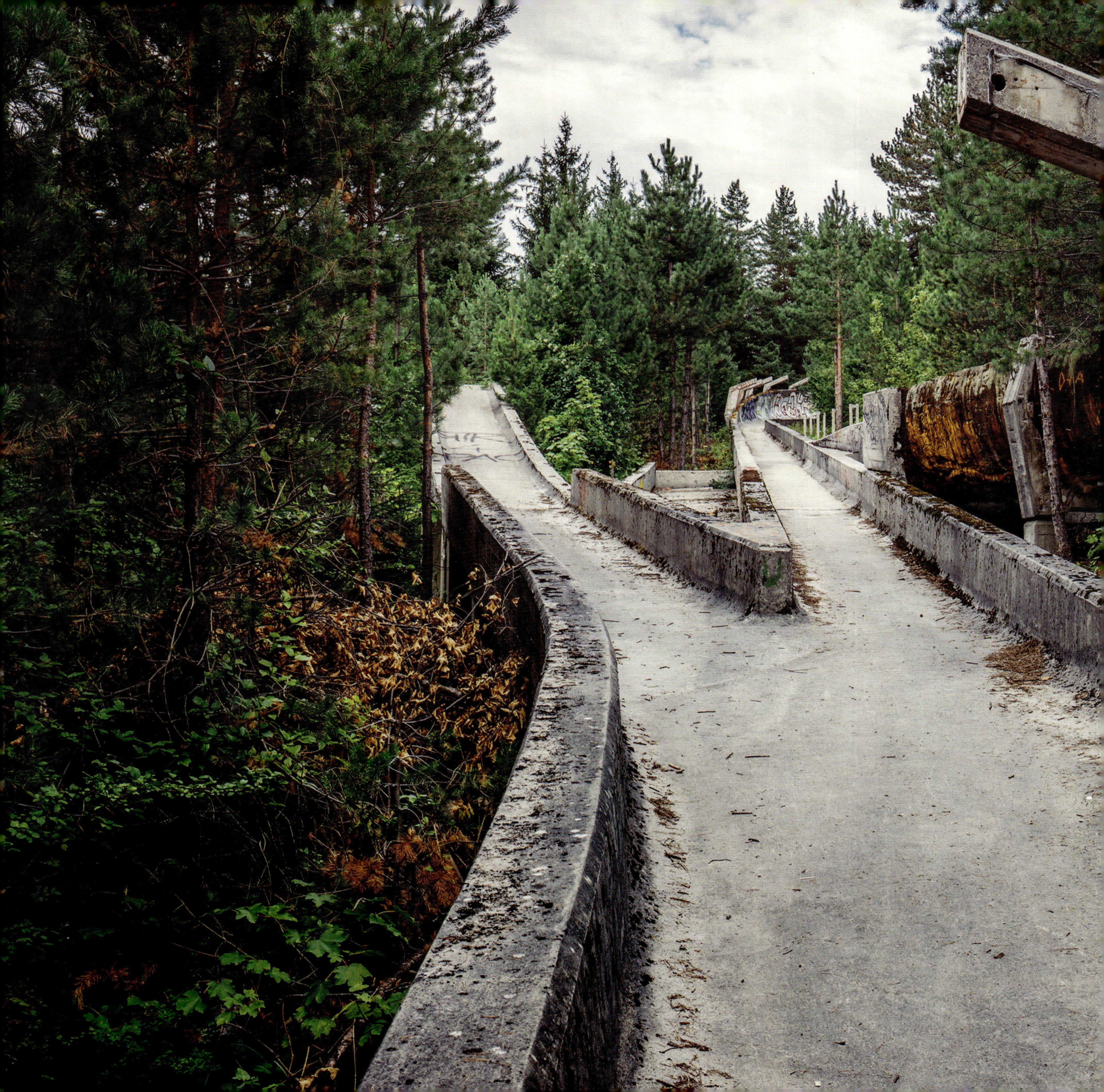

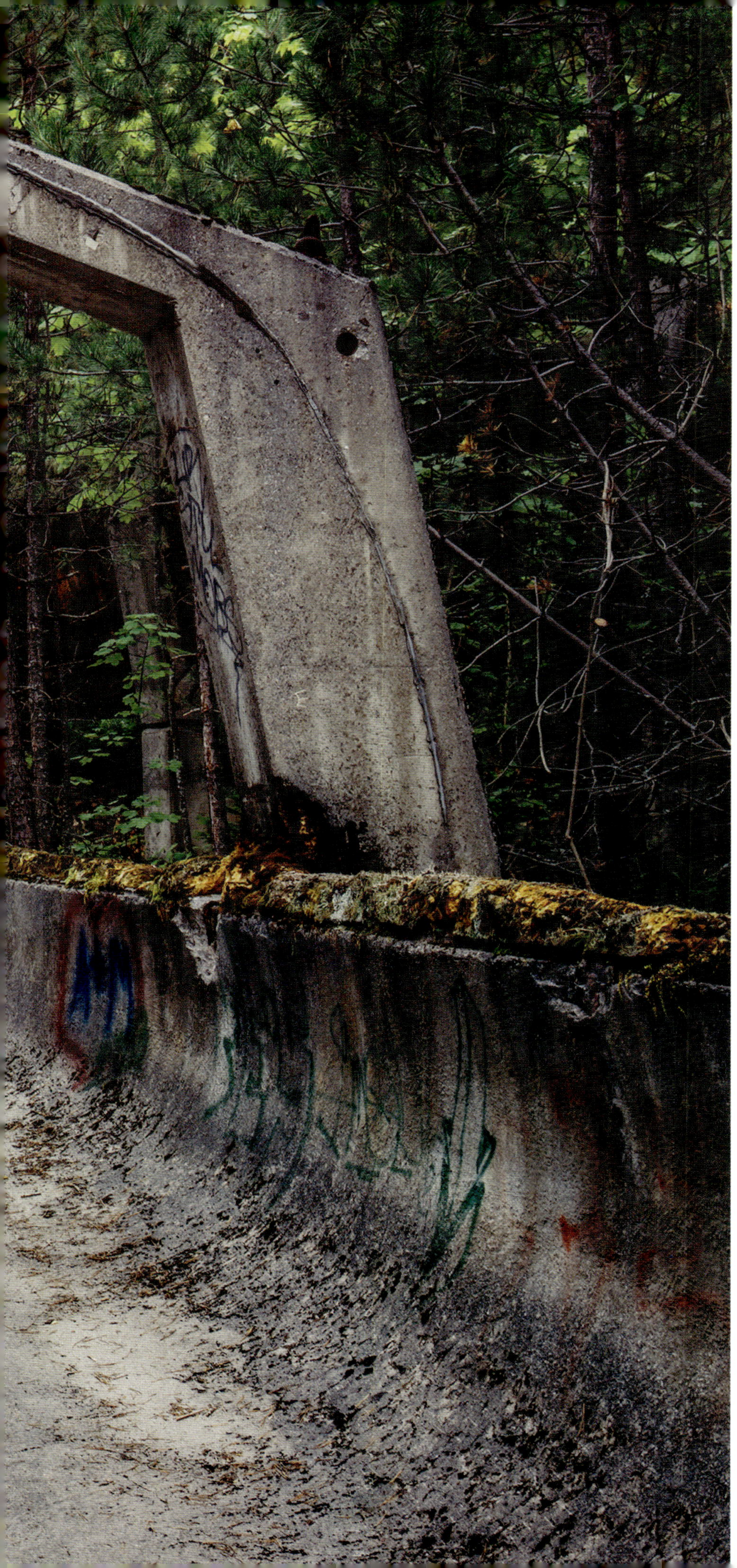

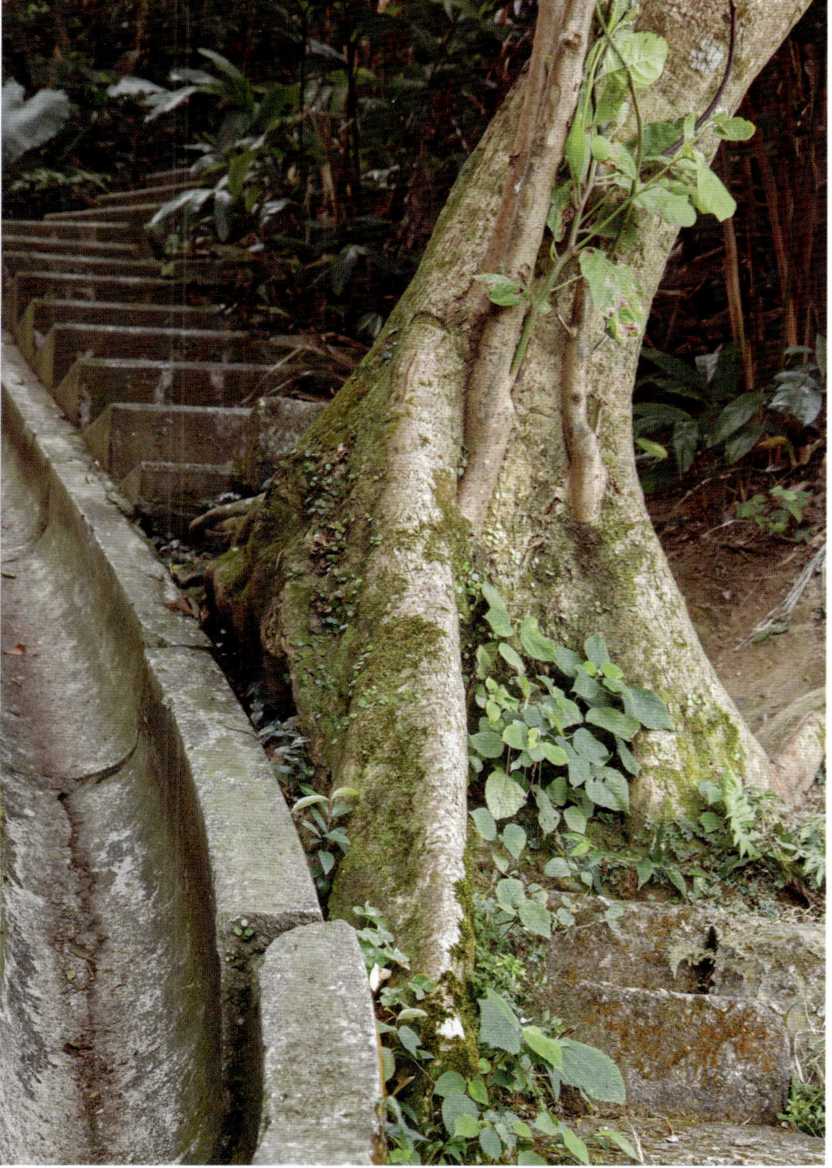

shock therapy of sudden change to a Western, market-based model and the competition it brought from foreign alternatives more efficiently produced. Already enduring an extreme economic crisis, it was a matter of time before the Kadykchan mine was closed, and in 1996 an explosion that killed six people dealt the death blow. A town which in the mid-1980s had been home to more than 10,000 people, since 2010 has been completely deserted – a slowly decaying relic of a political experiment that failed.

Above: *A tree grows in an abandoned staircase.*
Left: *Abandoned bobsleigh and luge track from the 1984 Winter Olympics in Sarajevo, Bosnia and Herzegovina.*

Lost Islands

Whether remote and daunting or simply hellish, there are islands across the world whose once-thriving settlements are now bereft of human presence.

The Whaling Stations of South Georgia

At the southern end of the earth, the island of South Georgia, still a British Overseas Territory, was once the whaling capital of the world, with a string of seven whaling stations along the island's east coast. Between them and Antarctica was the wild Southern Ocean where, in the twentieth century's first six decades, vast fortunes were made in these maritime killing fields. Britain abandoned the whale trade in the 1960s, and the whaling stations with it, but the rusting ruins of several of these old blubber towns can still be seen clustered in the island's sheltered bays. Larger stations such as Leith Harbour (*see* right) and Grytviken (*see* page 111) were home to hundreds of men at the height of the trade, but today their tumbledown sheds and shacks of wood and corrugated iron lined with asbestos are too dangerous to visit for any traveller with the wherewithal to reach such an inhospitable place, leaving these long-vacant stations to the elephant seals that breed there in the spring every year.

St Kilda

South Georgia is one of the most isolated places on earth and so cold and forbidding that a permanent community never took root. But other islands with long histories of occupation are no less vulnerable, not only to economic change, but to the movements of people that have shaped the modern world.

Right: *Leith Harbour whaling station factory, South Georgia.*

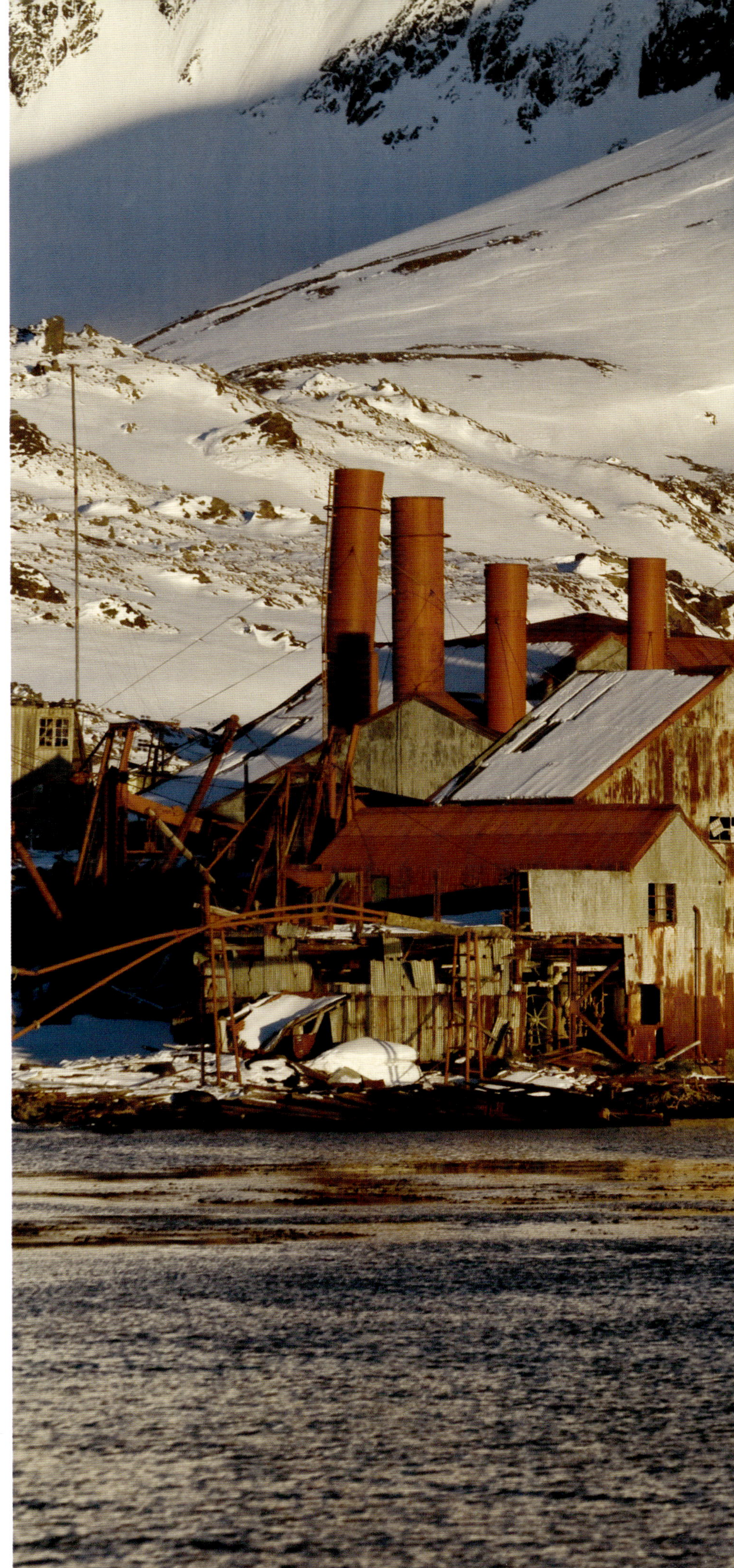

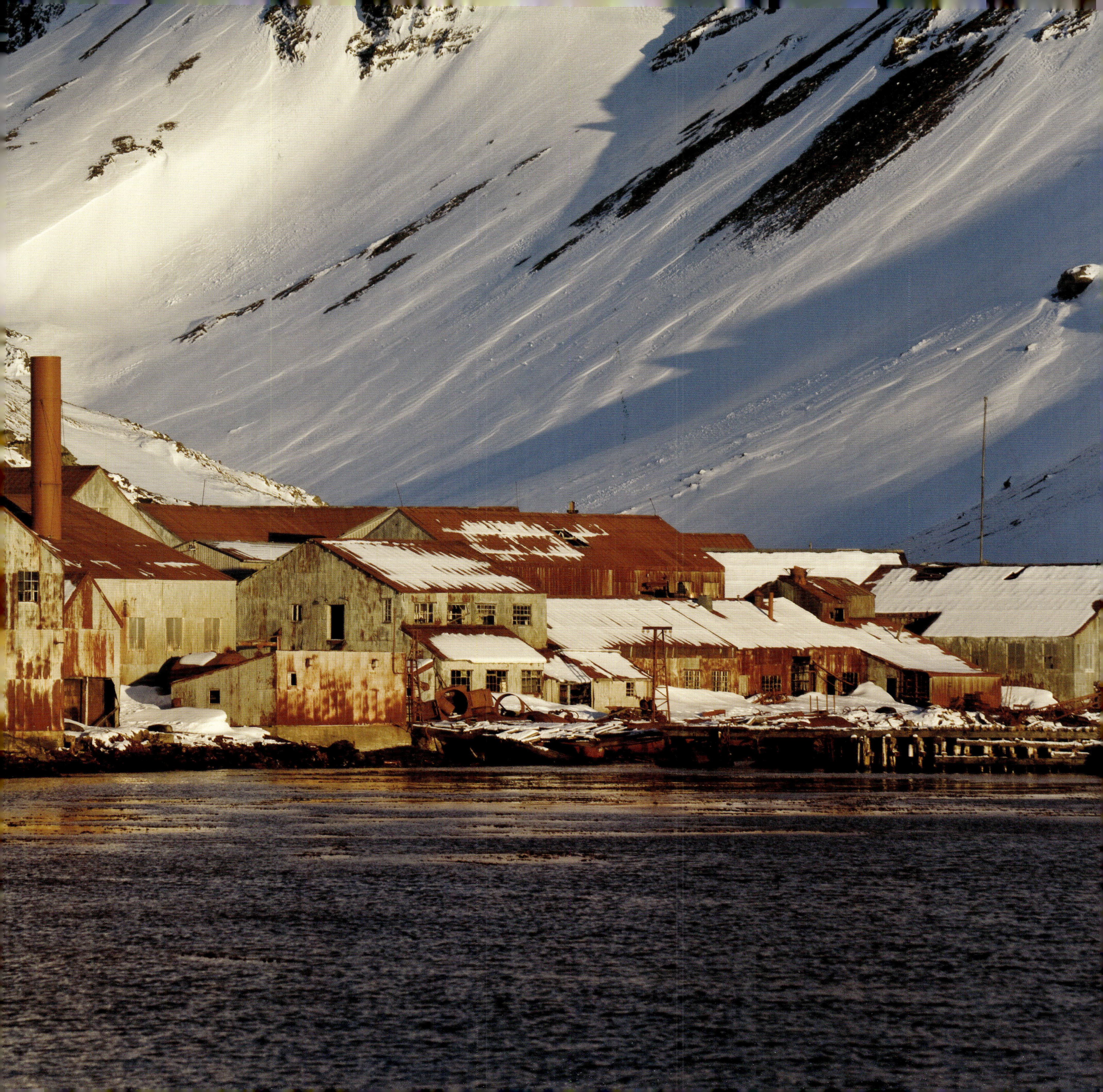

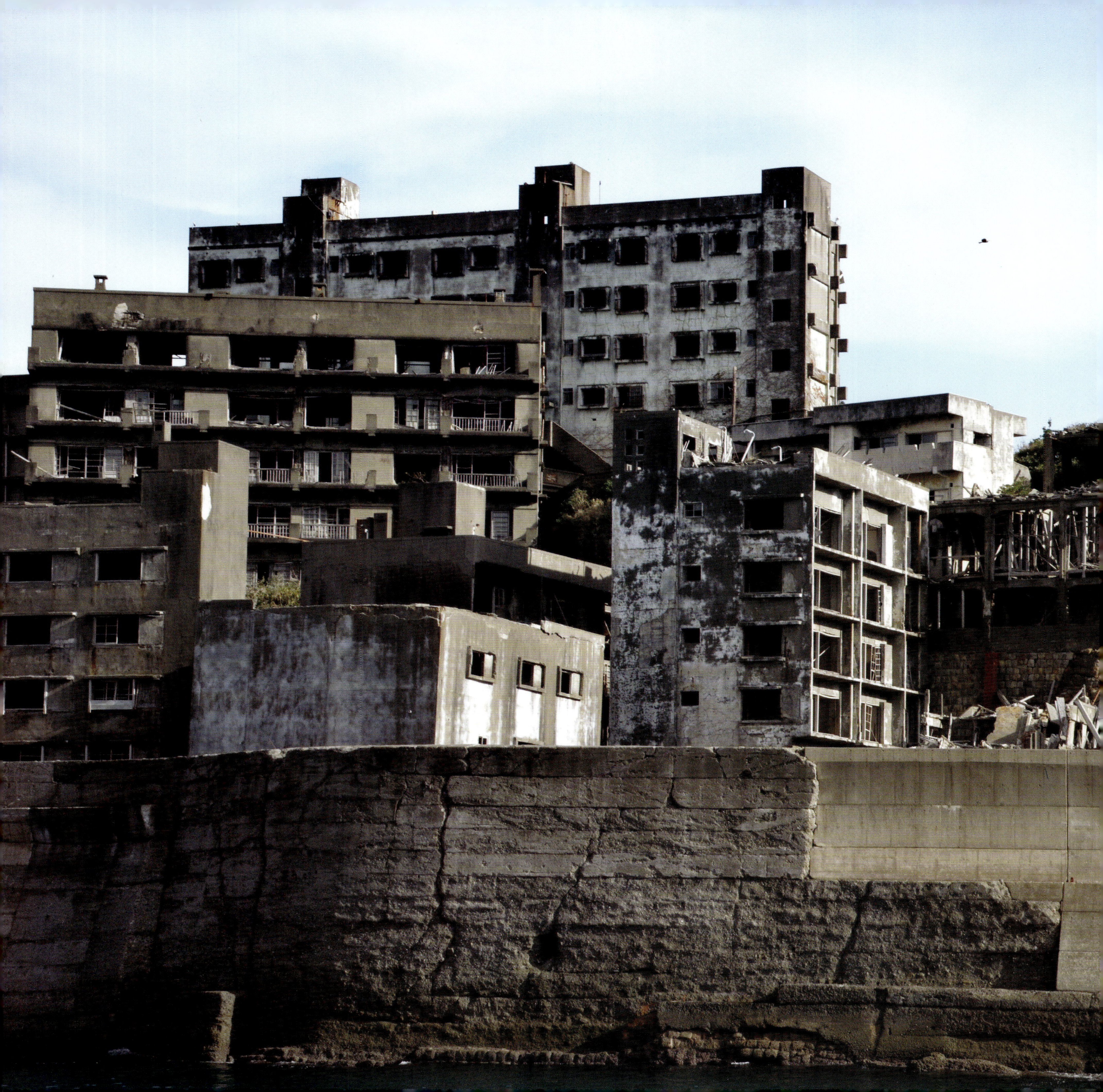

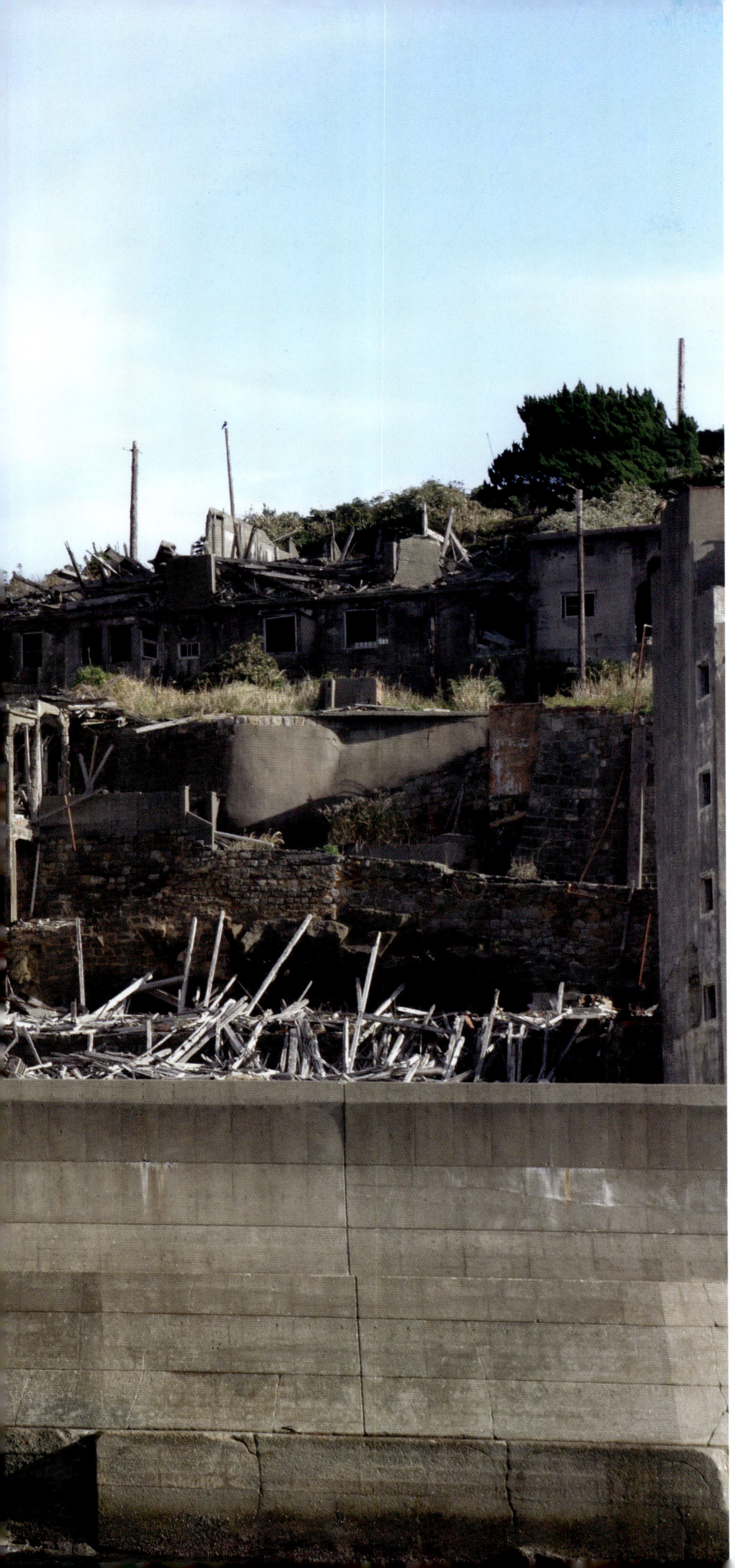

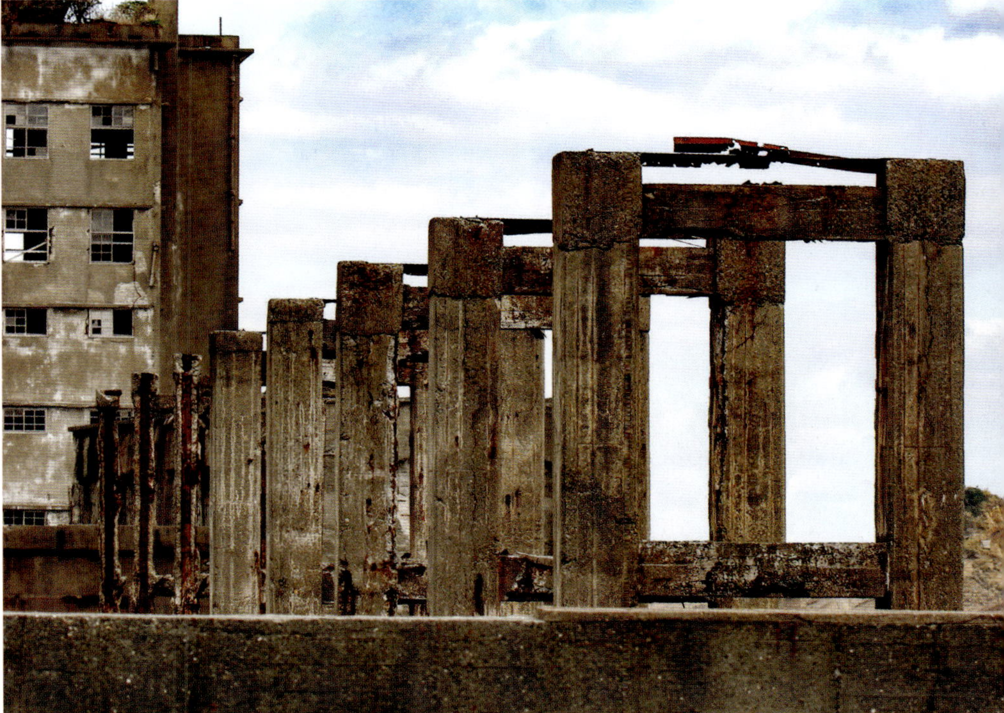

Above: *Ruined apartment building, Gunkanjima, Nagasaki, Japan.*

Britain's westernmost lands, the archipelago of St Kilda (*see* page 109) that is part of the Outer Hebrides in Scotland, were abandoned in 1930 after significant depopulation over many decades, thus ending more than two millennia of continuous occupation since the Bronze Age.

Houtouwan

And as recently as the early 1990s, the far more accessible fishing village of Houtouwan on Shengshan Island, just 40 miles east of Shanghai in China, where a community of thousands had lived for centuries, was more or less abandoned as most of its residents moved to the mainland in search of an easier life. In little over 20 years, the village's many buildings have been overrun with both picturesque creeping vines and hordes of tourists who visit every year, among whom are some of the one-time residents, who come to pay respects to their former lives.

Left: *Gunkanjima, Nagasaki, Japan.*

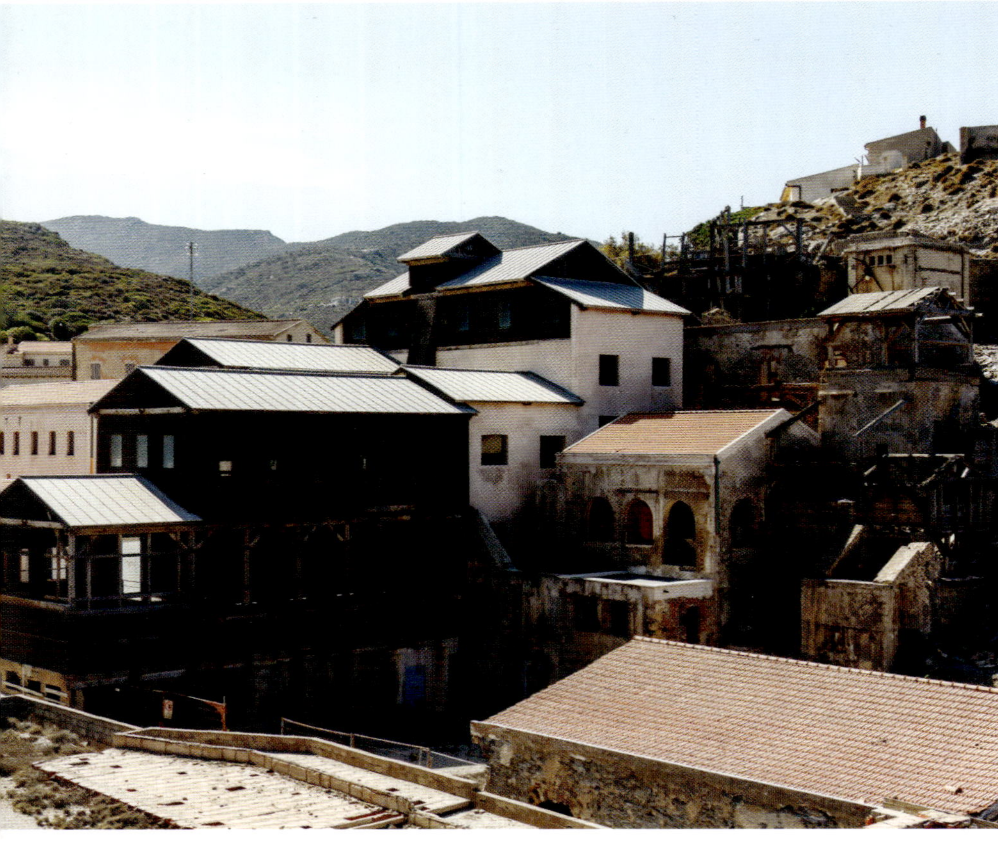

***Above:** Old silver mine at Argentiera, Sardinia.*

Hashima Island

Perhaps the most extraordinary of all abandoned islands is Gunkanjima, or Hashima Island, which lies just offshore a few miles to the south of Nagasaki in Japan. Undersea coal deposits were first discovered here in 1810, and when the country industrialized in the late nineteenth century, a significant mining operation began on this tiny islet – just a few hundred metres long – which saw the population peak at more than 5,000 people in 1959. But the workforce had not always been voluntary: during the period of Japanese imperial expansion from the 1930s up to 1945, thousands of conscripted Koreans and Chinese prisoners of war were forced to work there under terrible duress. Something of this oppressive history can still

***Right:** Nowadays, only sheep and huge flocks of seabirds live on the abandoned Scottish islands of St Kilda in the Outer Hebrides, after the last residents all left in 1930.*

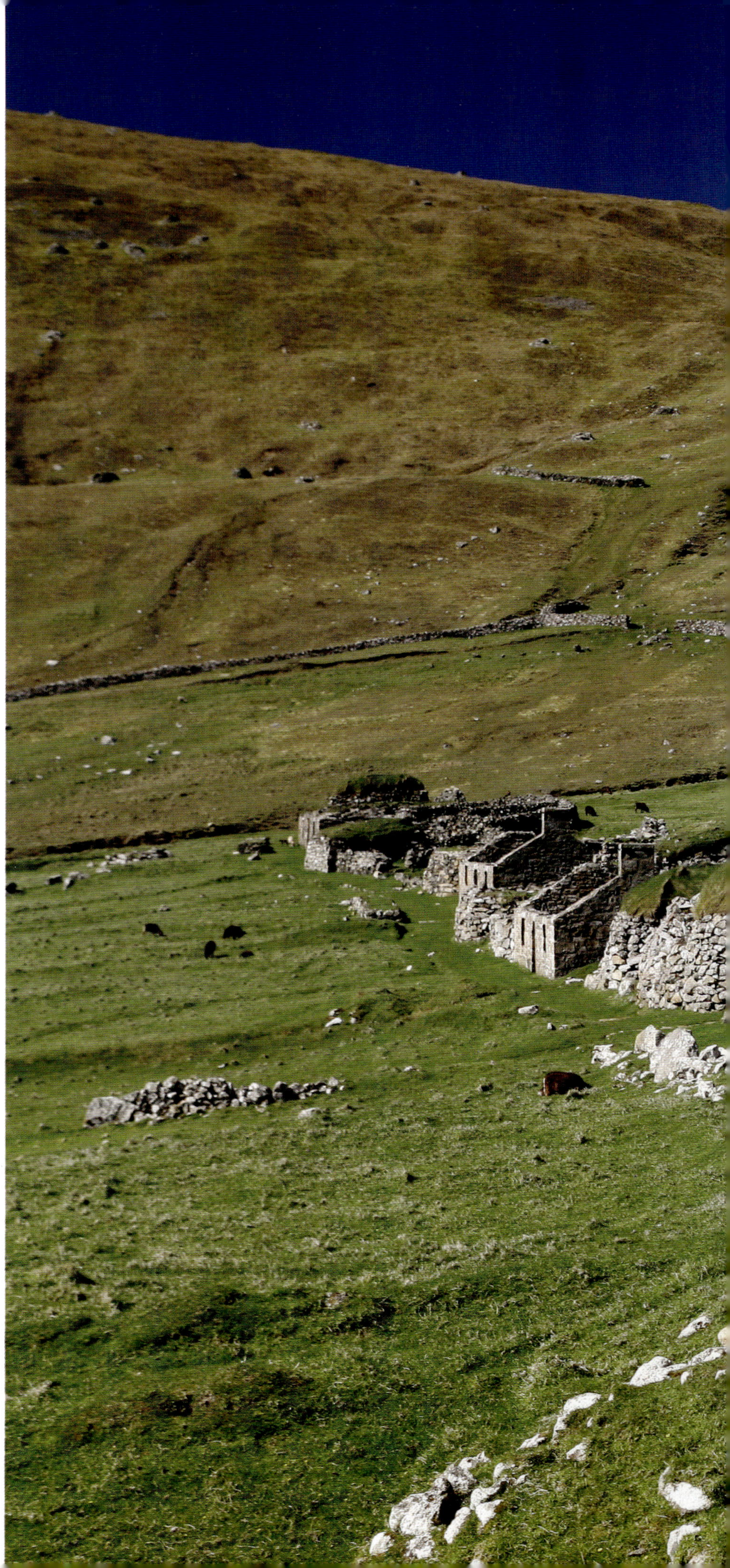

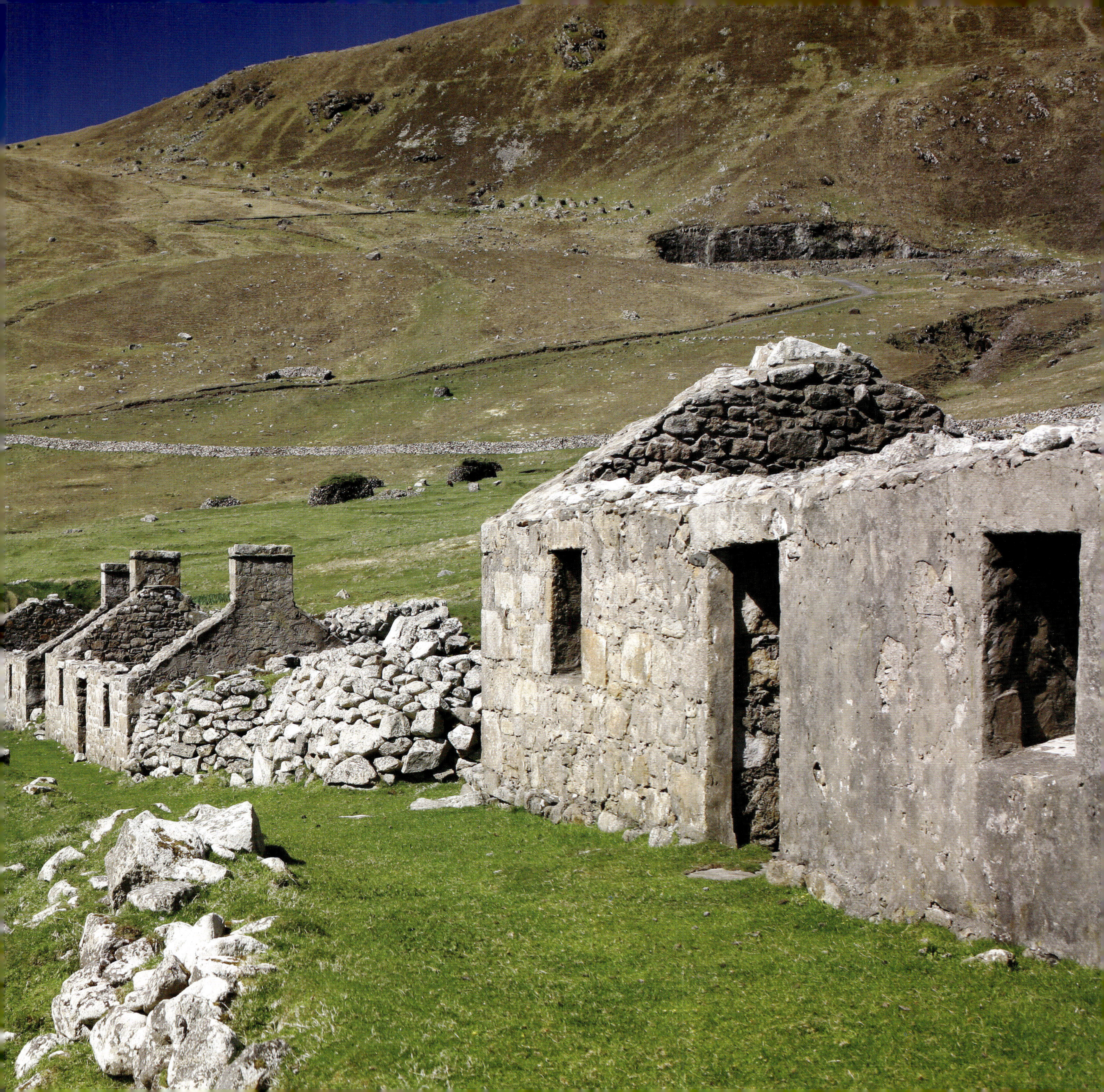

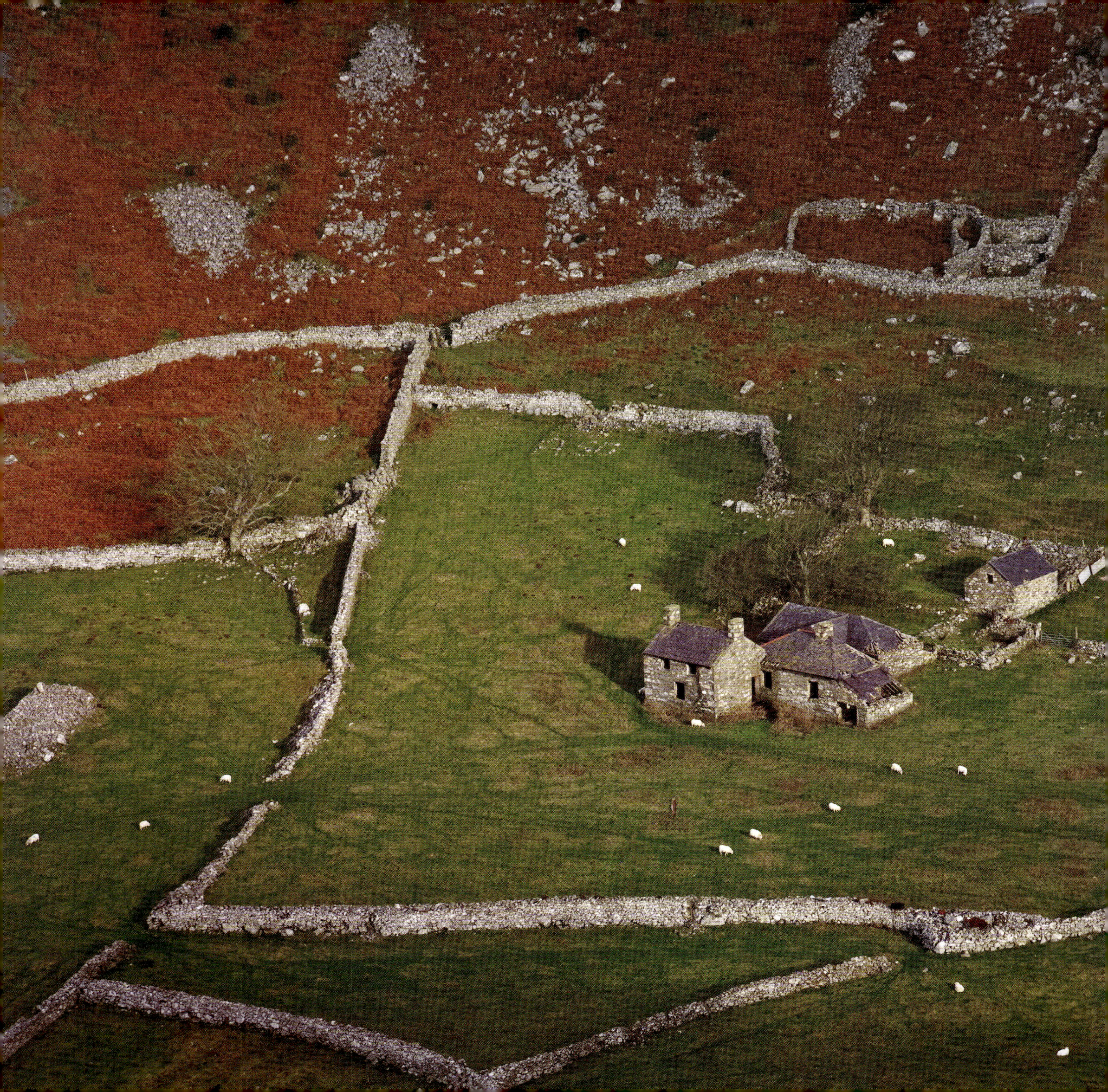

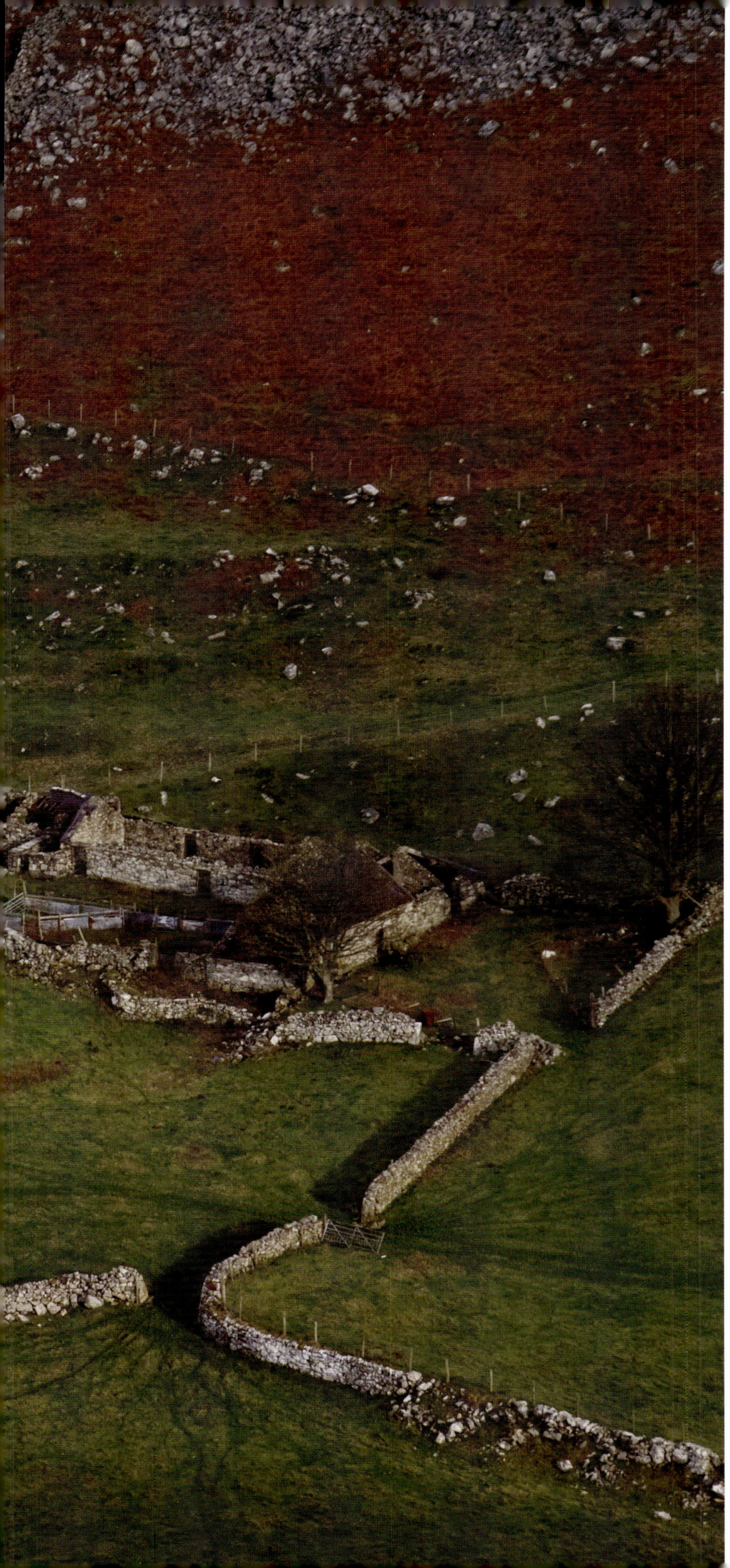

be felt among the ruined high-rise apartments of the citadel in which workers had to live, and which, towering above the seawall that encircled it, earned Hashima the nickname Battleship Island, after the vessel it resembles from afar. As ever with resource-extraction boomtowns, after the peak the fall was precipitous, and with the end of mining in 1974, Hashima Island was abandoned to its ghosts.

Left: *The abandoned quarrying village Porth y Nant, near Llithfaen, North Wales.*
Below: *Abandoned whaling station at Grytviken, the former capital of South Georgia.*

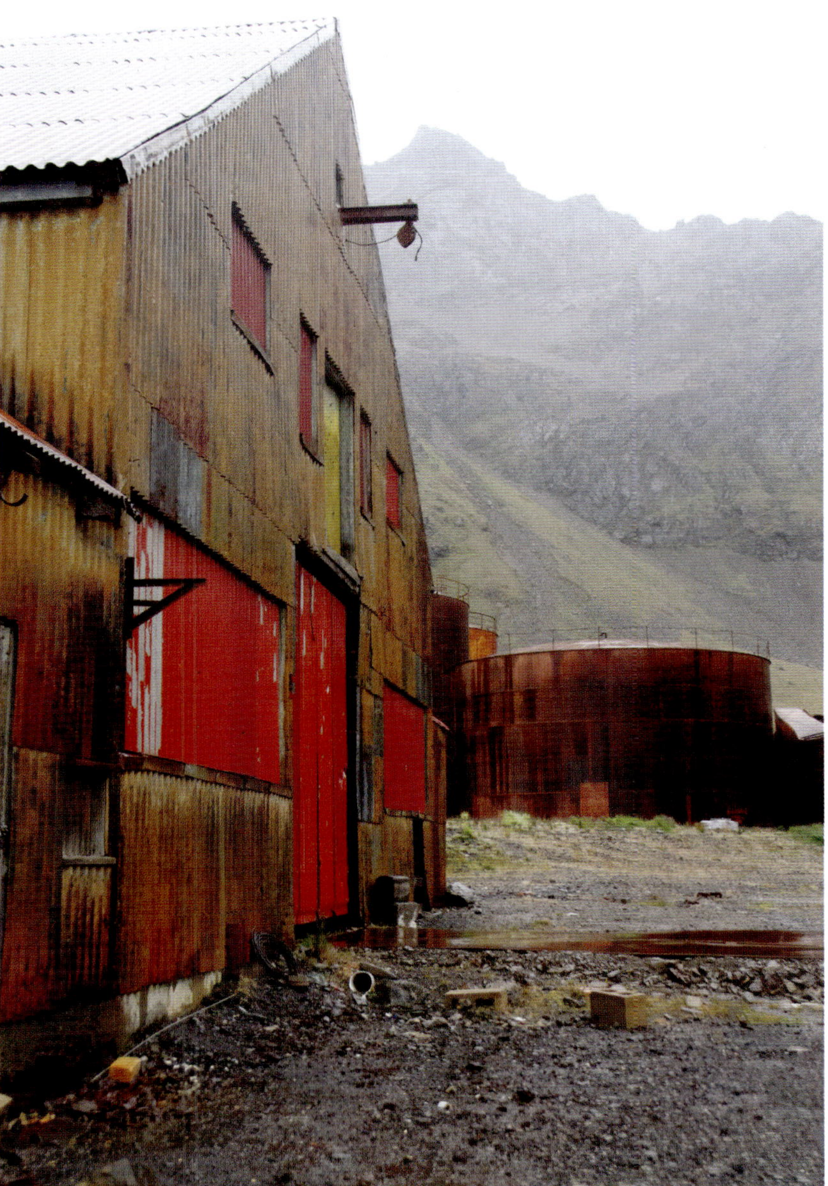

Empty Cities

From empty worker towns to glistening forests of modern apartments, there is no end of well-intentioned schemes where no one wants to live

Fordlândia

Hashima was in fact a company town, owned by the Mitsubishi Corporation, and while ethically dubious it does at least seem to have been a commercially successful venture. The same cannot be said of Fordlândia, these days a district of the city of Aveiro in northern Brazil. This stillborn town was dreamt up by Henry Ford and thus represents a rare failure from one of the shrewdest business brains of all time. Motor cars need rubber for tyres and synthetic rubber was then still a distant dream. So Ford's idea to establish a factory close to the source of a large

Right and Below: *Abandoned buildings in China.*

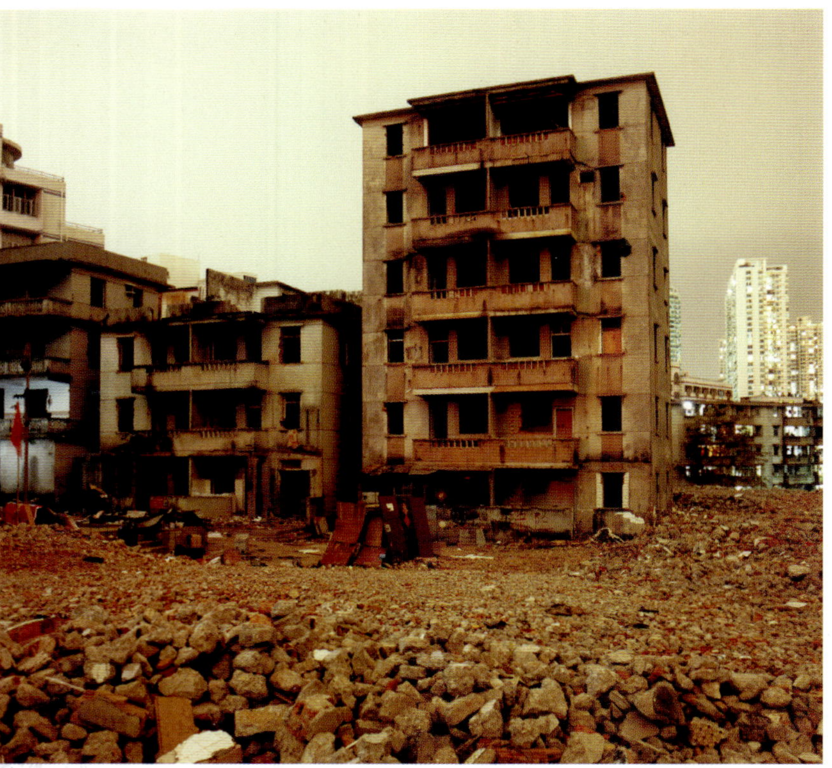

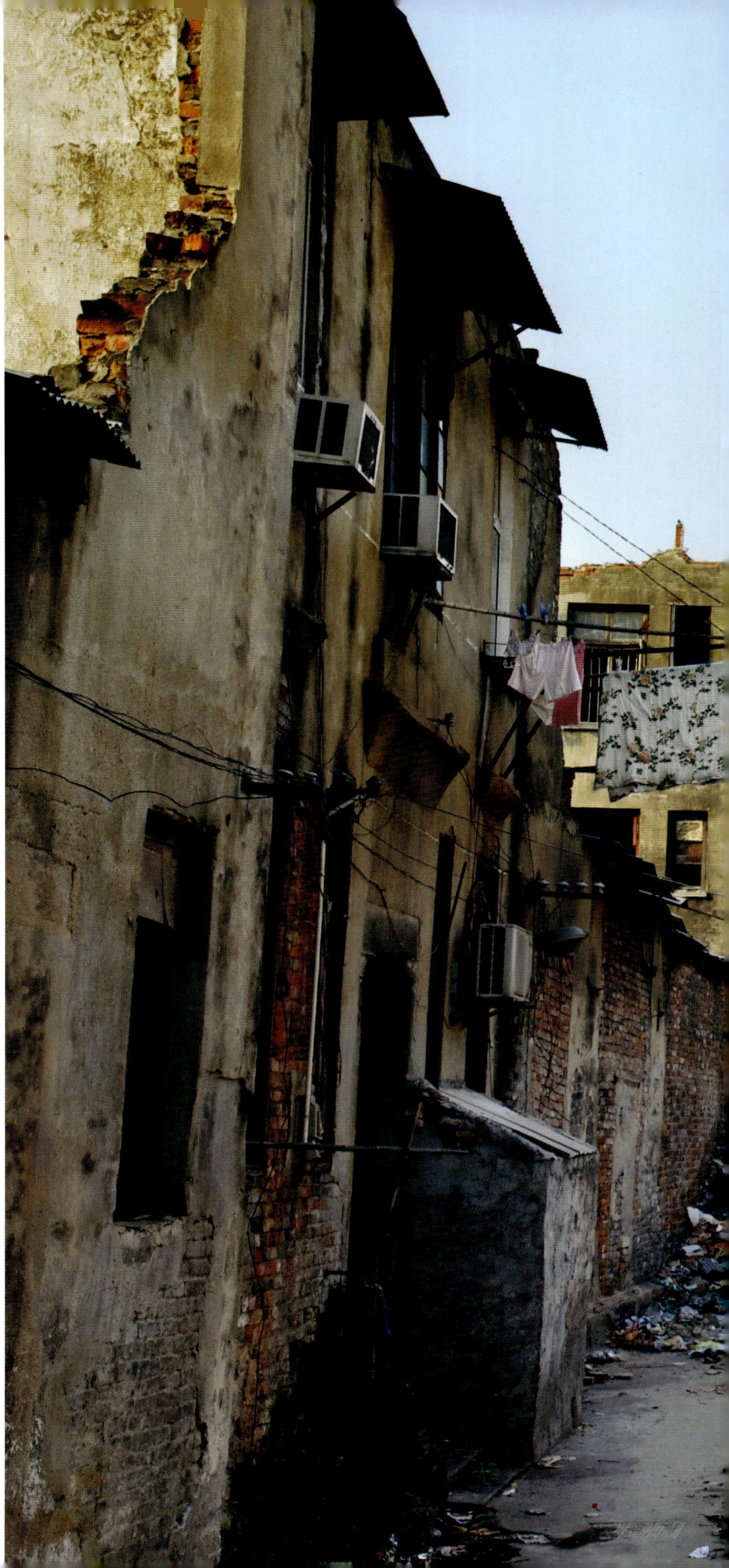

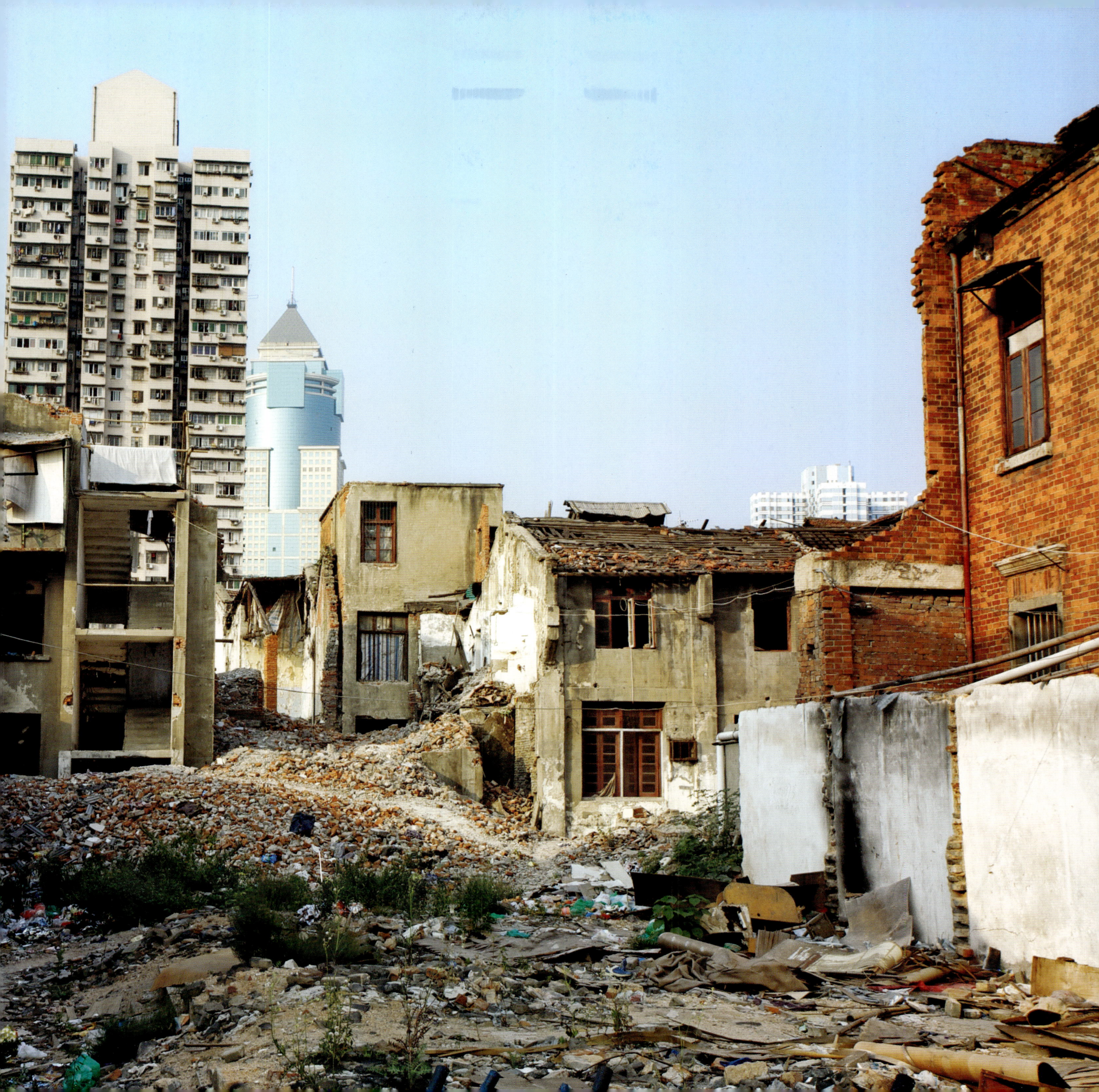

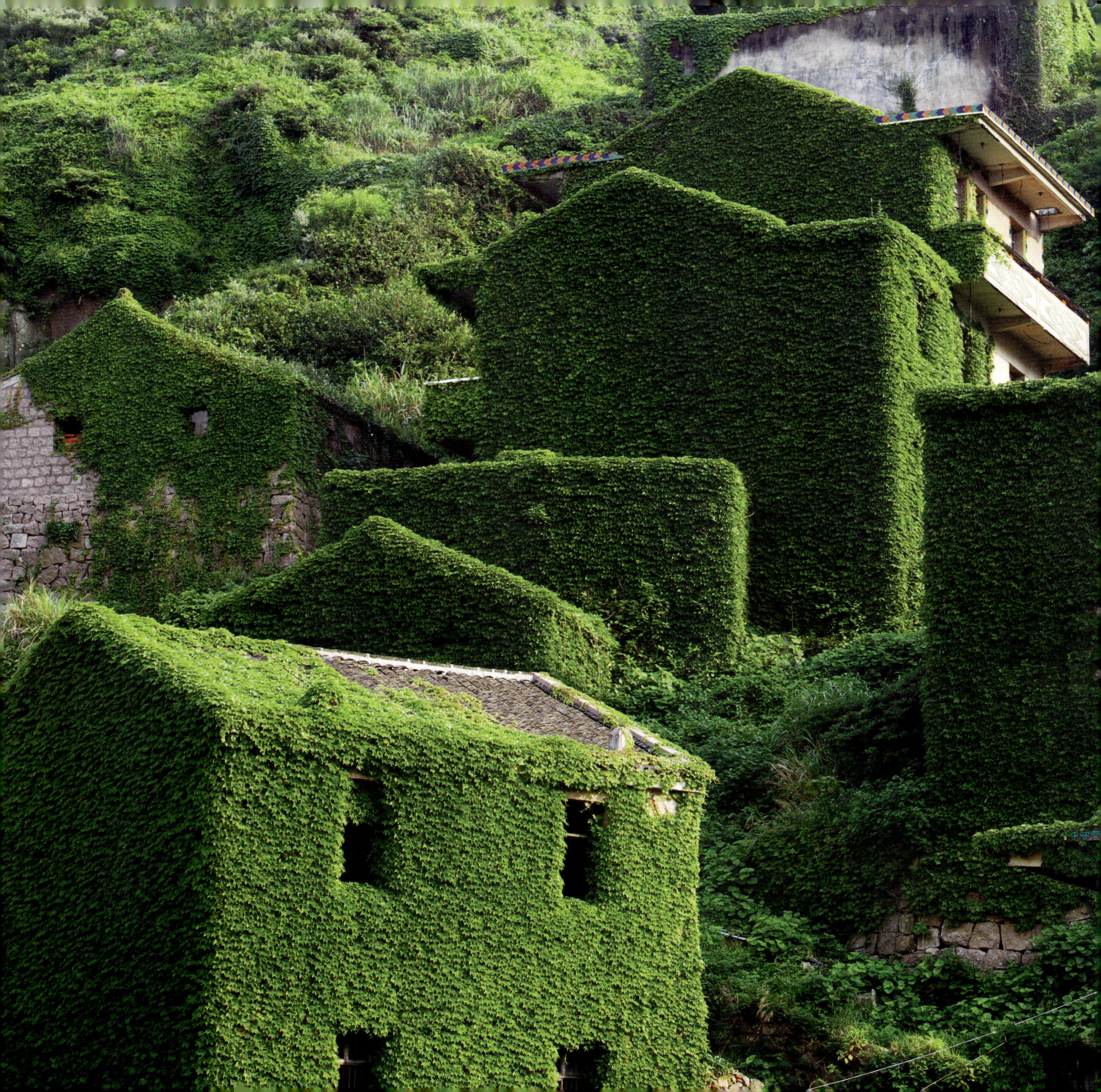

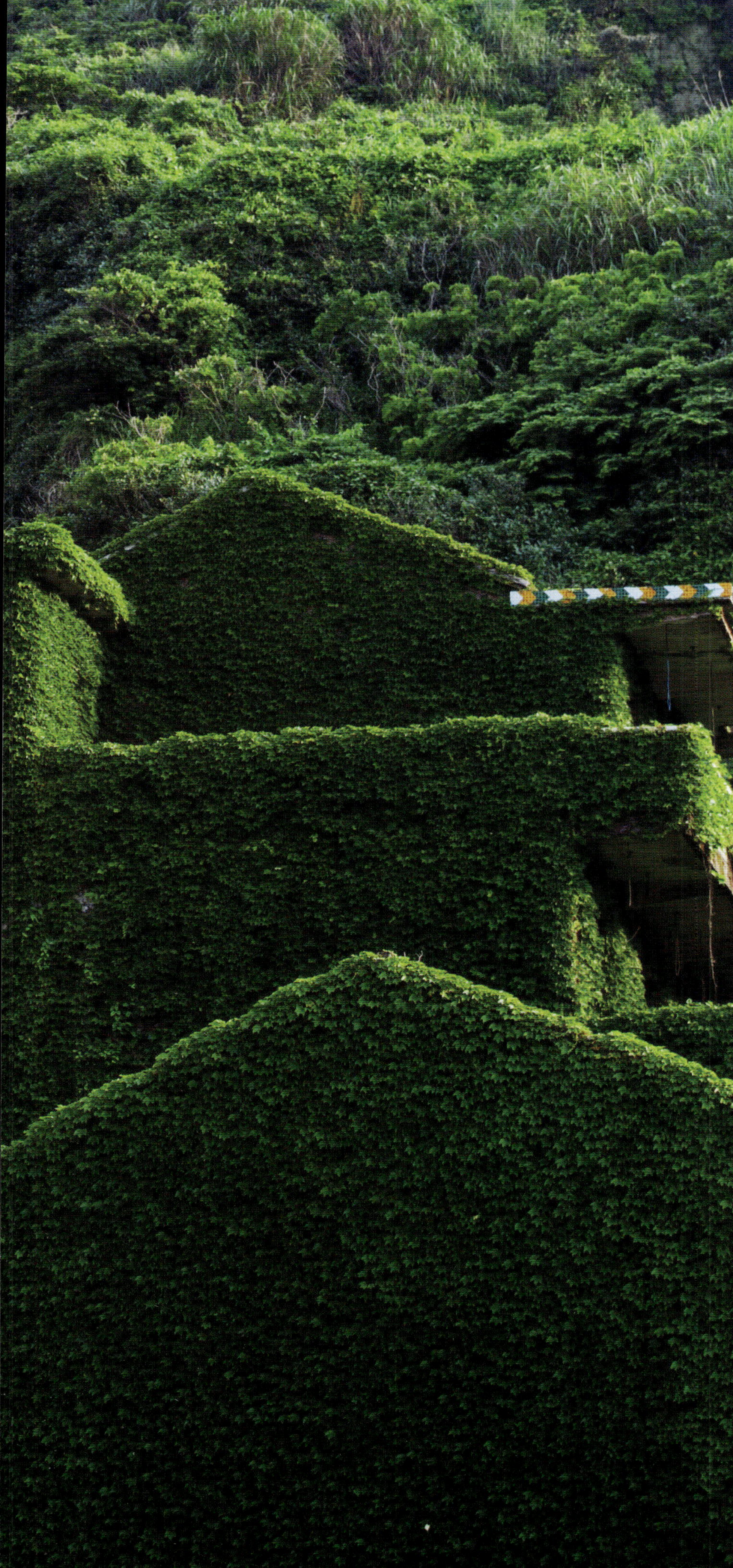

potential supply of cultivated rubber on a company plantation in the heart of the Amazon Rainforest seems commercially quite sound.

By 1926, the Ford Motor Company was so successful that he probably thought nothing of investing a large sum of money in building a city, bearing his name, in which company workers could live close to their place of work. But despite the planned conurbation boasting all the modern amenities enjoyed by American workers, the venture was beset by problems from the start. Brazilians who came to work there disliked the American food they were served in the company canteens, they disliked the rigid working conditions, and at times there was open revolt. The rubber too was difficult to grow in this area, and in 1934, just six years after it opened, the plantation was moved downriver, and Fordlândia became a ghost town overnight.

Chinese Ghost Cities

Henry Ford's forward planning may not have come off, but successful societies always look to the future. The same confidence has been central to the Chinese economic miracle of recent decades, in which hundreds of millions have abandoned the old rural life and flocked to newly built cities for the promise of much higher wages and a better standard of living, a demographic movement accompanied – some would say driven – by a building boom of unprecedented haste. This has led to the growth of so-called ghost cities, with vast plantations of tall apartment blocks apparently unoccupied for want of enough people who can yet afford them. But a construction programme of such ambition has never been attempted before, and it does seem as if once-deserted districts in cities like Dantu and Ordos Kangbashi are slowly beginning to fill up with a rapidly growing middle class.

Left: *Abandoned houses in the fishing village on Shengshan Island, China.*
Next page: *Uninhabited mining town of Sewell, Chile.*

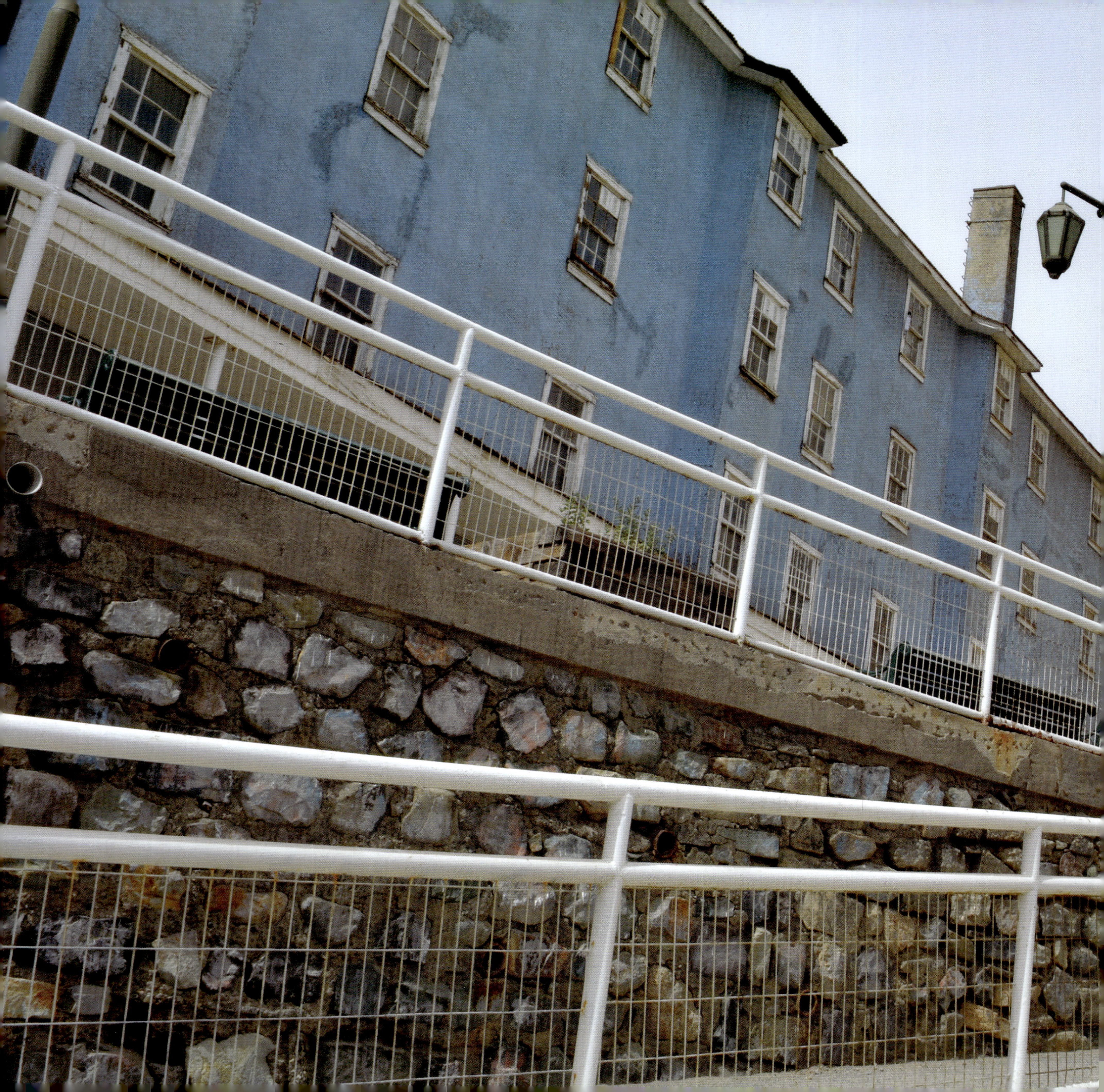

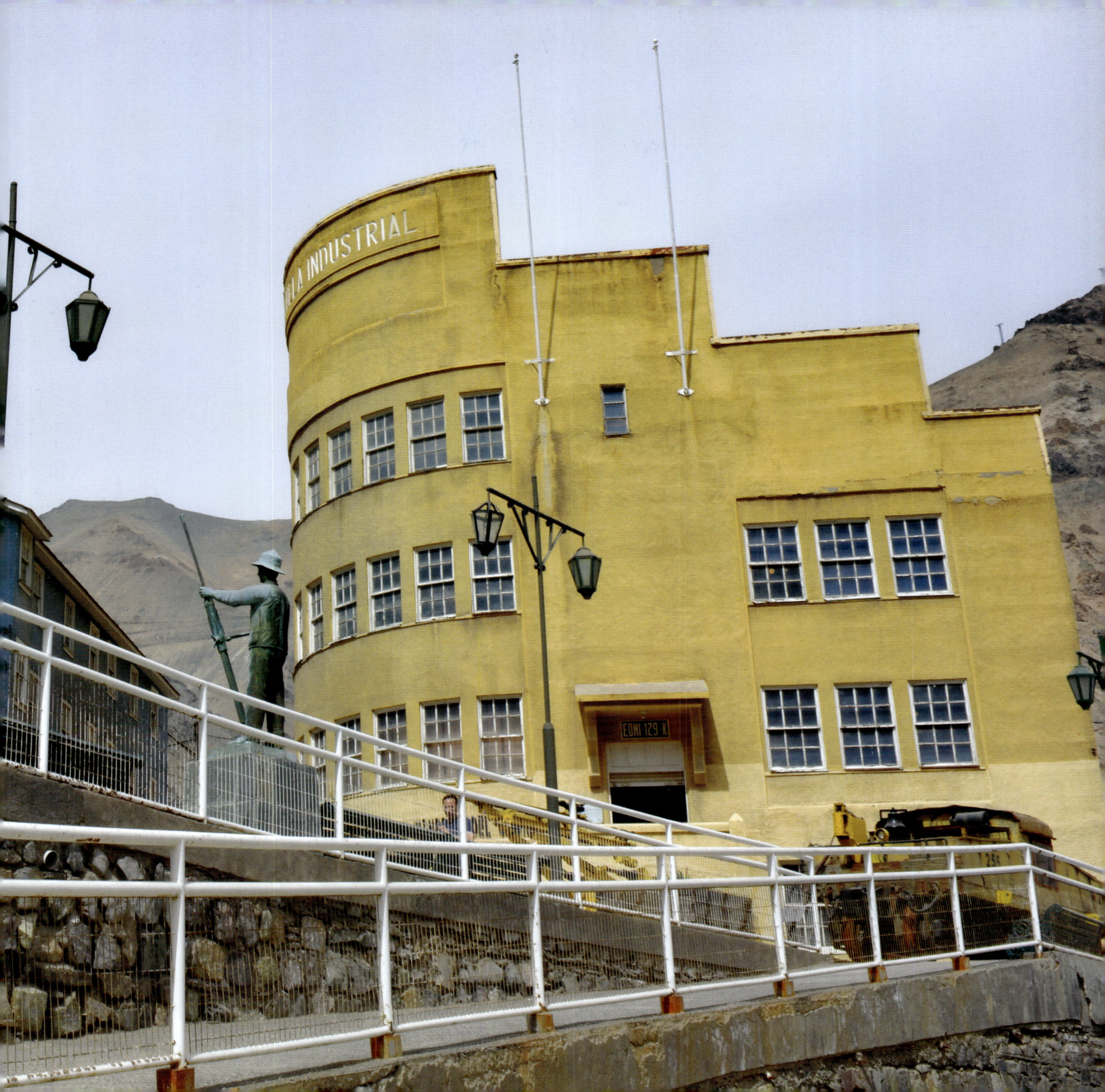
INDUSTRIAL
EDNI 129 K

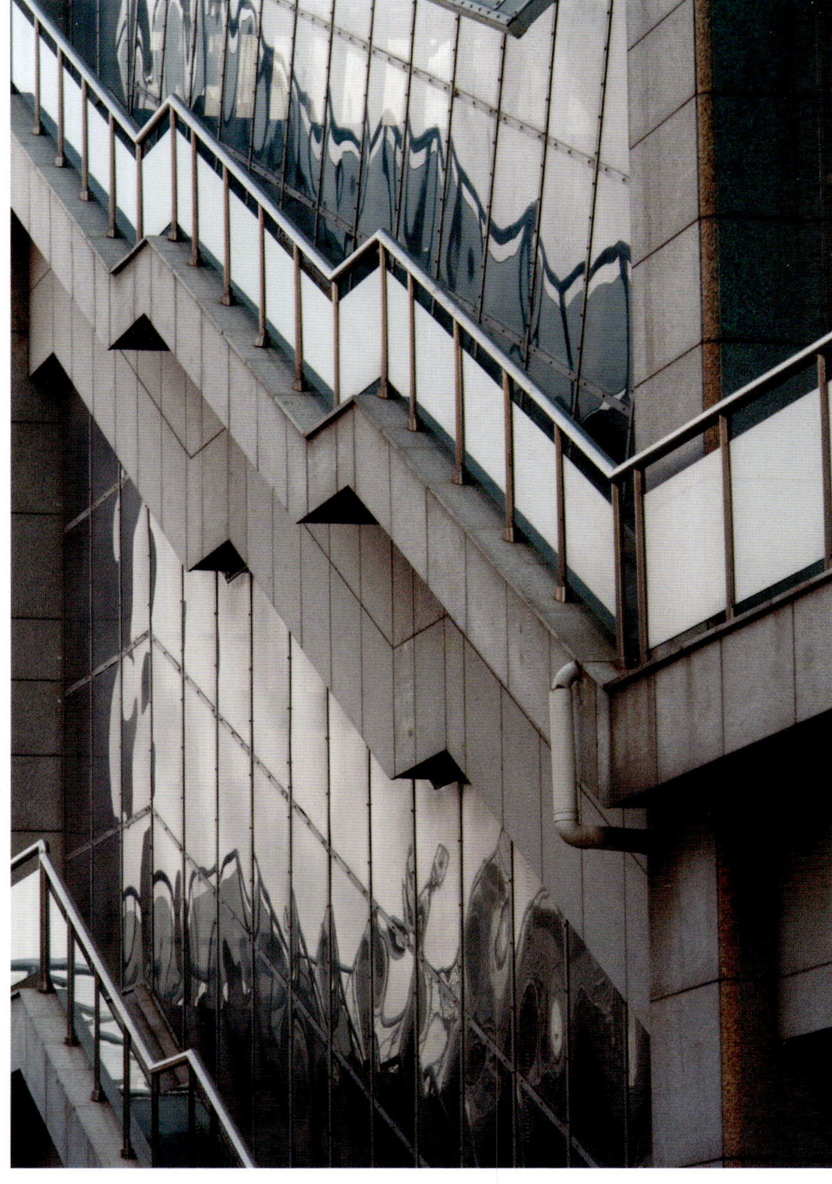

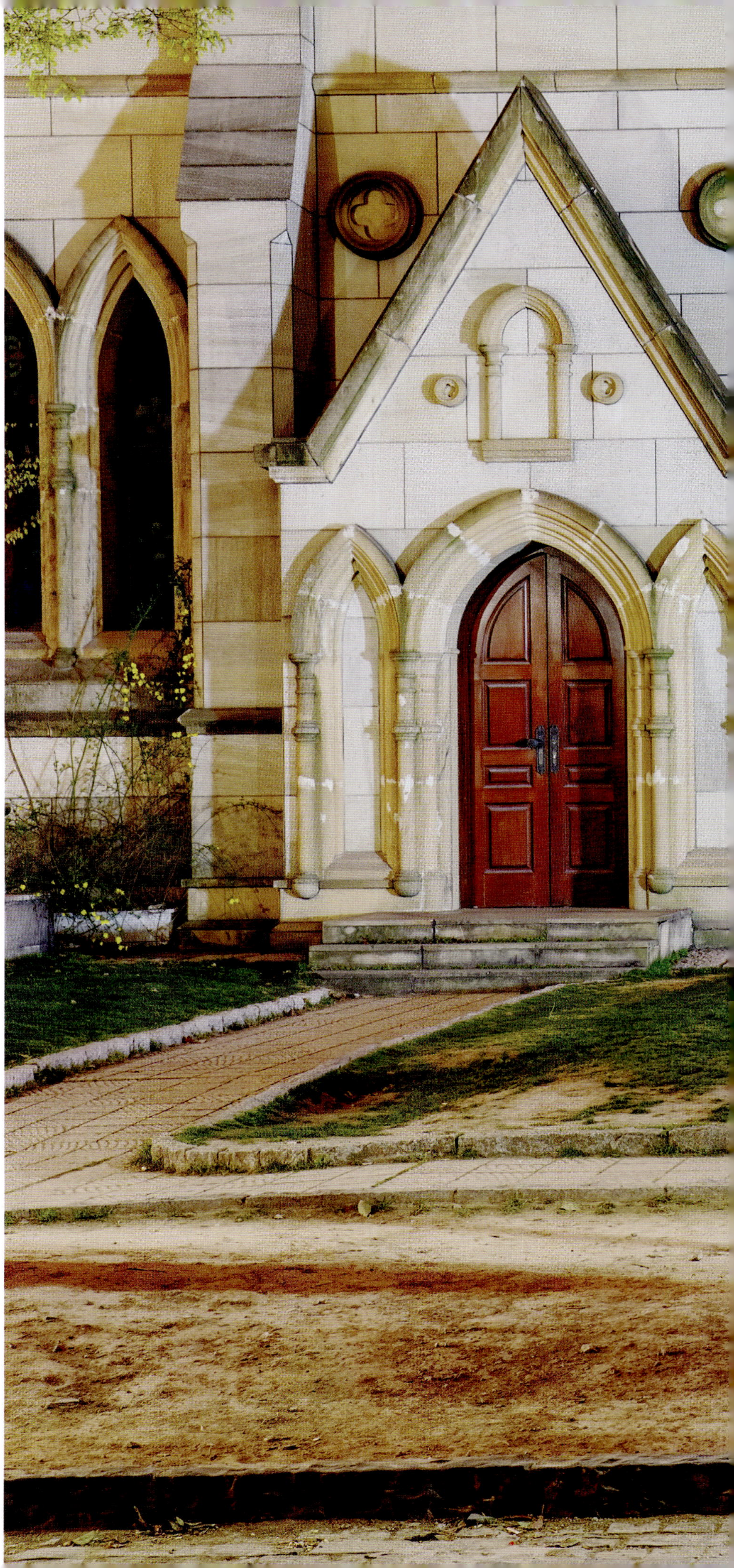

More unfortunate are the still-deserted pastiche districts in assorted European styles, such as Thames Town in Shanghai, a simulation that would fit right into the English home counties; or the perfect replica of the Austrian town of Hallstatt, standing close to the world's largest ghost mall in the city of Guangdong. These empty cultural imports are among hundreds of similar copycat towns in cities across China, all of which have been built since the turn of the century.

Above: *Building in Binhai, Tianjin, China.*
Right: *Thames Town in Shanghai, China simulates an English village, though very few people actually live there..*

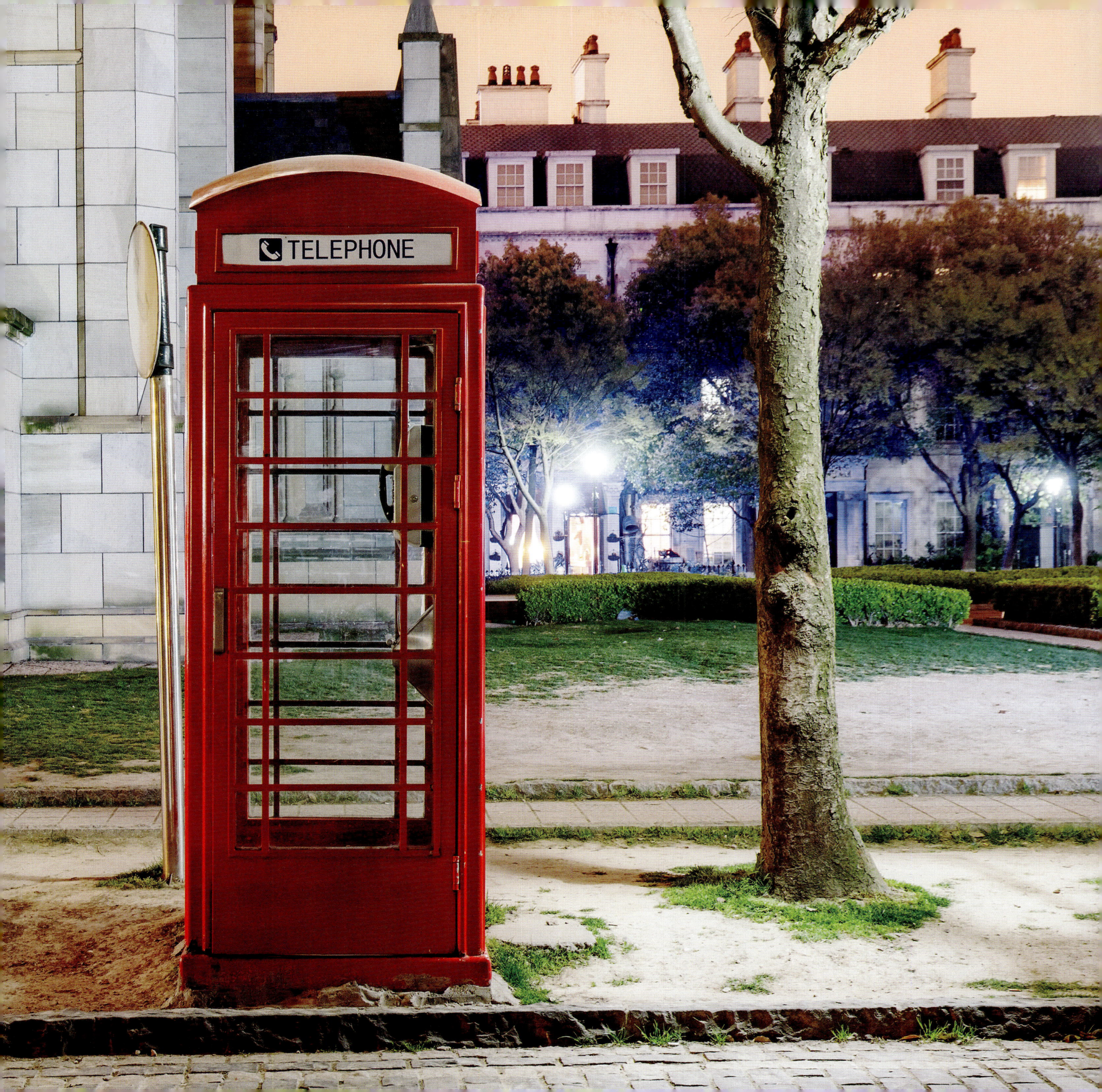
TELEPHONE

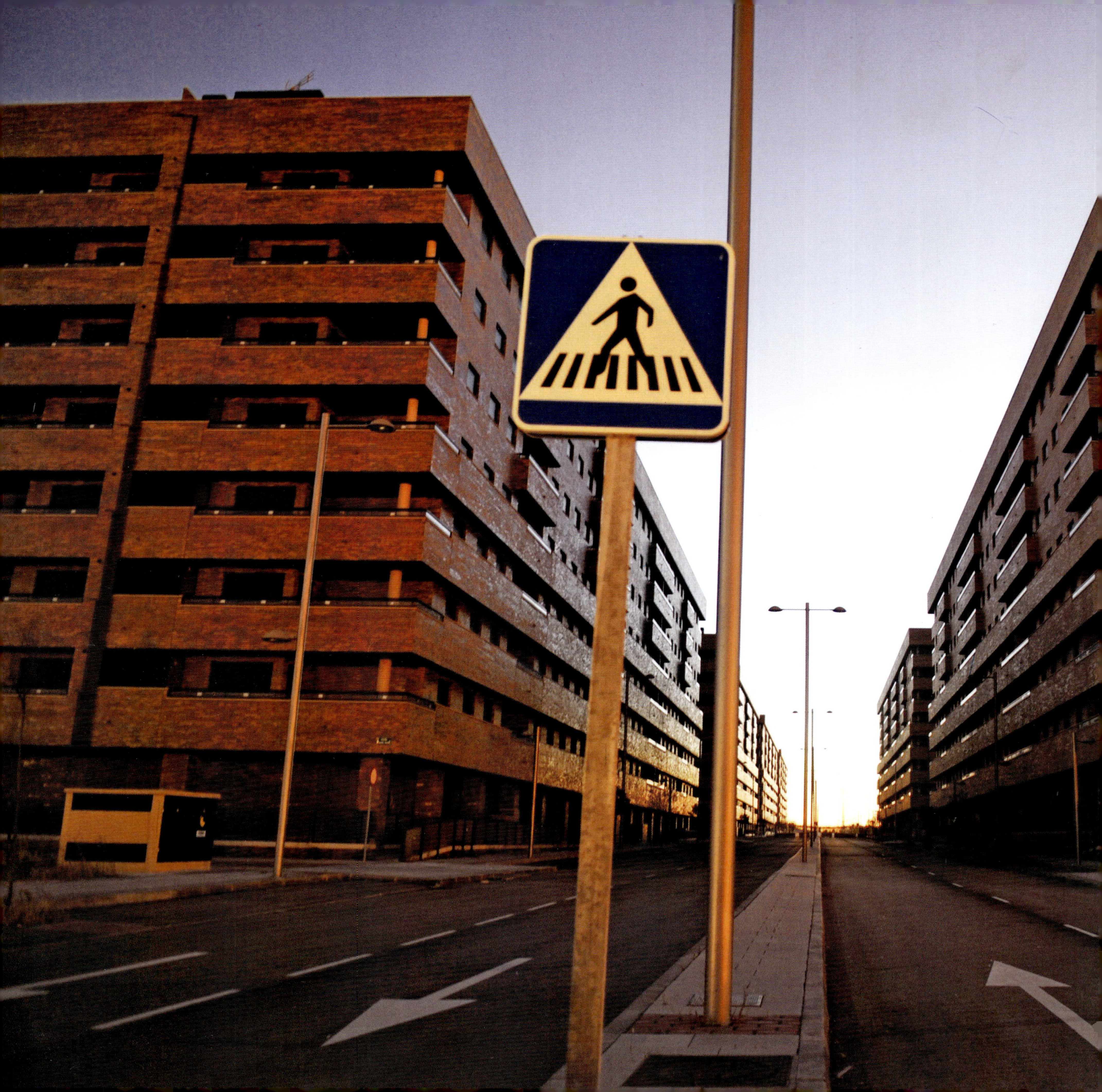

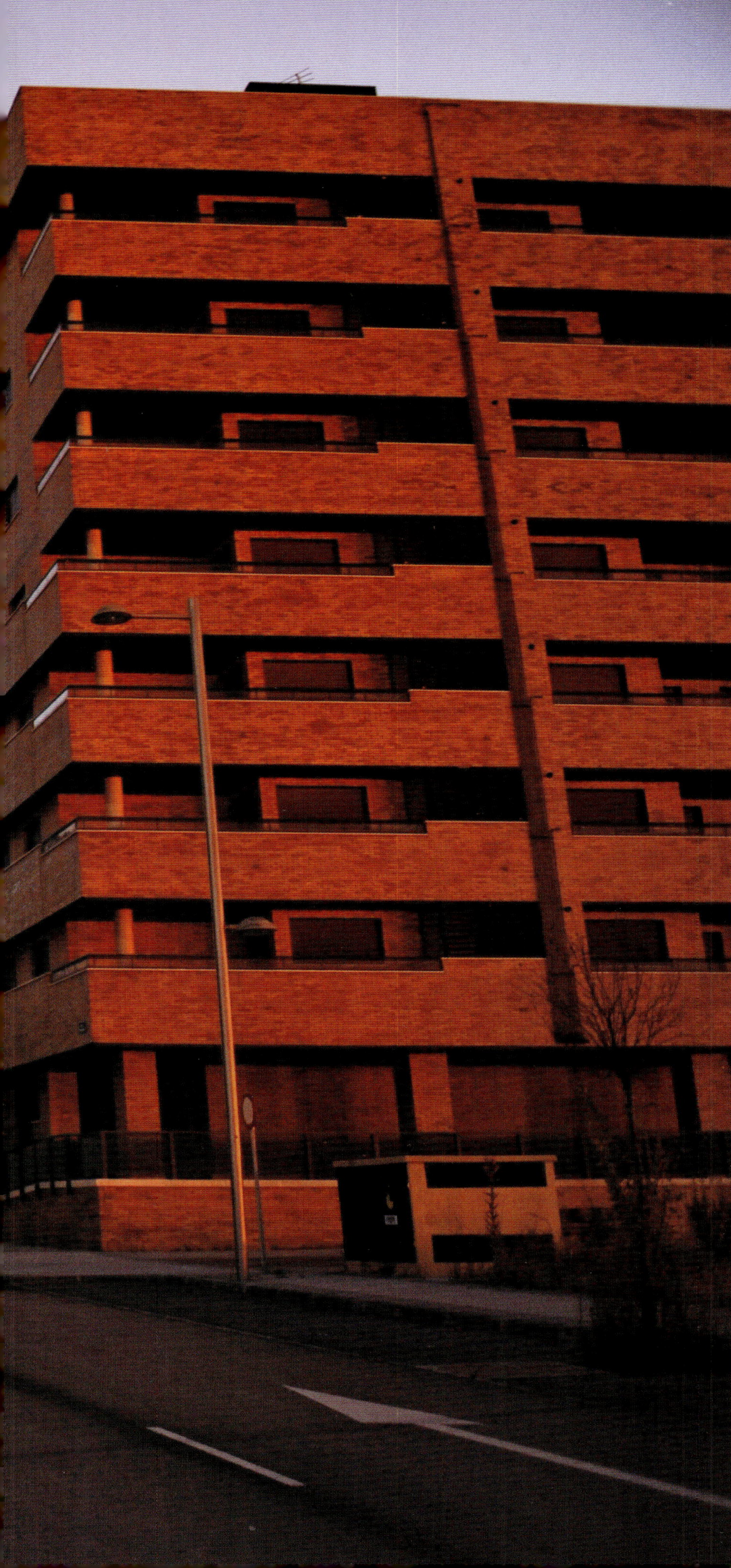

Economic Crises

China's economy may well be robust enough to cope with the financial hazard of so many projects built ahead of demand, confident that the country's still enormous rural populace will soon take them up. But similar speculation in countries more vulnerable than China has had ruinous effects.

The Pain in Spain

Spain's brand of woe in the financial crisis of 2008 stemmed from banks lending money for developments that were never occupied after the economy crashed and large numbers of people lost their jobs. Madrid satellite cities like Seseña (*see* left) and Ciudad Valdeluz were intended as dormitory towns for thousands of the capital's workers, but have struggled to attract a fraction of that number to fill the majority of apartments that still lie empty. And in some places the clock was stopped even before the buildings went up, leaving networks of empty roads with nothing to serve, still printed on the landscape like an indecipherable message to ancient gods.

Ghosts of the Future and the Past

A similar story played out in Ireland during the same period, with some estimates of as many as 1,000 new housing estates like Castlemoyne and Belmayne close to Dublin, built in a bubble of speculation in the pre-crash years, still largely or even wholly unoccupied several years later.

Left: *The speculative property boom in Spain came to an abrupt end with the financial crisis of 2008 and the euro crisis that followed, leaving thousands of unfilled apartments.*

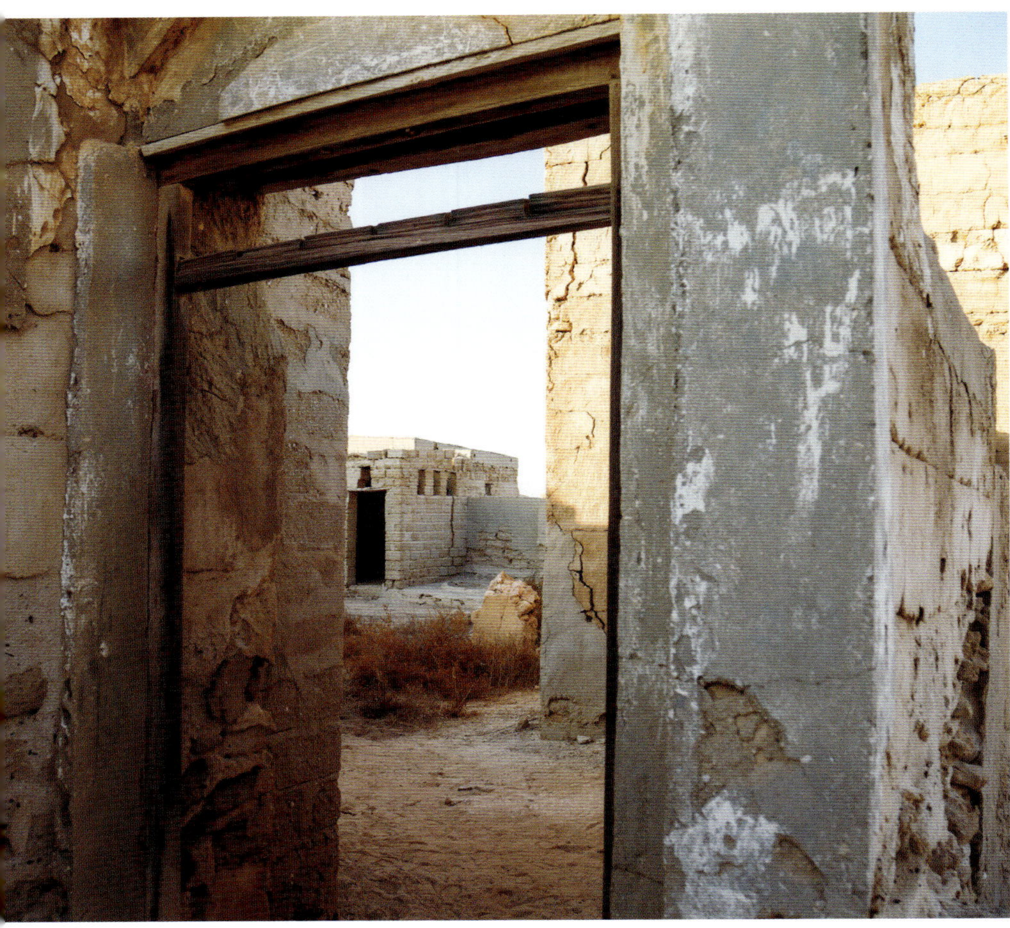

***Above:** Al Jazirah Al Hamra in the United Arab Emirates is known for its collection of abandoned houses.*

Facing the bald fact of an oversupply of homes that will never be filled, in 2013 the Irish government ordered the demolition of 40 such estates, but in spite of this, the flood of people away from rural communities towards the promise of an affluent life in towns and cities in Ireland and abroad has continued. Depopulation has been a constant of Irish life for centuries, as during the same period the main global demographic has switched from a rural, agrarian existence to an urban and now post-industrial life. Scores of Greek villages as well as hundreds the length of Italy – particularly in the south – have been wholly abandoned or left with a dwindling, ageing populace that will not be replaced.

***Right:** The ex-mining town of Linda in Tasmania has been a ghost town for half a century.*
***Next page:** Ruins of the church of La Mussara in Tarragona, Spain.*

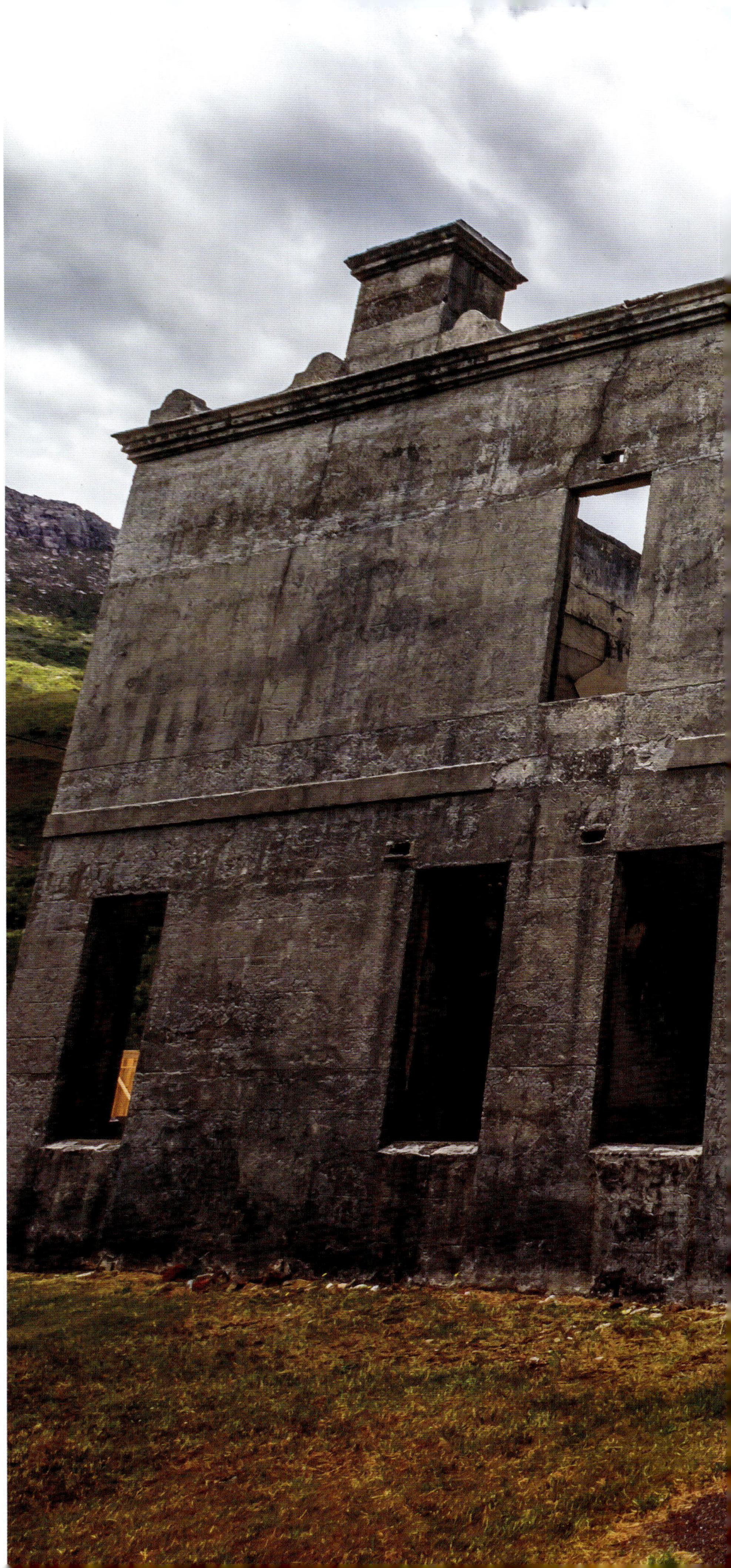

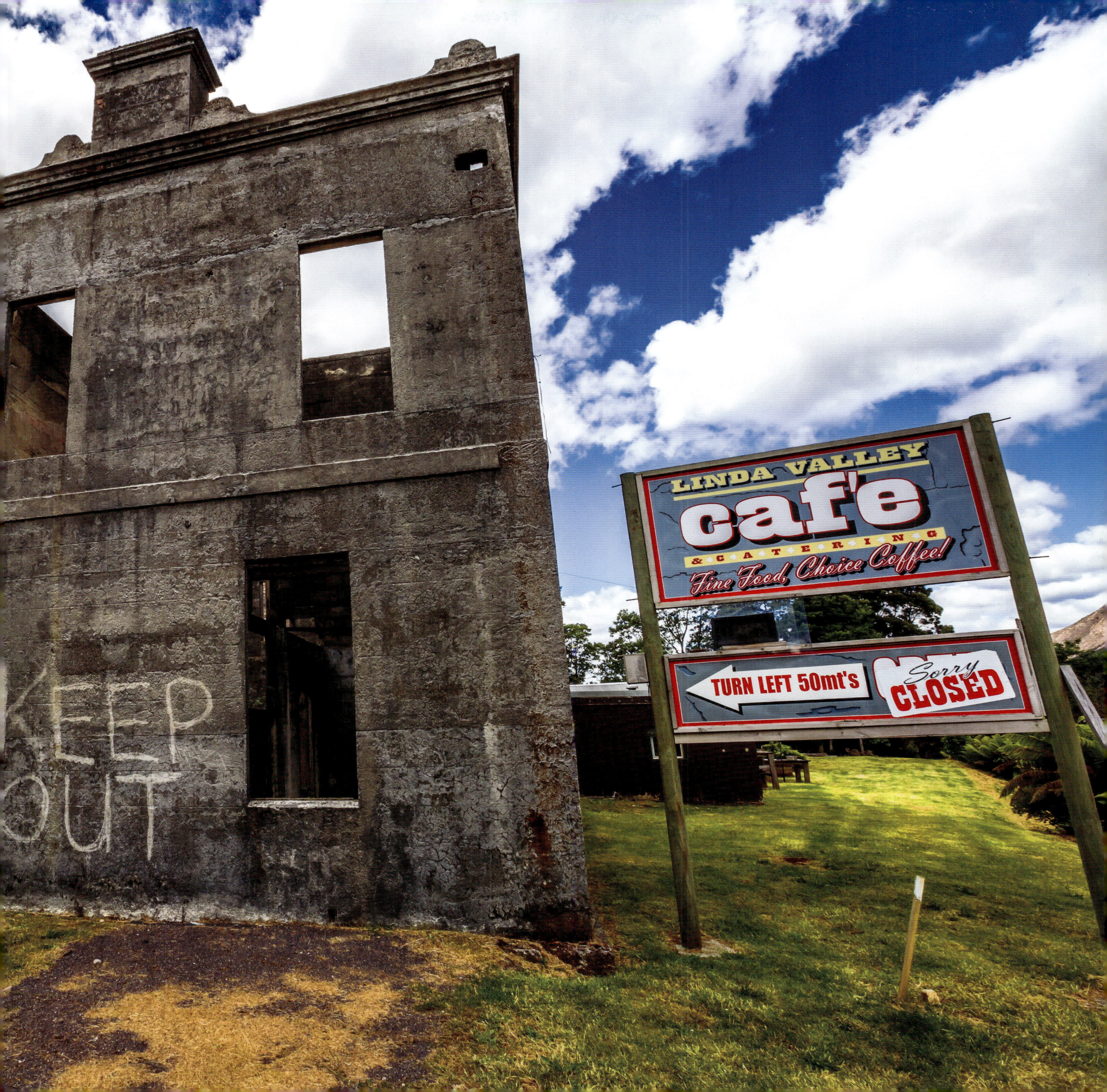
KEEP
OUT
LINDA VALLEY
café
& CATERING
Fine Food, Choice Coffee!
TURN LEFT 50mt's
Sorry
CLOSED

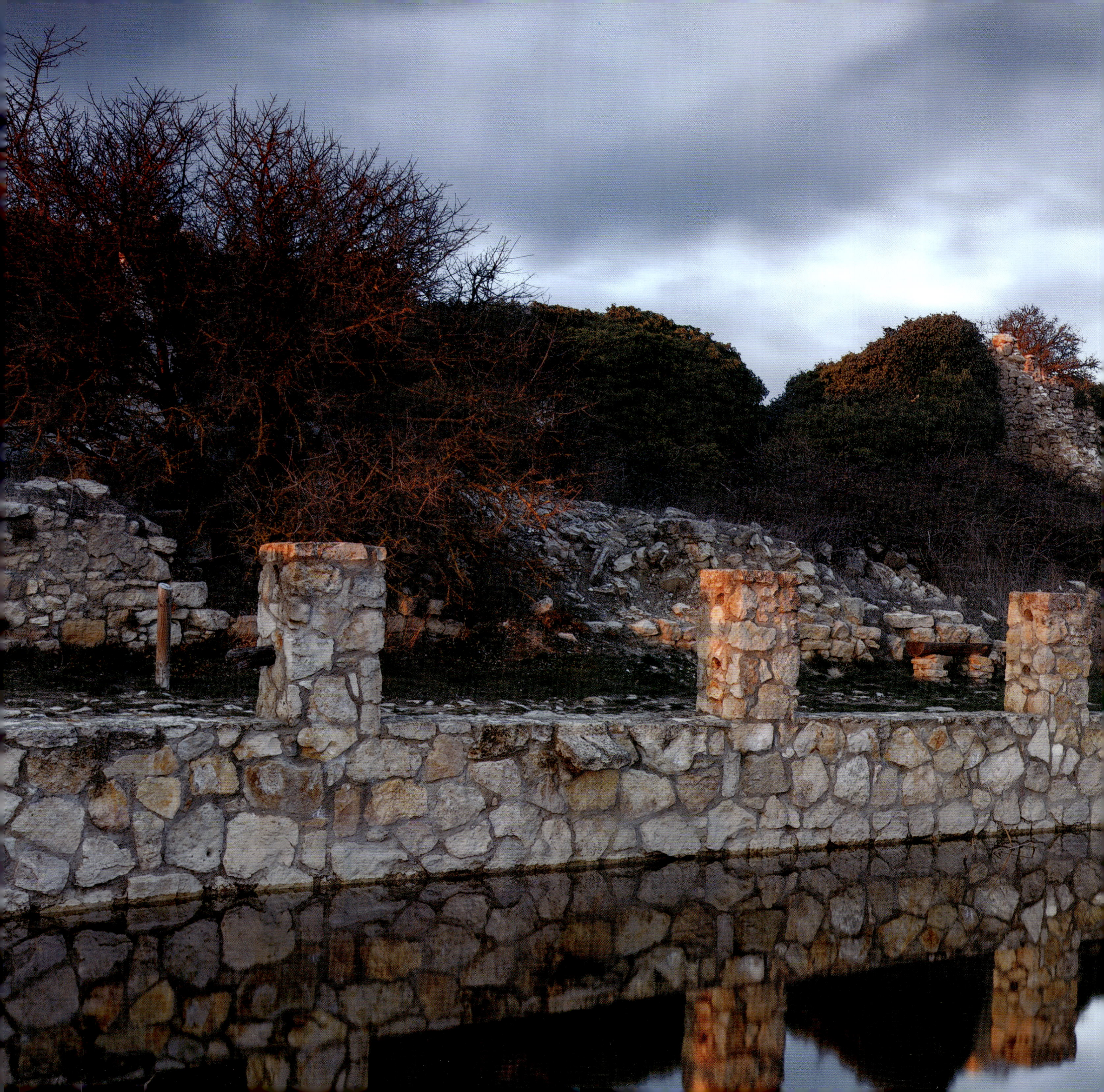

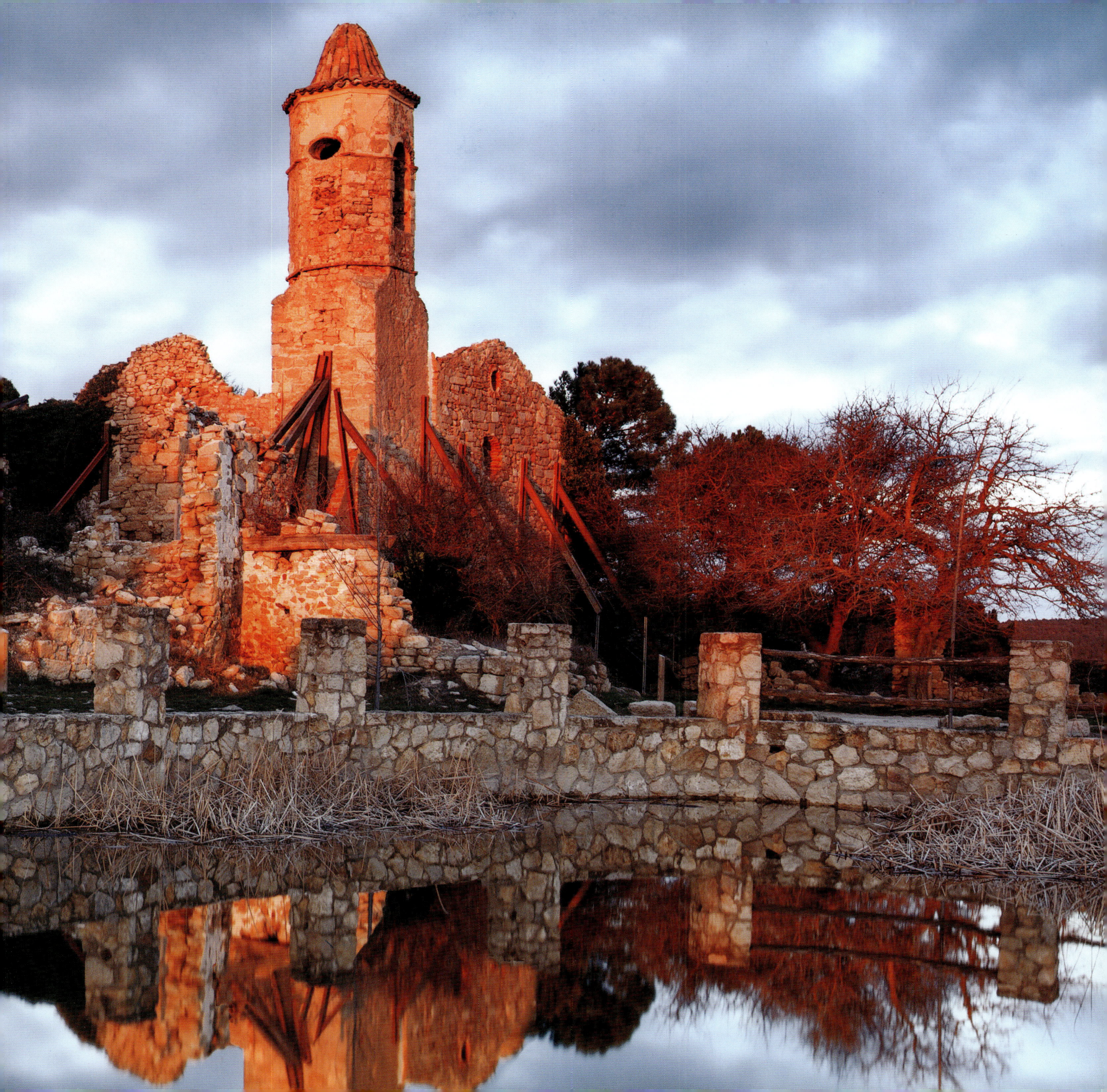

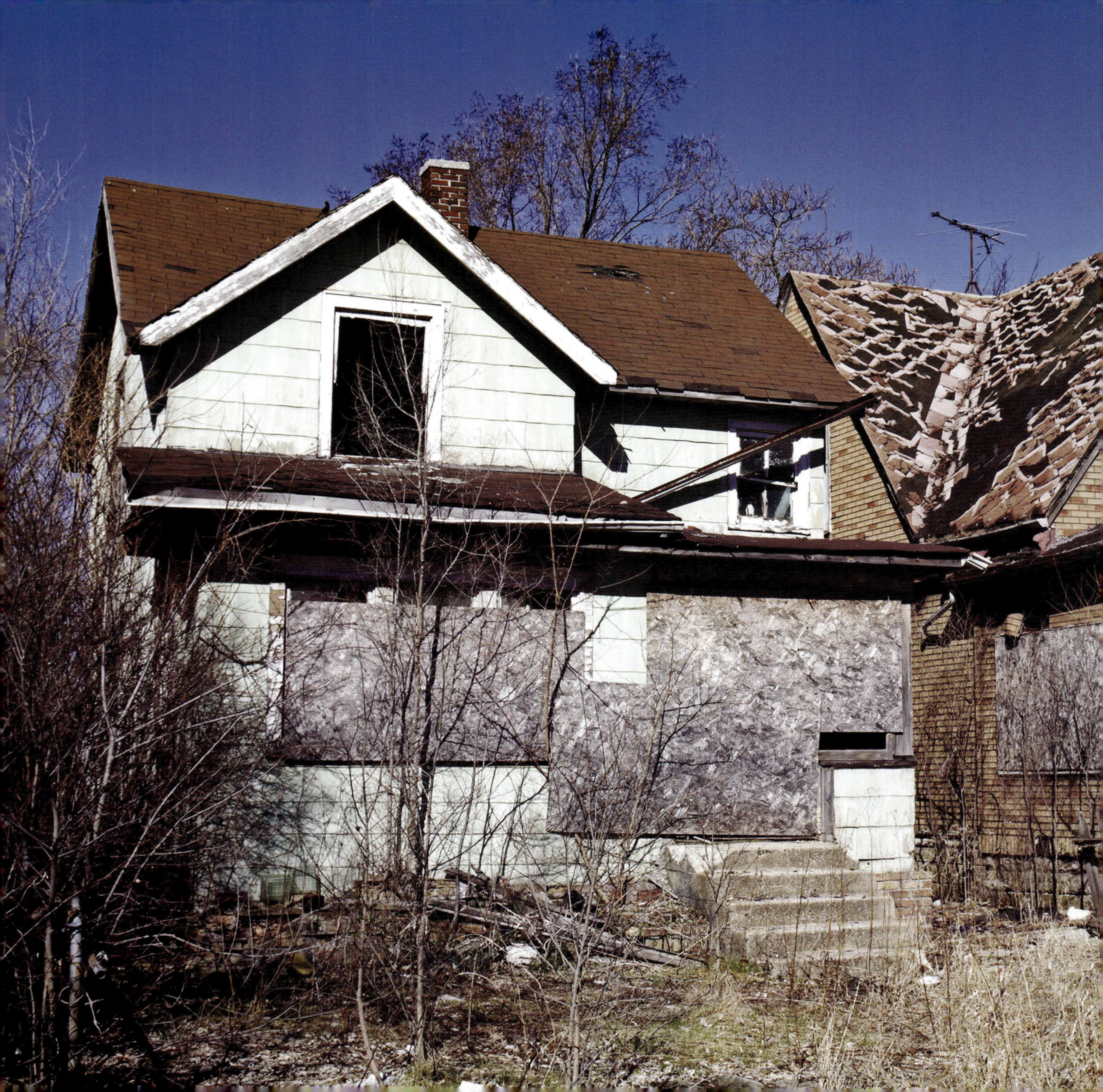

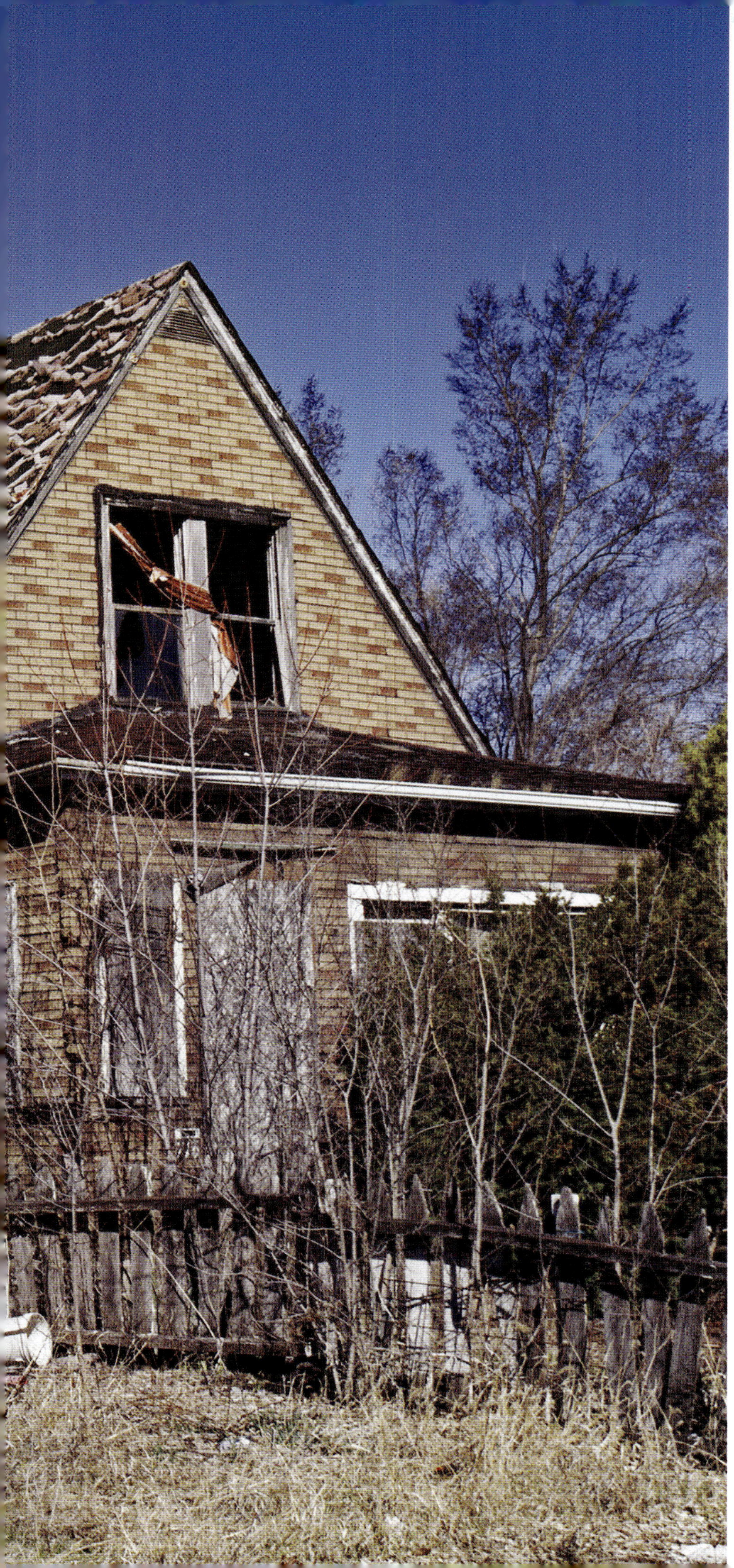

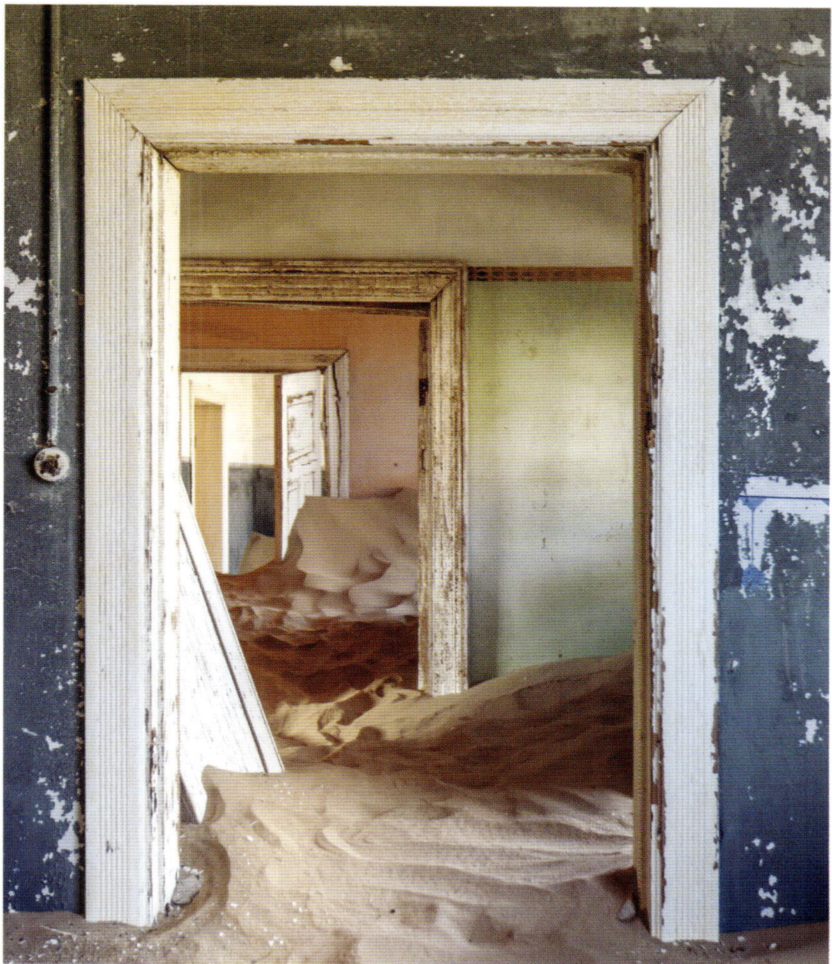

Above: *The once-thriving town of Kolmanskop in the Namib Desert grew rich when a diamond field was discovered here in 1908, but within 50 years had been abandoned to the sands.*

America's Shrinking Cities

The same economic storms have swept across the world, and in the USA, the most affluent country on earth, after the subprime crash of 2007 even large and well-established places such as the now bankrupt city of Stockton, California, have been hollowed out by the high number of foreclosures and a fall in local tax revenues as people lost their homes. Economic distress has brought with it a host of other problems such as drug abuse and crime,

Left: *Since 1960, the population of Gary, Indiana, once one of America's main steelmaking cities, has dropped by more than half as the industry slowly collapsed and people left for good.*
Next page: *Abandoned in 1970, the company town of Humberstone is the most famous of a number of former saltpetre 'nitrate towns' in the Atacama desert of northern Chile.*

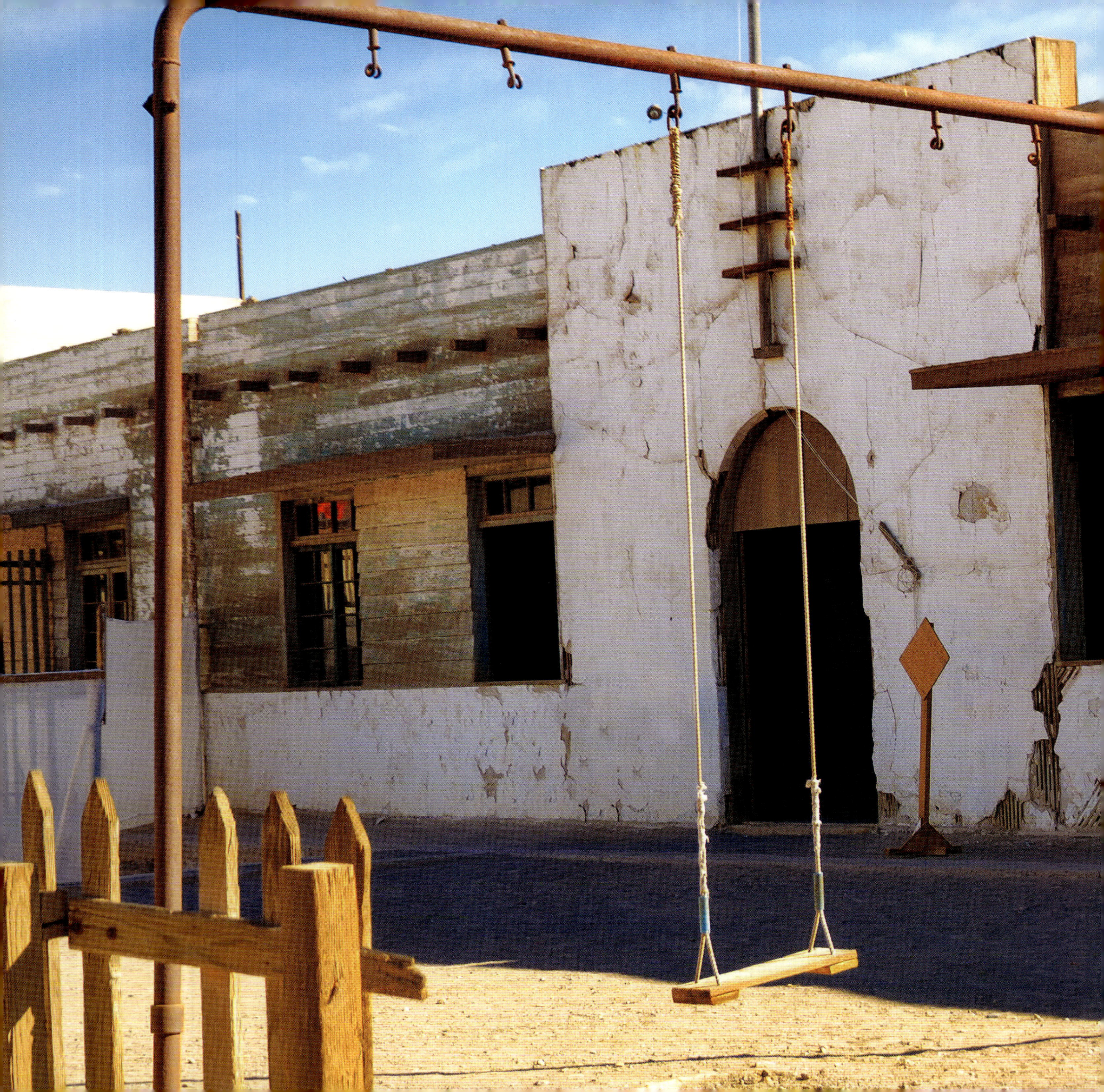

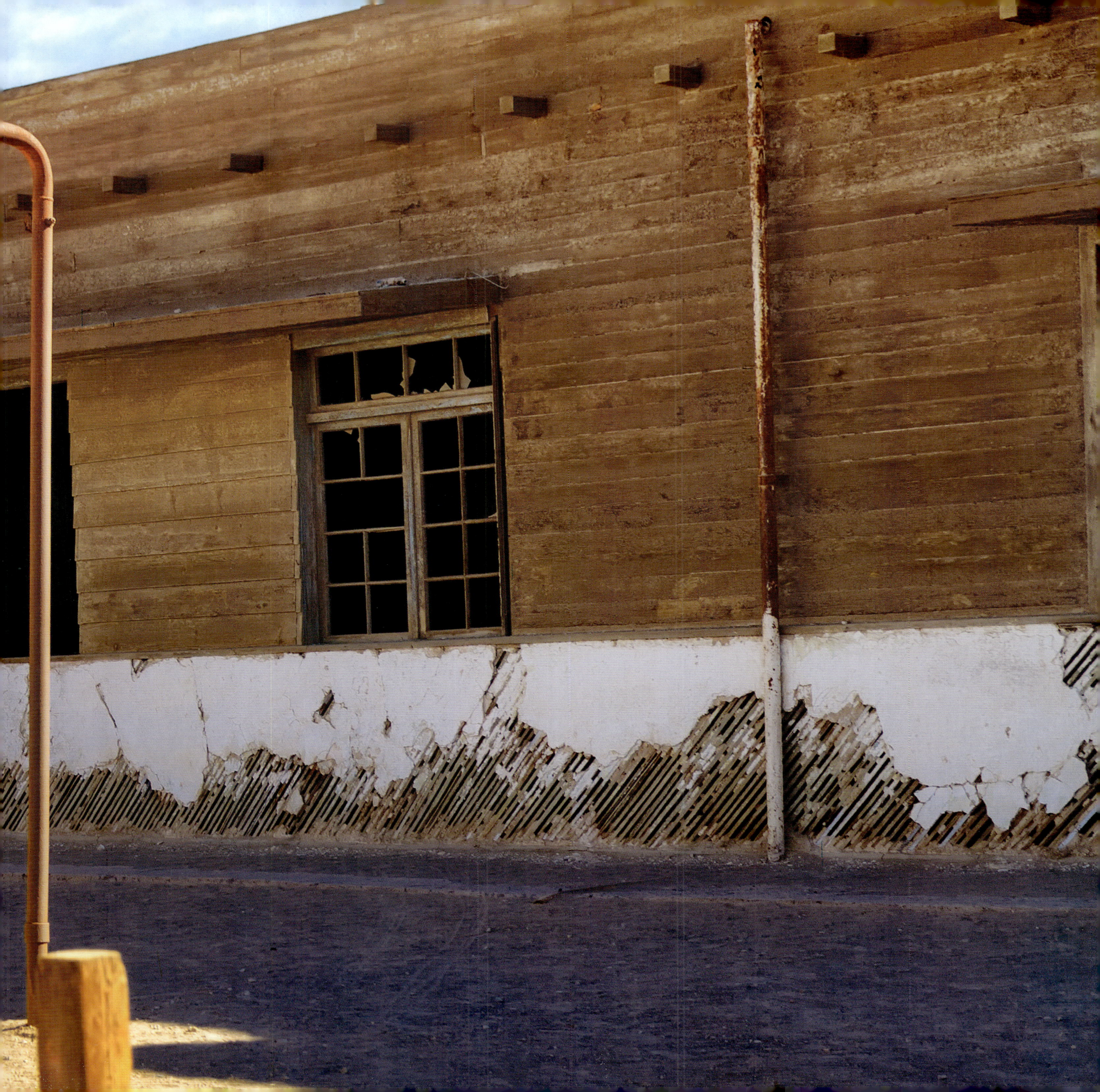

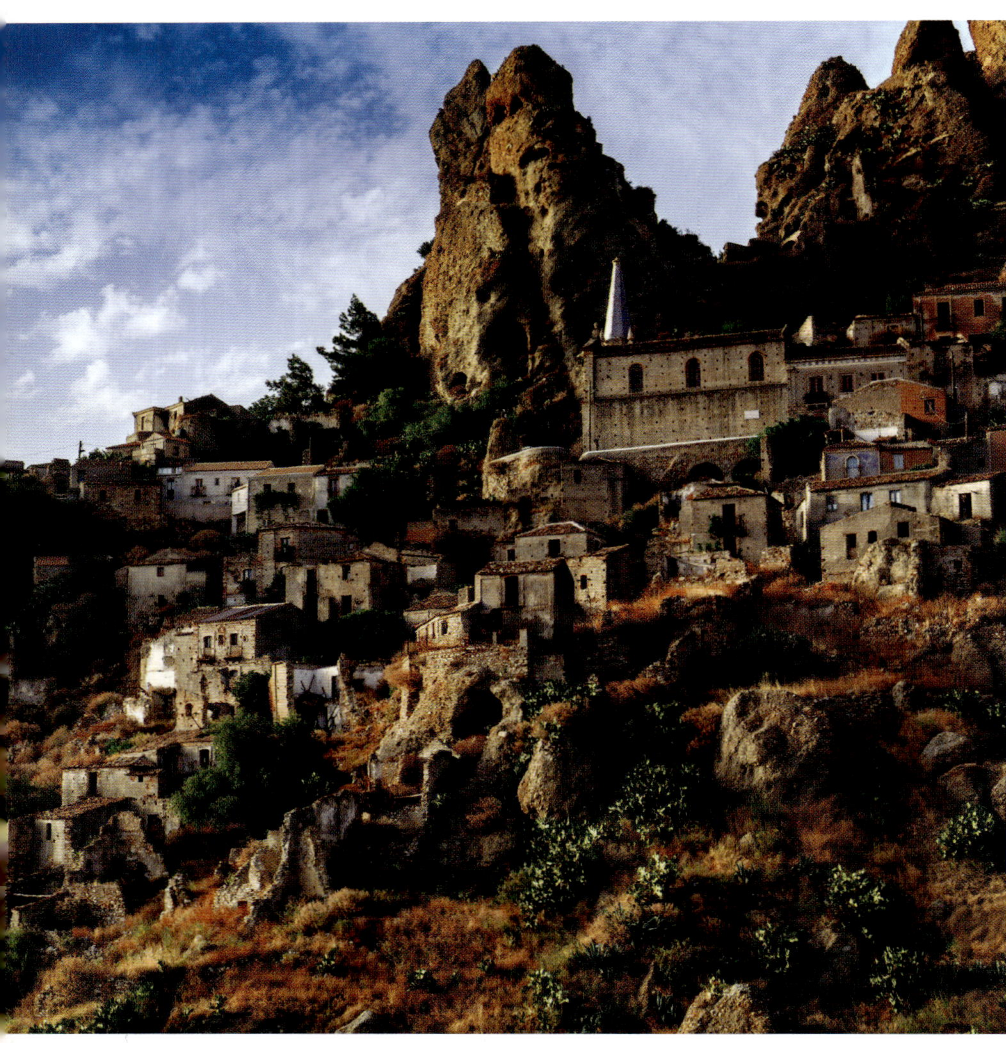

Above: *The abandoned village of Pentedattilo, Italy.*

while the effects of long-term industrial decline in once prosperous, now decaying cities like Gary, Indiana (*see* page 126) or Youngstown, Ohio have seen whole neighbourhoods and once industrious factories simply left to rot. The case of Detroit is especially poignant, as the principal industry of the Motor City of Henry Ford has collapsed over time. With the city's population now little more than a third of its peak figure of more than 1.8 million in 1950, at least 70,000 buildings and more than 30,000 homes lie abandoned in a place that was once an emblem of the American Dream.

Right: *Alley in Civita di Bagnoreggio, Italy.*

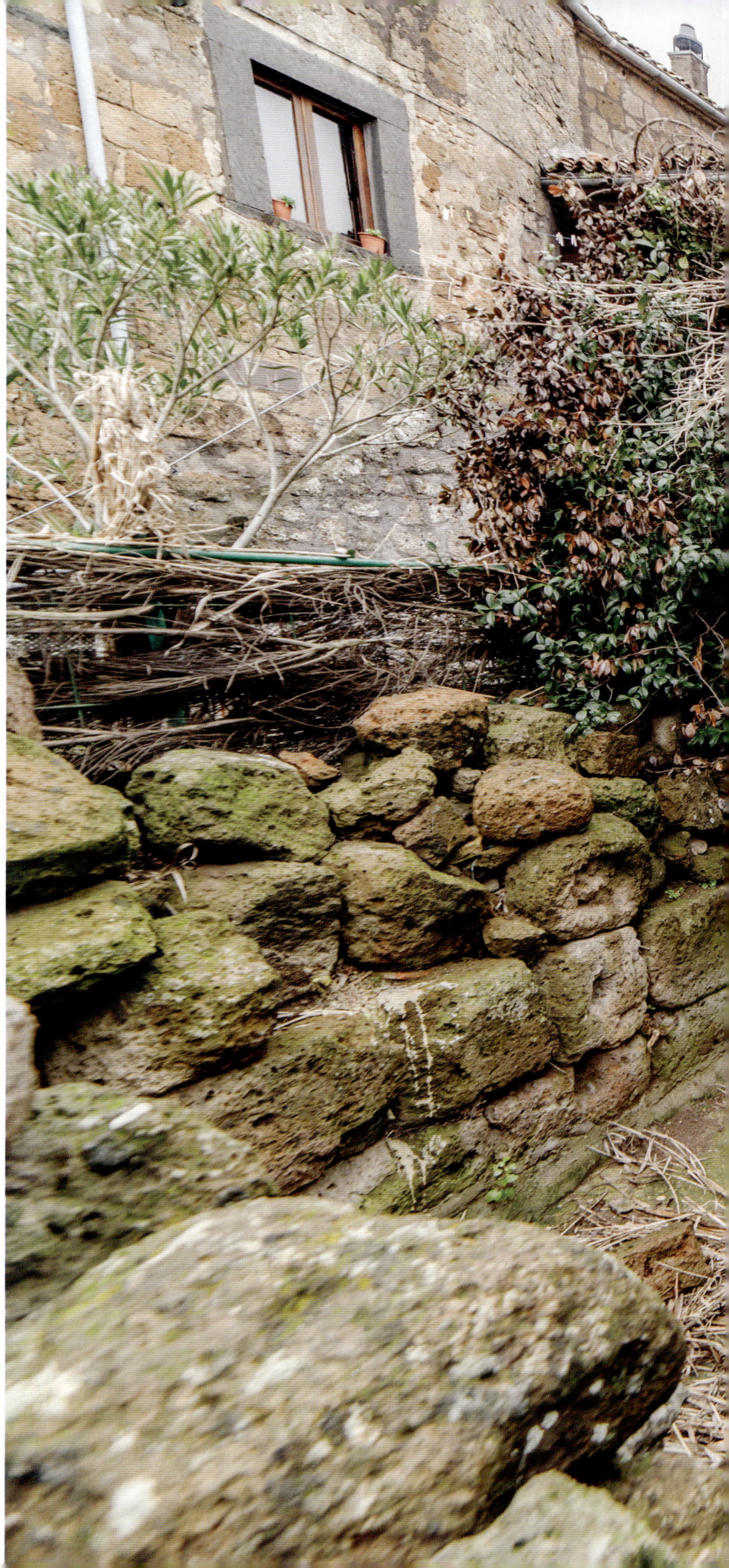

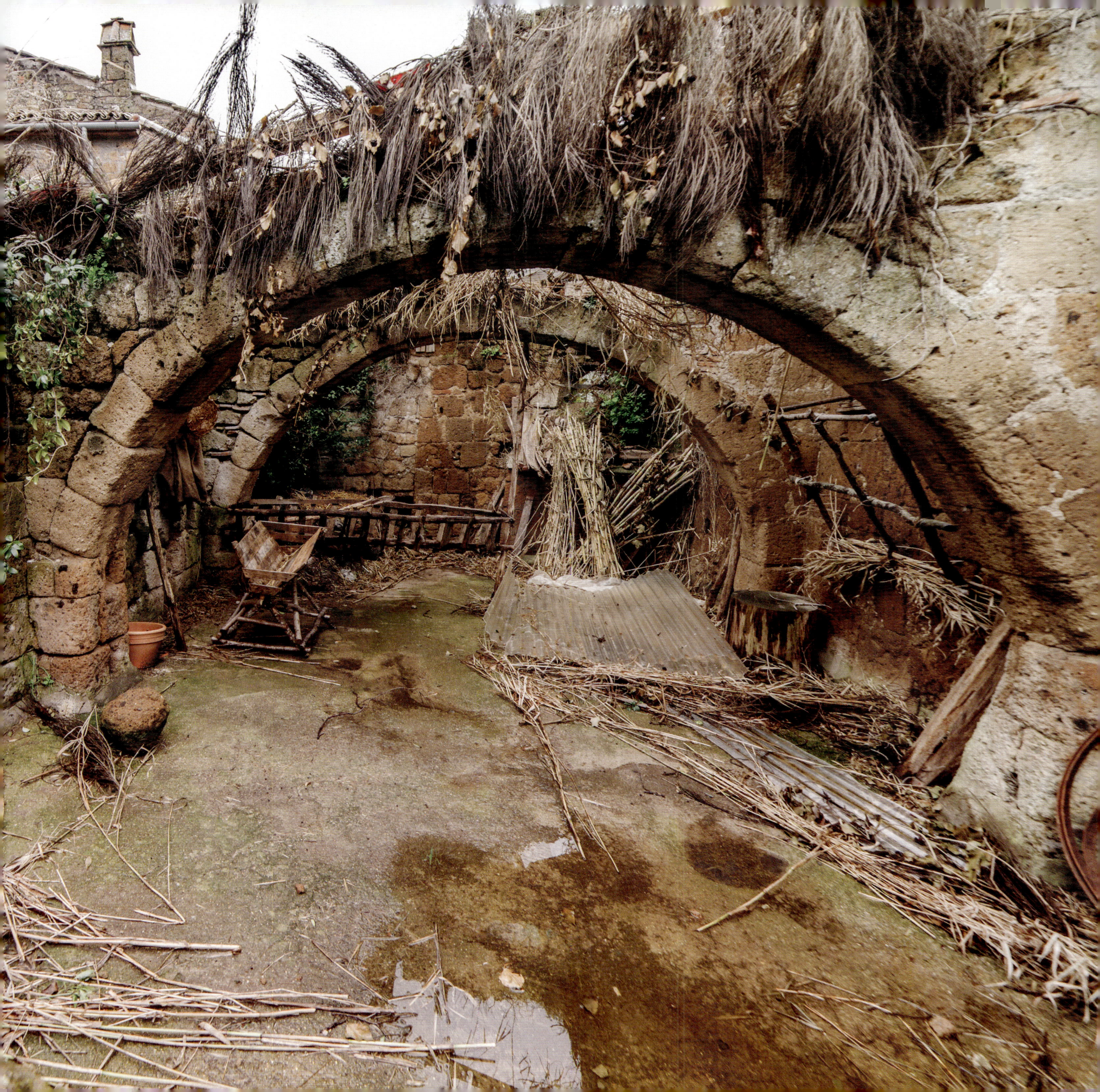

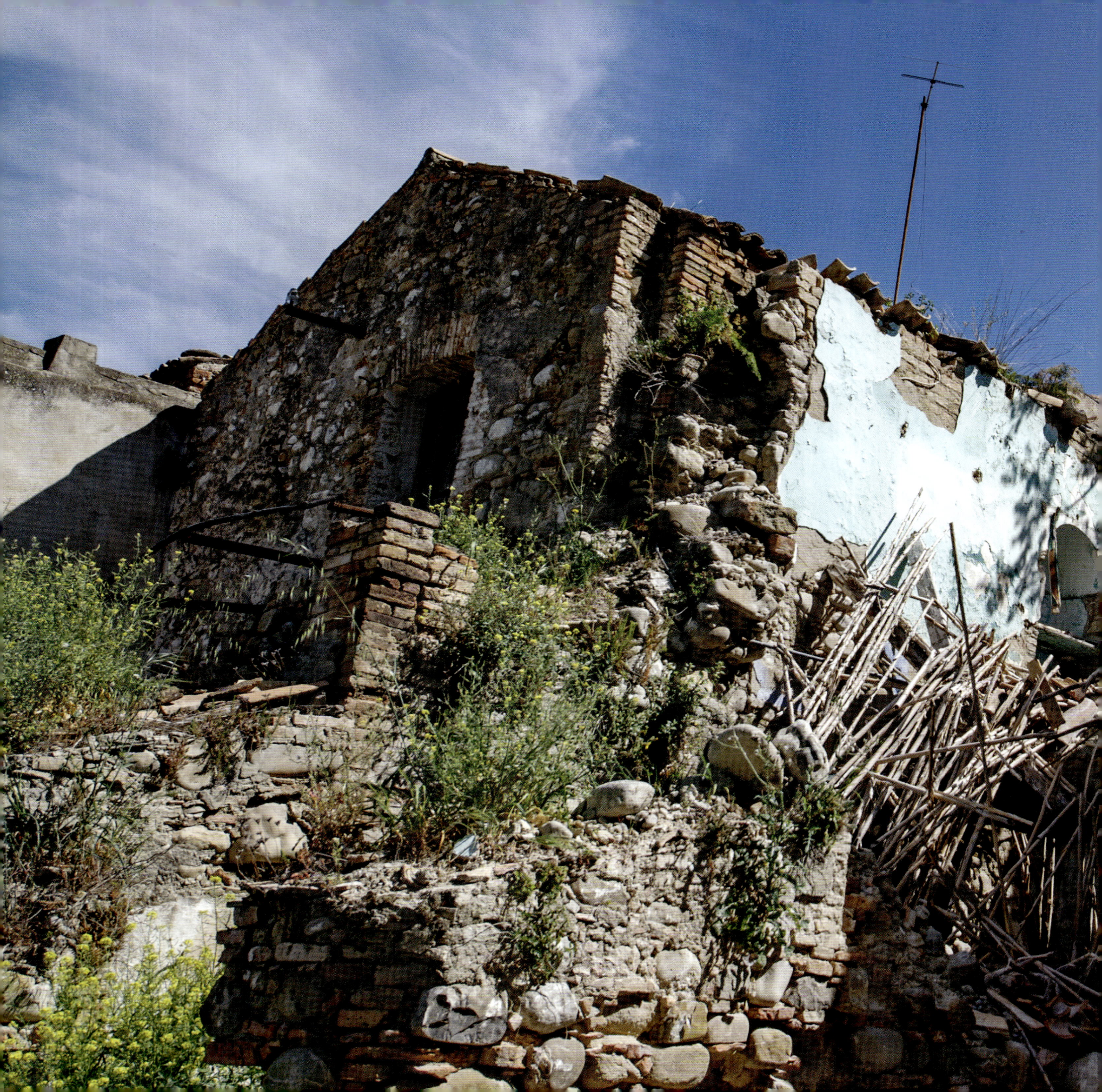

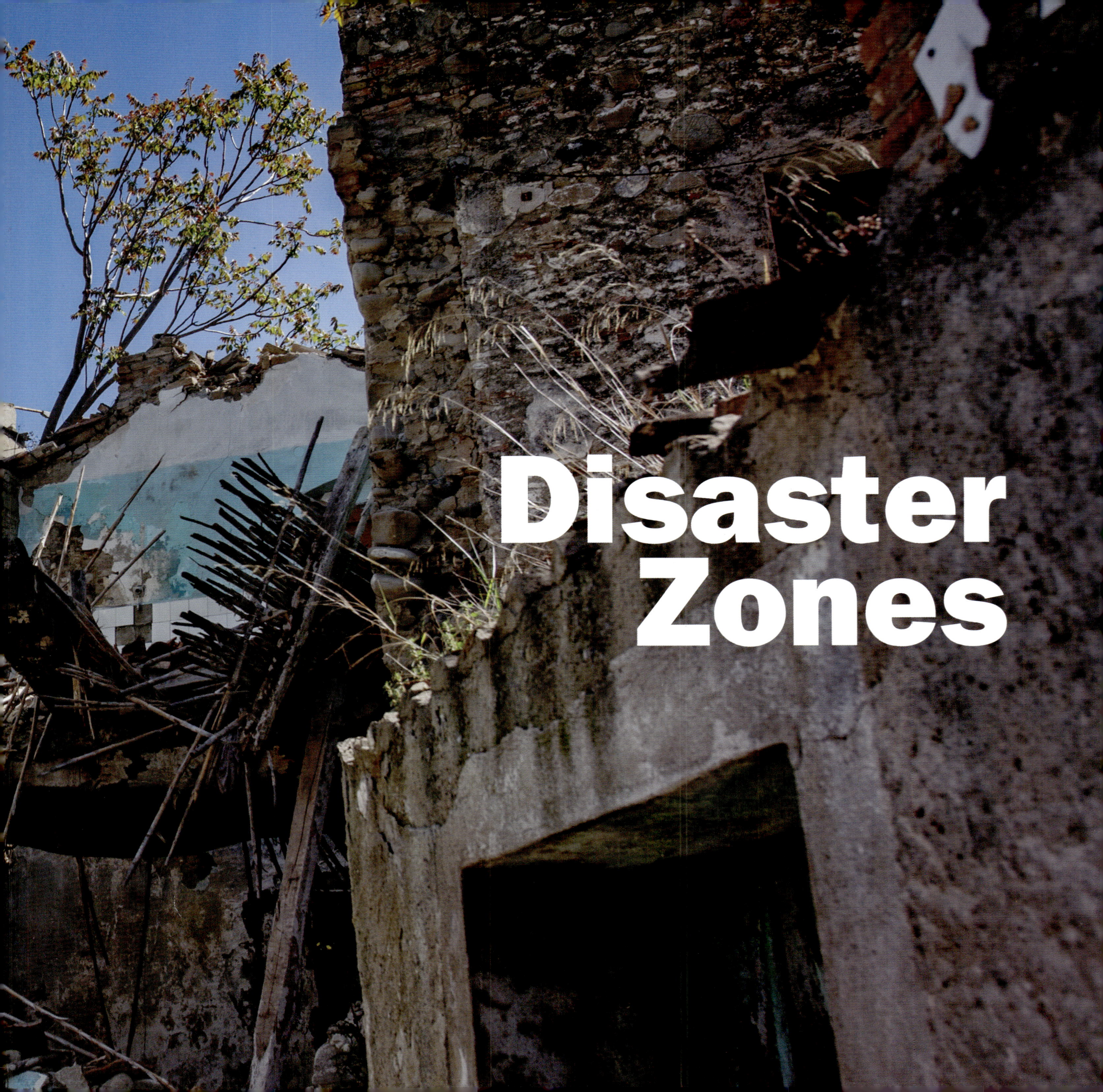

Disaster Zones

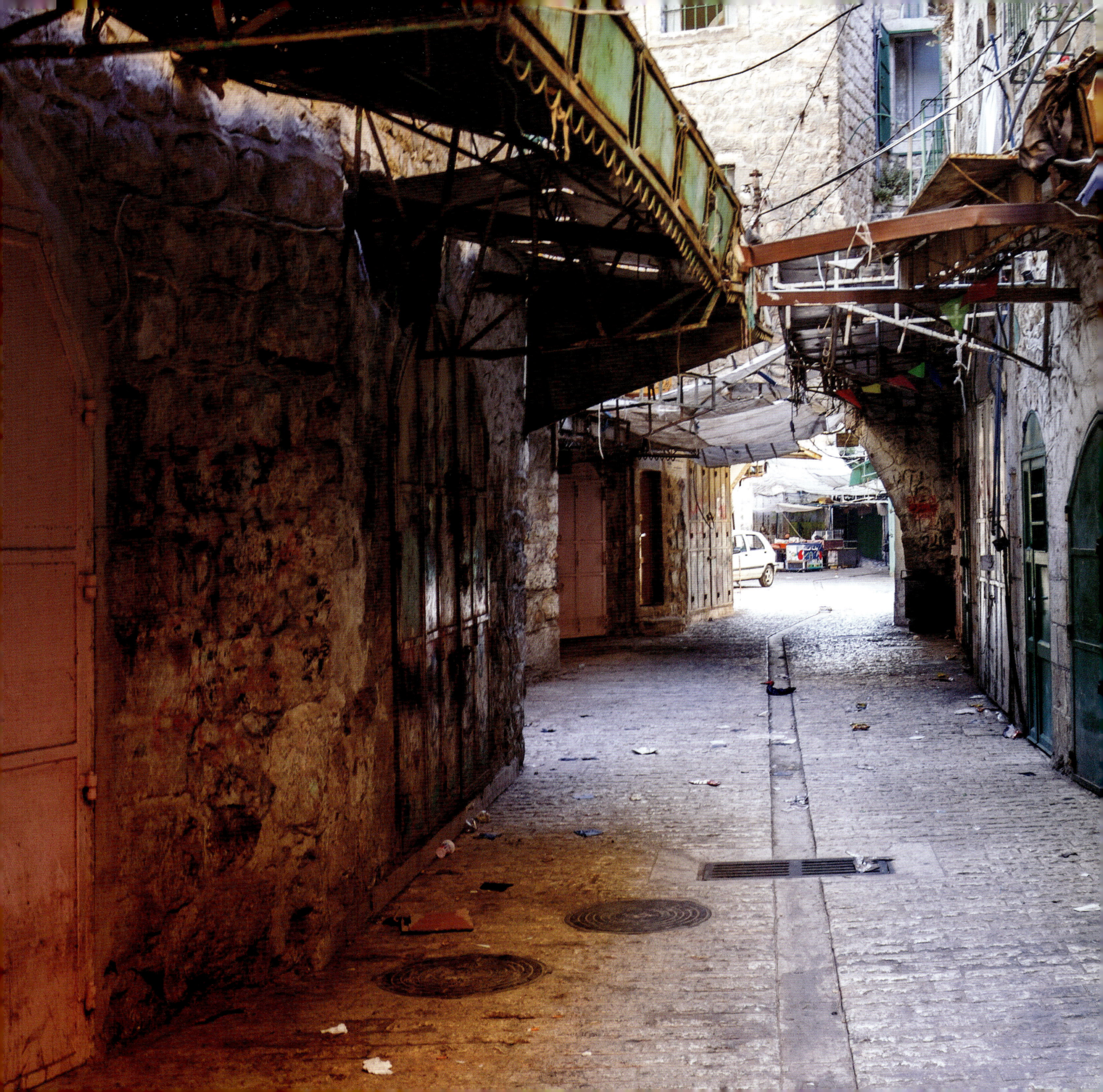

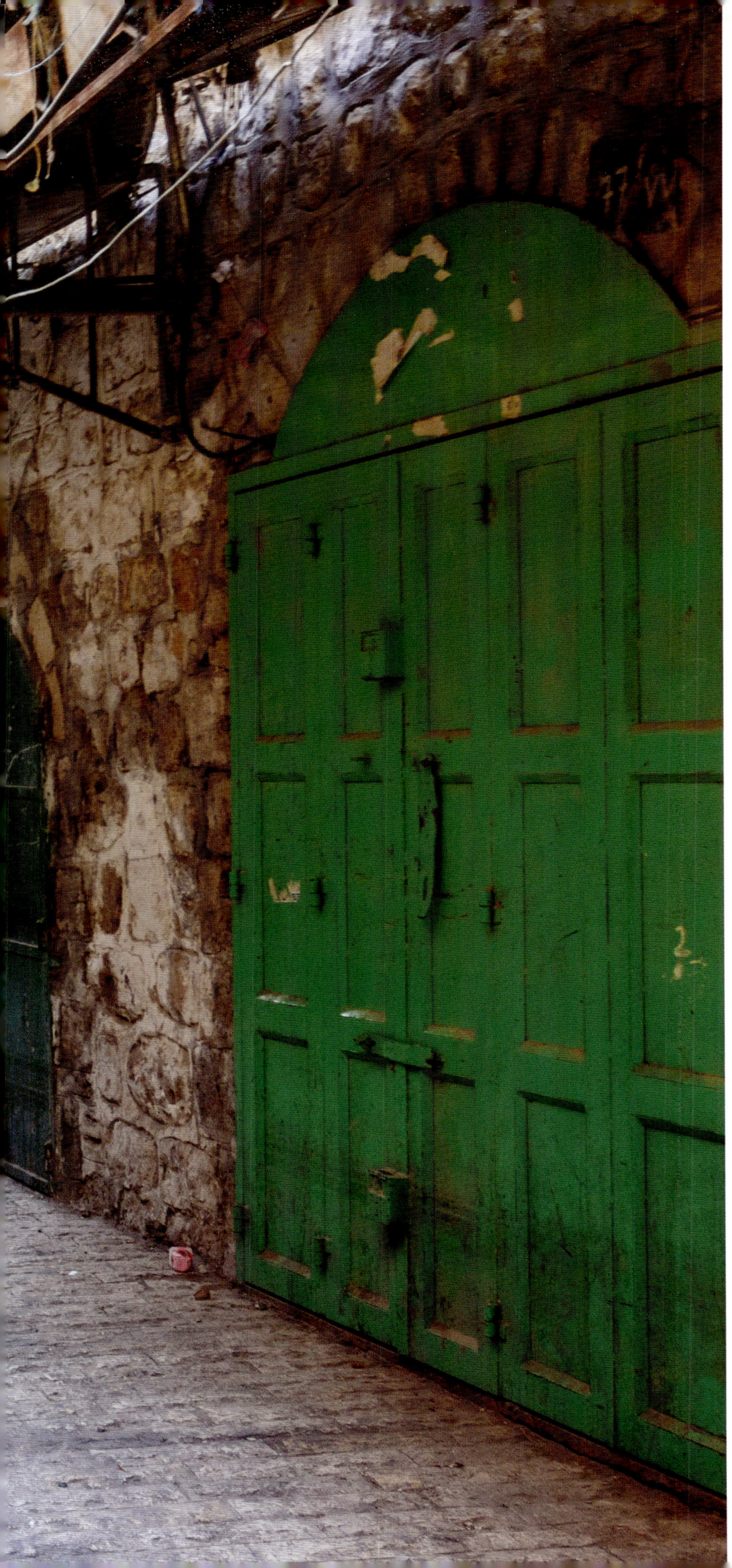

Persistence of Tragedy

If the decline of once thriving towns owes much to human greed and the injustice it fosters, there are forces more powerful and more direct that can tip them very suddenly into ruin. For all our ingenuity as a species, geological forces such as earthquakes or volcanic eruptions, as well as floods, fires and the ravages of war, can still cut us down to size.

And as the numerous tragic events that have happened in the past few decades show, we are as vulnerable to these same catastrophes as were the unsuspecting citizens of ancient Akrotiri or affluent Pompeii or magnificent Persepolis in Achaemenid Persia before disaster struck. Moreover, pollution, contamination and new forms of warfare, not to mention the collateral damage of well-intentioned public works, have added to the reasons that once thriving settlements can be suddenly abandoned or their pecple wiped out.

Previous page: *Abandoned town in old Aliano, Italy.*
Left: *An abandoned street of Hebron's old market, Israel.*
Below: *The ruins of the leper colony closed in the 1950s on Spinalonga island, Crete*

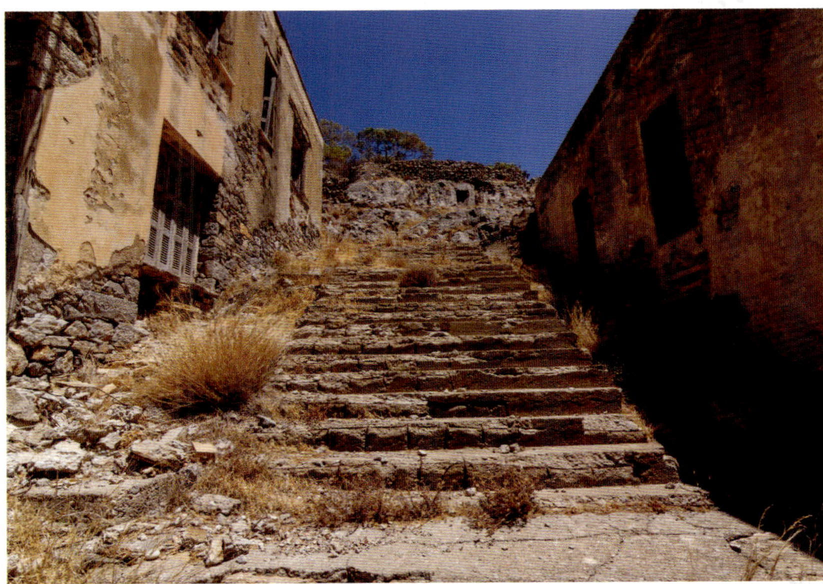

Geological Disasters

Disasters with a geological cause are both horrible and humbling, reminding us of a power that is greater than our own. Earthquakes and volcanoes are existential foes whose many thousands of victims, time and again, have been helped by a divided world, which has come together to assist. But if the ability to rebuild cities and settlements destroyed by such calamities is greater than ever, quite often the destruction is so complete that it is simply better to start again.

The Erasing of Yungay

Yungay in Peru was a thriving city of some 20,000 people when on 31 May 1970, an undersea earthquake off the coast caused an avalanche of glacial debris to collapse on to this interior mountain town. Travelling at speeds of some 200 miles an hour, the monstrous juggernaut of rock, ice and mud overwhelmed Yungay and its citizens in a matter of minutes. Only 92 people had time to make it to ground high enough to escape the torrent, which buried the town along with its dead. A new Yungay later grew up a mile away from the scene of the tragedy and numbers some 10,000 people today; but the site of the old town was declared a national cemetery on which nothing can be built.

The Horror of Armero

A similar apocalypse annihilated the Colombian town of Armero (*see* page 138) in 1985 when a sudden eruption of the Nevado del Ruiz volcano sent pyroclastic flows gushing from the crater, melting the glaciers

Right: *Houses destroyed after a volcanic eruption in Chaitén, Chile.*

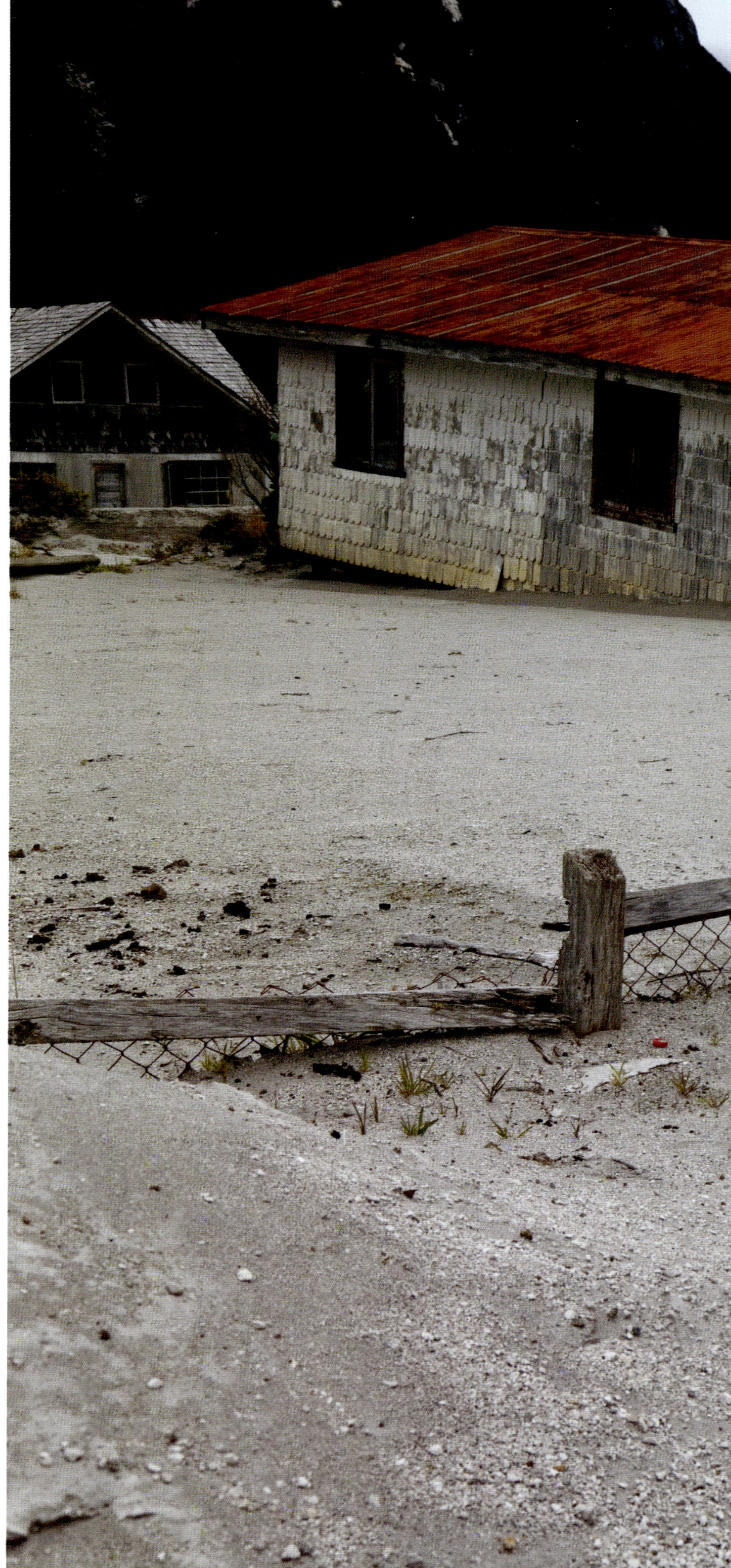

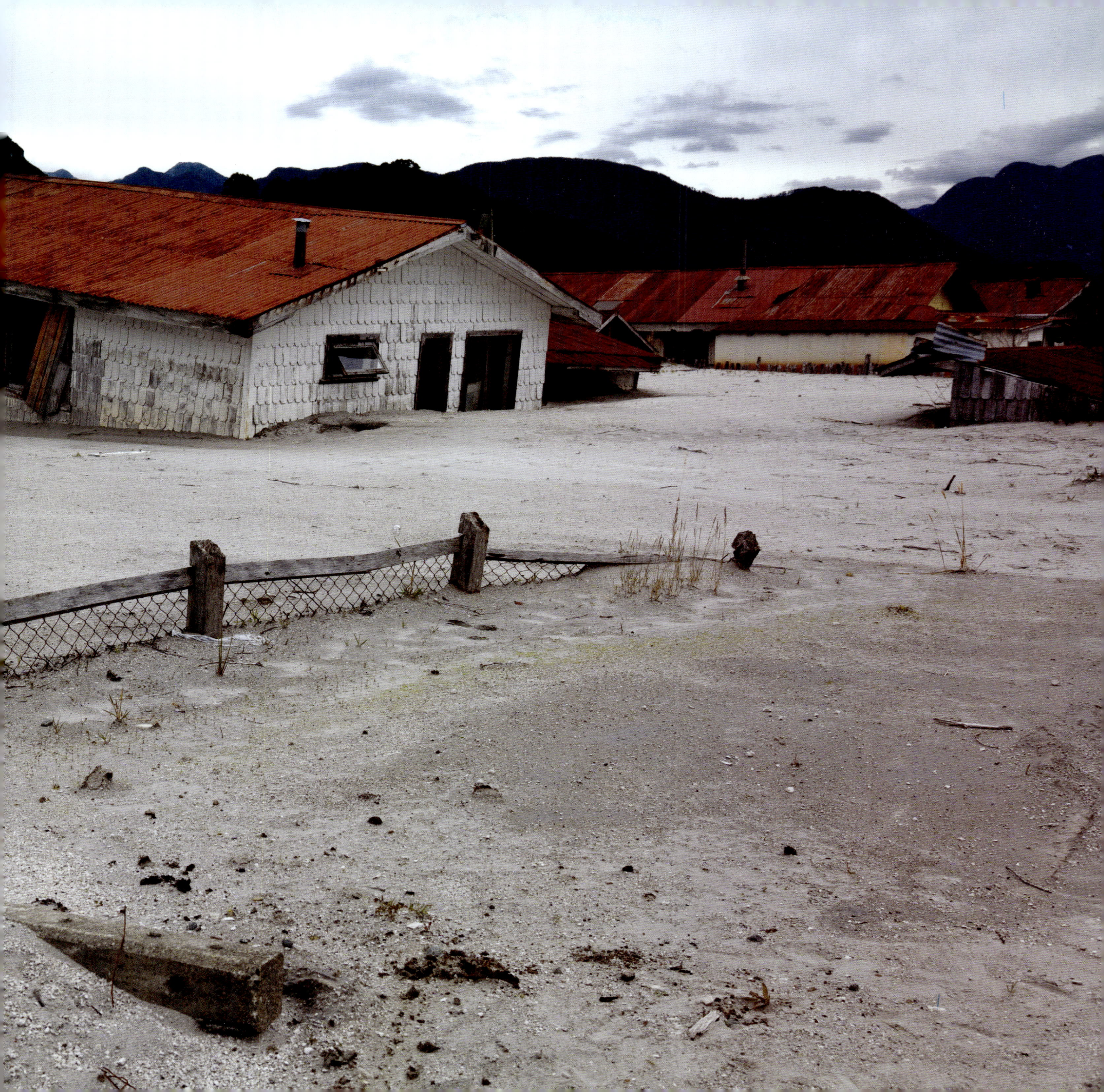

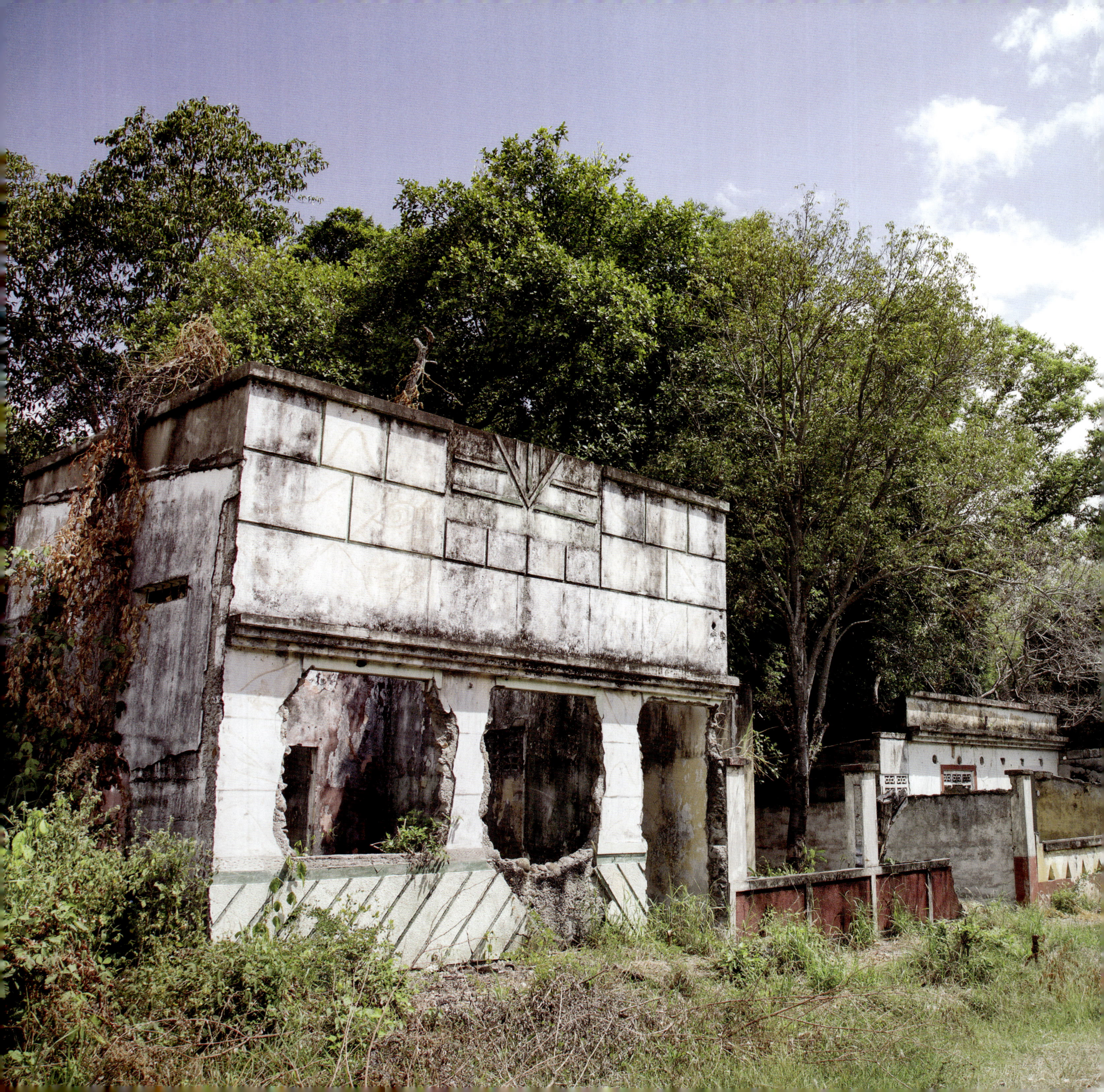

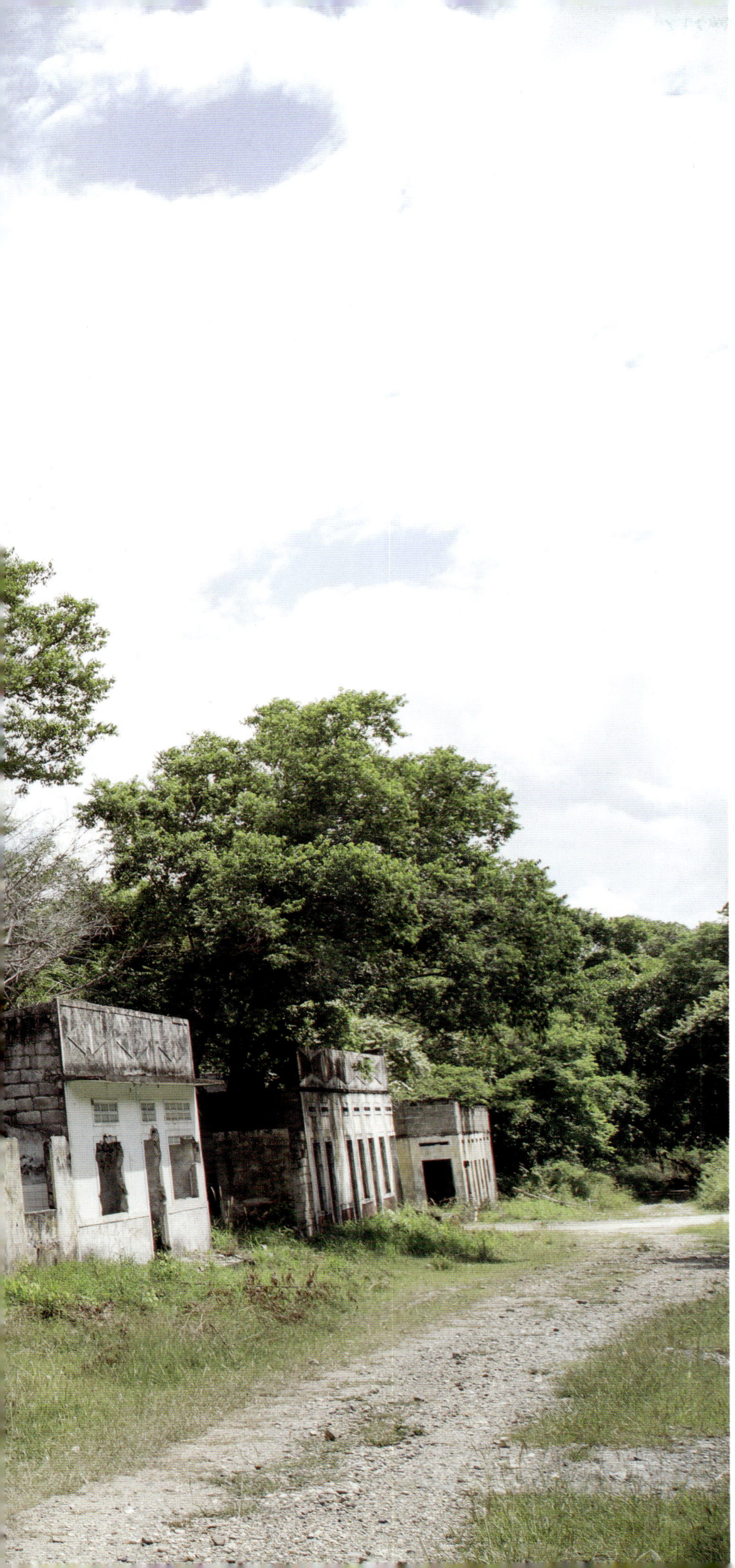

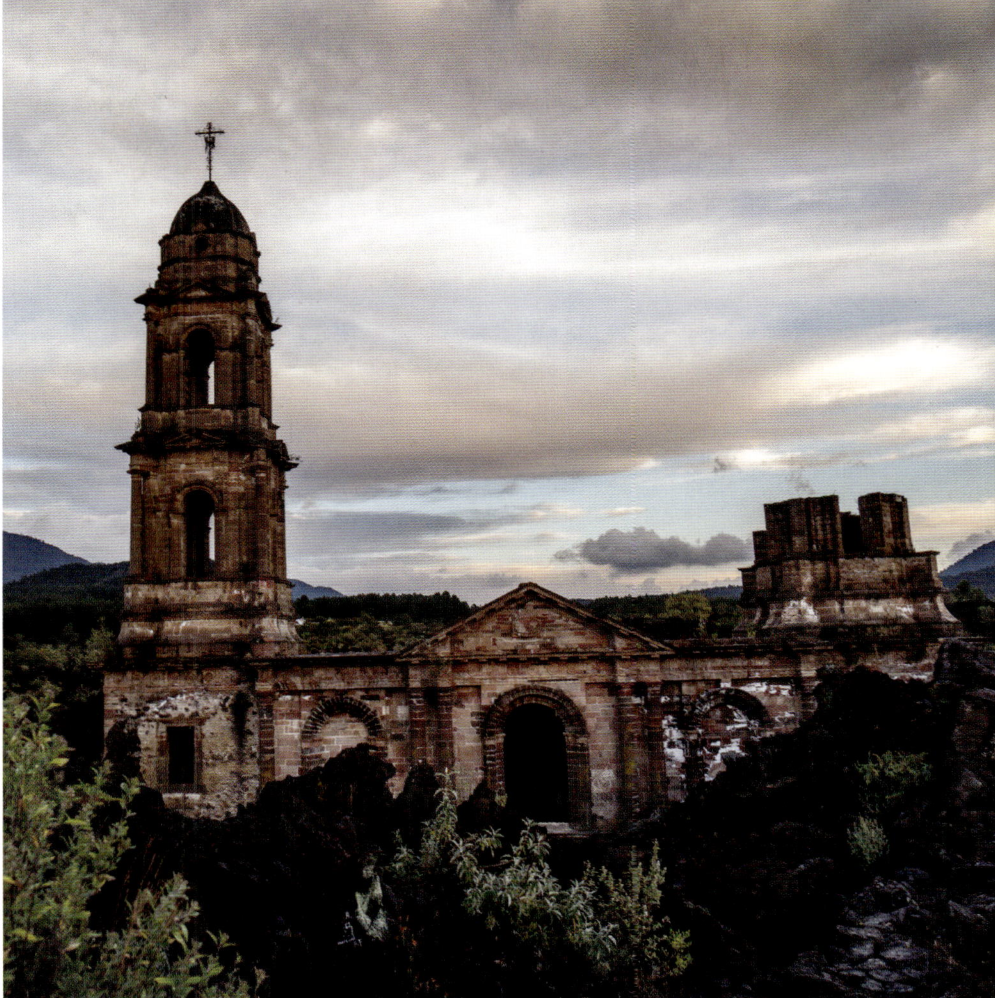

Above: *Church ruins of the original San Juan Parangaricutiro, Mexico.*

and sending four huge landslides mixed with mud and debris cascading down the mountain to the settlements around its base. When ash starting raining on Armero, the town worst affected, its 28,000 residents were counselled that, after all, it was perfectly safe to stay in their homes. It was bad advice, and the deadly flows gathered pace and volume as they descended on Armero. When the liquid wall of rock, pumice, ice and mud reached the town that night, there was no warning and little chance of escape. Nearly every building was engulfed by the flow, and some 23,000 people lost their lives. Those who survived moved to other towns, leaving only scattered ruins amid a river of mud.

Left: *Ruins in Armero, Colombia, resulting from the eruption of the volcano Nevado del Ruiz in 1985.*

The Museum City of Beichuan

In a comparable trauma with a still greater loss of life, on 12 May 2008, a massive earthquake struck the province of Sichuan in central China. Almost 70,000 people lost their lives in the worst earthquake the country had suffered in more than 30 years, and many cities in the region were badly damaged. Worst affected by far was Beichuan (*see* right), a town of 20,000 people where a huge number died, including more than 1,000 children who perished when school buildings collapsed as the earthquake struck. What was left of the town was thought too tragic to see, and too unsafe, but such was the need to make sense of the disaster that the following year, 100,000 people came to Beichuan to pay their respects. The Chinese government stabilized the ruins that could be saved and set aside this modern ghost town as an open-air museum and memorial park to a terrible tragedy that shocked the world.

The Misery of Port-au-Prince

As the poorest country in the Western Hemisphere, Haiti already faced massive challenges when, on 12 January 2010, a magnitude 7.3 earthquake struck the Caribbean island of Hispaniola, of which Haiti is the western part, close to the capital city, Port-au-Prince. A staggering 316,000 people, some three per cent of the country's population, died as a direct result – more than the total number killed across 18 countries in the Asian Tsunami of 2004. Some 300,000 homes and other buildings were damaged or destroyed, leaving 1.5 million people homeless, while piles of bodies lying in the streets had to be buried in mass graves. To compound the trauma, an outbreak of cholera in the squalid conditions that followed the disaster claimed thousands more lives. And in 2016, further destruction caused by Hurricane Matthew heaped yet more misery on Haiti; seven years after the quake some 50,000 people are still in temporary accommodation and many buildings remain in ruins.

Right: *Apartment block destroyed after an earthquake at Beichuan, China.*

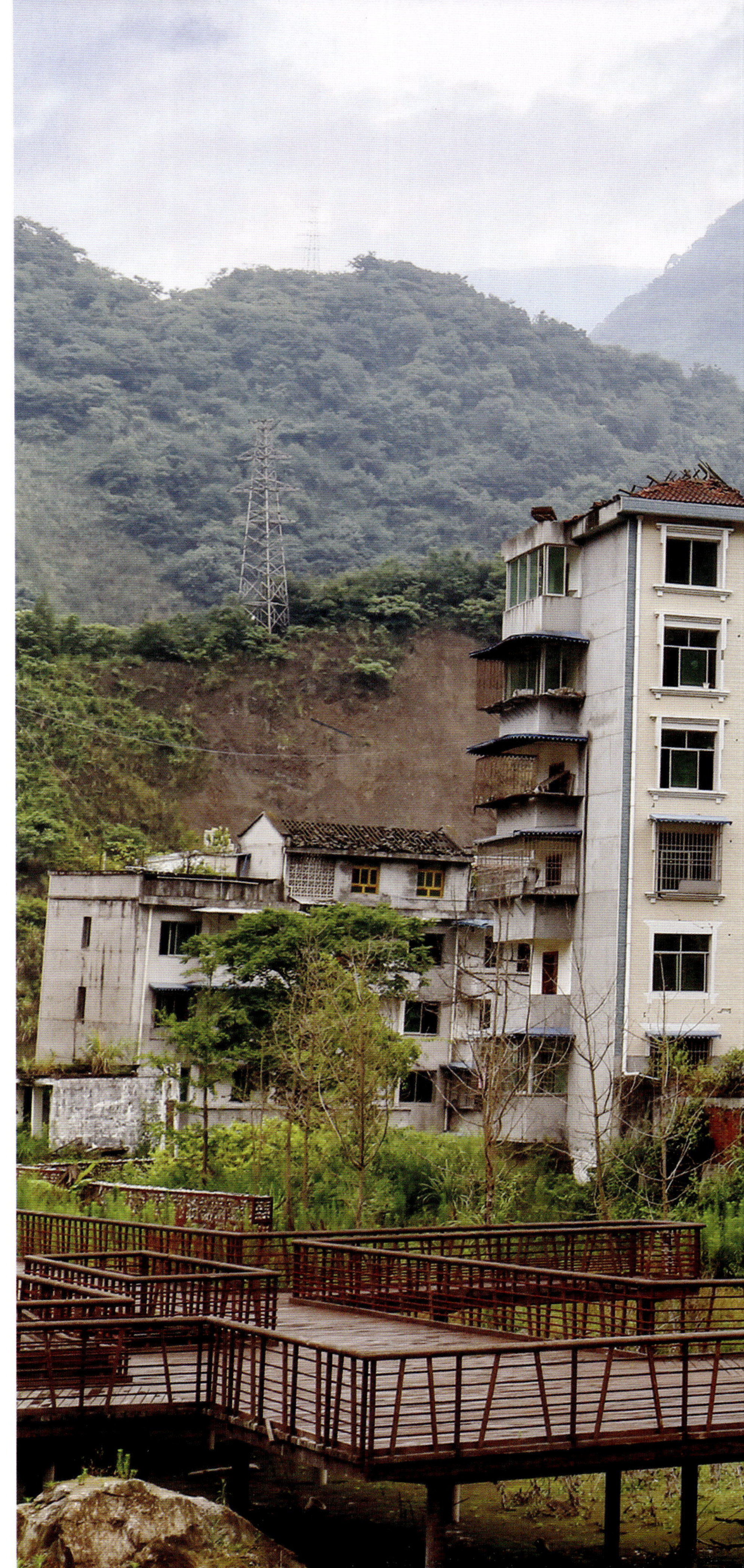

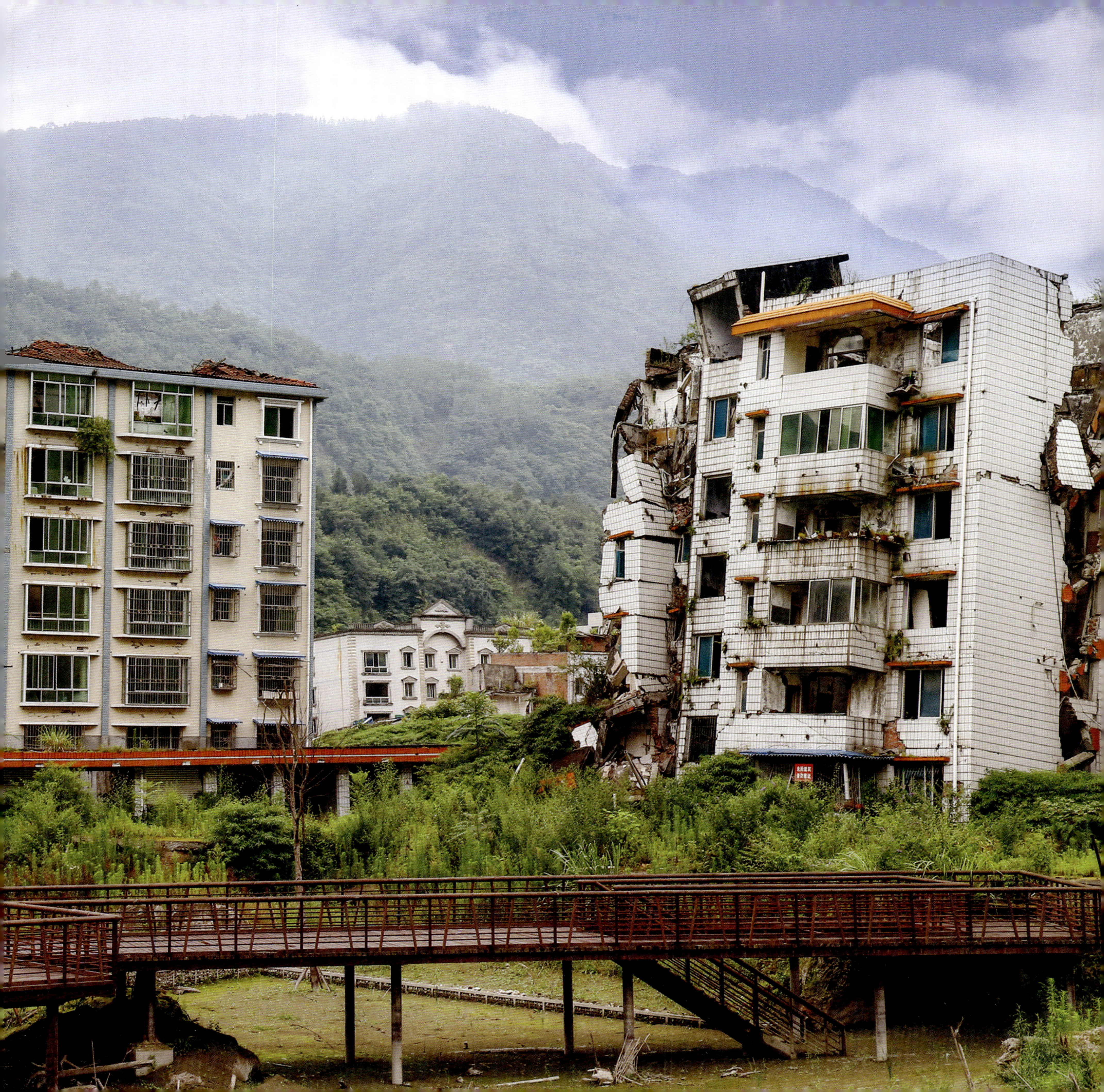

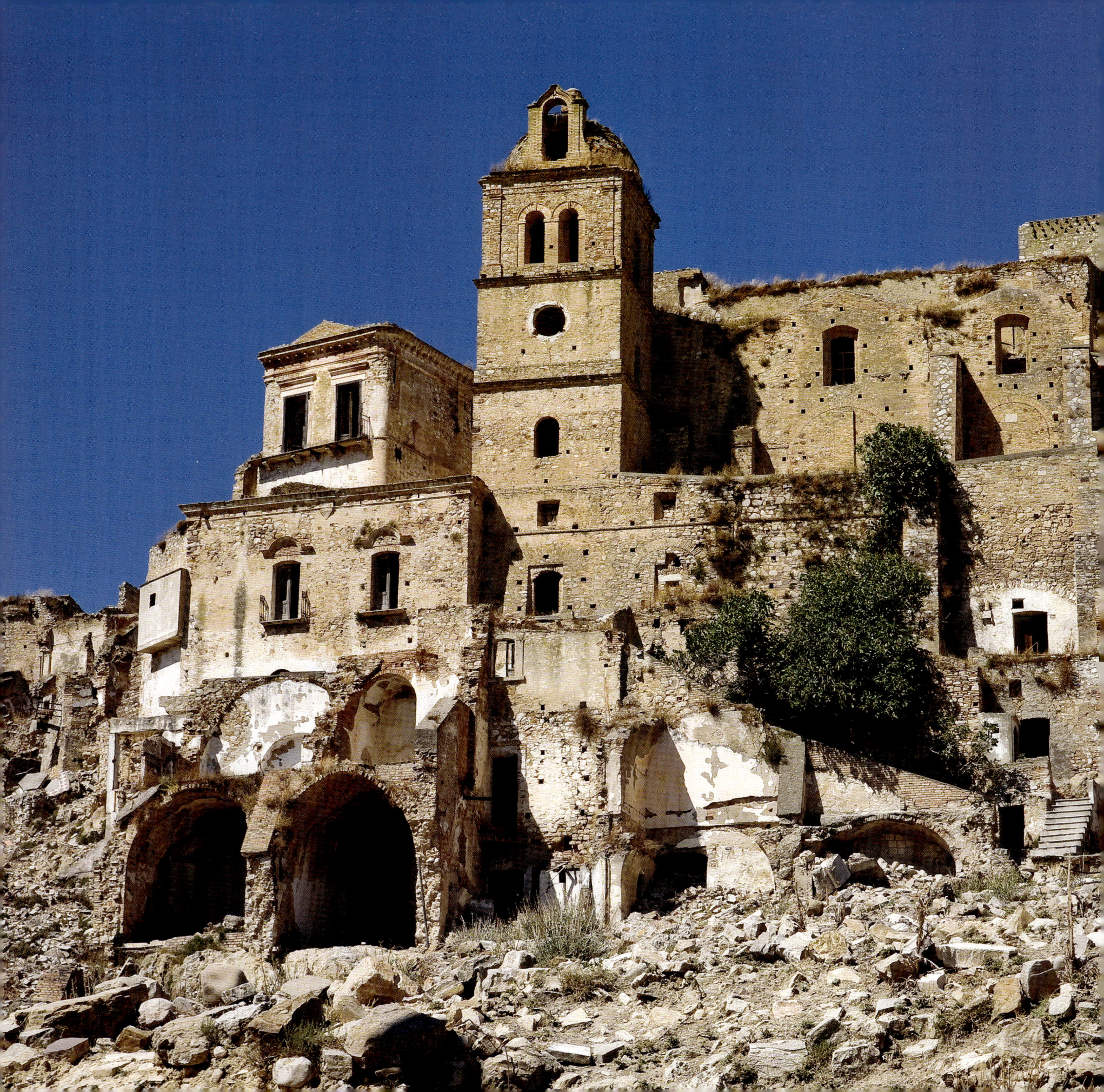

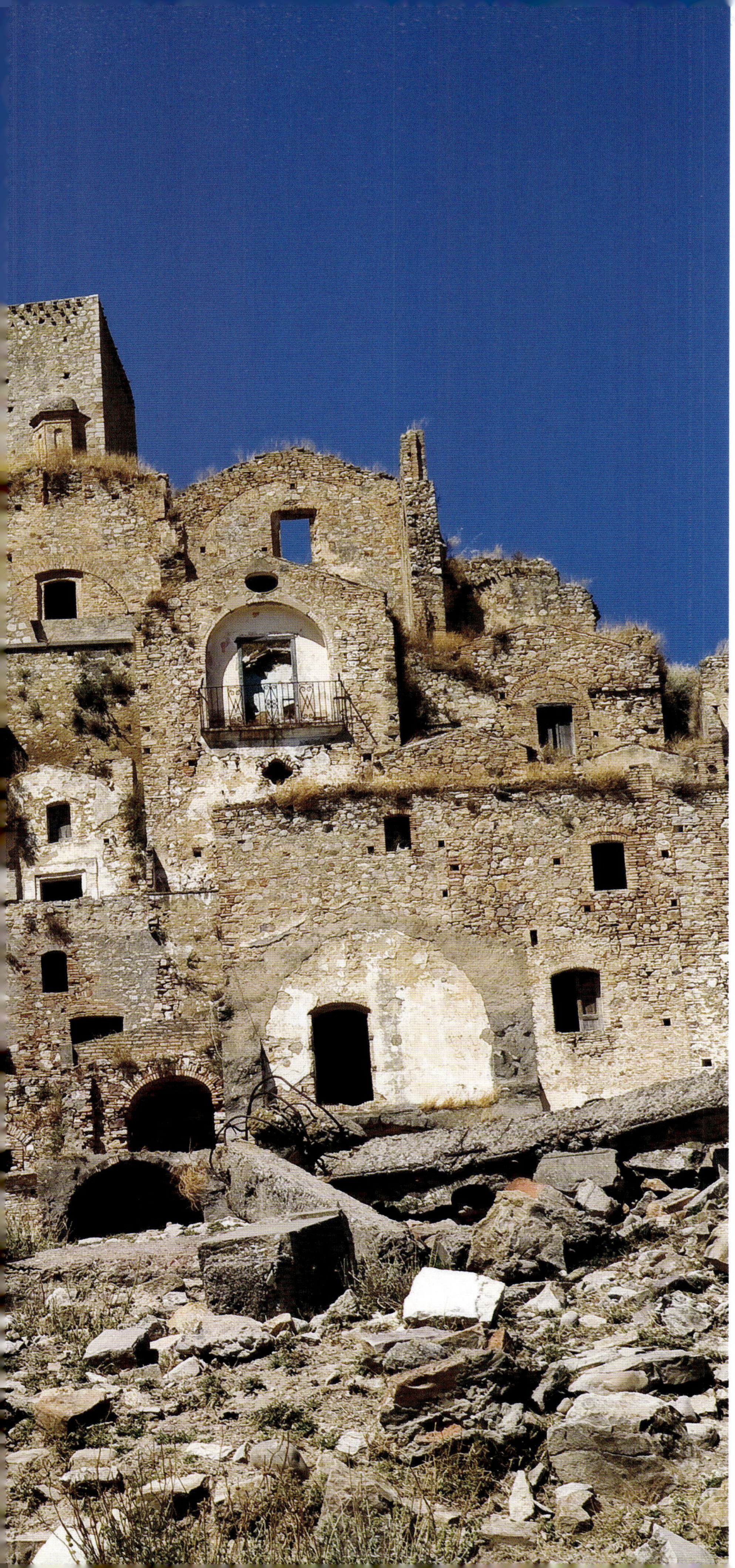

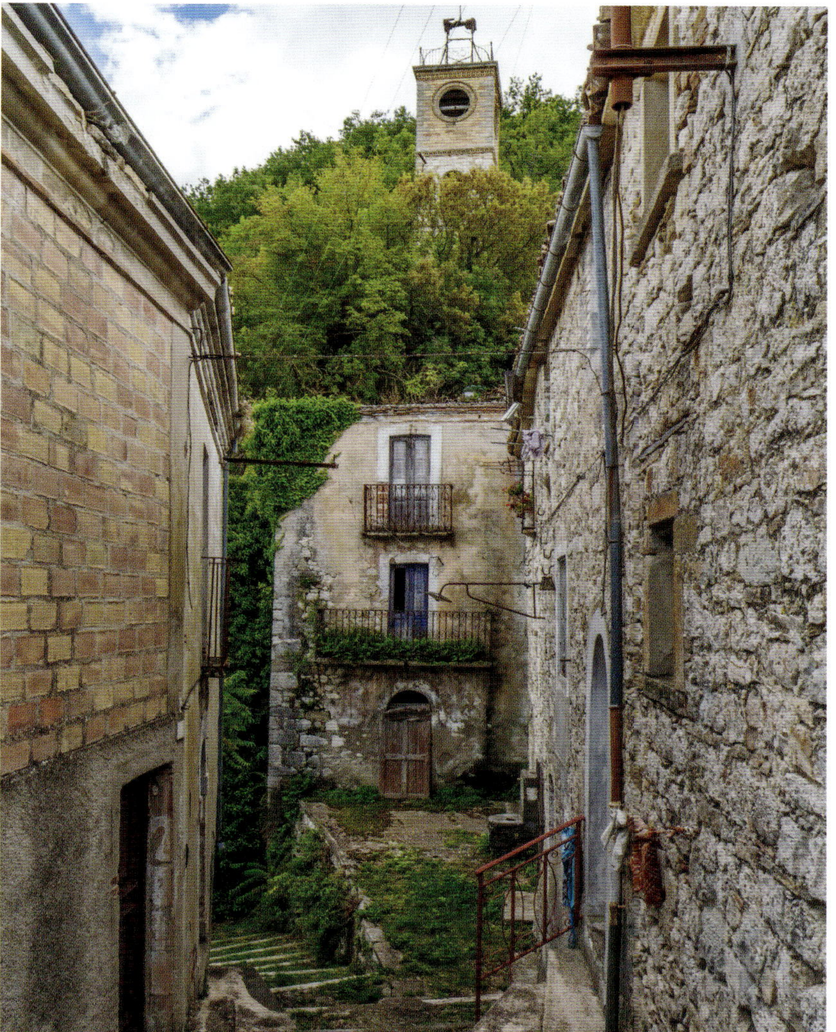

Above: *Buonanotte, a village in Abruzzo, Italy, was abandoned after a landslide destroyed many of the buildings. It is one of many Italian mountain villages to have suffered a similar fate.*
Left: *View of Craco, Italy.*

The Abandonment of Craco

Italy's medieval towns and villages were often built on the ridges of mountains, which made them easy to defend but also structurally vulnerable to the earthquakes to which Italy is more prone than any other European country. The mountain villages of Tocco Caudio and Romagnano al Monte were so badly damaged in the Irpinia earthquake in 1980 that residents were moved to newly built communities on sites nearby, leaving behind them ghost villages sufficiently intact for tourists to explore.

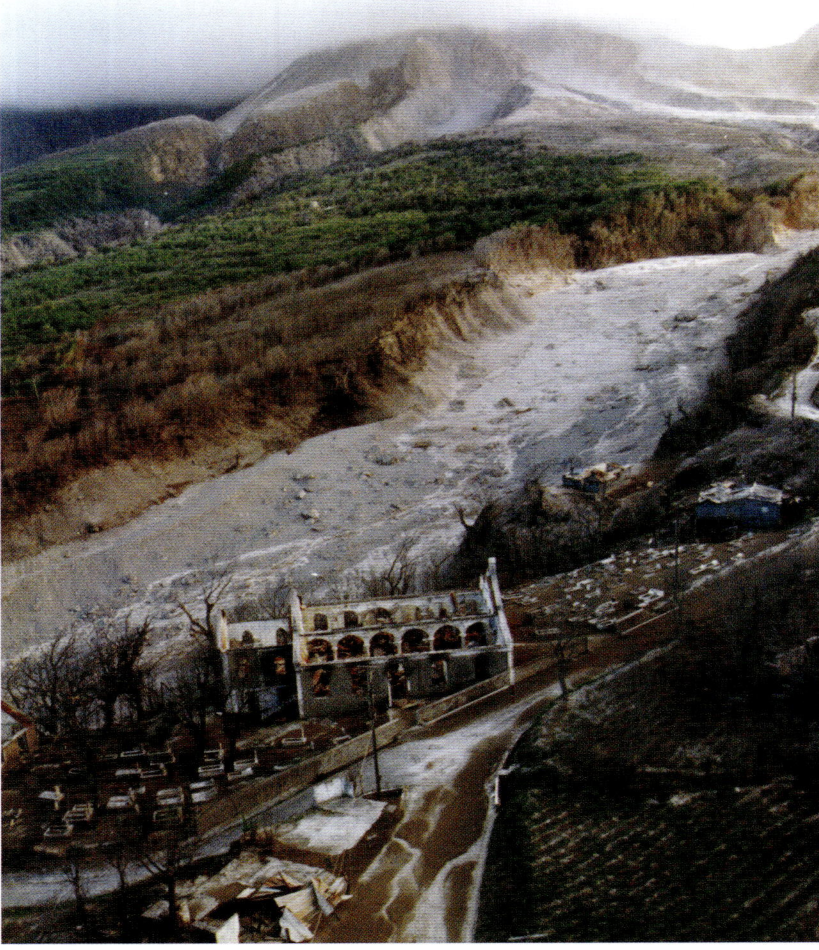

Above: *The eruption of the dormant Soufrière Hills volcano on the Caribbean island of Montserrat in 1995 was completely unexpected and buried the capital city, Plymouth, under 12 metres of mud.*

The beautiful town of Craco (*see* page 142), located on the top of a mountain on the instep of Italy's boot, is perhaps the most striking example, with a thousand-year history that was broken off more than half a century ago. The challenges had been many, including a steady migration from Italy to America in the early twentieth century, which saw some 1,300 people leave from Craco. Then in 1963, a landslide made life there untenable, leading to mass evacuation to the valley below. For those residents who hoped to return one day, the idea was ruled out once and for all when the Irpinia earthquake further weakened the already vulnerable buildings of this ruined hilltop town.

Right: *The village of Poggioreale, along with those of Gibellina and Salaparuta, was rendered uninhabitable by an earthquake that hit the Belice Valley of western Sicily in 1968.*

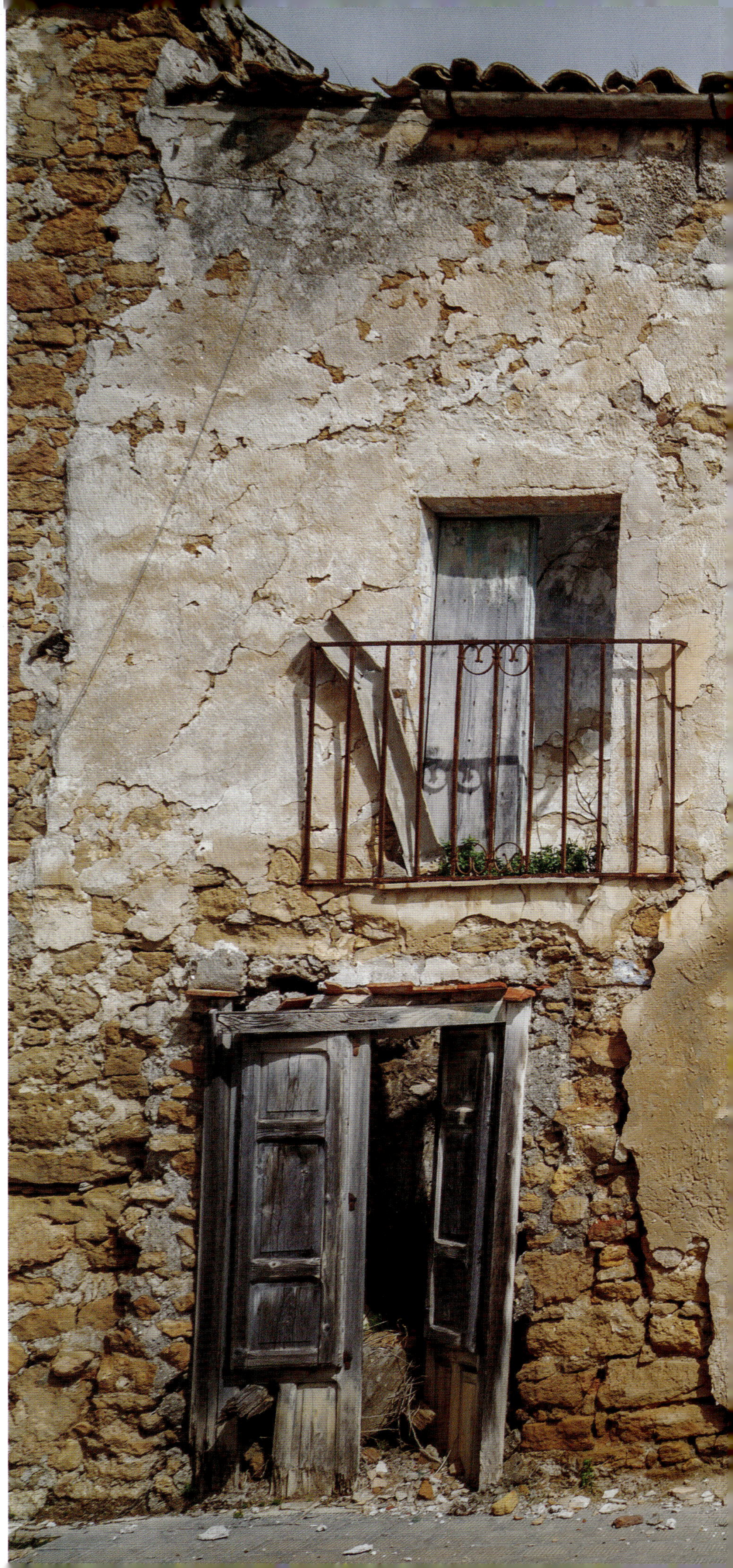

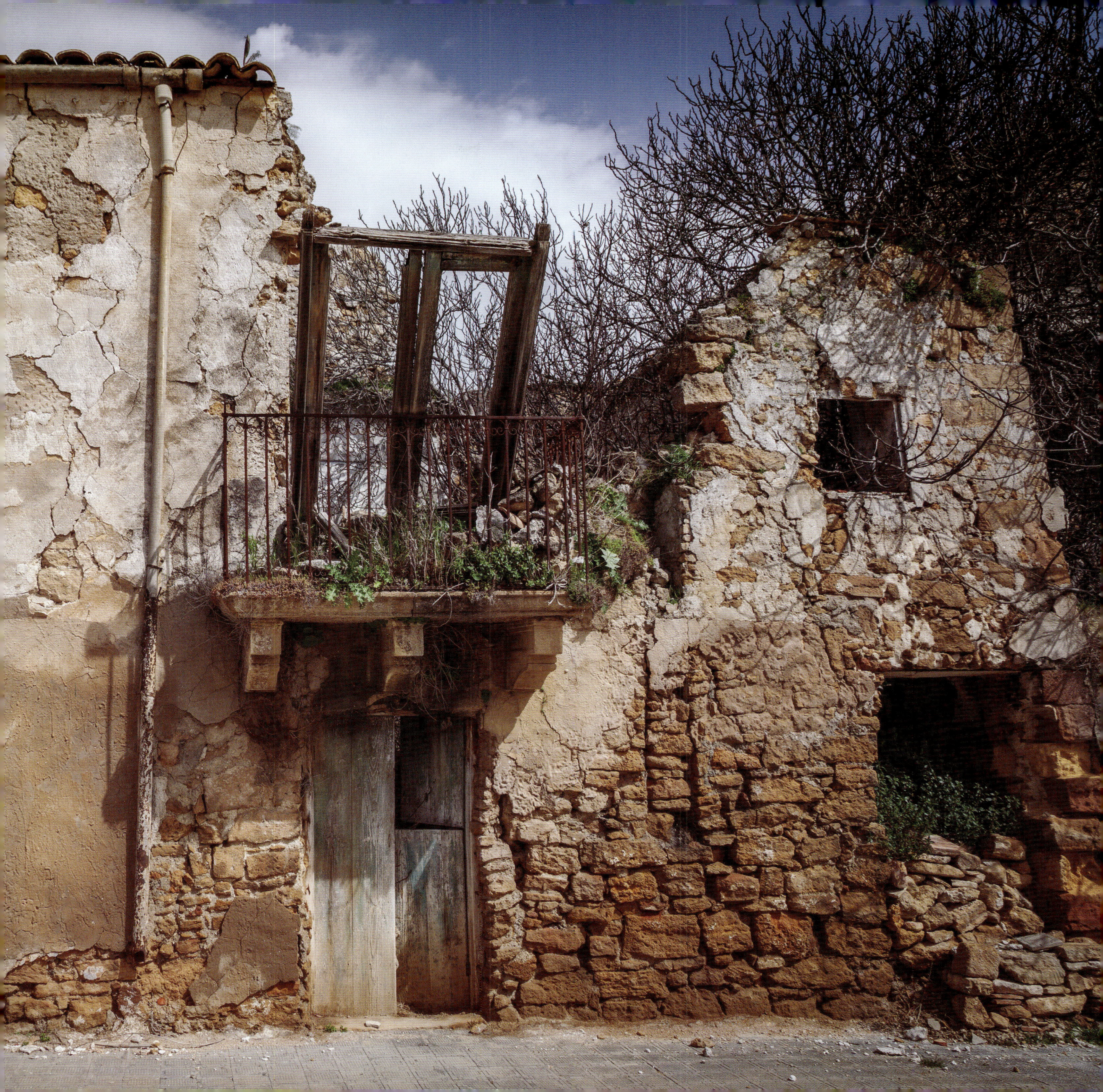

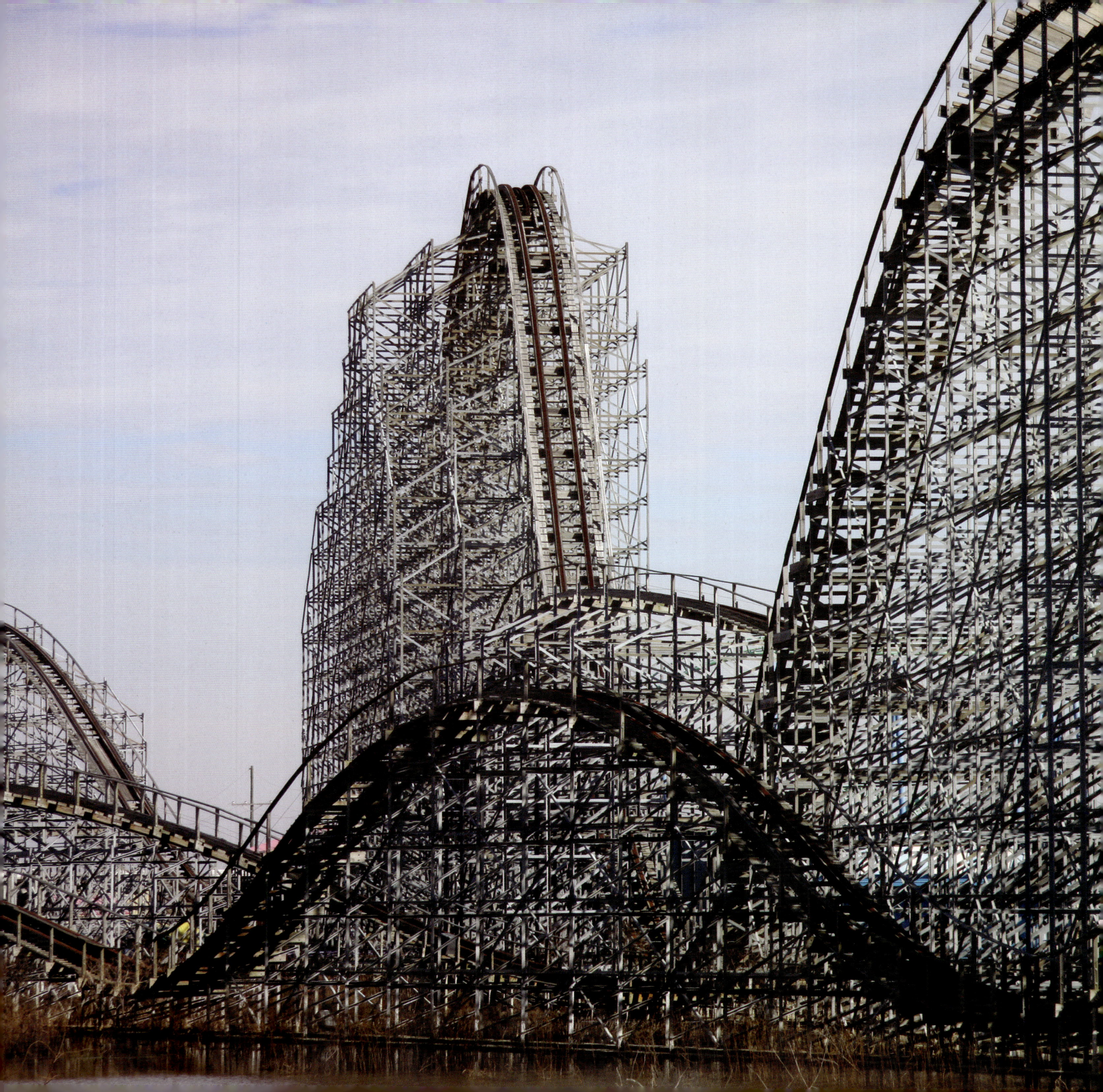

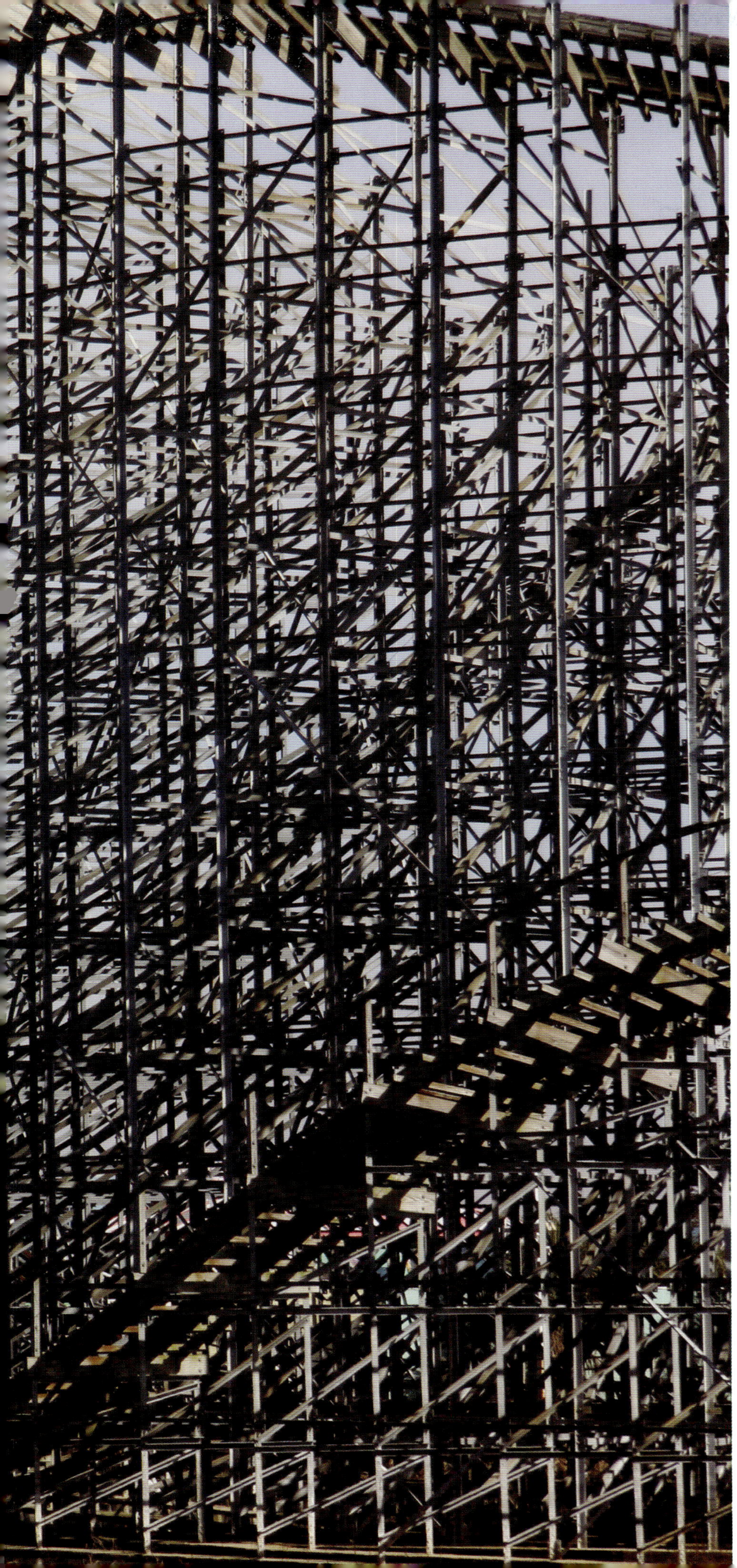

Wind & Water

People who live in dangerous places tend to be pragmatic about the risks. Caribbean communities battered by hurricanes every year are well drilled in battening down hatches and bouncing back, though even then, nature can make a mockery of the most determined plan.

A Hurricane Named Katrina

In 2005, Hurricane Katrina broke through the levees of New Orleans, which for centuries had succeeded in keeping out the sea, bringing with it the biblical inundation the city had always feared (*see* left and below). Poor wards such as the Lower Ninth, which was flooded by Hurricane Betsy back in 1965, were submerged in some cases up to roof level, and today are still unrenovated districts, full of empty houses to which evacuated residents have yet to return. But while there is still hope for the Lower Ninth, in some cases there is simply nothing left to restore.

Left: *A rollercoaster in New Orleans, USA, stands surrounded by water five years after Hurricane Katrina.*
Below: *A boat still sits parked in front of a New Orleans home a year after the floods of Hurricane Katrina washed it there from a marina over a mile away.*

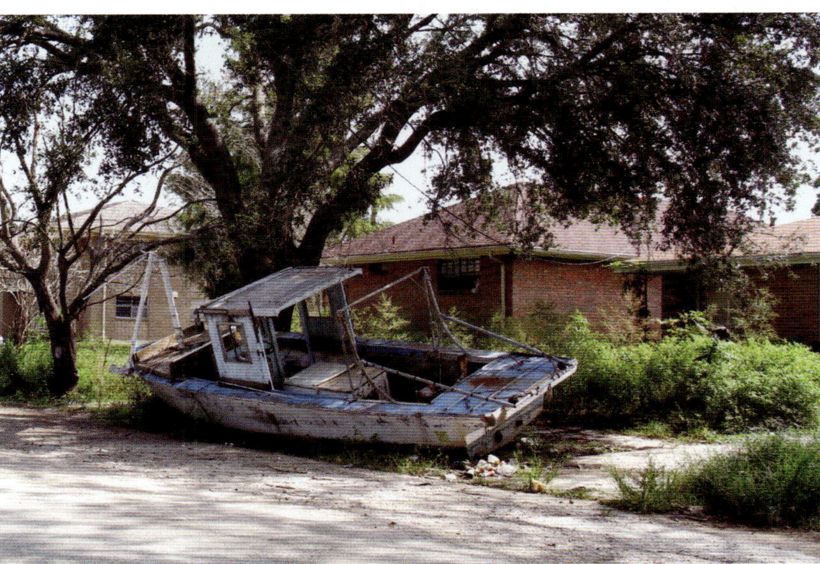

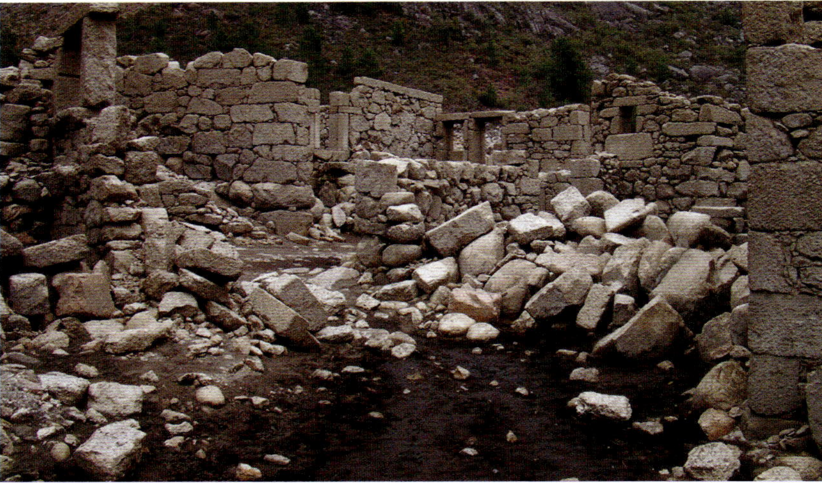

Above: *The ruins of the village of Vilarinho da Fuma in Portugal emerge during dry spells from the lake named for it, since the damming of the River Homem in 1972.*

The Destruction of Dhanushkodi

The Indian town of Dhanushkodi (*see* right), in the southern state of Tamil Nadu, was founded on a finger of land off Rameswaram Island, which was itself connected to the mainland by a bridge. Despite being vulnerable to cyclones, the town had many advantages and, just a few miles from Sri Lanka, was the main port for ferries to that island's northern tip.

Then, on 22 December 1964, a super-cyclone with winds close to 200 mph tore across the gulf, bringing 20-foot tidal waves in its wake. Some 1,800 people died, including 115 aboard a train crossing the bridge from the mainland when the cyclone struck. The effect on Dhanushkodi was dramatic, as most parts of the town dropped by some 15 feet, disappearing into the sea. With most of it lying underwater, the Indian government declared the site a ghost town; but, 40 years later, an unhappy resurrection occurred when, on Boxing Day 2004, as a giant tsunami approached the coast of Tamil Nadu, the ruins of Dhanushkodi emerged briefly from the deep as the sea receded far enough to expose them before consigning them once again to the waves.

Right: *Little remains today of the former port town of Dhanushkodi in southern India after a super-cyclone in 1964 caused most of its buildings to sink into the sea.* ***Next page:*** *The flooded village of Movada, Italy.*

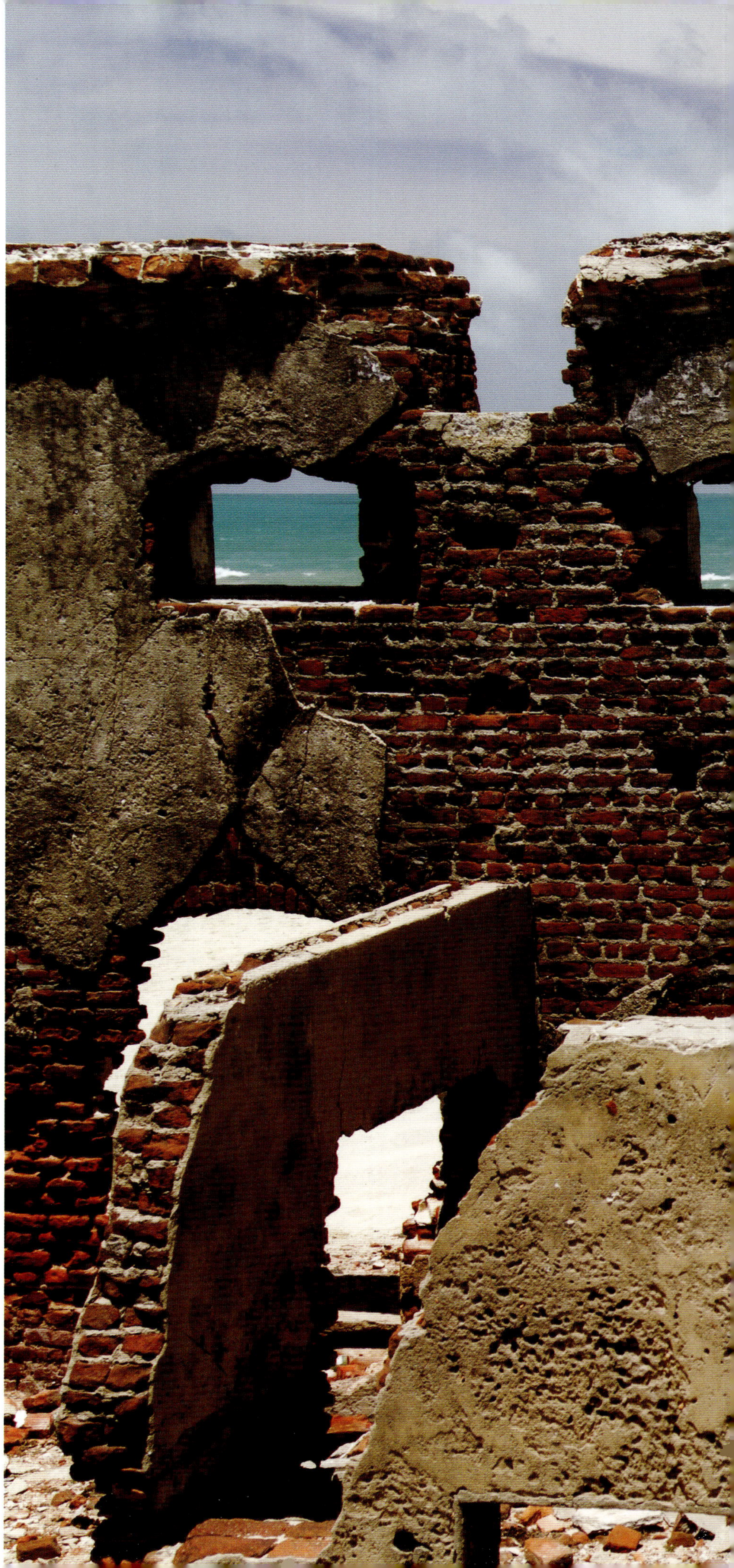

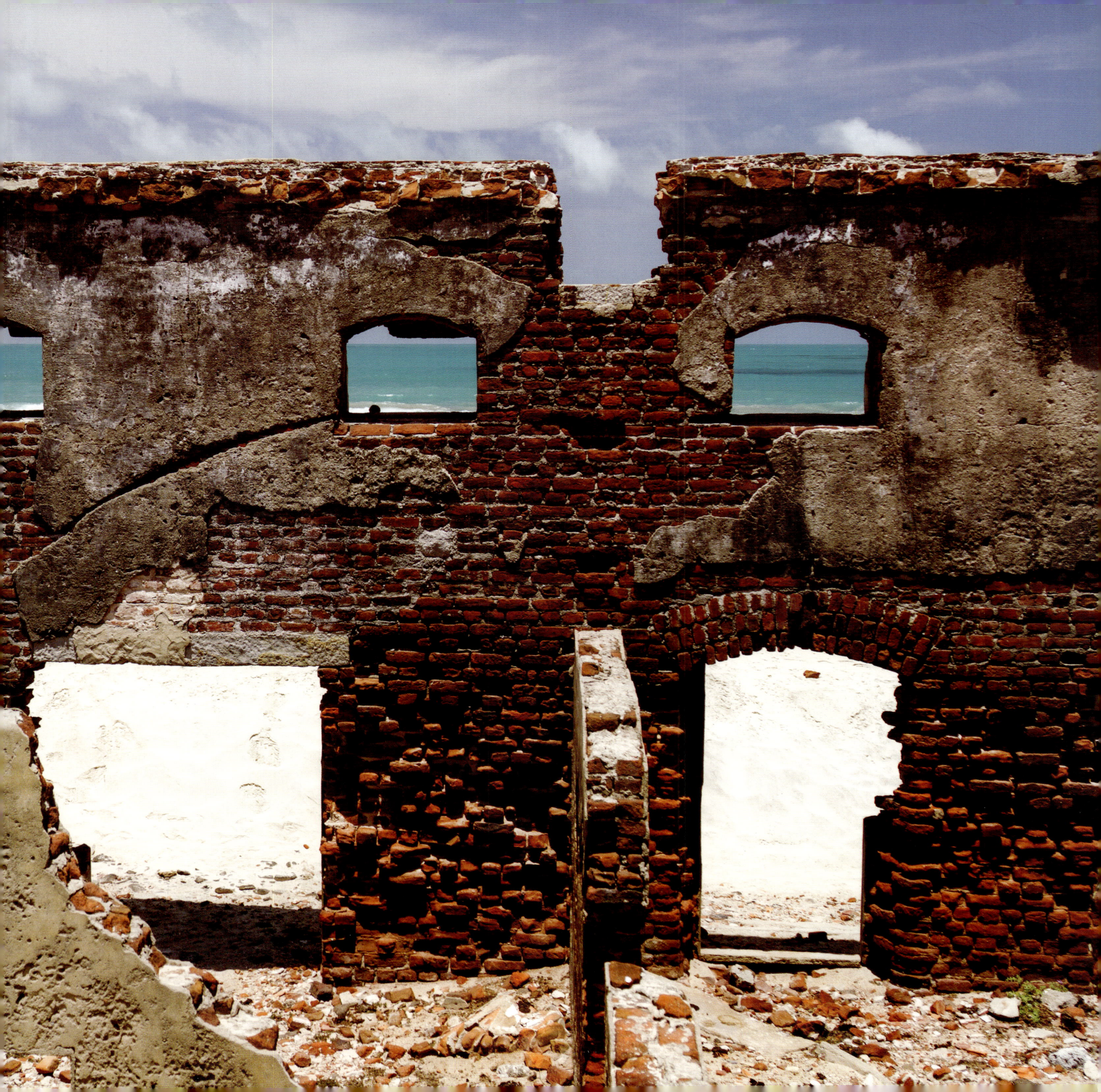

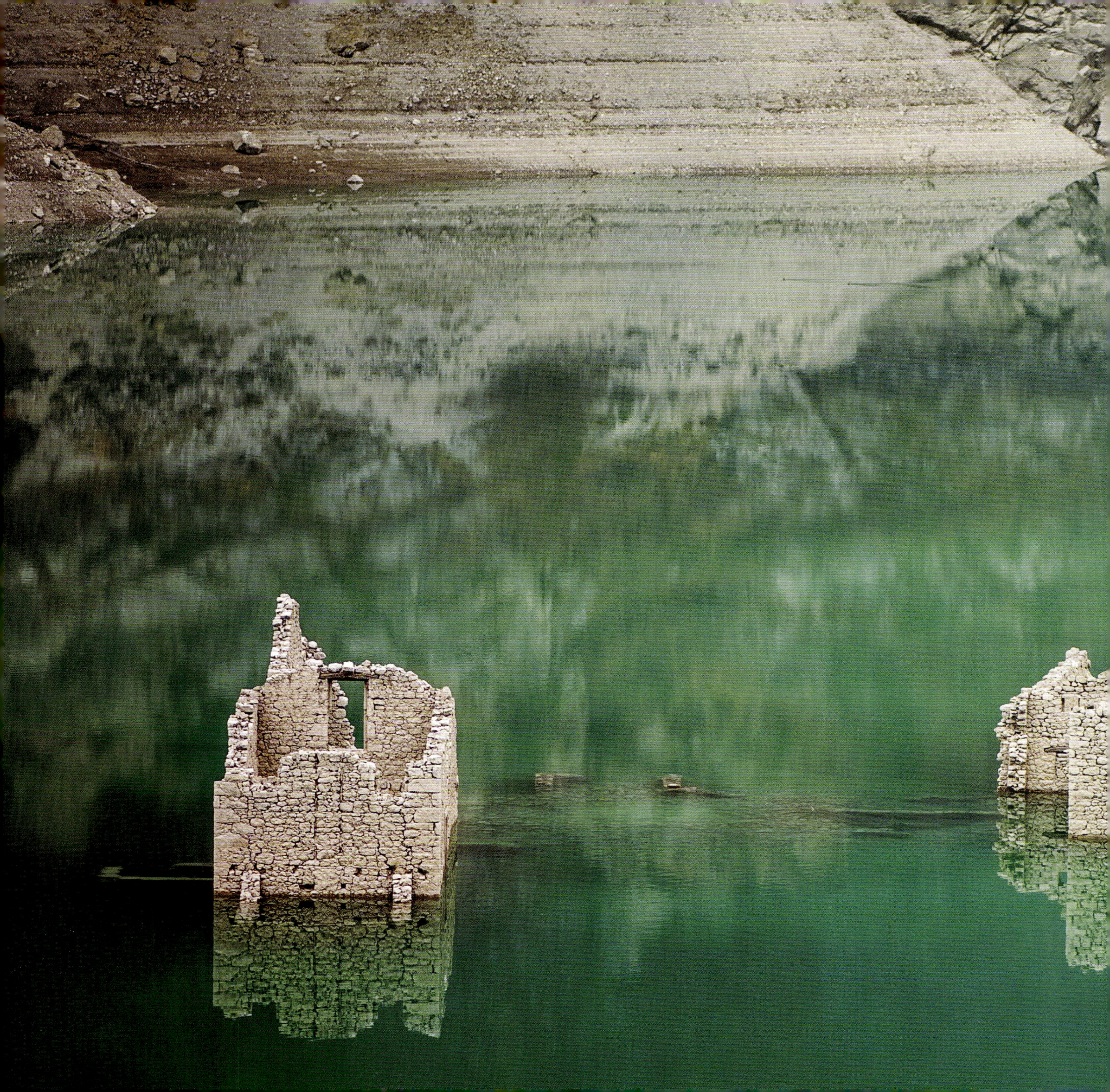

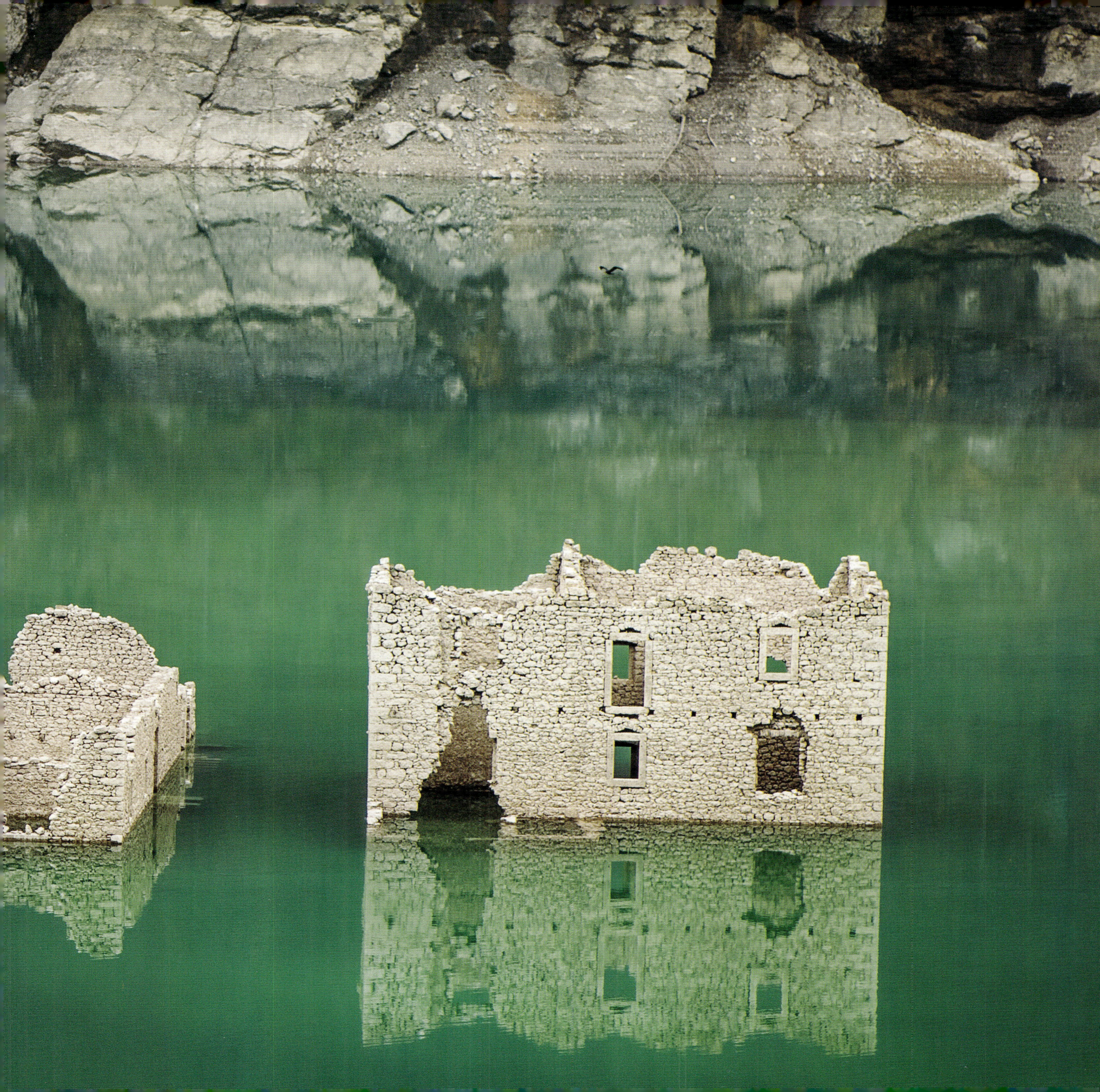

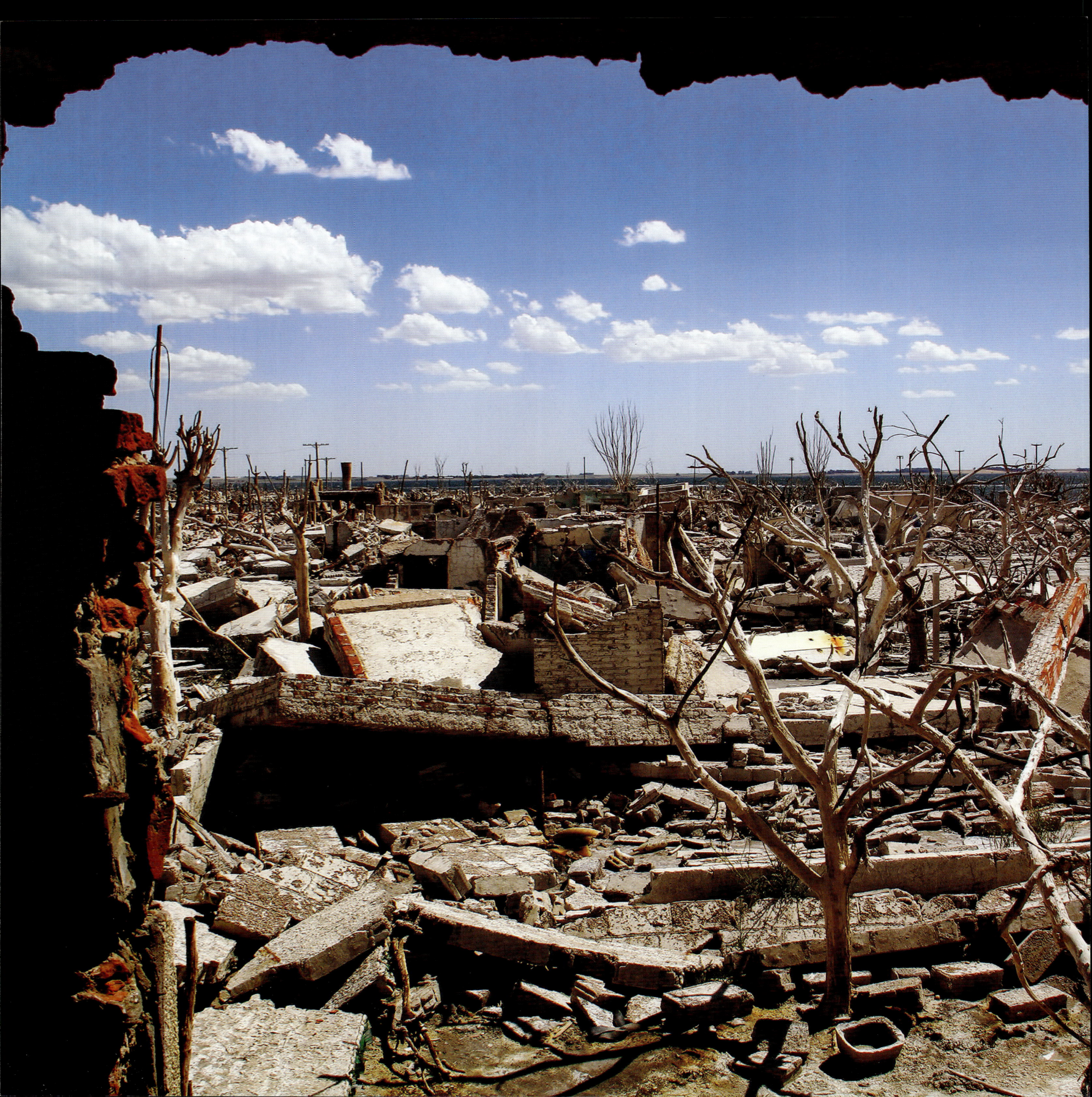

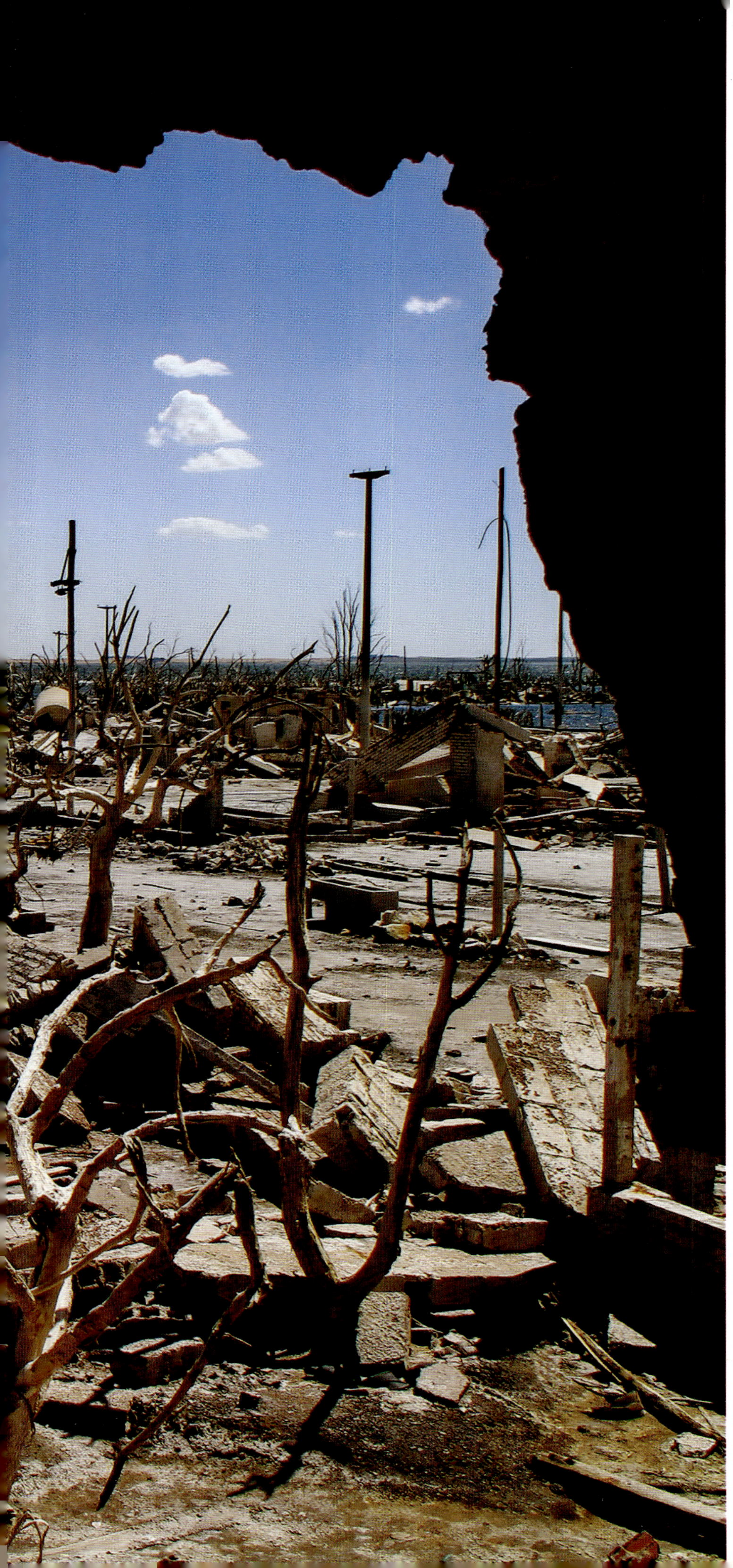

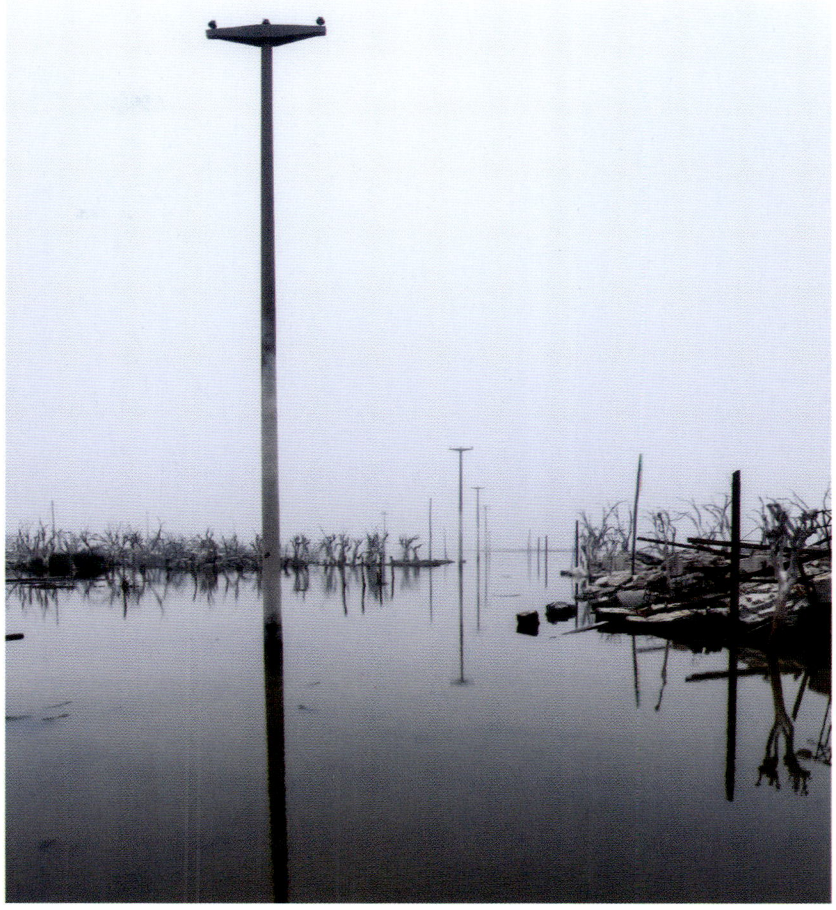

The Town in the Lake

Another place that re-emerged from a watery grave is Villa Epecuén in Argentina (*see* left). Built in the 1920s as a tourist resort, at its height the town housed some 5,000 residents and 25,000 tourist visitors to the hotels and guesthouses which catered to the trade. Then on 6 November a seiche, or standing wave, from the lake on which it stood broke through first a dam and then the dyke that protected the town. The water level continued rising and Villa Epecuén was slowly abandoned over several years until by 1993, it was fully submerged to a depth of some 30 feet. Thus it remained until 2009, when the process went into reverse, revealing ruins only decades old, but broken and bleached and beyond recognition of what they had been.

Above: *Utility poles in a flooded village.*
Left: *The resort town of Villa Epecuén in Argentina was once swallowed by rising waters from a nearby lake.*

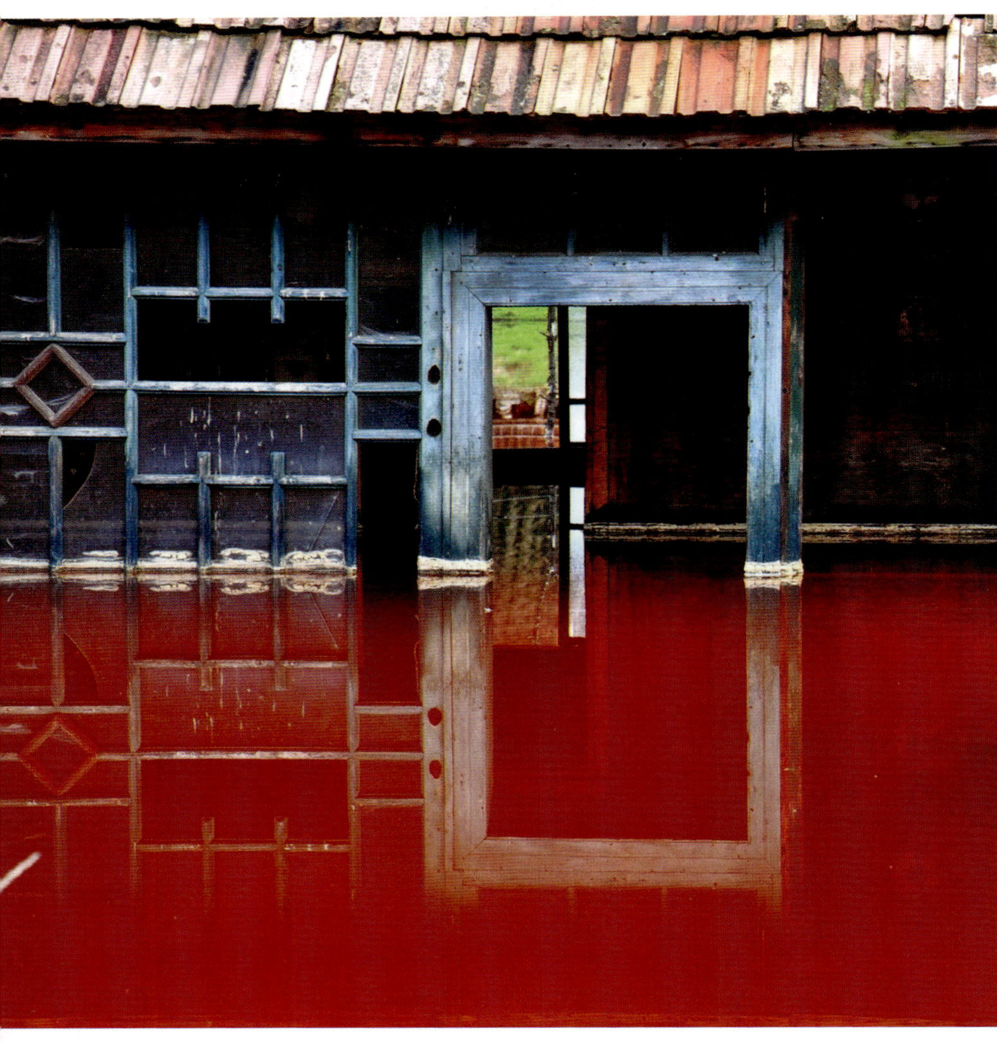

Above: *Abandoned home in Geamana, Romania.*

The Drowned Village of Geamana

The Communist system was crude and often brutal, perhaps nowhere more so than in Romania, which under the systematization programme of dictator Nicolai Ceaușescu saw thousands of traditional buildings in cities, towns and villages across the country torn down and replaced with faceless modern blocks of often monumental size. The ultimate fate of the traditional village of Geamana was no different from that of hundreds of others across Romania; only the manner of its death marks it out.

Right: *The steeple of the hilltop church of Geamana is all that remains of the centre of the former Romanian village above the surface of a toxic lake.*

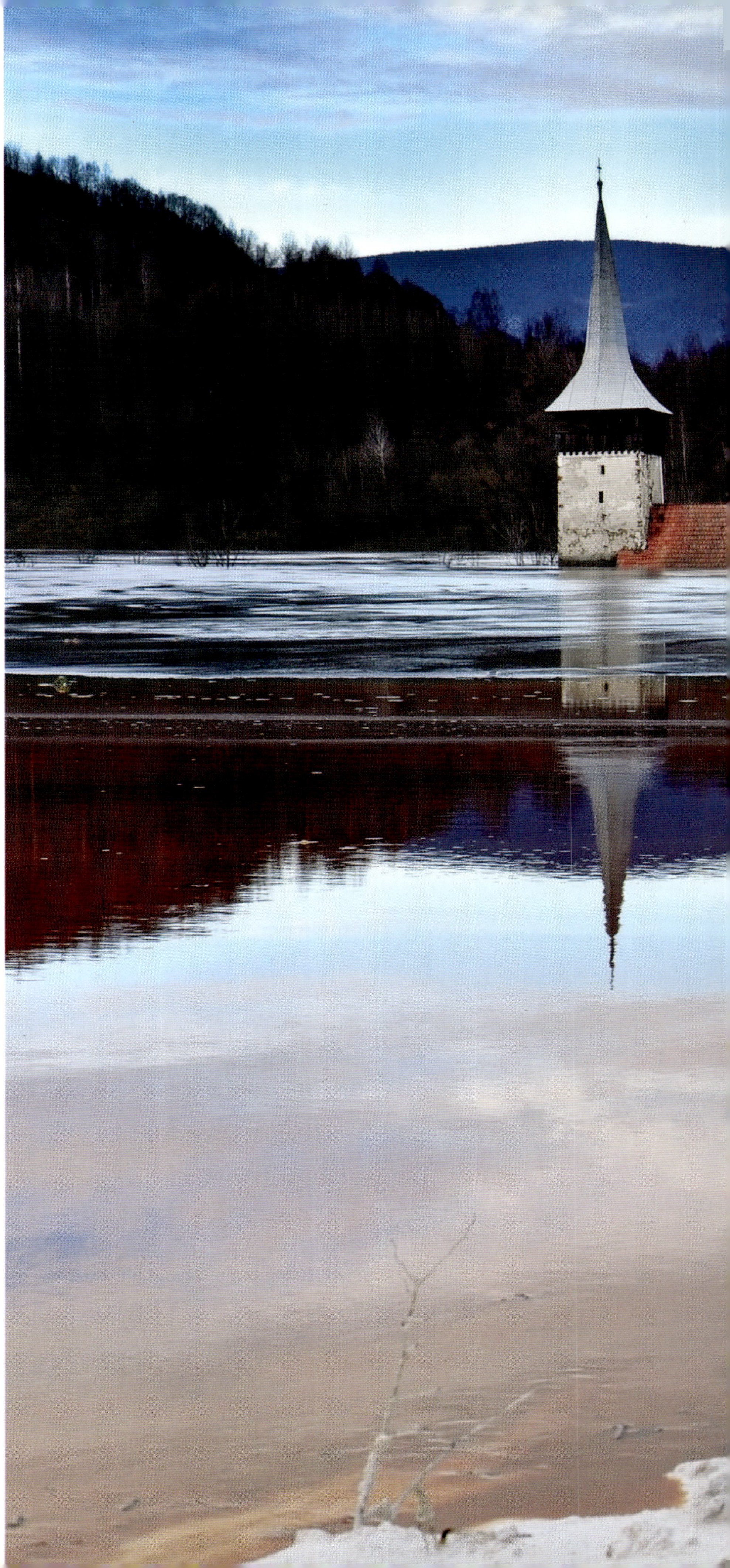

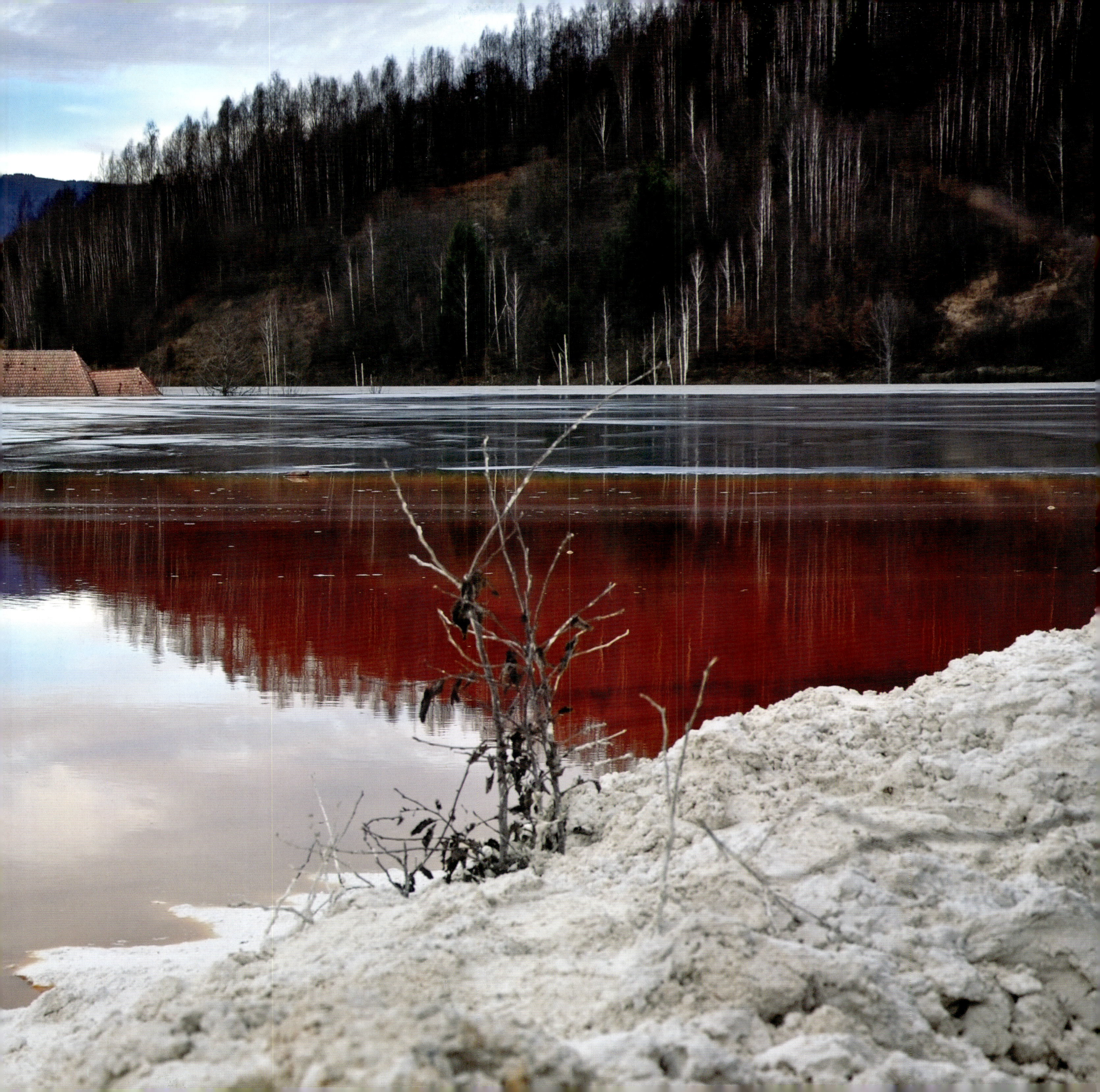

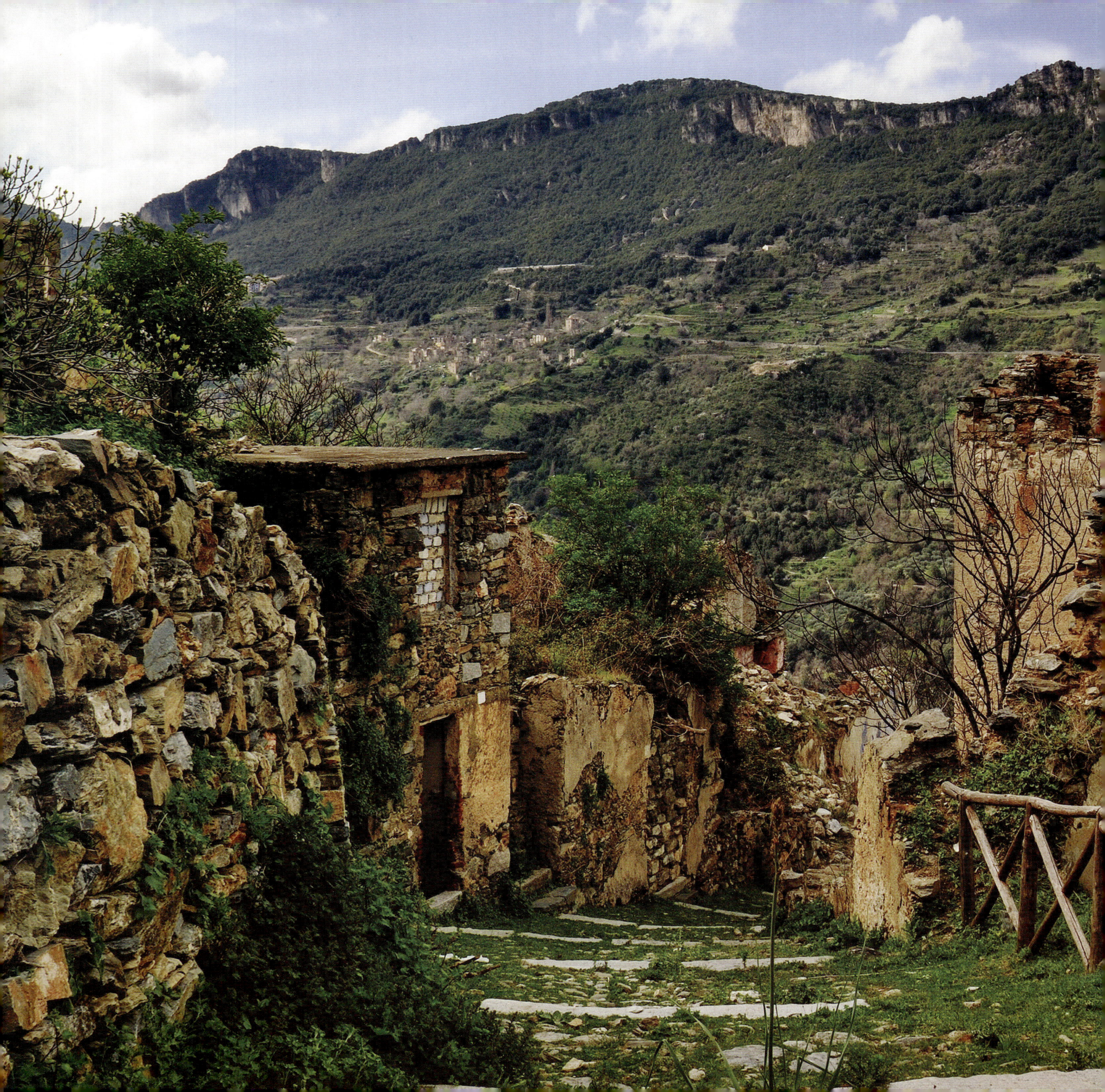

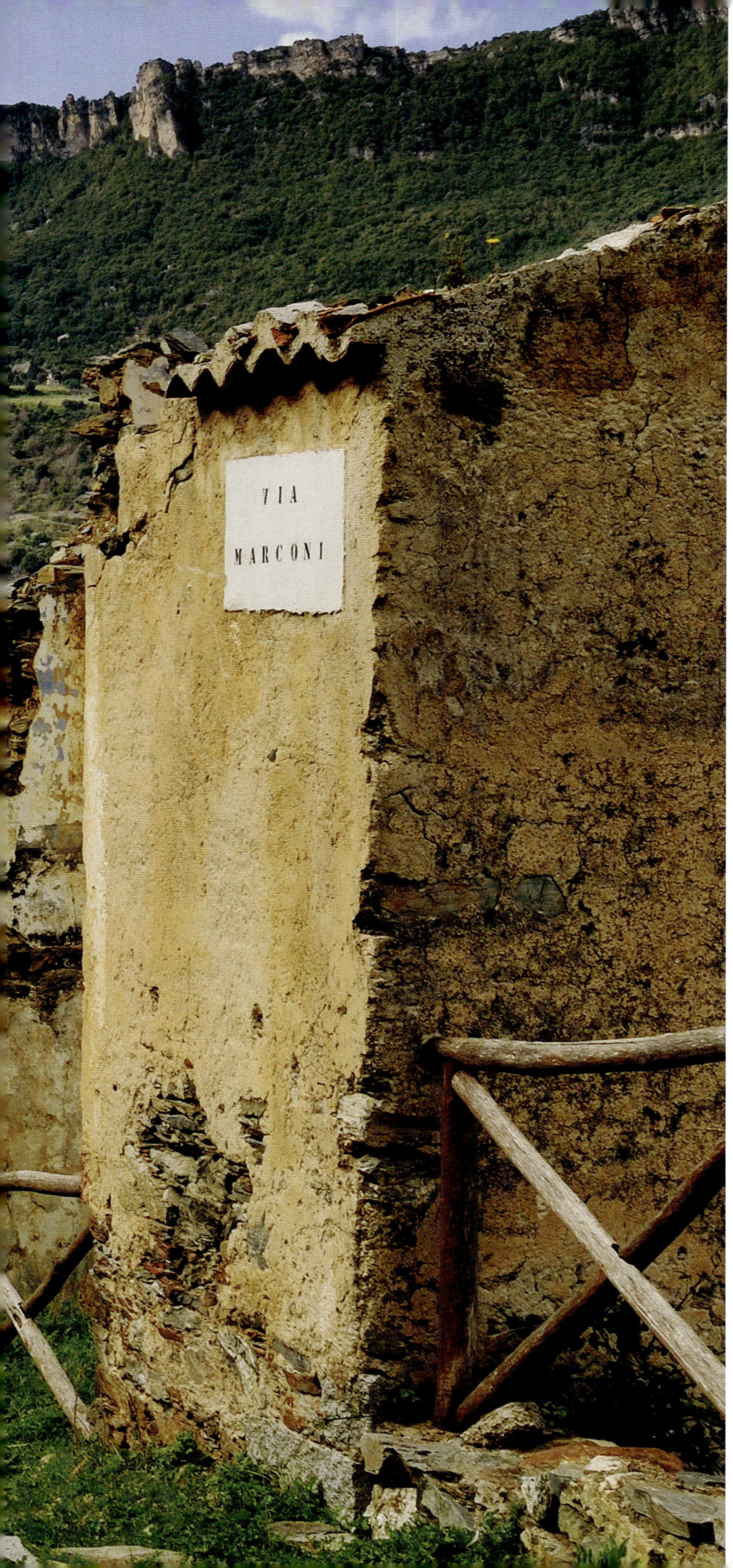

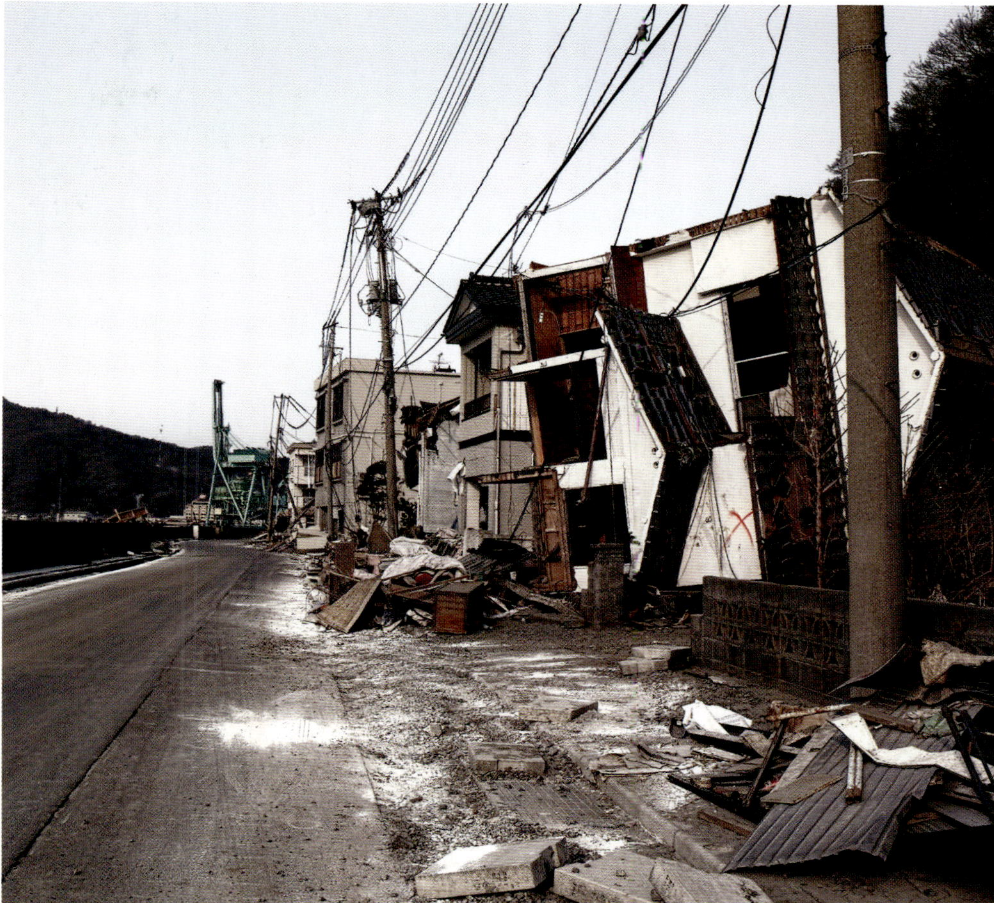

Above: *The earthquake and tsunami which struck the east coast of Honshu Island, Japan, in March 2011 destroyed hundreds of thousands of buildings across a wide area.*

In 1977, a large copper deposit was discovered in the mountains above the valley in which the village once stood – an idyllic setting with a huddle of old wooden buildings watched over by an elegant little church on a hill above Geamana's historic heart (*see* page 155). As mining began, the government made residents move out, as the valley slowly filled with the toxic sludge that slid down the mountain from the mine. Today, the lake that grew gradually is stained a range of filthy colours from orange to brown, while the centre of Geamana lies deep down below, with only the church's steeple still breaking the toxic surface, reaching up for a God whose help will never come.

Left: *Old Gairo in Sardinia was partially destroyed by a flood in 1951, and in 1963, it was completely abandoned.*

Pollution

Industrialization has brought many benefits to the lives of hundreds of millions in Western countries and now to increasing millions in developing countries too. But for some, this material progress has come at a terrible cost.

The Toxic Towns of Oklahoma

In the mining towns of Picher (*see* right) and Cardin in Oklahoma, it gradually dawned on people that something wasn't right. In particular, the children of Picher were diagnosed with learning difficulties in unusually large numbers and, for some reason, there were three kidney dialysis centres in the area for a population of just 30,000.

The cause of the problem wasn't hard to identify. People started looking at what the mining companies left behind, once the mines closed down in the 1950s, because of fears even then about their environmental impact. Sure enough, the water of Tar Creek was found to be poisoned with heavy metals such as cadmium, zinc and lead, and for years the huge mounds of tailings from the mine had blown dust across the town of Picher and into the lungs of its unsuspecting citizens. Not only that, but with large parts of the area undermined in years gone by, huge excavated chasms below populated areas were now at imminent risk of collapse. Today, these two towns are deserted, and the clean-up operation across the whole area – known as the Tar Creek Superfund site – will go on for many more years.

The Dust of Wittenoom

Like so many American mining towns, the community of Wittenoom in Western Australia (*see* page 160) developed rapidly when deposits of blue

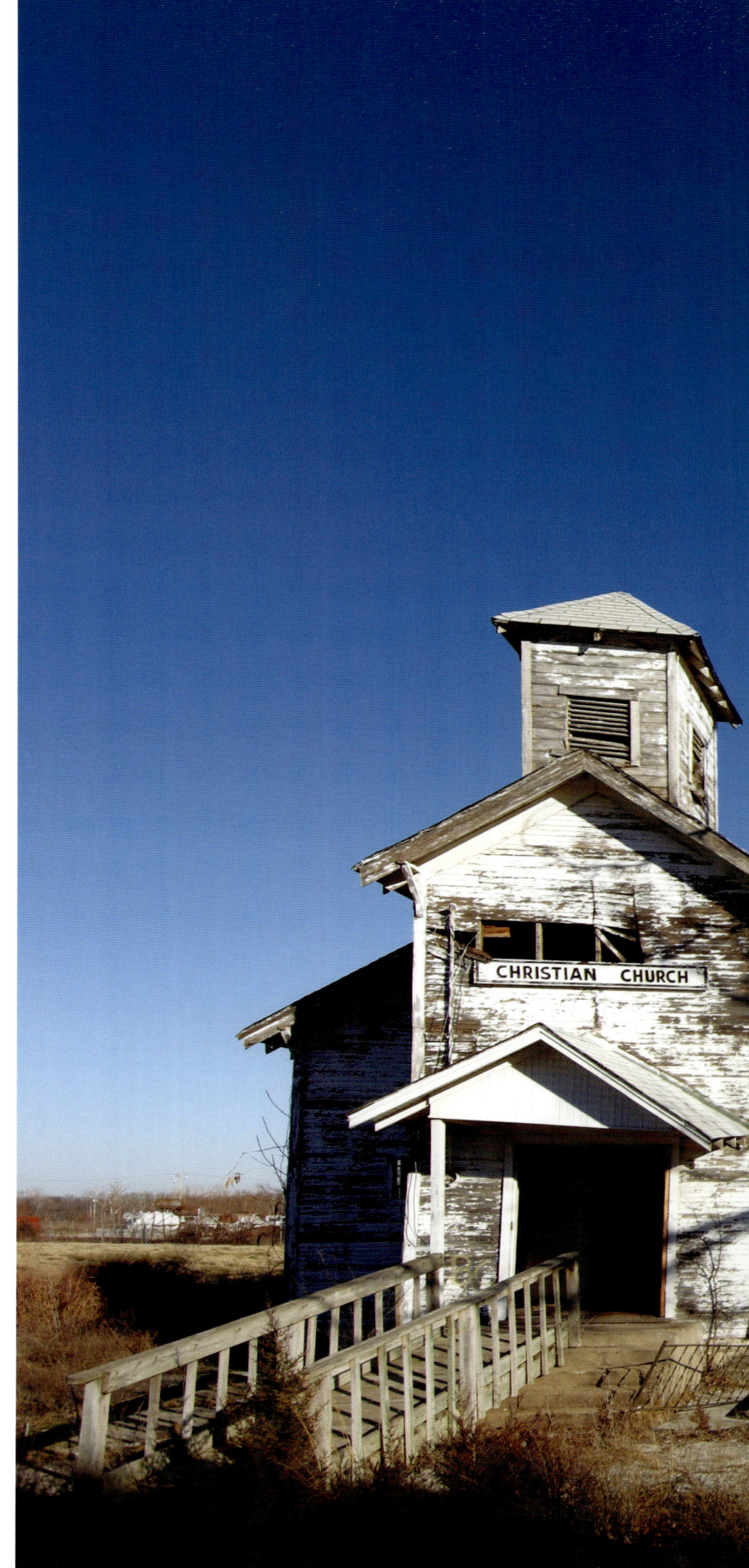

Right: *Abandoned church in Picher, Oklahoma, USA.*

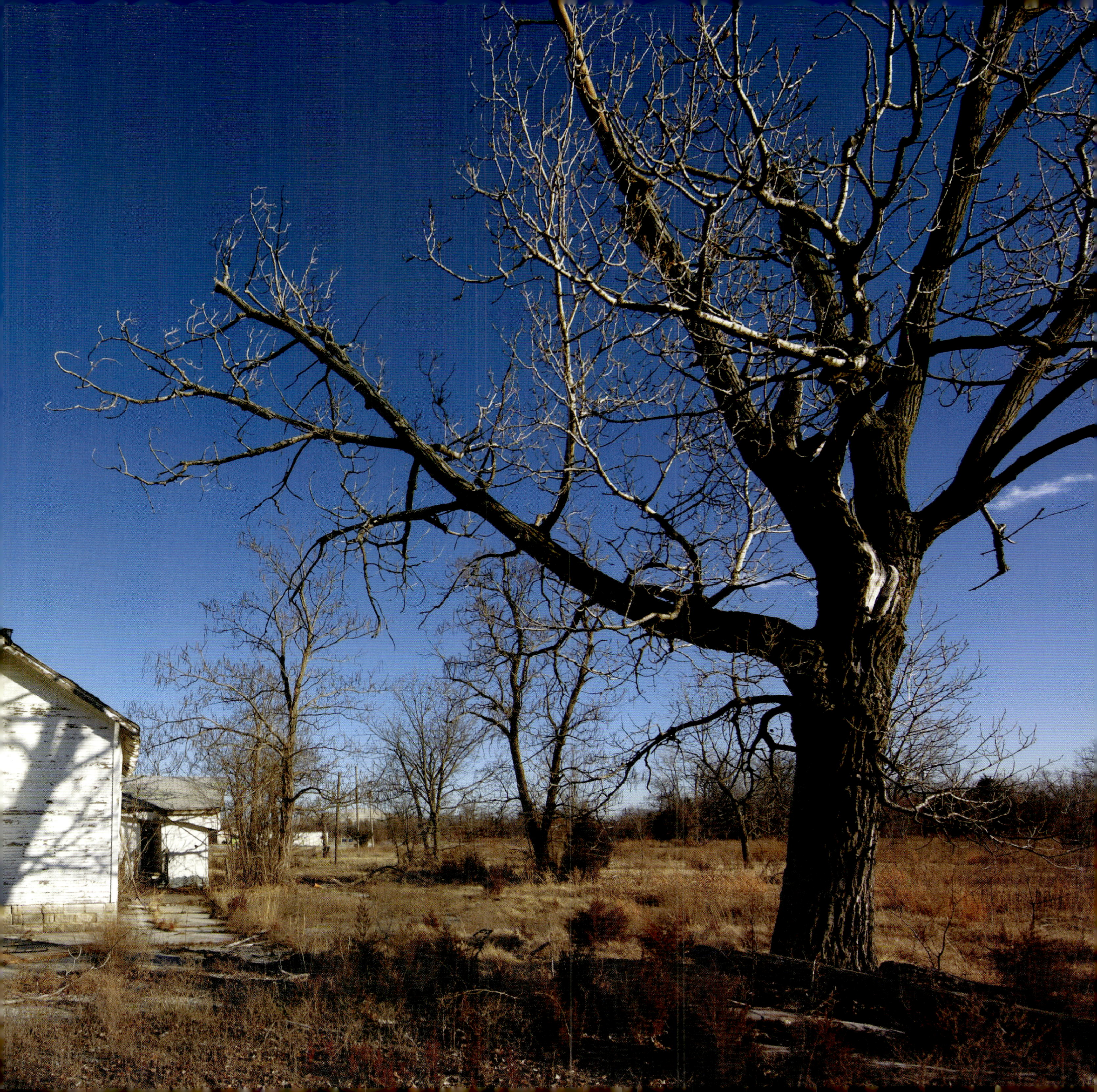

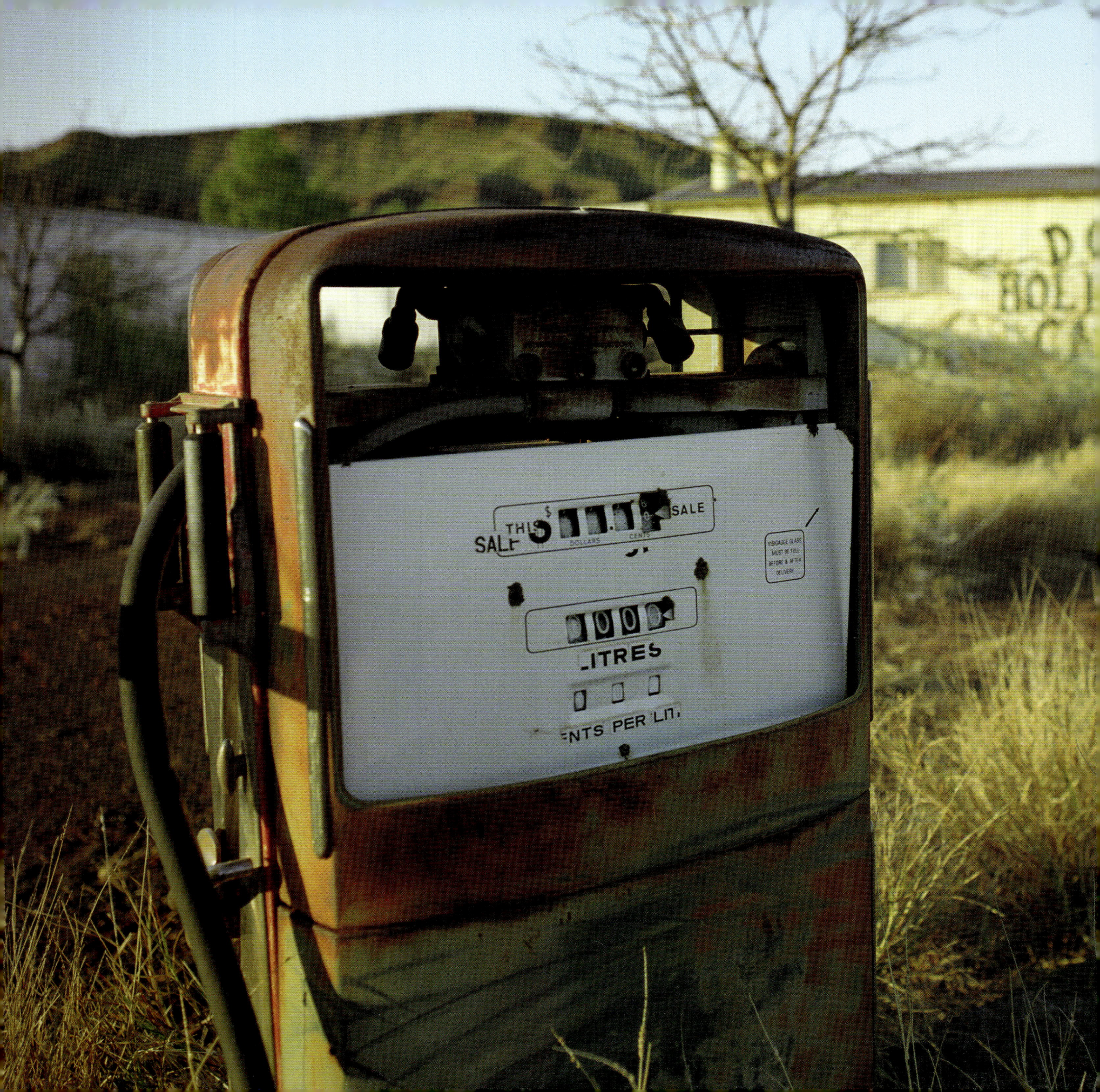
THIS SALE
DOLLARS
CENTS
LITRES
PER

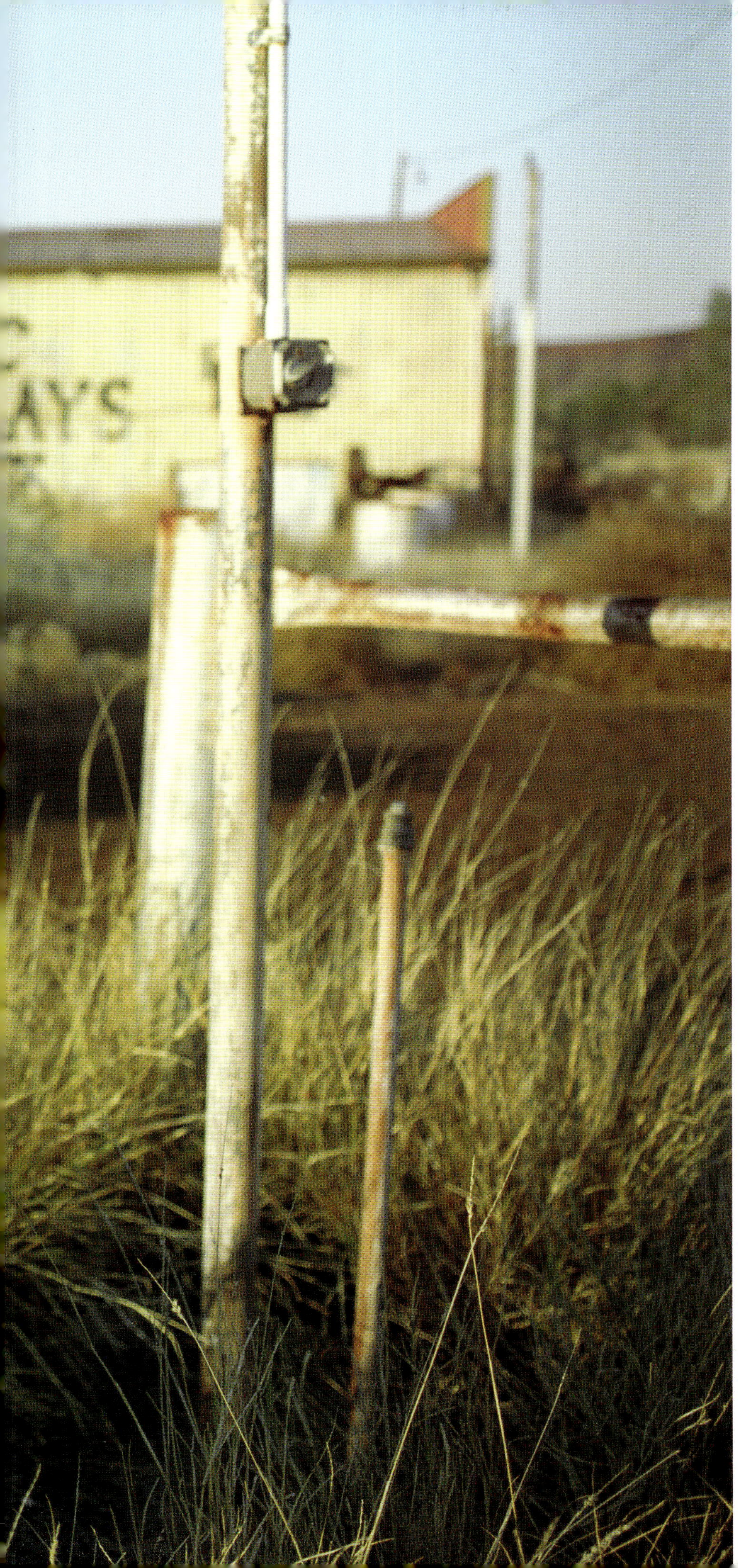

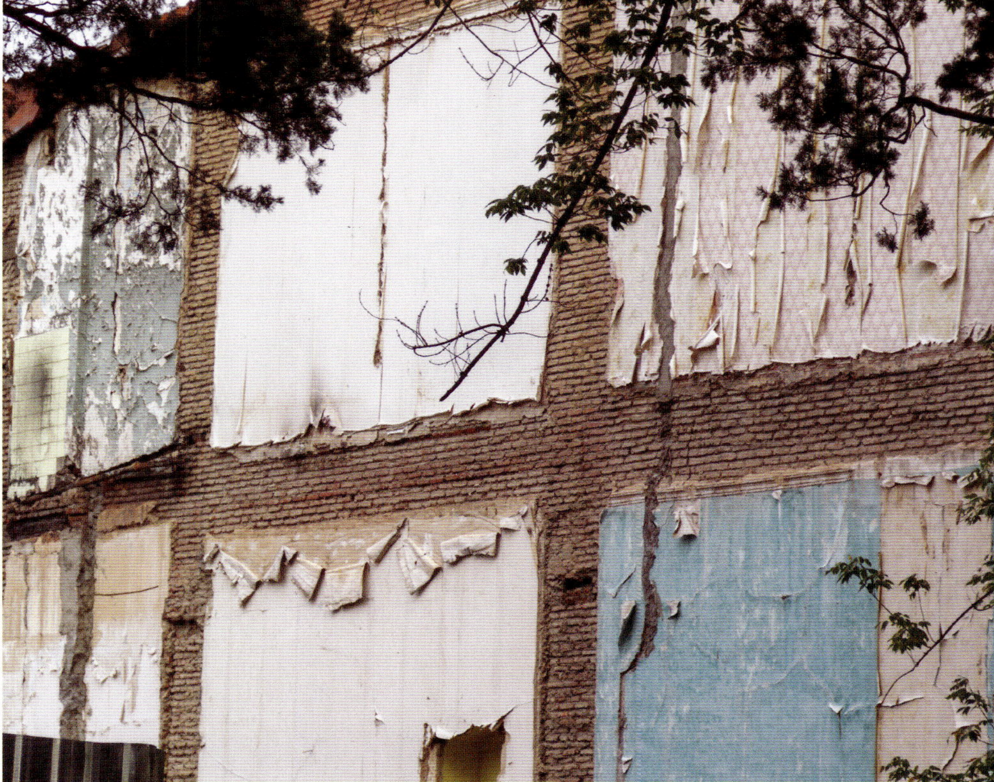

Above: *Old houses in Tbilisi, Georgia.*

asbestos were found in the area in 1943. The government knew of the hazards of asbestos even then, and cases of asbestosis began appearing just a few years later. But warnings were ignored, despite the children playing in the dusty streets kicking up clouds of deadly fibres that had floated to the surface from the mines where their fathers worked and where dust clouds of fibres filled the air.

When in the mid-1960s asbestos was proven to be a mortal danger to health, the mine was closed and the area declared unfit for human habitation, though many residents decided to remain there despite the risks. But the damage had been done, and to date some 2,000 of the 20,000 people who lived there have died of asbestos-related diseases like

Left: *Old petrol pump in Wittenoom, Australia.*

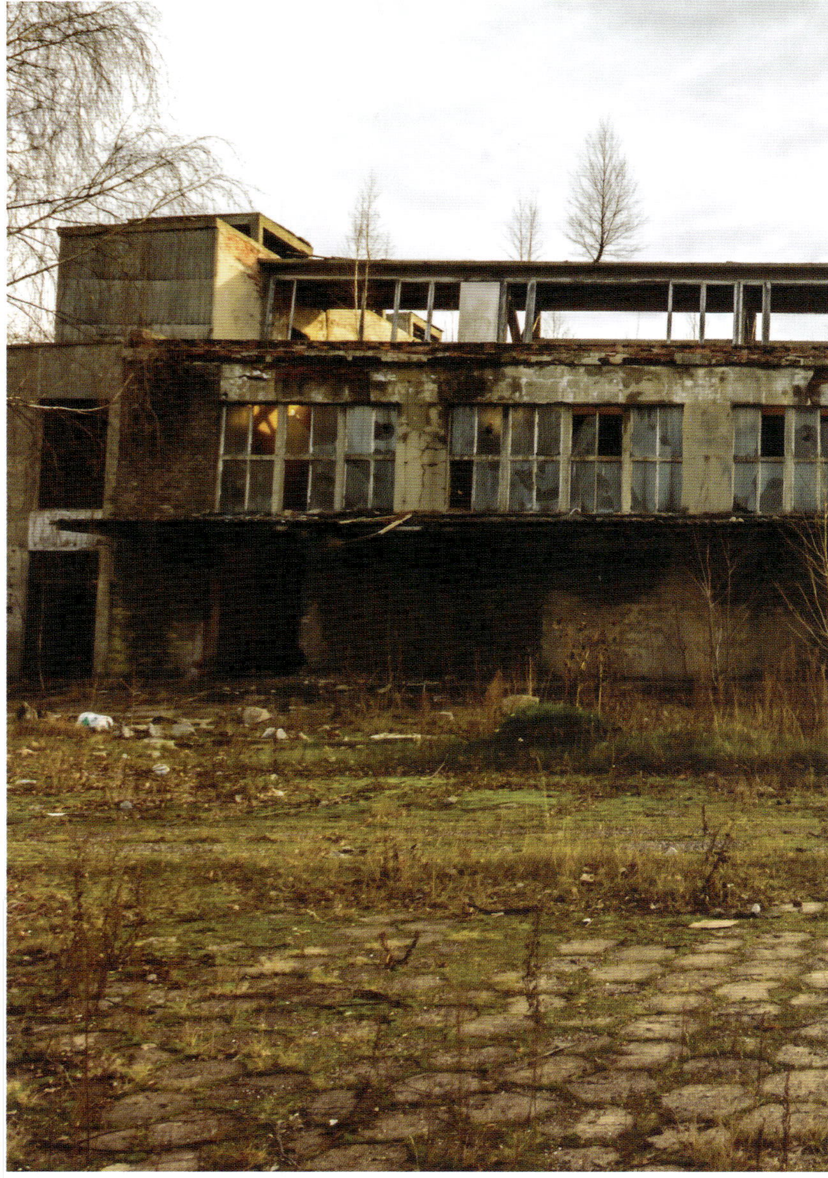

Above: *Ruins of a very heavily polluted industrial factory in Europe.*

asbestosis and mesothelioma. Today, after failed initiatives to clean the place up, Wittenoom has been all but abandoned, with essential services no longer supplied to the town. The three people who still cling on there elected to move there long after the dangers were known, drawn by the lonely beauty of this place of poison dust.

Right: *Abandoned power plant at Tkvarcheli in Abkhazia.*

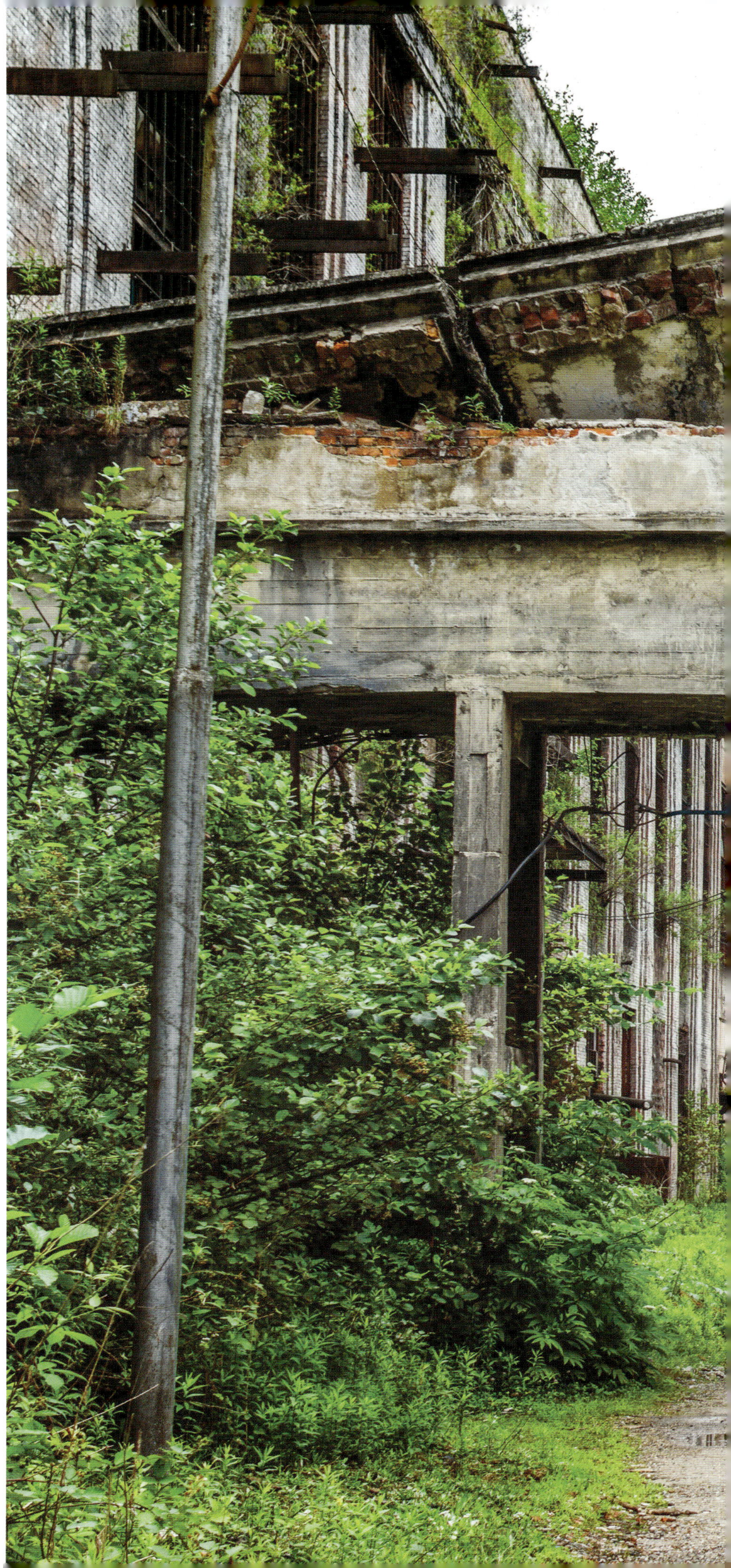

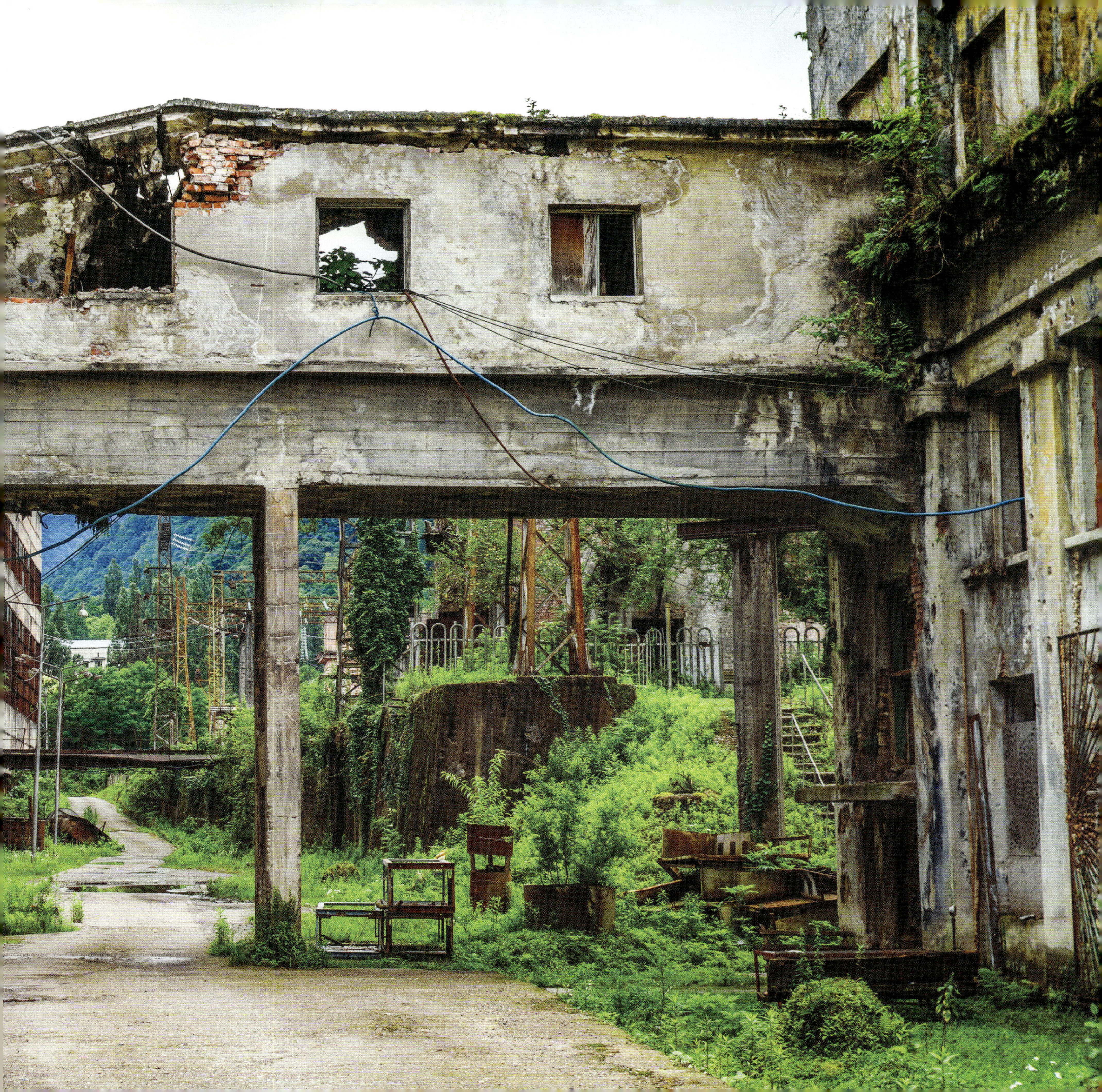

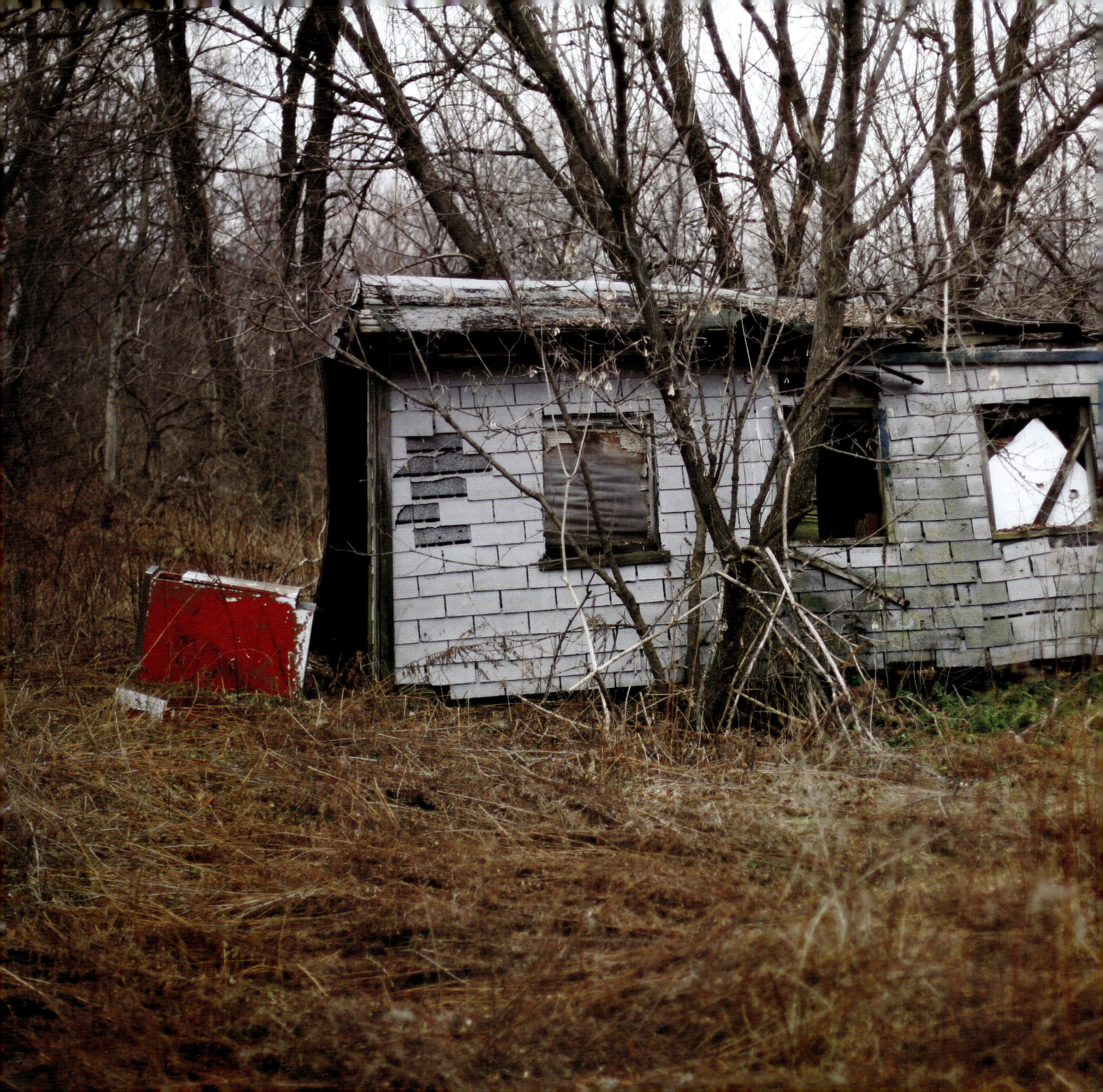

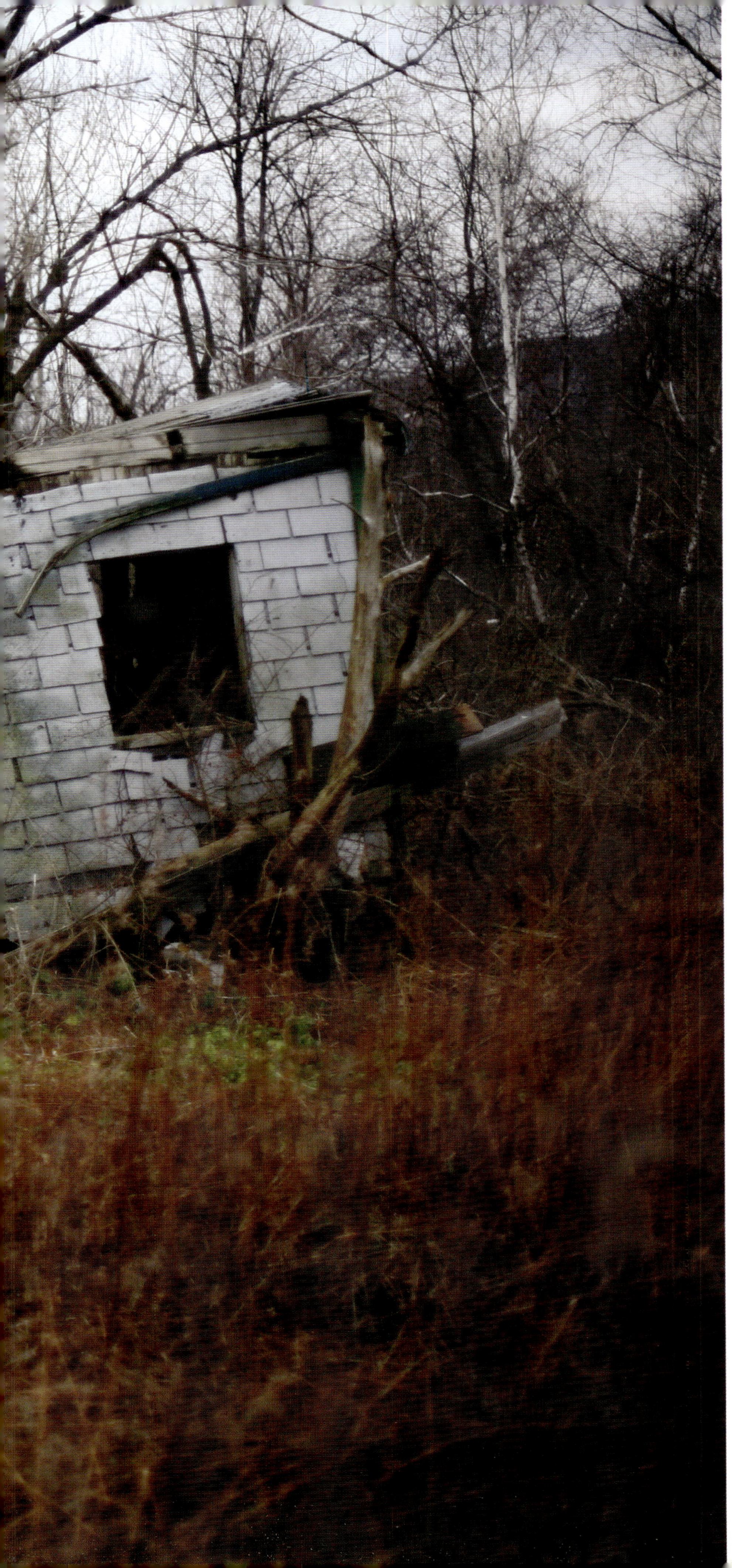

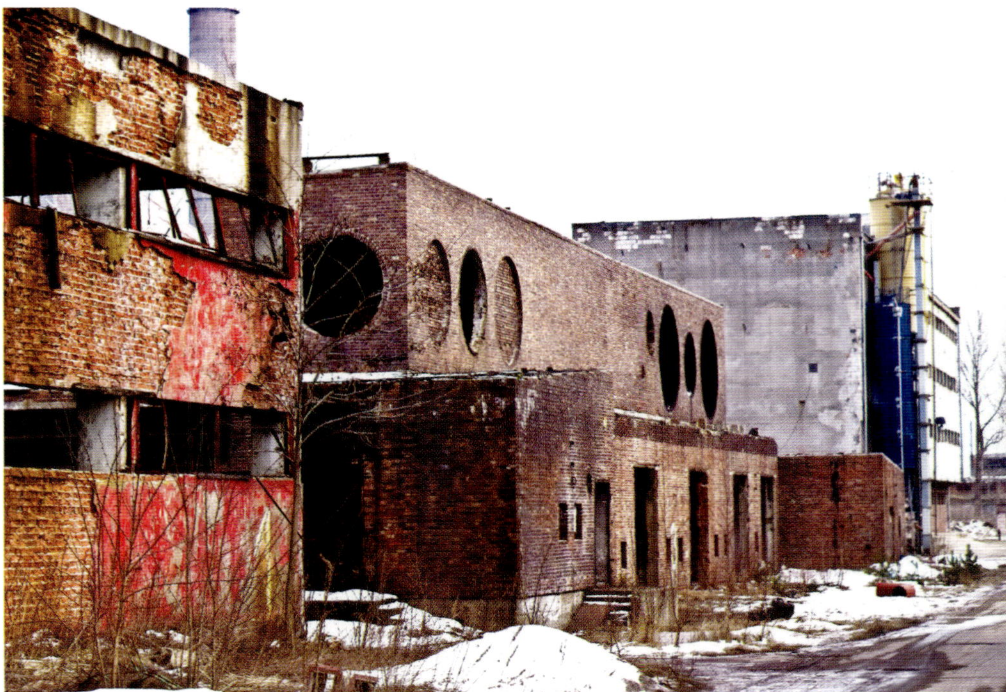

Above: *A heavily polluted industrial site in Europe.*

Life at the Hellmouth

A similar number of holdouts still live in the community of Centralia in Pennsylvania, where a fire ignited in a coal seam in a mine beneath the town is still burning more than 50 years after it started. In 1962, when the fire was discovered, failed attempts were made to put it out, but life continued anyway for years afterwards. The true extent of the danger became apparent only in the early 1980s when underground measurements found hazardous levels of gases, including carbon monoxide, which were linked to the health problems reported by residents of Centralia. In 1984, most families agreed to leave, and most of the buildings were torn down, while signs and barriers prevent anyone today from driving in on roads that are buckled and broken from the heat of the fire. But a few cussed souls remain there, unfazed by the plumes of smoke that issue from fissures in the ground in this suburban entrance to hell.

Left: *Derelict building in Centralia, Pennsylvania, USA.*

Danger Zones

While towns like Centralia are quarantined when a mishap occurs, some are built from the outset with a hazardous purpose, and for that reason established in places where no accidental visitor will find them.

The Deadly Secret of Kantubek

The ghost town of Kantubek in modern Uzbekistan was in a little-known part of the Soviet Union when its first buildings went up. The town's obscure position on an island in the middle of the Aral Sea was in fact the main reason why the Soviet army chose Vozrozhdeniye Island as the site to develop a secret program of deadly biological weapons, such as smallpox and anthrax, for military use. From the mid-1950s until the collapse of the Soviet system, thousands of hapless animals were subjected to the deadliest diseases known to humanity; made more so by Soviet scientists engineering strains resistant to all known vaccines that could counter them.

Kantubek was built as a workers' village close to the testing facility but then abandoned in 1992, along with the labs, when the USSR collapsed. Since then, international teams have removed the lethal holdings of anthrax, but other deadly hazards still lurk within the soil. And a further menace today is the increasing accessibility of Kantubek, as the island on which it was built has disappeared since the Cold War ended, as rivers that fed the Aral Sea were diverted for irrigation and what was once the world's fourth-largest freshwater lake has all but dried up.

Right: *View from the roof of a 16-storey apartment in Pripyat, near Chernobyl, Ukraine.*

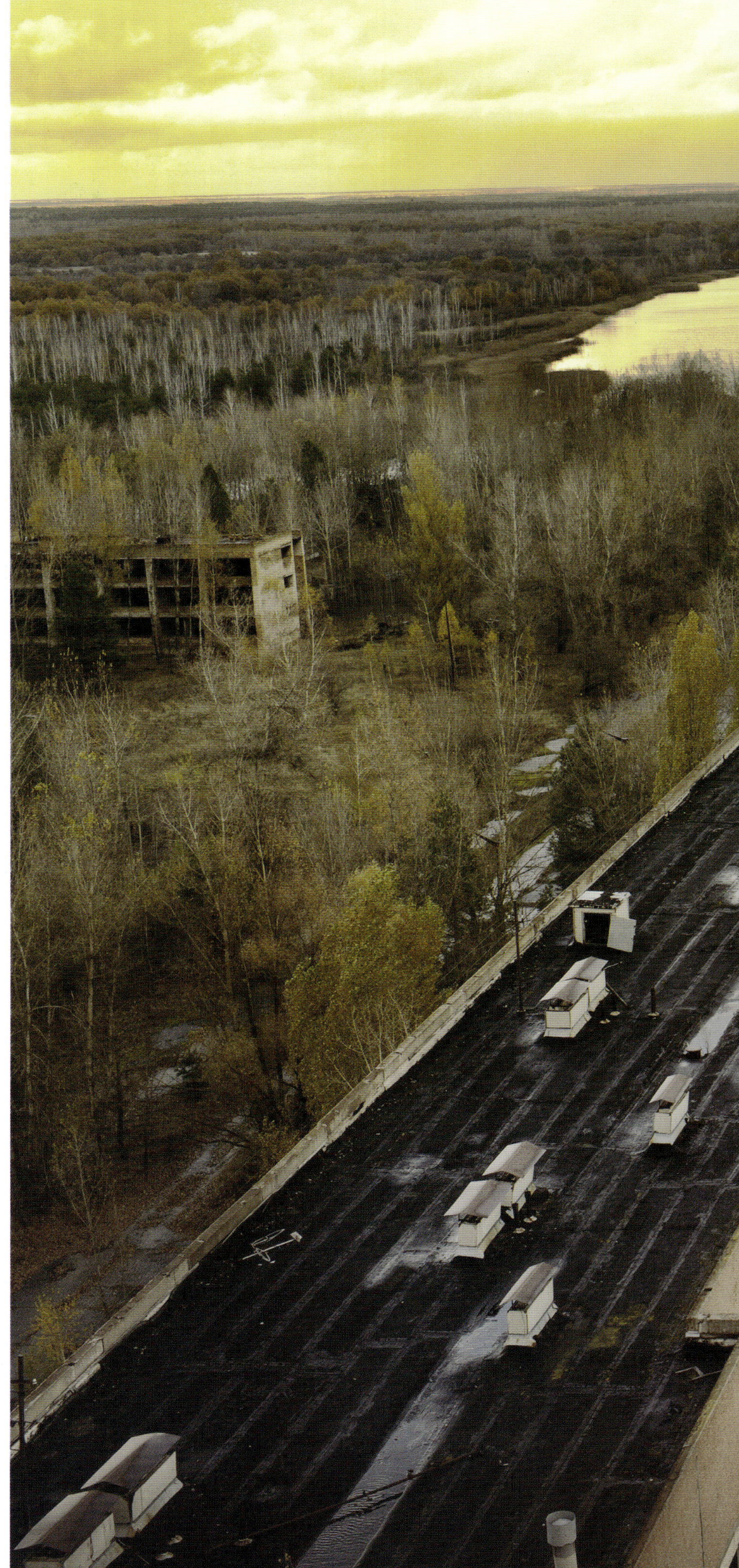

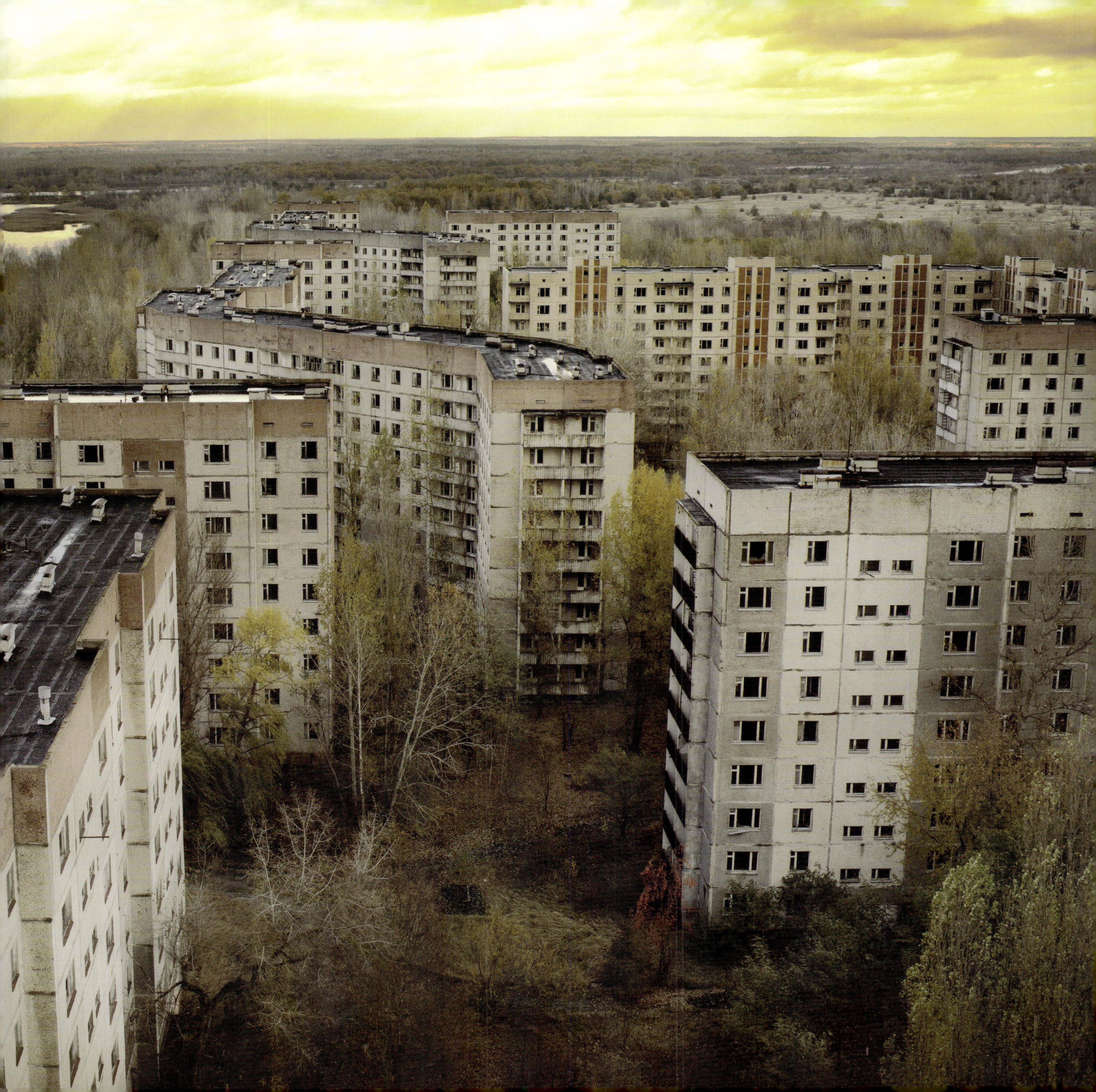

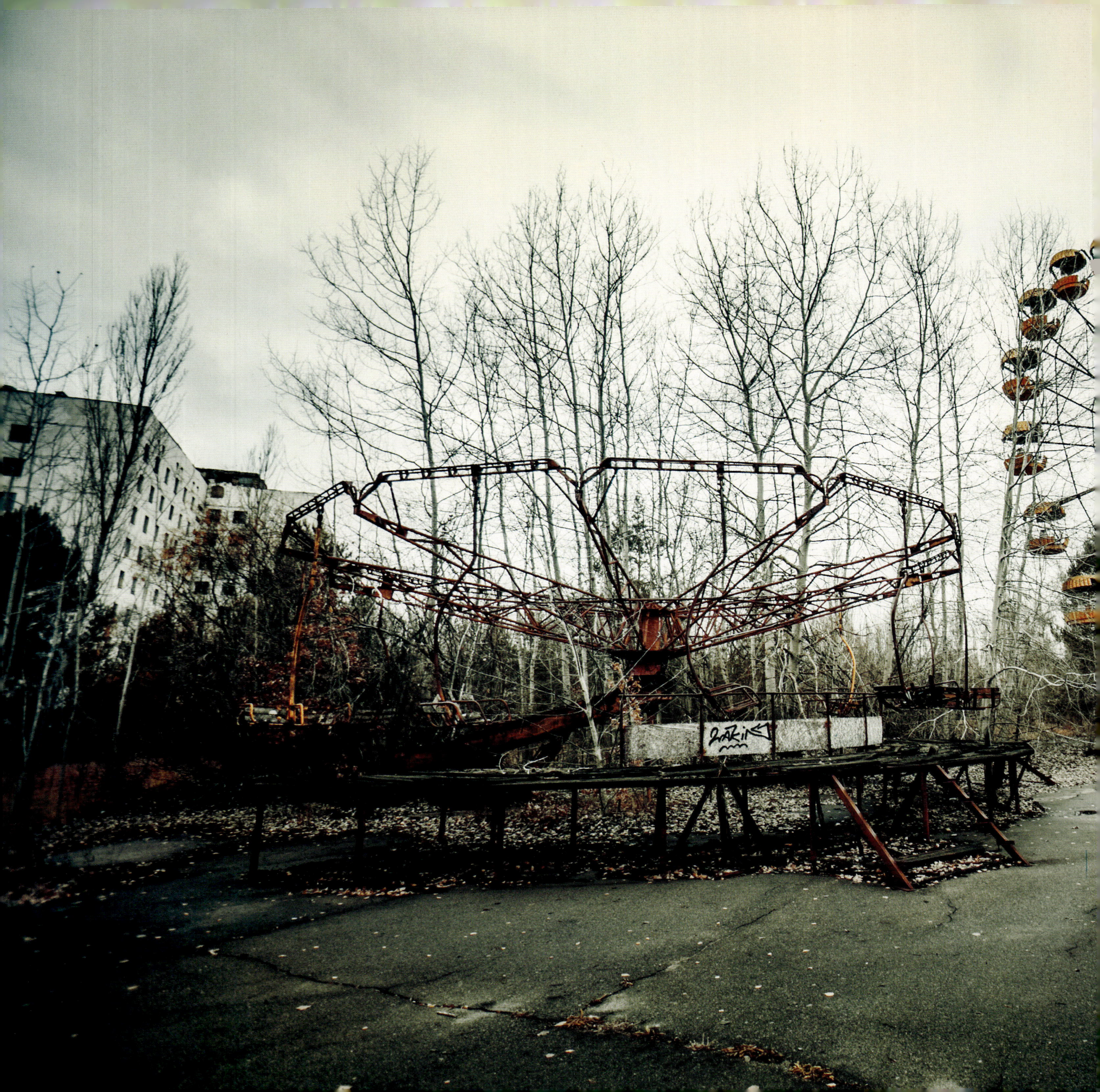

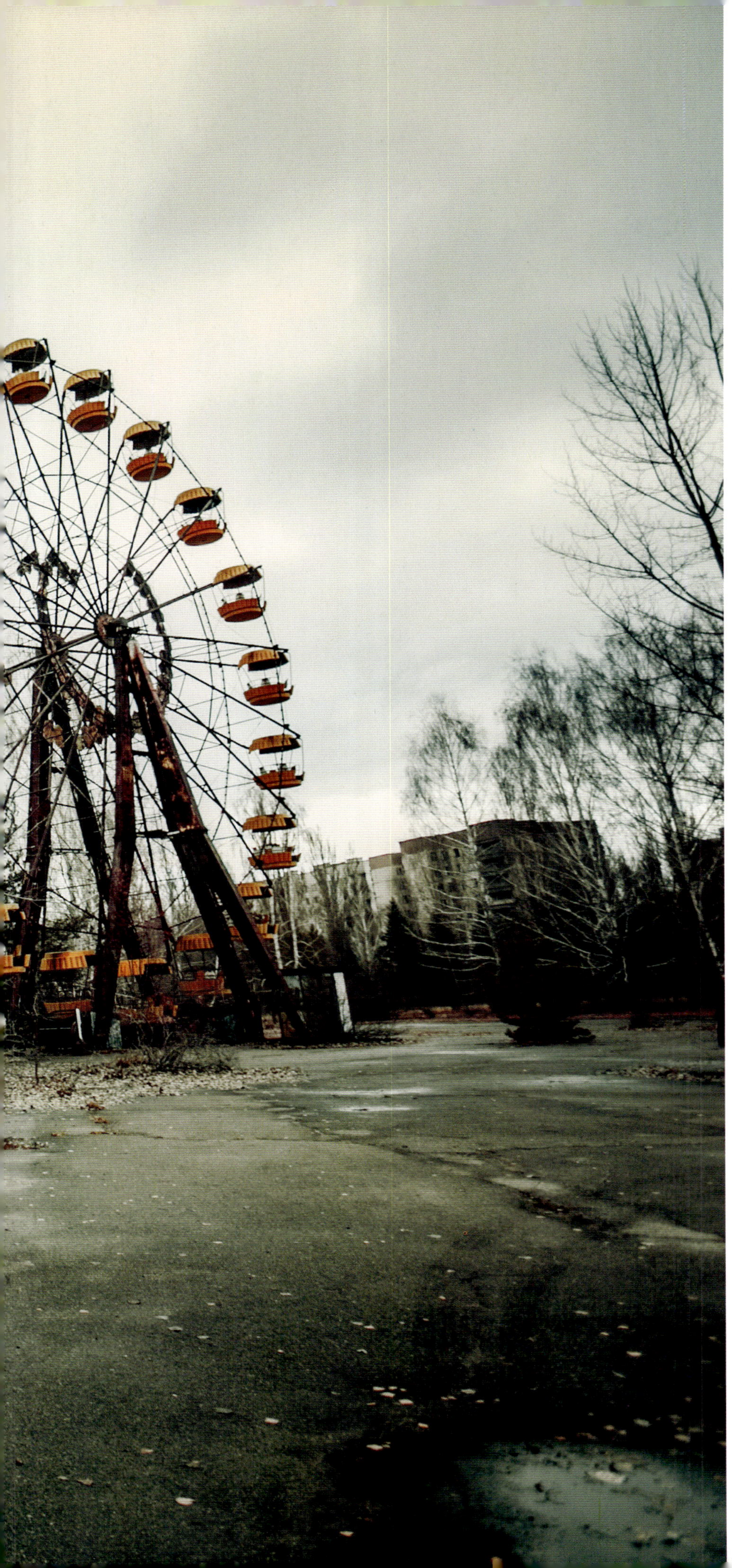

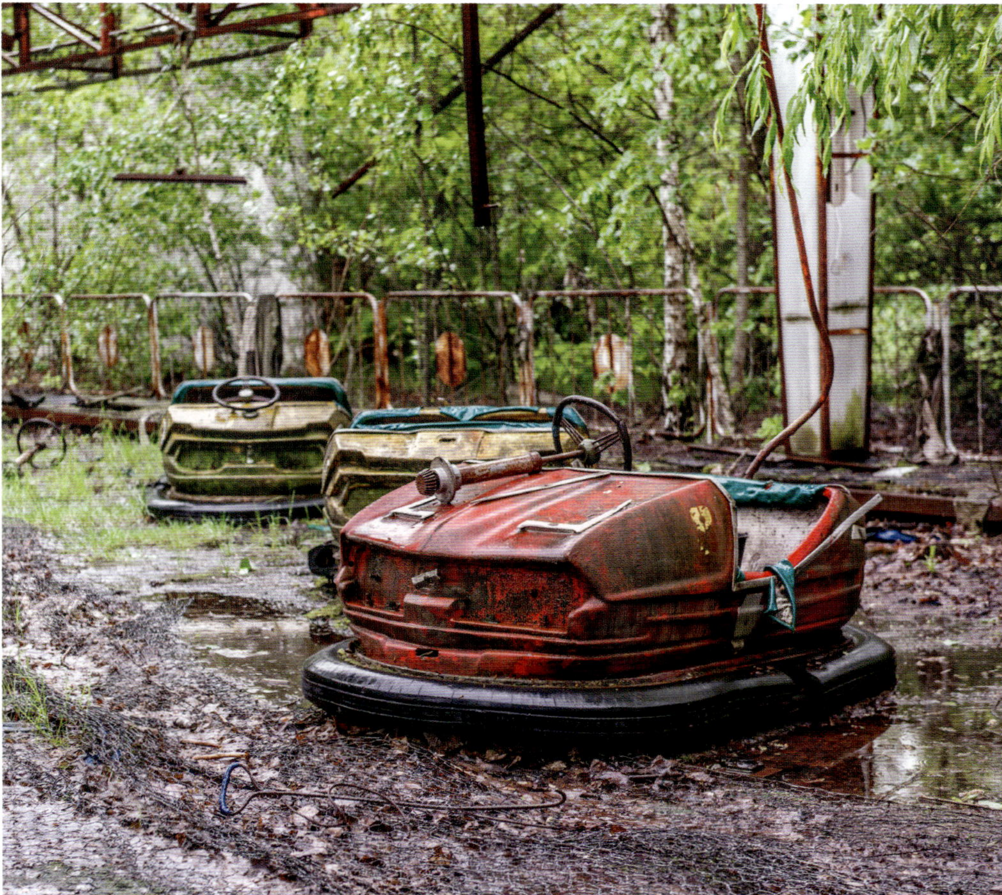

Above: *Abandoned amusement park in Pripyat, near Chernobyl, Ukraine.*

The Half-Life of Pripyat

The use of nuclear energy has always been controversial and the accident at Three Mile Island in Pennsylvania in 1979 – though disaster was averted on that occasion – only reinforced existing worries about the dangers of this otherwise very clean source of power. These fears came to pass on 26 April 1986 when a massive explosion destroyed the No.4 reactor at the Chernobyl nuclear power plant in what today is northern Ukraine but was then a part of the USSR. Two employees were killed instantly and a further 29 people would die from the effects of radiation in the months that followed. The destroyed reactor was encased in concrete and has since been further

Left: *No one will ever return to live in Pripyat, the city closest to the Chernobyl nuclear power plant where in 1986 a reactor exploded, spreading poisonous radiation across the region.*

enclosed, but nuclear contamination had already drifted on prevailing winds across Western Europe and especially over a concentrated area surrounding the plant.

Entire populations in hundreds of towns and villages were immediately evacuated, never to return; some half a million Ukrainians were quickly resettled outside the exclusion zone of 1,000 square miles – an area which, though overrun by wildlife today, will remain unfit for human habitation for another 20,000 years. Inside the contaminated region are hundreds of ghost villages, towns and cities, the best-known being Pripyat, closest to the plant (*see* pages 167–69). This time-capsule city of some 49,000 people was evacuated in less than two days following the accident, and the suddenness of departure comes across strongly in photos of the ghost town taken in recent years. Trees and shrubs have since burst through concrete pavements and now overtop decrepit buildings, which for the next twenty millennia will decay very slowly into rubble and dust.

The Double Disaster of Fukushima

For a quarter of a century there were no more nuclear accidents, then on 11 March 2011 an undersea earthquake, off the east coast of Japan's largest island, swept a 15-metre tsunami over hundreds of towns and villages in the Tōhoku area, killing some 16,000 people and displacing 340,000 in all. The nuclear plant in Fukushima was built to withstand the unavoidable earthquakes Japan endures, but the tsunami was unexpected and defences insufficient: the wave knocked out the emergency generators that kicked in after the earthquake to cool the plant's reactors, a catastrophic failure that tipped three of the four reactors into meltdown, spreading radiation to a wider area than just those towns directly hit by the wave.

Right: *The radioactively polluted city of Chernobyl, Ukraine.*

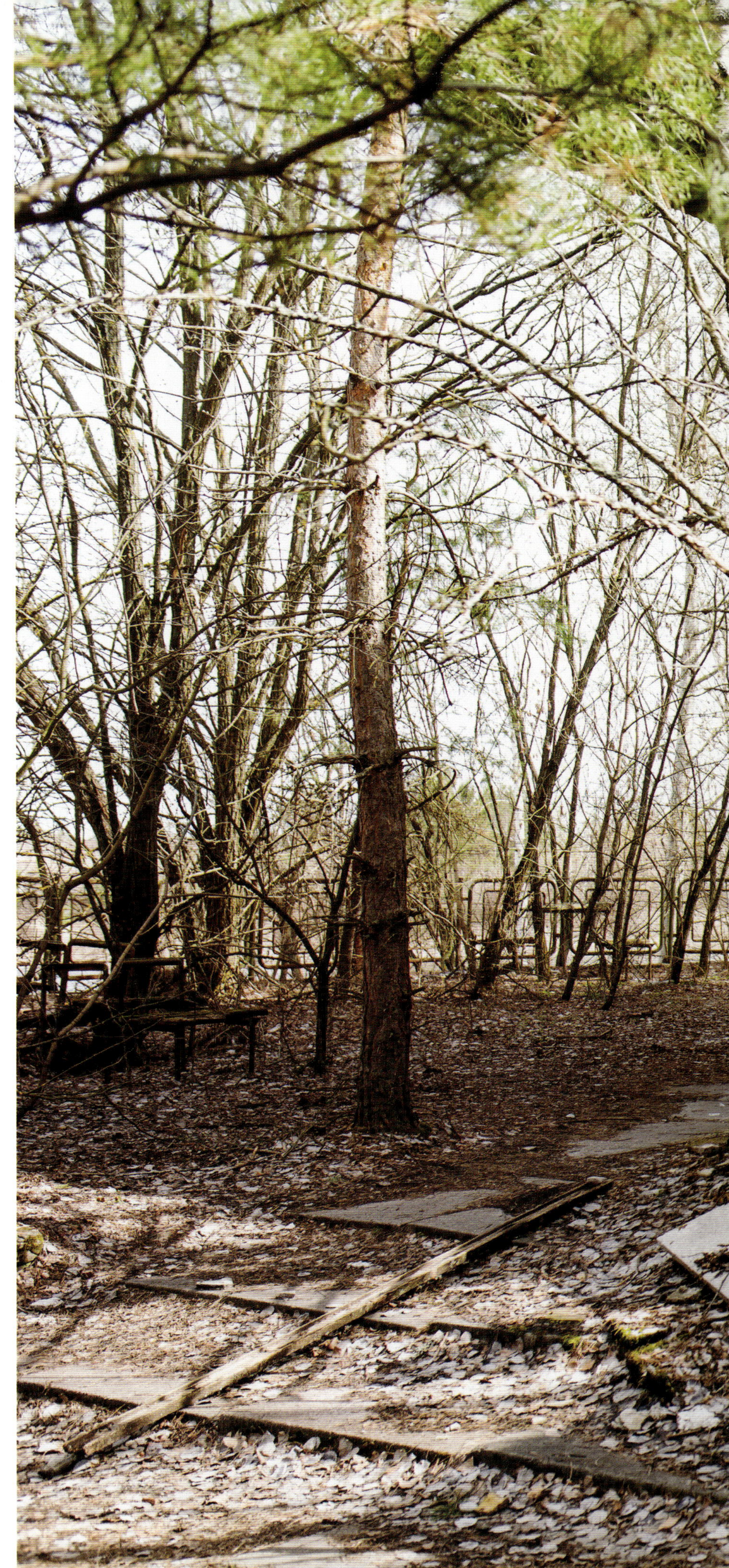

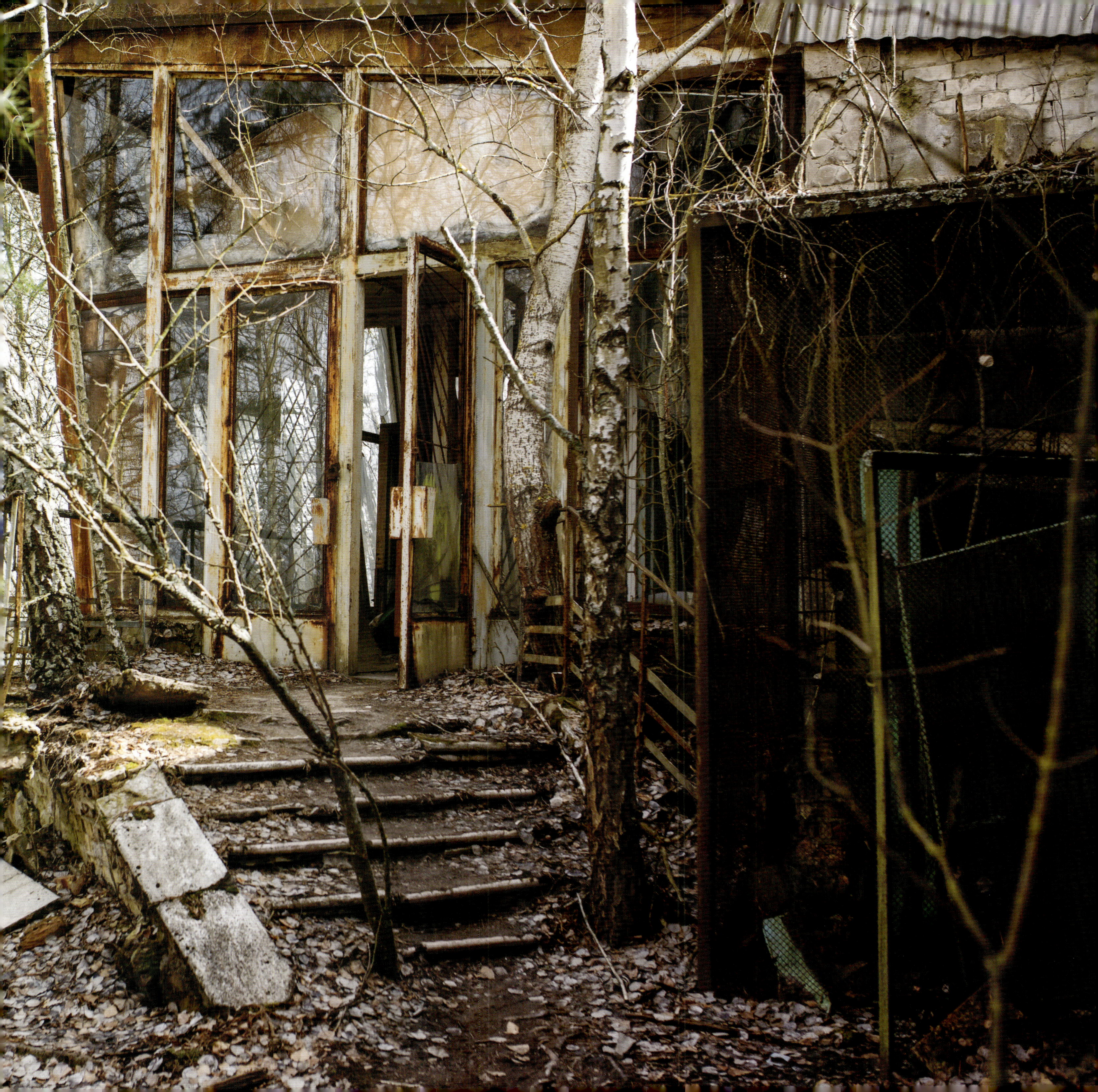

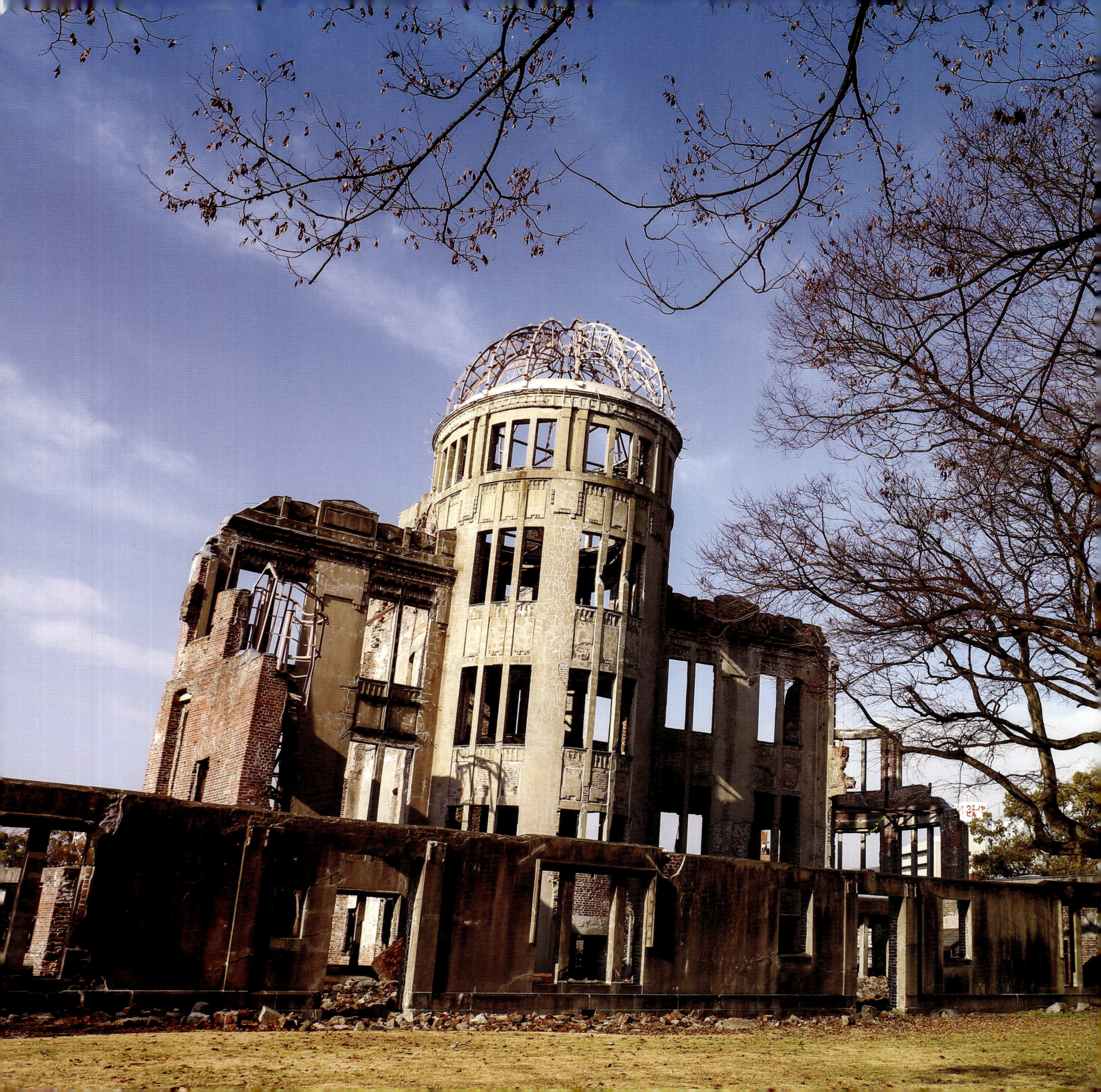

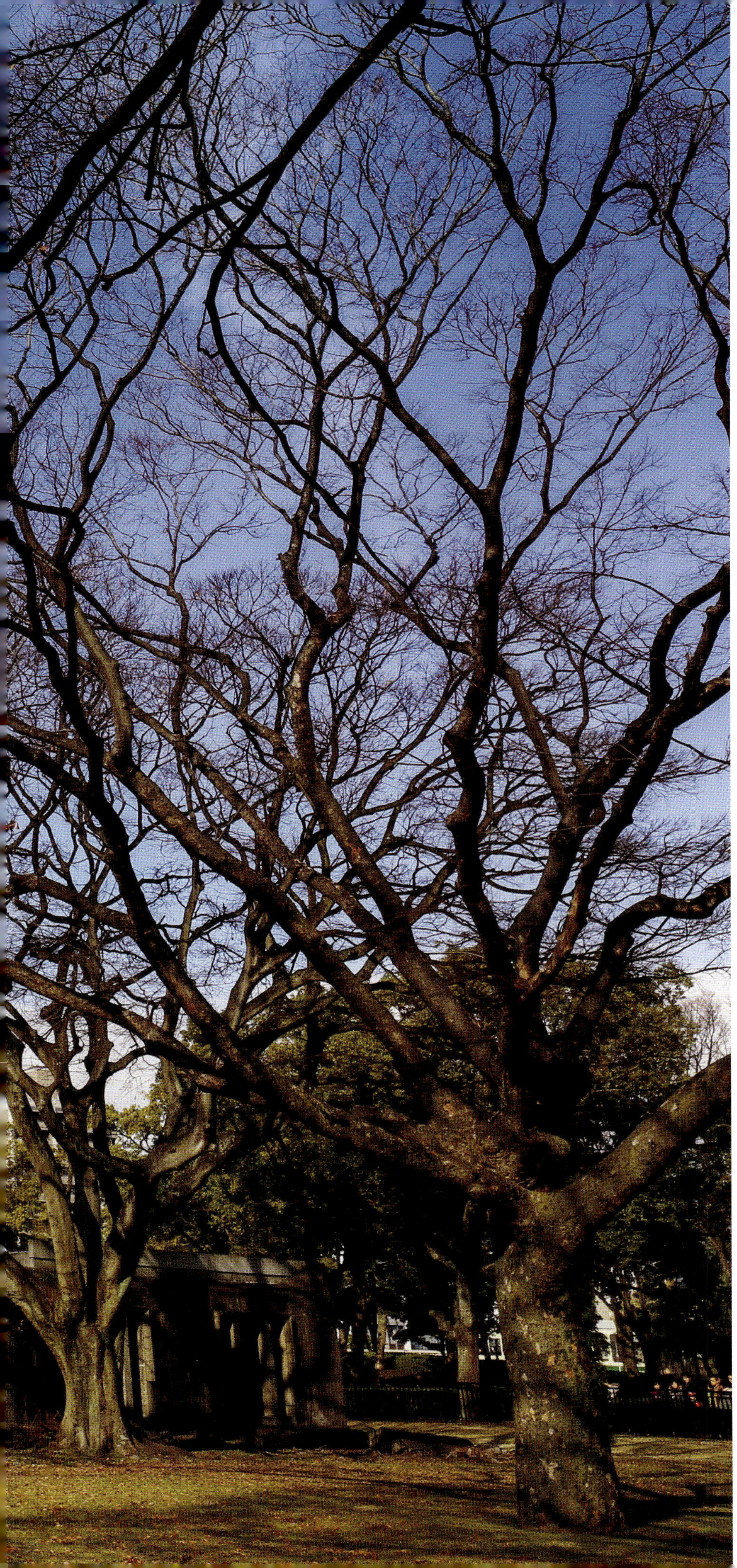

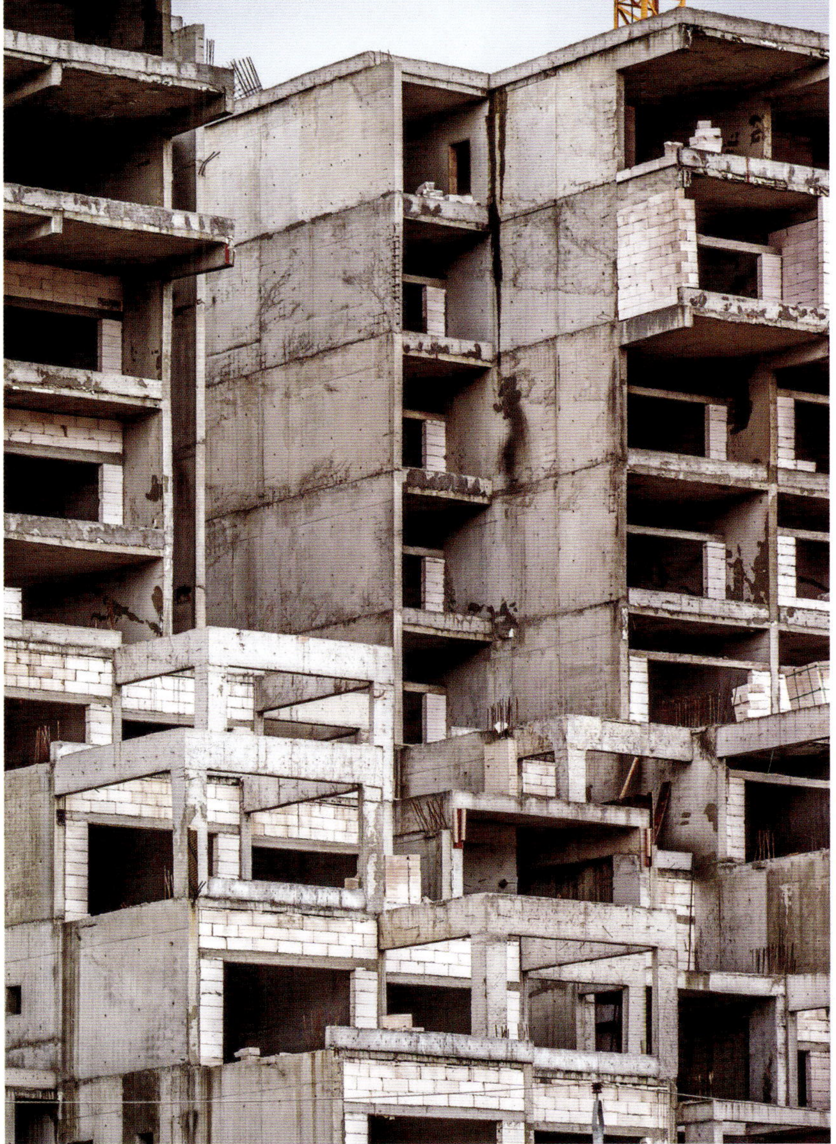

Above: *Abandoned buildings in Iraq.*

A mass evacuation took place and today, with levels of radiation inside the 20 km evacuation zone still unsafe, residents are forbidden to return. But among those who have ventured into places such as the deserted wreckage of Namie-machi, a city close to the Fukushima plant, some have photographed the eerie remnants of that first disaster, suspended at the moment of their destruction by the legacy of a second.

Left: *Hiroshima Peace Memorial, Japan.*

Devastation of War

No one intends a nuclear accident, as terrible as they are, but war is a different thing altogether.

The Deserted Resort of Varosha

In the case of Varosha in northern Cyprus (*see* right), war between Greece and Turkey caused this luxurious tourist resort to be abandoned quite suddenly in 1974. Part of the town of Famagusta, it was once the most glamorous resort on the island, whose high-rise hotels attracted a wealthy, jet-setting crowd. But when the Turkish army invaded on 20 July, the people fled and the area was seized by Turkish troops. Many of the 39,000 who once lived in Varosha hoped to return when the fighting finished; but entry has been forbidden ever since, its beaches now as invitingly empty as its one-time swanky hotels.

The Pyrrhic Victories of Ethnic Cleansing

The brief war in 1993 between Armenia and Azerbaijan was one of several ethnic and territorial conflicts to have arisen in the countries of the former Soviet Union over the past quarter century. Many villages in the disputed region of Nagorno-Karabakh have lain abandoned ever since, their populations expelled or forced to flee. But the biggest evacuation took place when Armenian forces began shelling the Azerbaijani city of Agdam (*see* page 176) and 29,000 people fled for their lives.

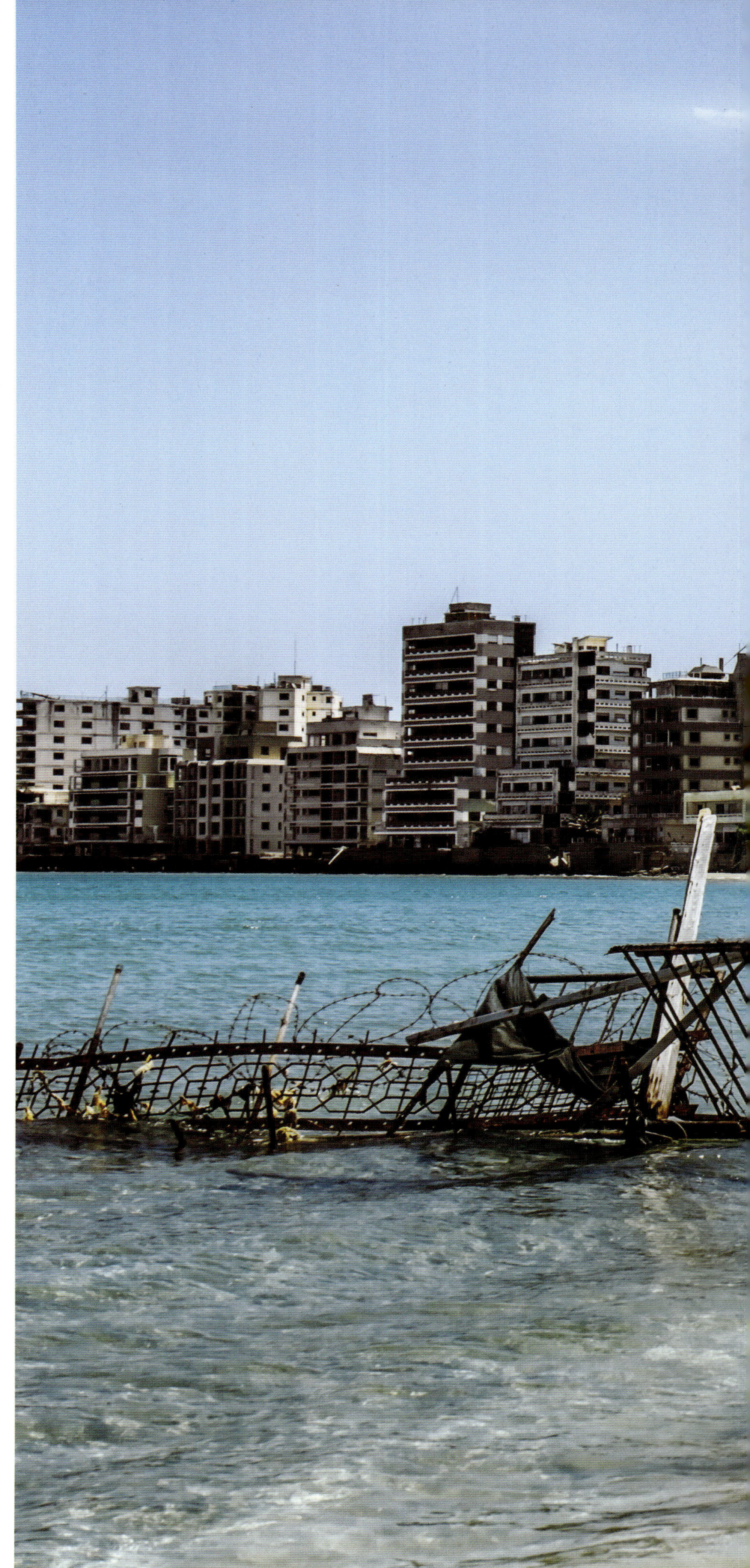

***Right:** Abandoned hotels at Varosha, Cyprus.*

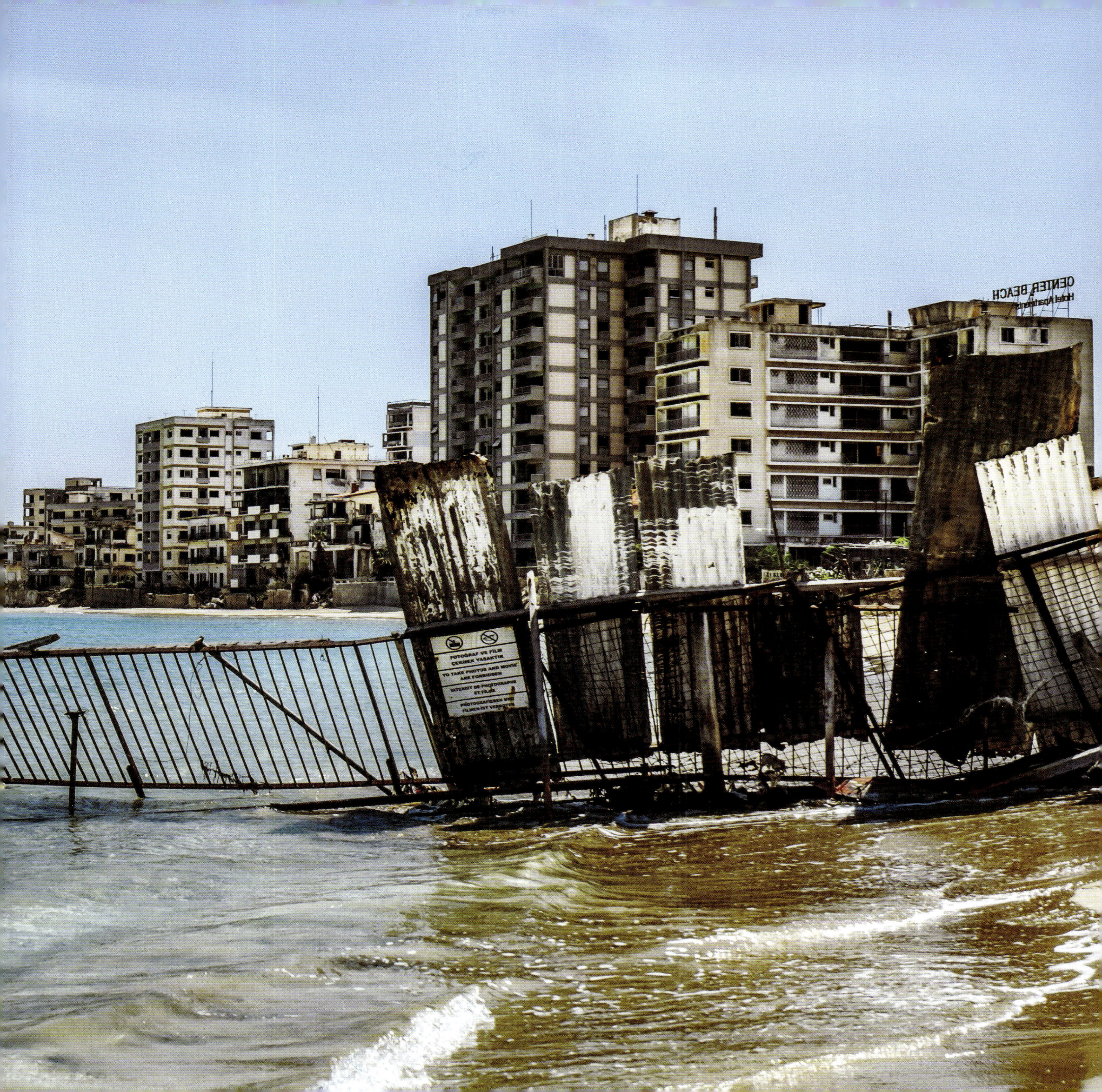
FOTOĞRAF VE FİLM
ÇEKMEK YASAKTIR
TO TAKE PHOTOS AND MOVIE
ARE FORBIDDEN

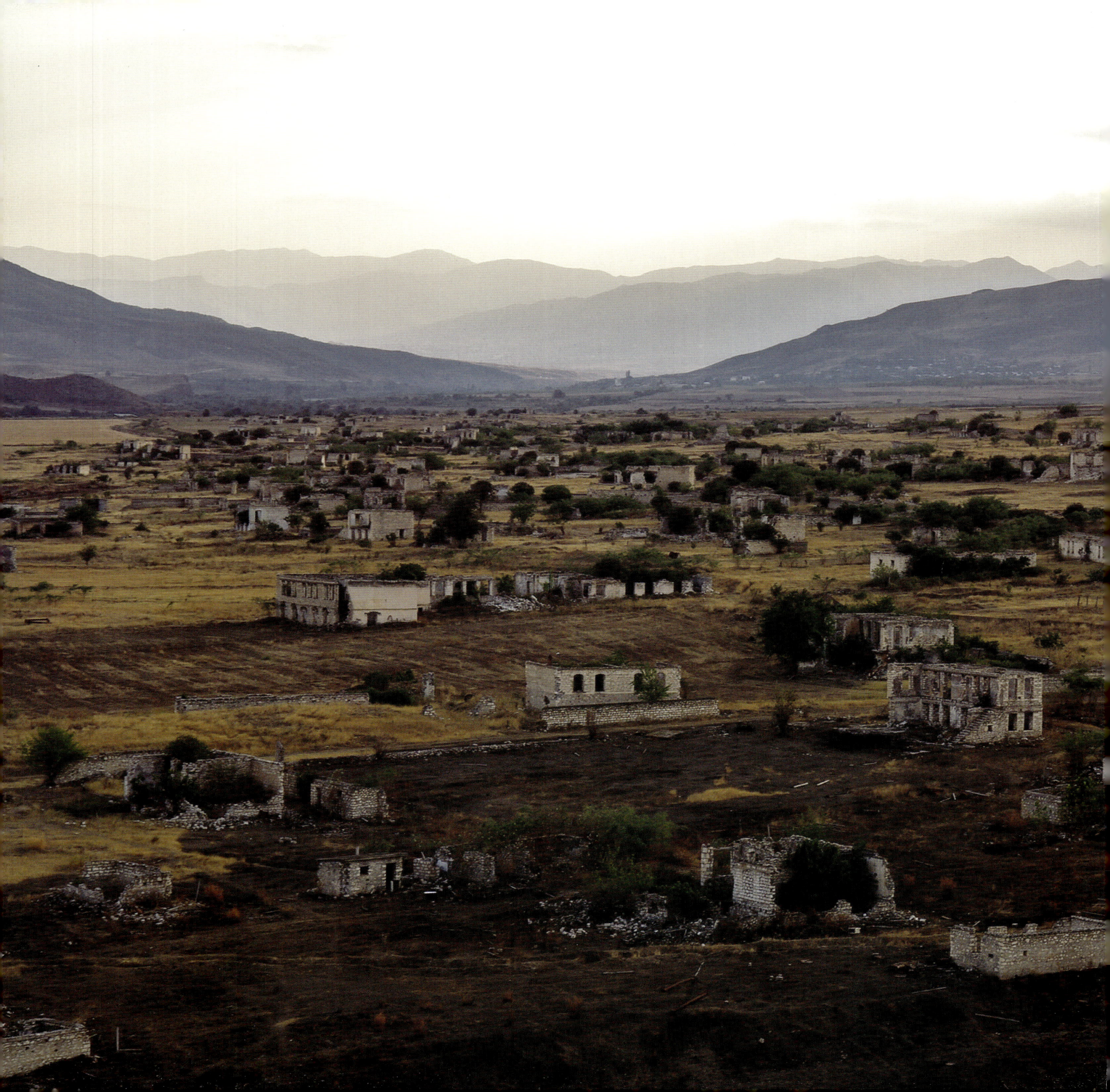

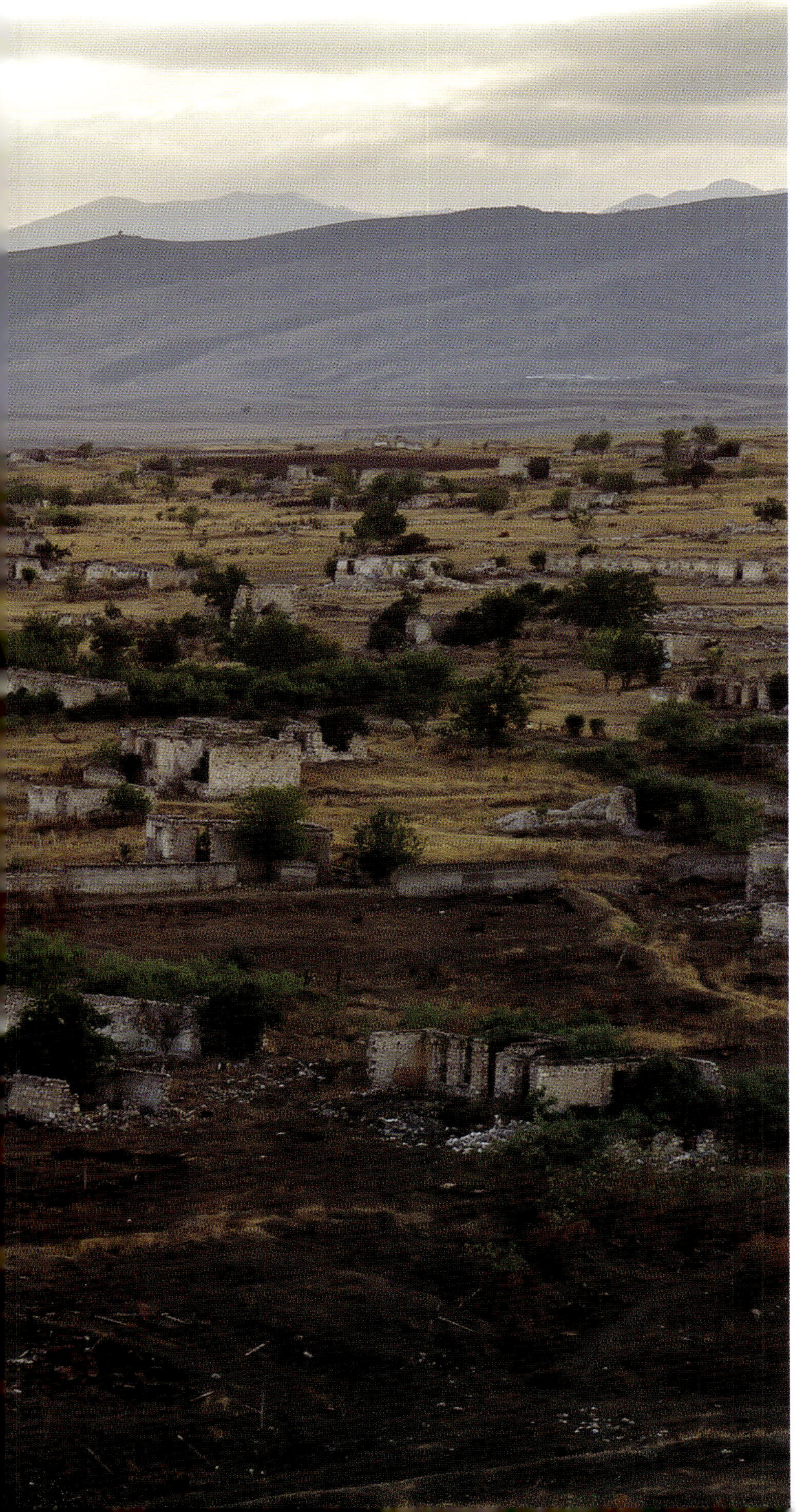

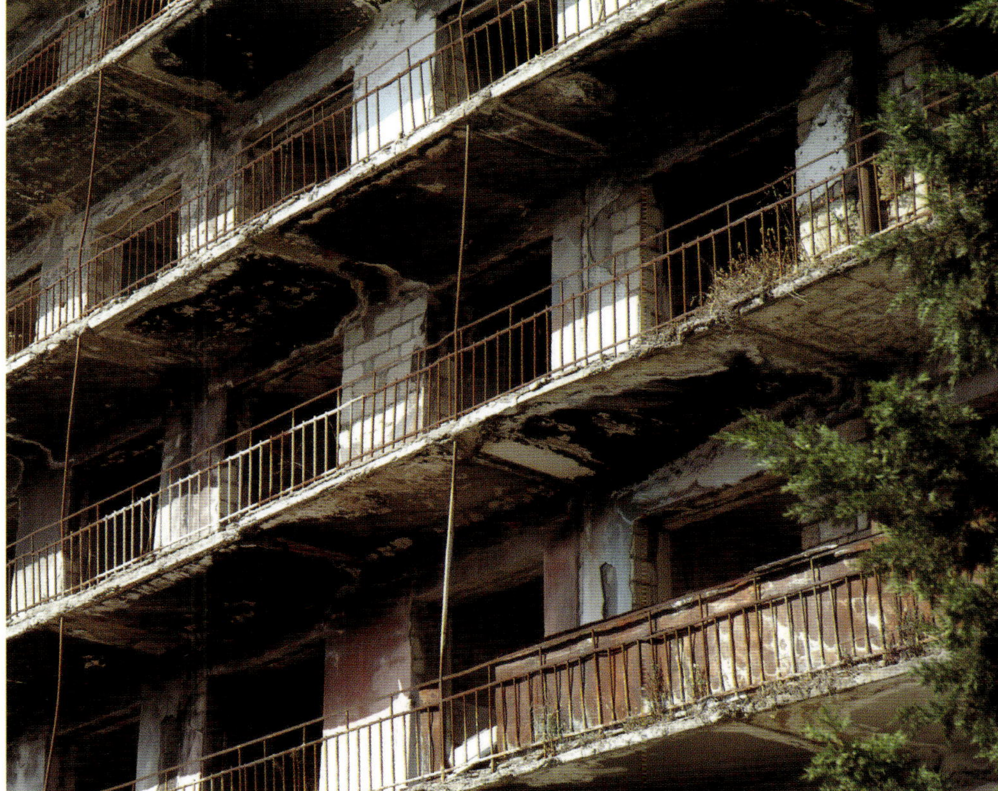

Above: *Before the war of 1992, the population of the town of Shusha in the disputed region of Nagorno-Karabakh stood at more than 15,000. Now barely 4,000 remain.*

In the months that followed, the occupying army of ethnic Armenians destroyed many buildings to dissuade its former population from ever coming back.

At the same time, another, similar ethnic–territorial dispute was raging in neighbouring Georgia over the now self-declared republic of Abkhazia. Former Soviet cities such as Ochamchire and Akarmara are now home to a fraction of the numbers who once lived there, after ethnic Georgians were expelled by Abkhaz forces. And local economies were so damaged by the loss of the majority population that many Abkhazis joined them in the years that followed, leaving deserted ruins as spoils of war.

Left: *Ruins of the city of Agdam in the Nagorno-Karabakh region, Azerbaijan.*

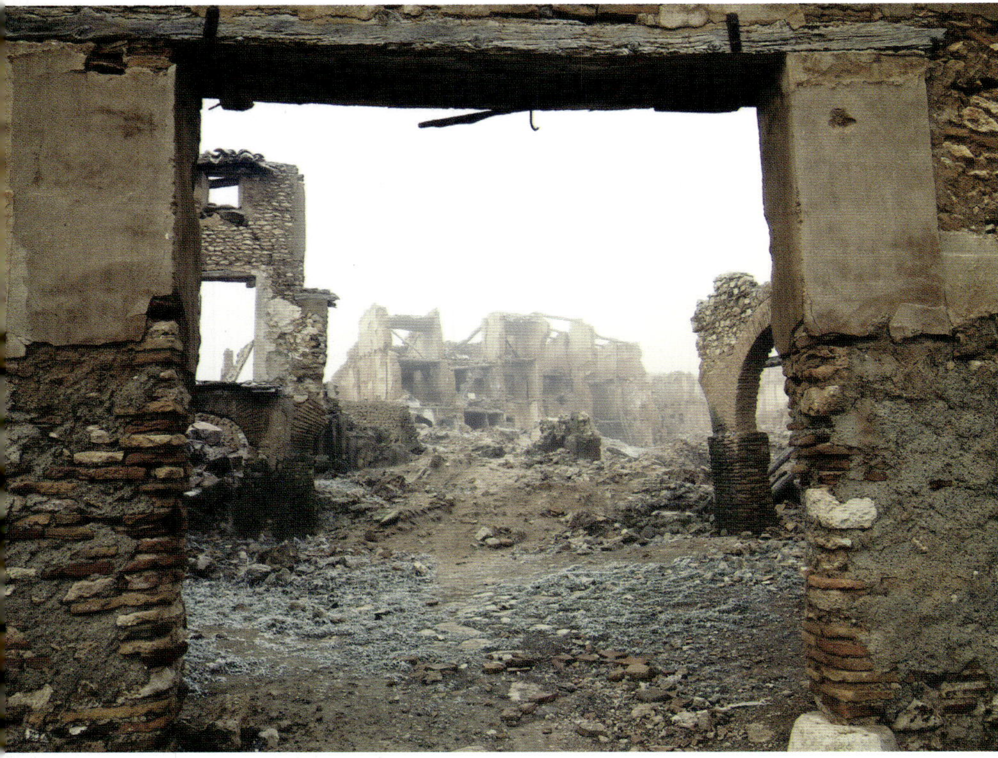

Above: *The town of Belchite was utterly destroyed in one of the worst battles of the Spanish Civil War and was later left as a memorial to that atrocious conflict.*

The Memorial Ruins of Belchite

The past hundred years have seen some of the worst wars in human history, and the need to remember them, so as not to repeat the same mistakes, has left a legacy of ruins intended to remind us of the true cost of conflict. One of the first of these memorial sites was Belchite (*see* above and page 184), a town near Zaragoza in northern Spain, where over two short weeks in the summer of 1938, one of the most destructive battles of the Spanish Civil War took place.

In launching their offensive against Nationalist forces occupying the town, the Republicans wanted to secure Belchite before closing in on

Right: *In 1923, the population exchange between Greece and Turkey following the end of the Ottoman Empire saw the Greek Orthodox village of Kayaköy in Turkey abandoned by its 2,000 inhabitants.*

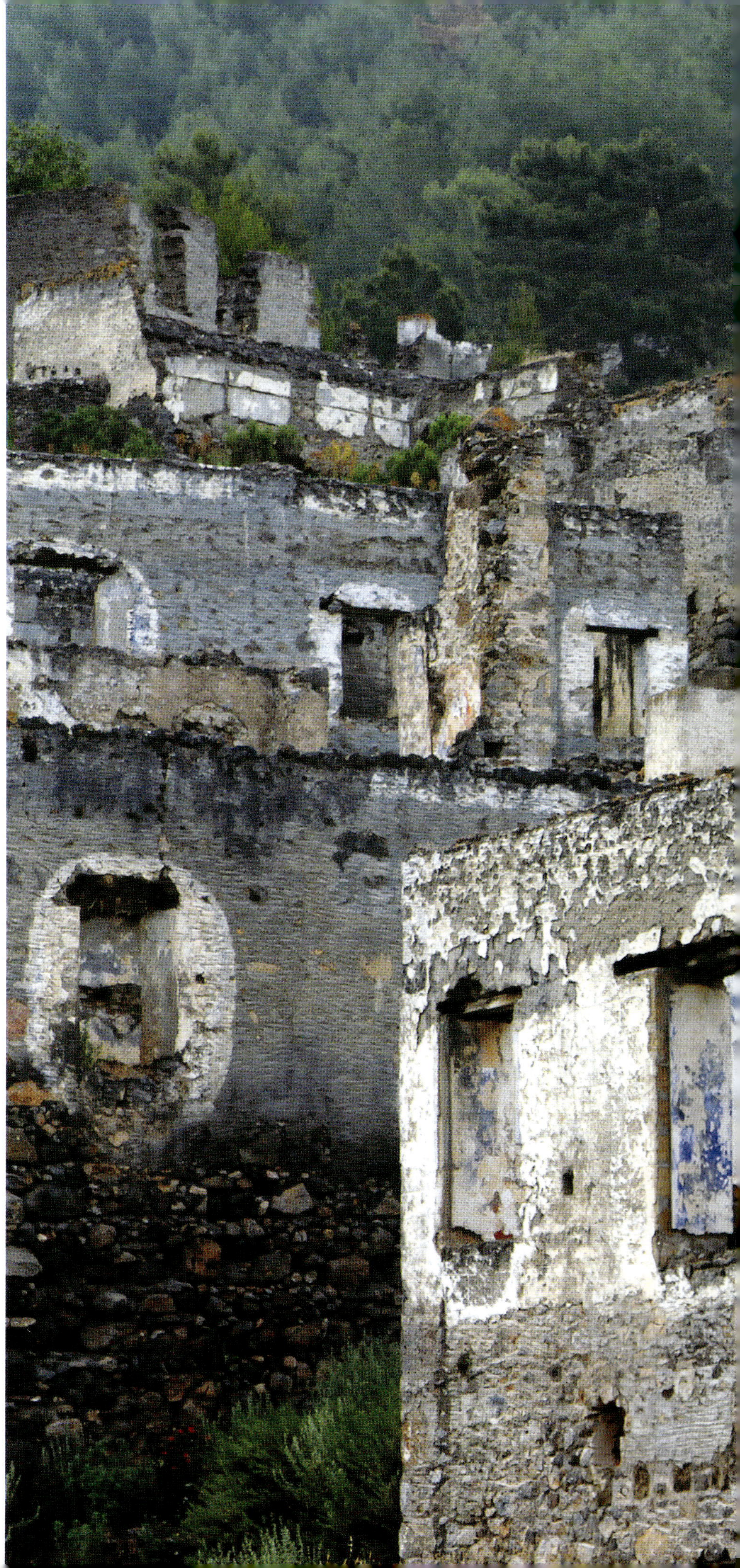

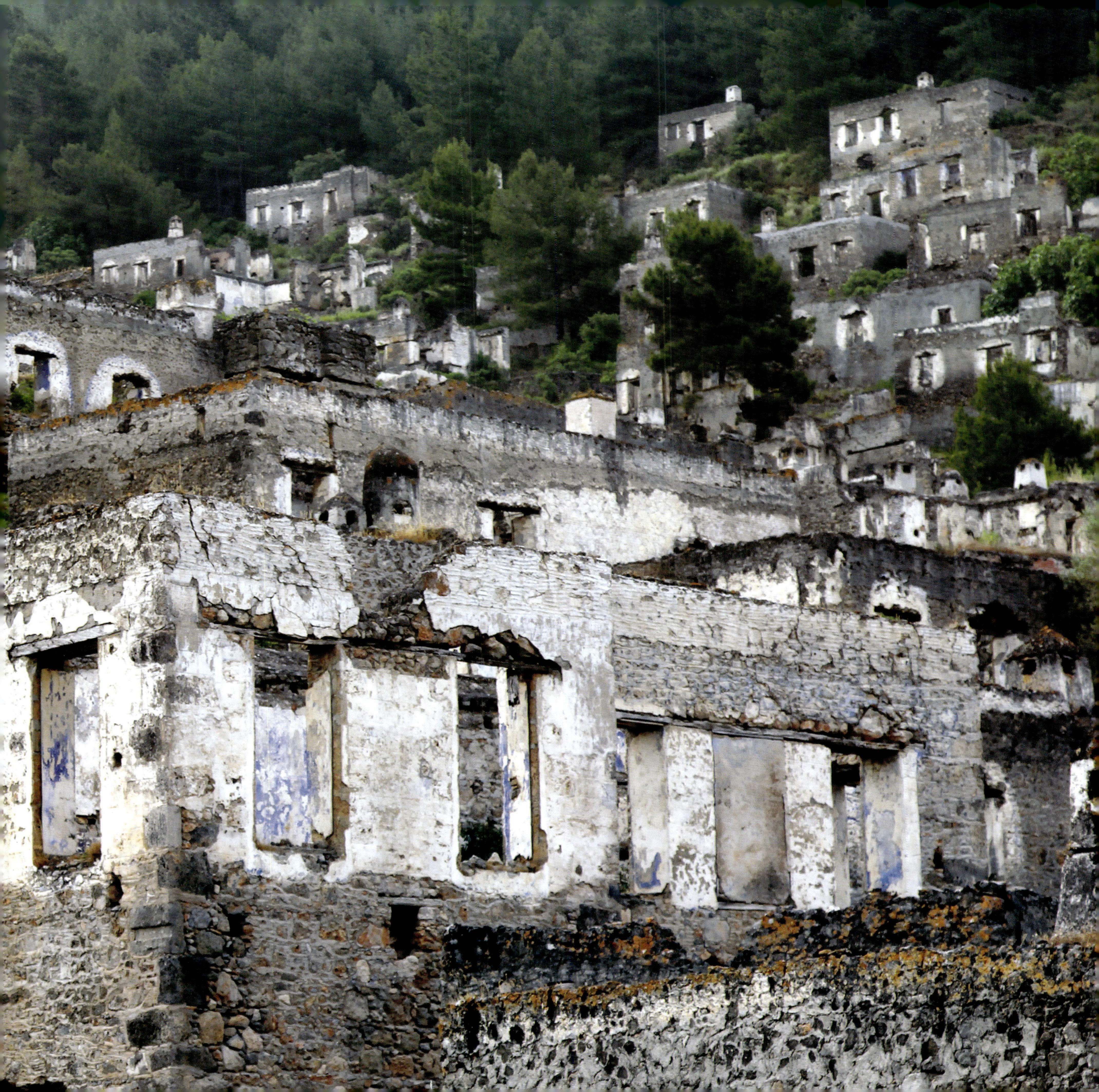

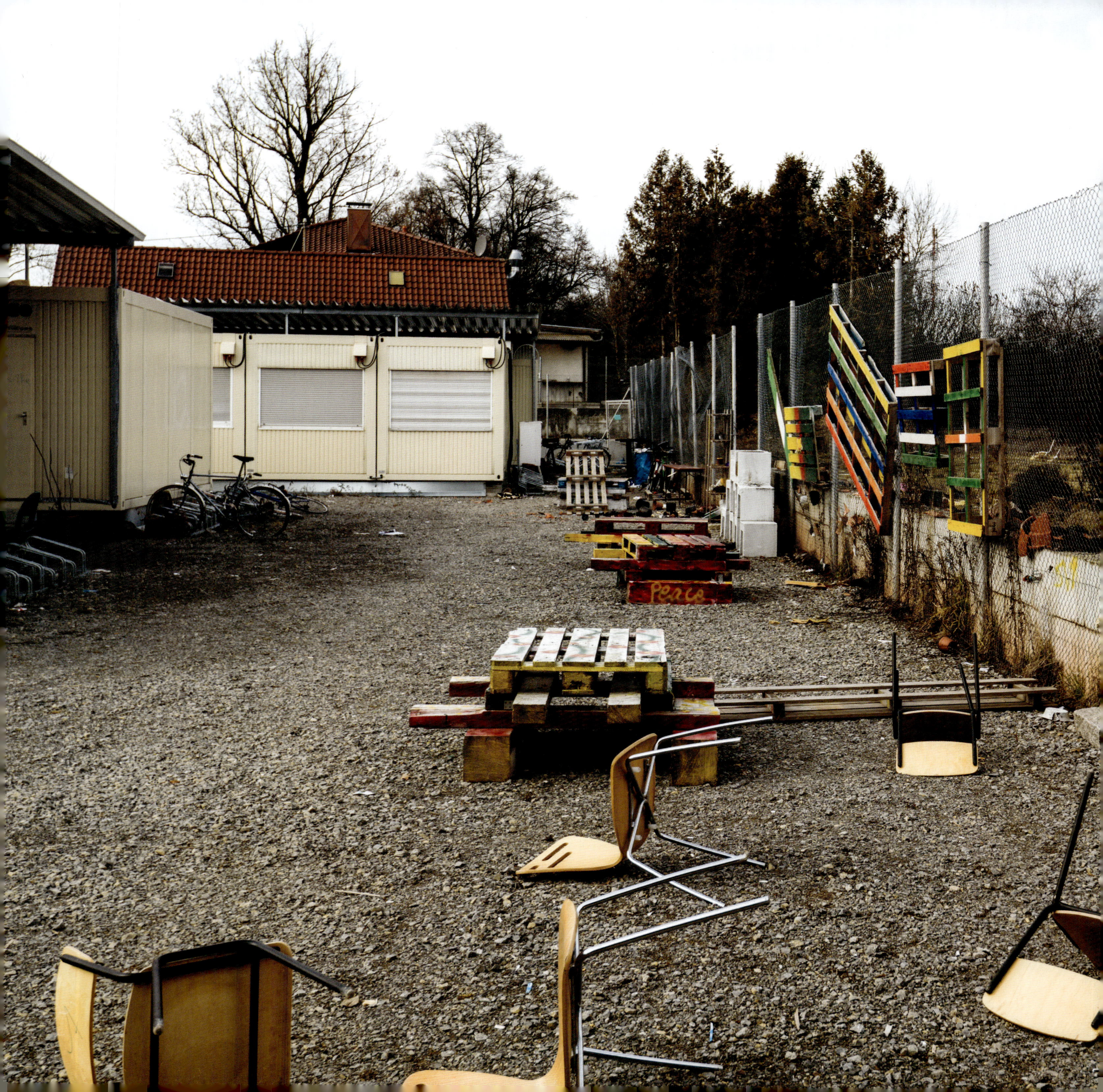
Peace

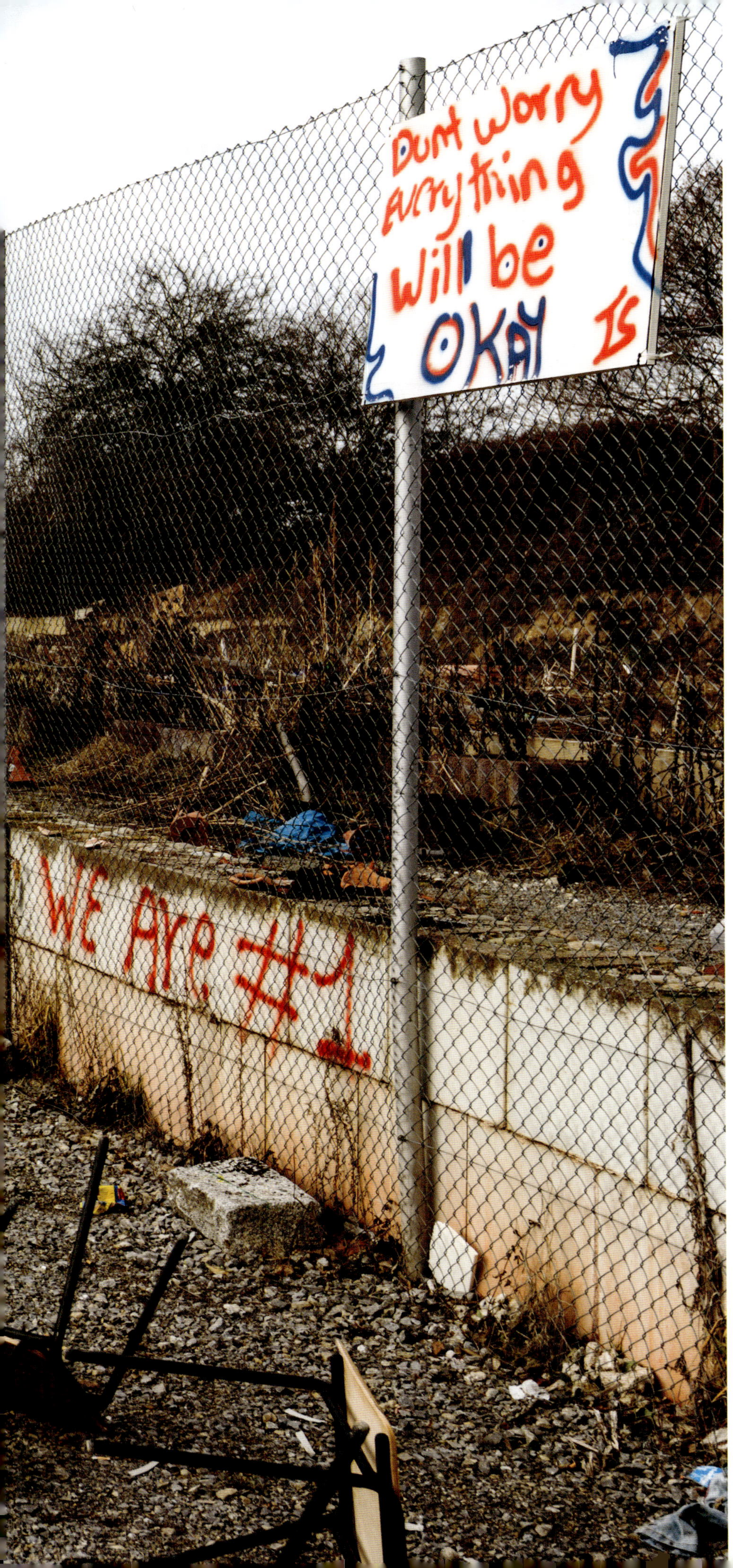

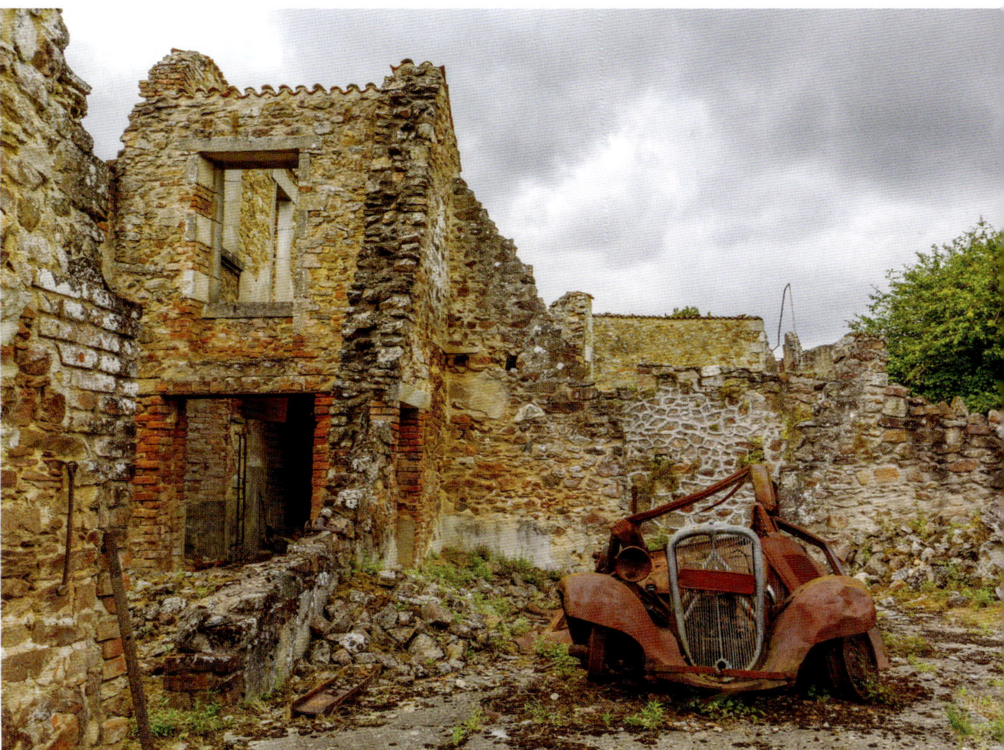

Above: *On 10 June 1944, almost the entire population of the French village of Oradour-sur-Glane was rounded up and killed – either shot or burned alive – by the Nazi Waffen SS.*
Left: *A temporary container city in Scharnhausen near Stuttgart, Germany, which served as a camp for refugees, now lies abandoned.*

Zaragoza, the greater prize; but the Nationalists held out and soon launched a counteroffensive. In the process of this brutal to and fro, Belchite was destroyed, and the war's eventual victor, the Nationalist leader General Franco, deliberately left the old town in ruins beside the new Belchite that was built next door. With this memorial gesture, the cruel dictator may have meant to remind his countrymen exactly who had won the conflict, but the ruins of Belchite now stand as a universal monument to the pointlessness of war.

The Massacre of Oradour-sur-Glane

That the atrocity in the village of Oradour-sur-Glane (*see* above) was not unusual in the Second World War reminds us of the unprecedented cruelty

Next page: *The Palestinian village of Lifta, near Jerusalem, was abandoned during the 1948 Arab–Israeli War and is now the last such ghost village not to have been bulldozed or redeveloped.*

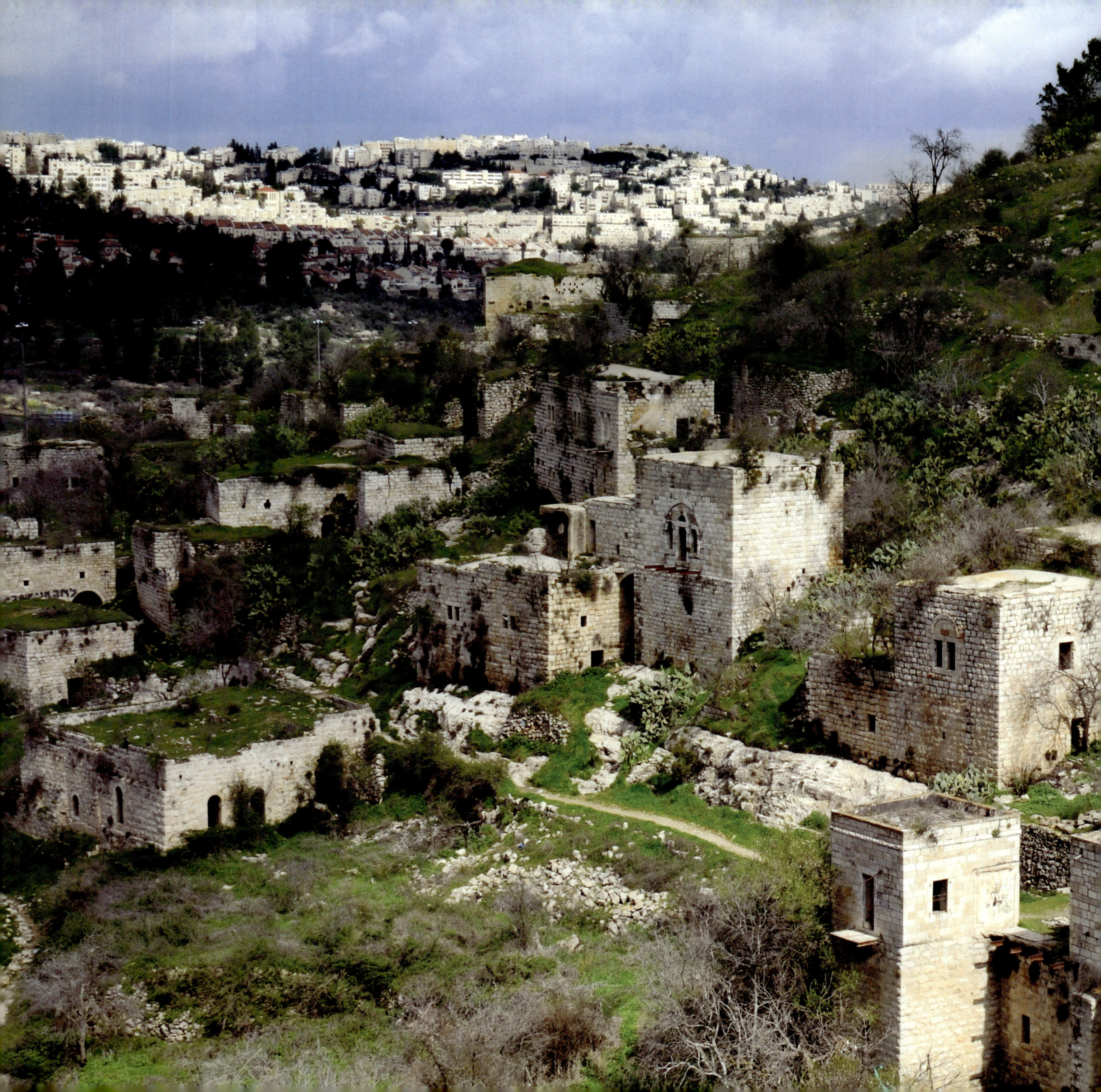

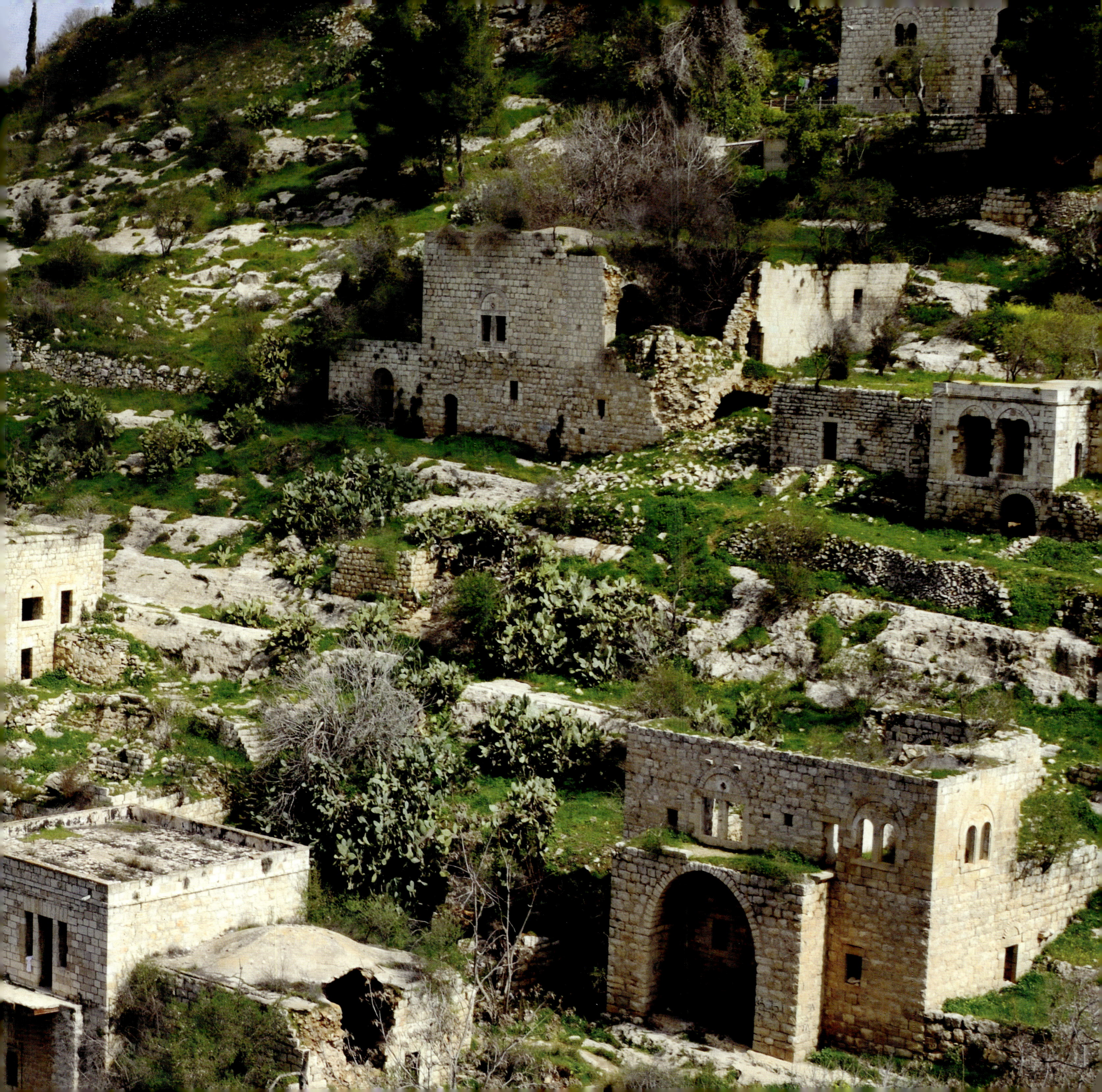

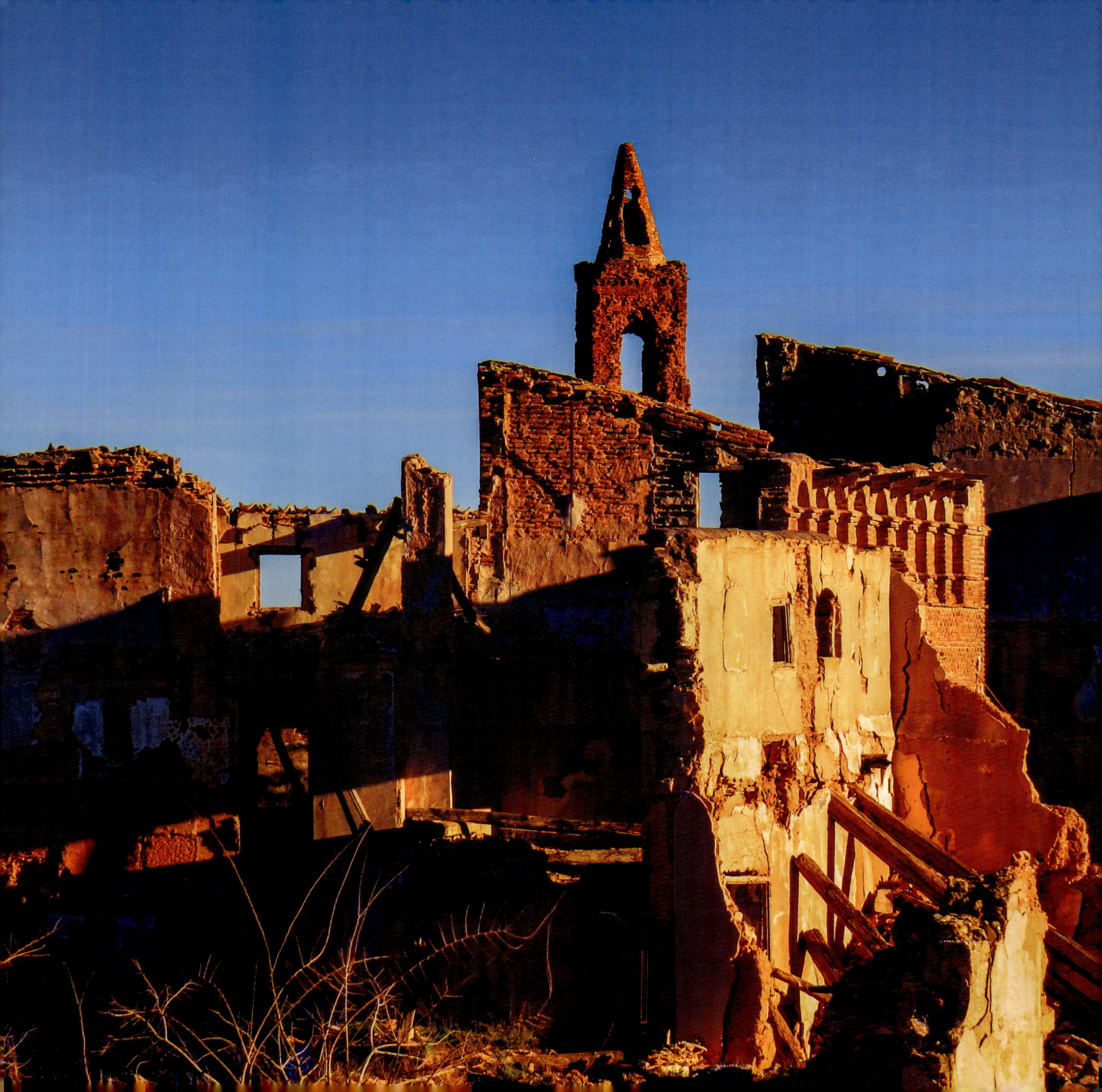

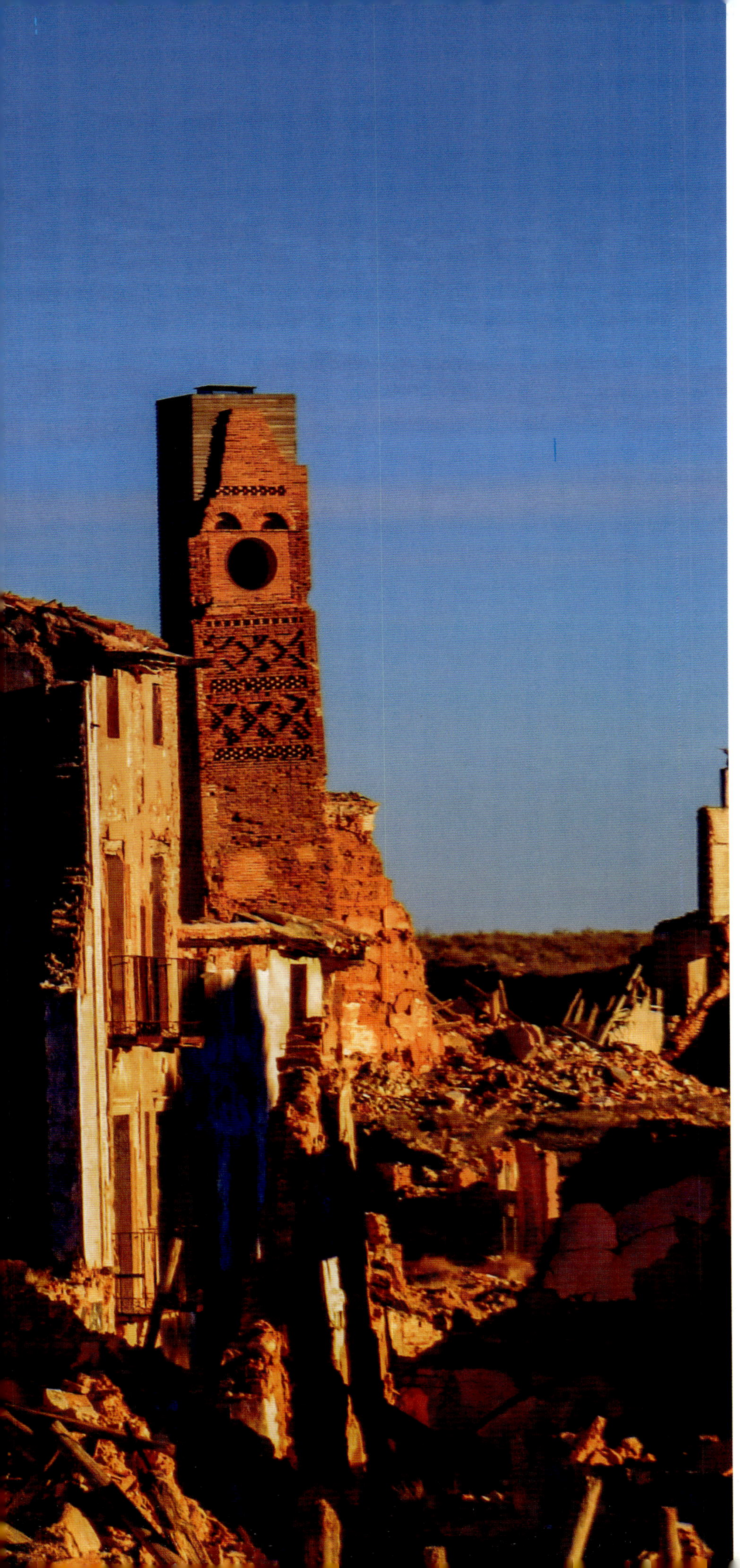

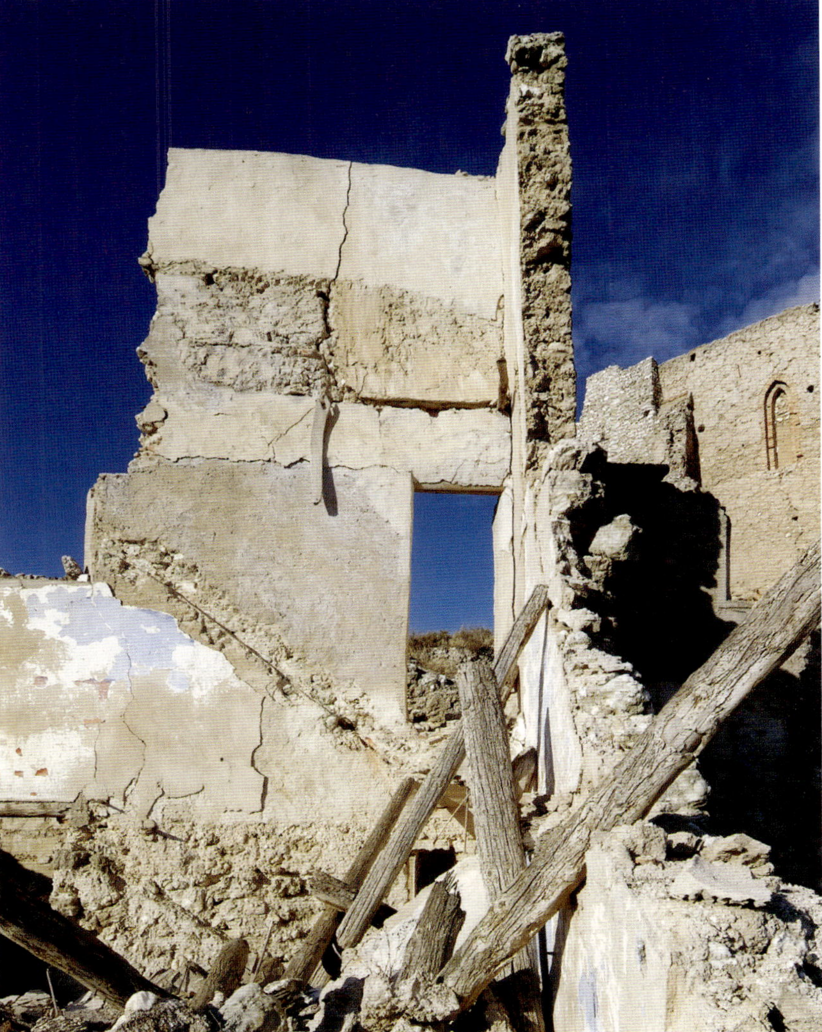

Above: *Village of Rodén in Zaragoza, Spain, which was destroyed by bombing during the Spanish Civil War.*

of the Nazi regime. On 10 June 1944, in response to the kidnapping of an SS officer by Resistance forces, the Waffen SS under SS-*Sturmbannführer* Adolf Diekmann ordered all the residents of the village, including several people who were just passing through, to be rounded up to have their papers checked.

The women and children were locked in the church, while the men of Oradour, some 190 in all, were taken away and shot. The Nazis then set the church on fire and machine-gunned any who tried to escape.

Left: *War-devastated buildings at Belchite, Spain.*

The village was looted and more or less razed to the ground, leaving 642 dead, almost the entire population. When the war was over, General de Gaulle, the leader of the Free French Forces, ordered that the ruins should be left as they were in memory of this unspeakable horror.

The Tragedy of Aleppo

There is no end to the misery humans are prepared to inflict on their fellow beings, or how much they are willing to destroy simply in order to come out on top. The latest country to bear witness to this awful truth is Syria, and of all the places torn apart by the civil war which has racked the country since 2011, none is more tragic than Aleppo. One of the oldest cities in the world, whose varied history over more than two millennia had endowed it with a cultural and architectural legacy of extraordinary richness, Syria's second city was also home to more than 2.3 million people at the start of the war. More than four years of almost constant bombardment from tanks and rockets and barrel bombs dropped from government helicopters has made ruins of places like the ancient Citadel and the famous Souk, and displaced a quarter of the citizens of Aleppo.

Hundreds of thousands throughout Syria have died in the fighting and millions have fled into neighbouring countries or to those parts of Europe that are willing to accept them. In our interconnected world, the disaster zone in a case like Syria is hard to contain and perhaps should not be contained. As we walk the ruins of Pompeii or Troy, we know there's nothing we can do now to aid the people who suffered all those centuries ago. The imagined dead can be a powerful presence in such places; but the dead make no demands. Only the living are currently suffering; only they cry out for our help.

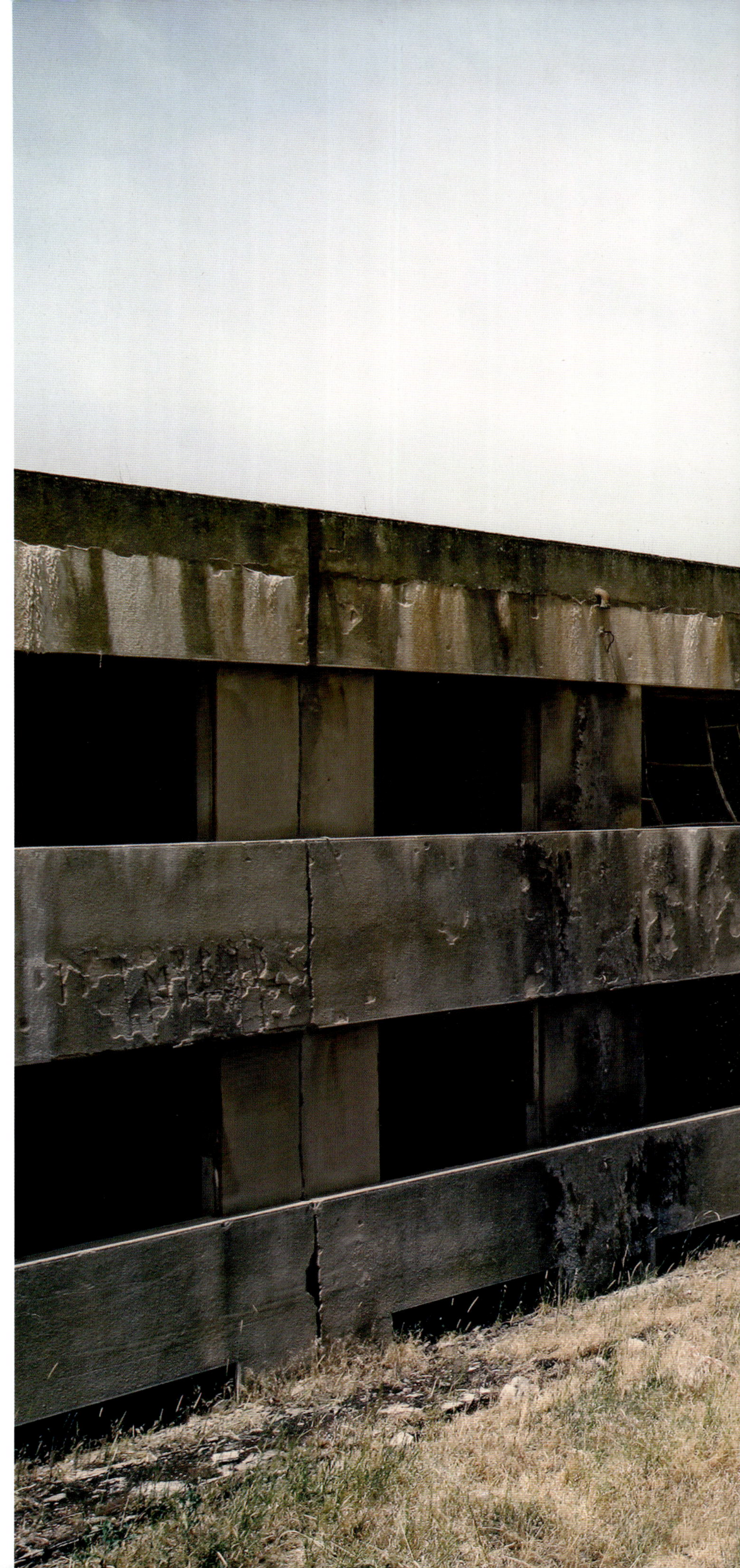

Right: *Having been captured and recaptured by Israeli and Syrian forces in two separate wars, the destroyed city of Quneitra in the Golan Heights in southern Syria was abandoned in 1974.*
Next page: *Destroyed houses show the after-effects of war in the Donetsk region of Ukraine.*

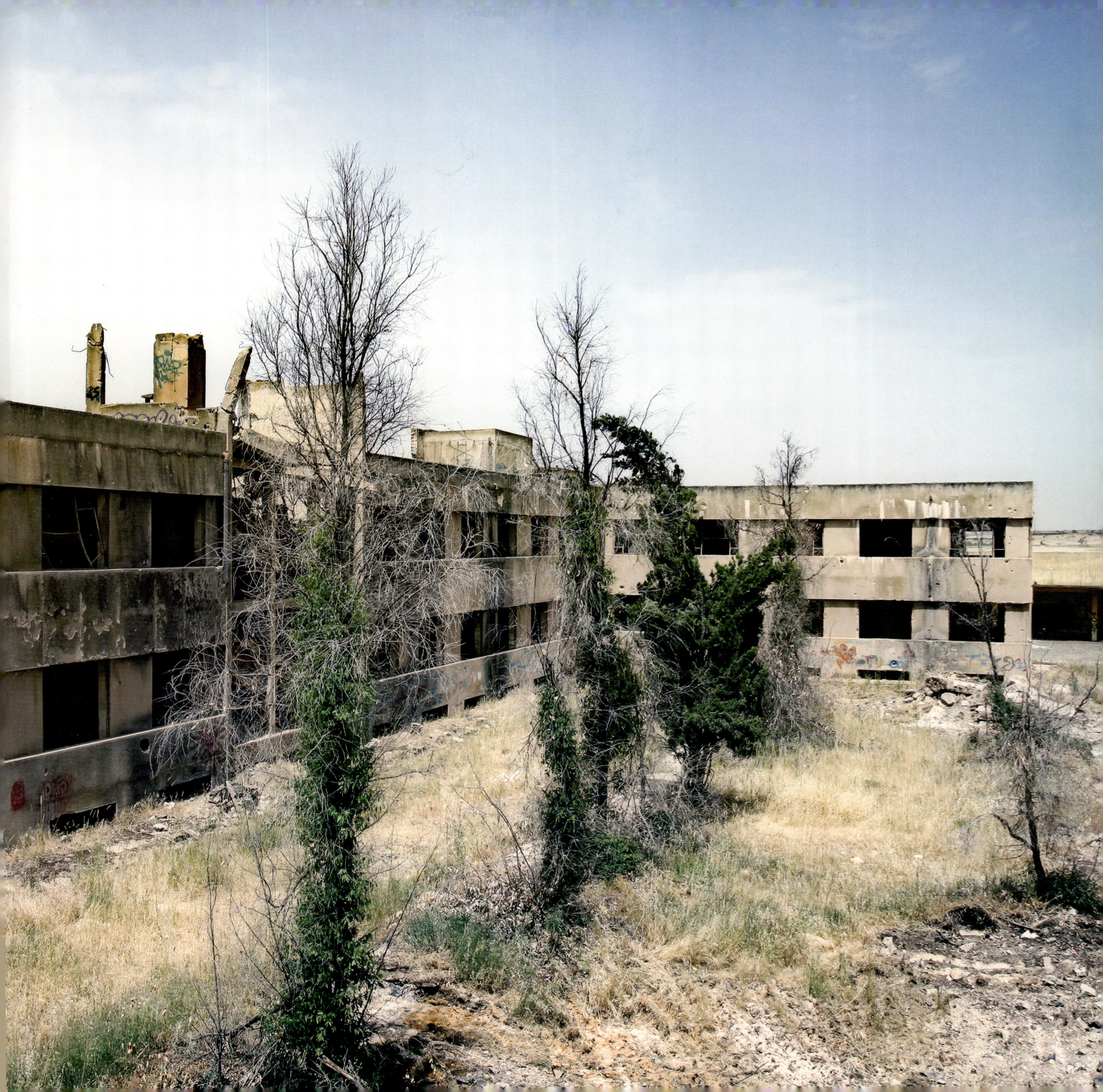

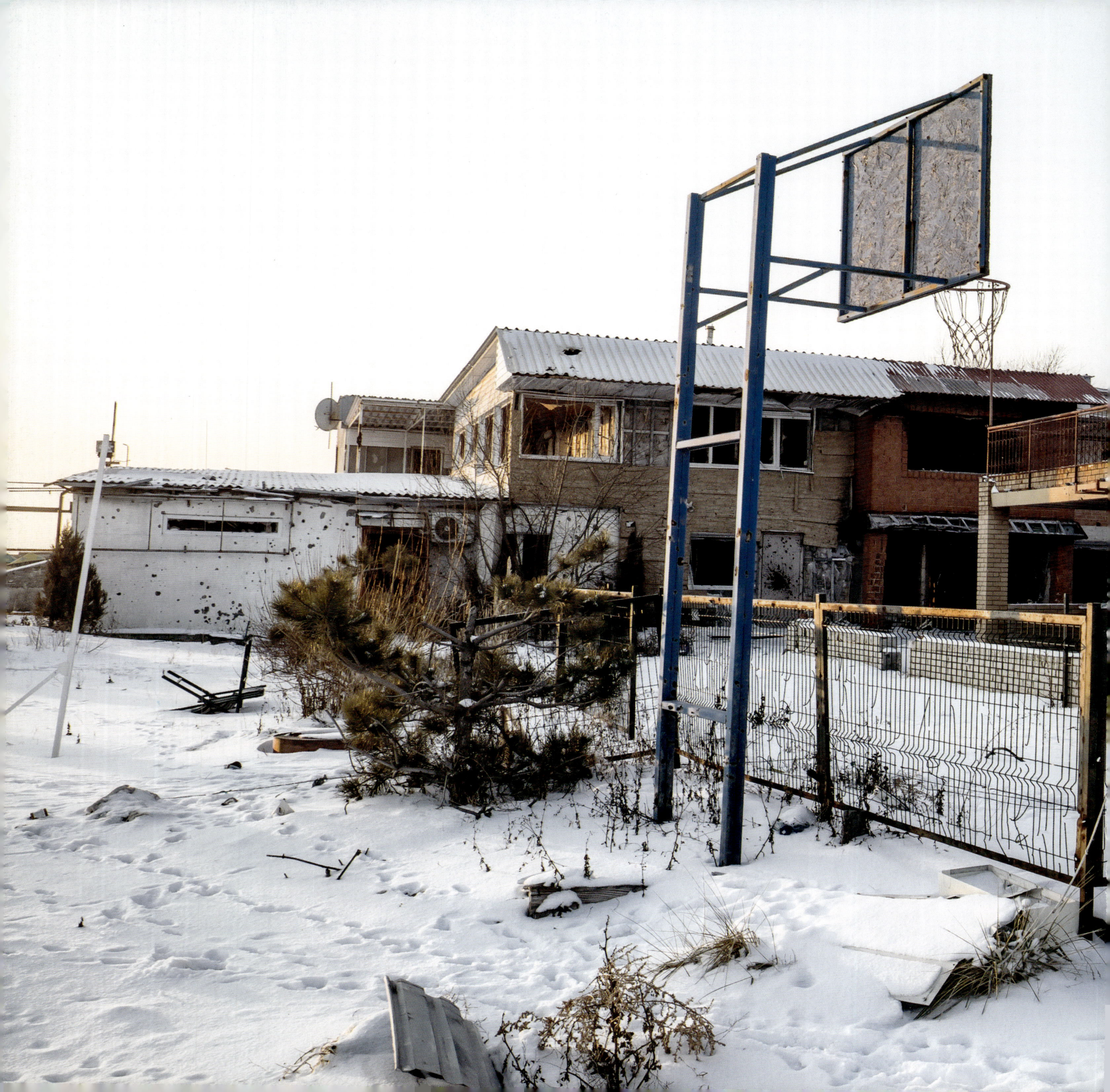

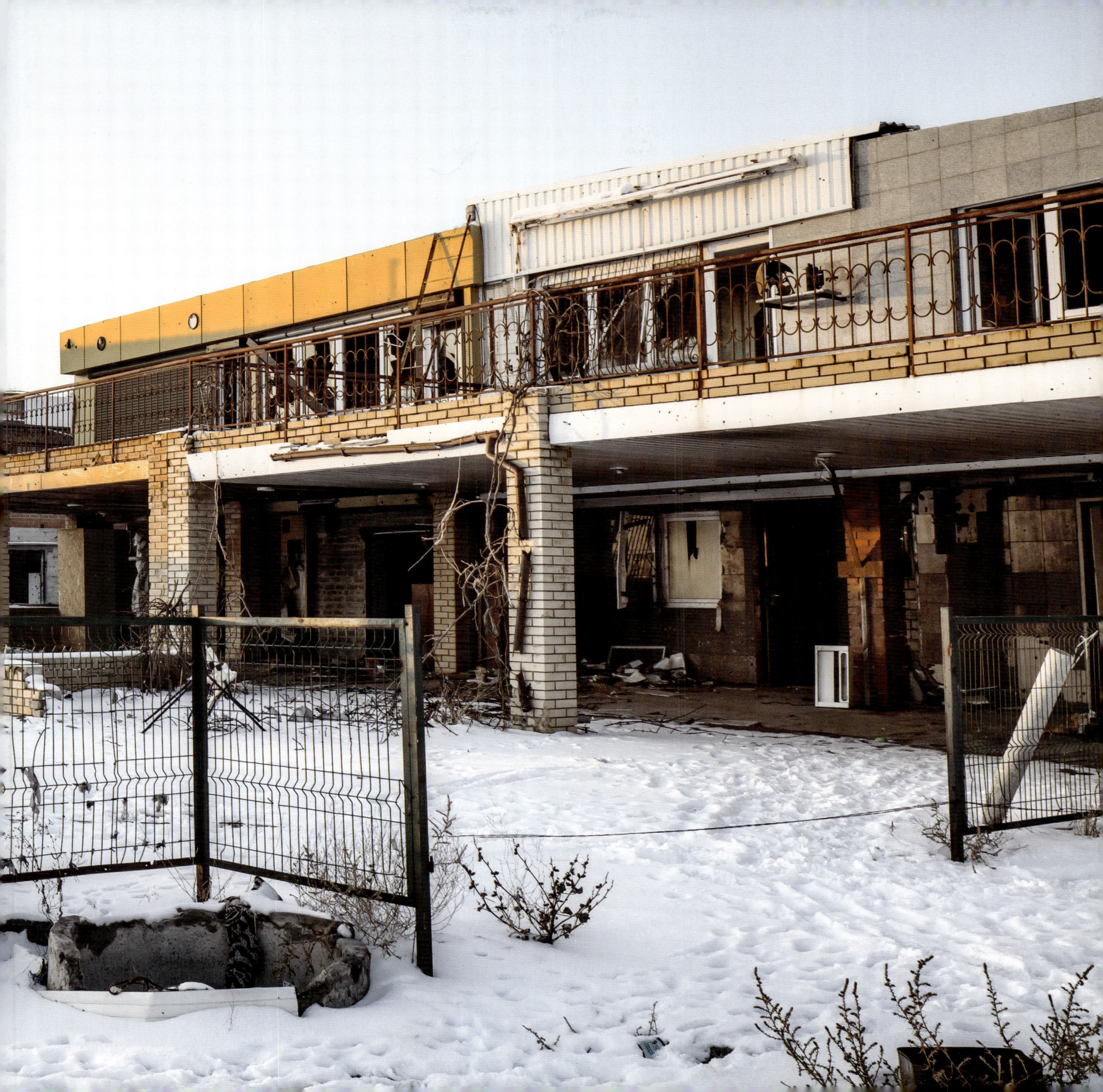

Index

Page numbers in *italics* indicate illustration captions.

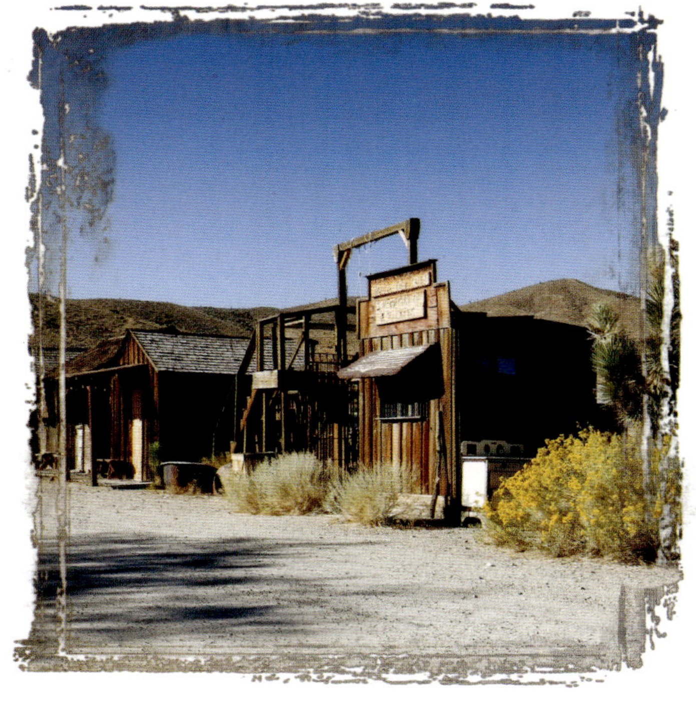

Wooden buildings in an abandoned town in Nevada, USA.